MASTERING LEADERSHIP

A Vital Resource for Health Care Organizations

Alan T. Belasen, PhD
Professor and Chair, MBA Program
SUNY Empire State College
Saratoga Springs, New York

Barry Eisenberg, PhD
Assistant Professor
SUNY Empire State College
Saratoga Springs, New York

John W. Huppertz, PhD
Associate Professor and Chair
MBA Healthcare Management Program
Union Graduate College
Schenectady, New York

JONES & BARTLETT
LEARNING

World Headquarters
Jones & Bartlett Learning
5 Wall Street
Burlington, MA 01803
978-443-5000
info@jblearning.com
www.jblearning.com

Jones & Bartlett Learning books and products are available through most bookstores and online book-sellers. To contact Jones & Bartlett Learning directly, call 800-832-0034, fax 978-443-8000, or visit our website, www.jblearning.com.

Production Credits

VP, Executive Publisher: David Cella
Publisher: Michael Brown
Editorial Assistant: Nicholas Alakel
Associate Production Editor: Rebekah Linga
Senior Marketing Manager: Sophie Fleck Teague
Manufacturing and Inventory Control
  Supervisor: Amy Bacus

Composition: Cenveo® Publisher Services
Cover Design: Scott Moden
Rights and Photo Research Coordinator:
  Mary Flatley
Cover Image: © kiko_kiko/Shutterstock, Inc.
Printing and Binding: Edwards Brothers Malloy
Cover Printing: Edwards Brothers Malloy

Library of Congress Cataloging-in-Publication Data
Belasen, Alan T., 1951-, author.
  Mastering leadership : a vital resource for health care organizations / Alan Belasen, Barry Eisenberg, and John Huppertz.
    p. ; cm.
  Includes bibliographical references and index.
  ISBN 978-1-284-04323-5 (paper)
  I. Eisenberg, Barry, 1954-, author. II. Huppertz, John, author. III. Title.
  [DNLM: 1. Health Services Administration. 2. Leadership. 3. Organizational Objectives. 4. Quality Improvement. W 84.1]
  RA971.35
  362.1068'3—dc23
                        2014038046
6048
Printed in the United States of America
19 18 17 16 15   10 9 8 7 6 5 4 3 2 1

Dedication

This book is dedicated in memory of my mother, Daisy Belasen, a woman of many talents and languages with the courage, passion, and respect for what is different ("Sovlanut"), who was always there for me and my family. I love you, Ema.

—Alan

I am honored to dedicate this book to my mother, Sylvia Eisenberg. She has endured life challenges that have tested her resilience and spirit, and she has come through with bountiful love and strength. She has my unwavering love and respect.

—Barry

I would like to dedicate this book to my wife, Diane Mastin, who has given me tremendous support, encouragement, and love throughout my career. She has inspired me with her unfailing kindness and consideration for all.

—John

Contents

PART A ▶ COMMUNICATION AND COLLABORATION

Chapter 2 ▶ Leading from the Middle Out *39*

Chapter 3 ▶ Understanding and Motivating Healthcare
Employees *73*

PART C ▶ COMPETITION AND COMMITMENT

Chapter 6 ▶ Leading with Vision: Competing Successfully in Healthcare Environments   *169*

Chapter 9 ▶ Patient Satisfaction and Quality Care: The Role of Leadership Communication   253

Chapter 10 ▶ Strategies for Maximizing Leadership Effectiveness in Healthcare Organizations   289

Foreword

Dr. Richard Boehler, President and CEO, St Joseph Hospital, Nashua, New Hampshire

In evolutionary biology, the theory describing rapid change between longer periods of relative stability is called punctuated equilibrium. Subsets of a species develop characteristics that give them an adaptive advantage to survive, and natural selection defines who will prosper and who will falter. We are in a state of change in health care today that closely mirrors this phenomenon.

There have been brief periods of flux: Medicare in 1965 and DRG payment mechanisms in the 1980s are perhaps the best examples. But between these changes there has been relative stability—until now. In response to rising costs, an explosion of healthcare information technology, growing numbers of under- and uninsured, and the Affordable Care Act, healthcare organizations are maximally stressed to rapidly evolve in order to survive.

In some respects, changing overnight to adapt to new payment mechanisms and incentives and to effectively do population health management is akin to walking out of the tidal pool or being the first to fly. When you consider how we have conducted our business, gotten paid, and delivered patient care to date, the necessity to quickly evolve or fall behind those who can is not all that different.

It follows that expectations for healthcare leaders are changing quickly as well, and that expanded content knowledge, strategic acumen, and self-awareness are requisites to succeed. Of course, no one individual can do this alone. This is where *Mastering Leadership: A Vital Resource for Health Care Organizations* can play a role. Whether an experienced practitioner or a student exploring a career in healthcare management, Belasen, Eisenberg, and Huppertz provide valuable insights into effective leadership behaviors and the characteristics of a motivated management team. The competing values framework helps to focus leaders on quadrants of personal strength or relative weakness and create a gap analysis for themselves and their team.

The text also gives the reader a strong sense of the growing importance of community collaboration and the moral obligation to become a high reliability organization—all necessary to succeed in the short run. Whether it's the incessant drive to eradicate hospital-acquired infections or implement error-free medication administration, we have to radically and quickly evolve to those states. The good news is that there are a growing number of organizations that are well along on this path, and we have unprecedented tools to help us get there. Successful practitioners will recognize the opportunities that exist and guide their organizations, using tools like *Mastering Leadership: A Vital Resource for Health Care Organizations* in that journey. I, for one, am optimistic about our adaptability and resilience to succeed, however fast the change needs to be.

Acknowledgments

Writing this book was particularly challenging because the Patient Protection and Affordable Care Act has altered the landscape of healthcare environments significantly by requiring a magnitude of organizational transformations (e.g., value-based purchasing, integrated care delivery) characterized by higher levels of depth, scope, and complexity never before experienced by the healthcare industry. It required us to be on the lookout for relevant and current knowledge, run ideas by different audiences and external reviewers, and constantly update the material while ensuring the integrity of content and quality of presentation. Writing this book was also challenging due to the publisher's tight deadlines and production schedule. This is exactly why this book benefited from considerable support in release time, research funds, data collection, case applications, feedback on earlier drafts, family and collegial support, and help from network enthusiasts, associates, and friends.

A number of individuals reviewed earlier drafts of the manuscript and helped improve the quality of this book and shape its overall direction: Dr. Richard Boehler, President and CEO, St. Joseph Hospital, Nashua, New Hampshire, whose rich skills and talent that combine clinical, administrative, and academic knowledge, stimulated our thinking about transformations in the industry, and Dr. Margaret Tally and Dr. Nancy Frank, who encouraged us to take the outside-in perspective by focusing on patients and communication. Many thanks go to Amy Eisenberg for the feedback and suggestions that shaped the discussion on patient satisfaction and patient–physician communications. Thanks to Dr. Ari Belasen of Southern Illinois University–Edwardsville who provided useful comments about hospital optimization and reimbursement models without the hardship of econometric and estimation models, making the discussion convincingly clear.

Many thanks to our colleagues at SUNY–Empire State College, University at Albany, and Union Graduate College for their collegial support and advice when needed. We are indebted to the 12 anonymous reviewers whose suggestions and insights helped fine-tune the structure and direction of this book. Special thanks to Michael Brown, Publisher at Jones & Bartlett Learning, and his staff specialists: Nick Alakel and Chloe Falivene, Editorial Assistants; Sophie Teague, Senior Marketing Manager; and Lindsey Mawhiney, Associate Editor. Special thanks to Jones & Bartlett Learning in-house Production and Permissions Editors Rebekah Linga and Mary Flatley.

We would like to acknowledge the logistical support of two individuals, Kathryn Fitzgerald and Neila Lachhander, for the instructor ancillaries as well as the references for the book. Neila was instrumental in creating the test bank for the supplemental material and Kathryn managed all of the internal communications, including the assembly of the various parts of the manuscript that were sent to the publisher. Both were helpful in helping us meet the tight deadline for completing the manuscript and instructor's manual on schedule.

Many thanks to Dr. Tai Arnold, Dean of ESC School for Graduate Studies, who provided Alan Belasen with the release time and resources to support the research and writing leading to this book. Thanks to Dean Bela Musits, School of Management, Union Graduate College, for helping to fund our participation in academic conferences in which topics from this book were presented. Special thanks go to our families for their enthusiastic support and encouragement, giving us the strength to complete the work on this important book. Finally, we would like to recognize our students for their feedback on many of the learning activities associated with this book.

Alan, Barry, and John

Introduction

LEARNING OBJECTIVES

Students will be able to:

- Learn about the purpose and structure of this book
- Gain insight into the leadership challenges in the environment of health care
- Recognize the components of the analytical framework used in this book
- Develop a broader view of the internal and external environments surrounding the master leader
- Become familiar with the tenets of the competing values framework (CVF)
- Appreciate the complexity of the interdependent roles that master leaders assume
- Learn about the importance of using transformational and transactional leadership roles

Managing and Leading

For decades, experts have highlighted the difference between managers and leaders, noting that managers are not automatically leaders, and the expectations of managers and leaders differ significantly. Managers deal with the present, leaders deal with the future. Managers work in a structured and predictable environment, leaders foresee and embrace opportunities brought about by the unpredictability of change. Managers organize and supervise people to produce expected results, leaders motivate others to achieve beyond expectations.

Implicit in this dichotomy is the assumption that one is either a leader or a manager—not both. In addition, we often assume that management is the easier of the two roles, in which leaders emerge from the ranks of successful managers, and that upon becoming a leader, the task of managing falls to those below, whose talents and skills are more suited to operating a day-to-day enterprise.

In health care, it is not so simple. Long considered an industry characterized by incrementalism and predictability, health care has entered an era of unprecedented change. Historically, the preponderance of management duties focused on operational soundness, a requirement that importantly, has not disappeared but has intensified in the face of increasing regulatory scrutiny and decreasing financial security. However the skills essential for this role are likely to prove insufficient as challenges descend on healthcare organizations with unparalleled fury. An inward management focus will ill-equip leaders who must now define a role for the organization in the context of relations with stakeholders external to the institution and environmental conditions that will weed out those unable to link a vision with a plan to achieve it. Healthcare leaders who can map their futures to a blueprint for actualizing their organizations' missions are more likely to succeed. At the same time, the work of the organization must continue, amid an extremely high level of scrutiny by outside regulatory authorities that are examining the quality of care, operational processes, and financial soundness. Operational failures cannot be tolerated, and the financial penalties for errors—not to mention the costs to our patients who entrust their well-being to us—are severe. Organizations with leaders who are able to integrate innovation and operations, planning and coordination, and adaptability and reputation management will have a more prosperous and enduring presence in the industry.

Managing and leading—creating an environment in which these roles are complementary and integrated—may emerge as the paramount challenge for healthcare organizations in the coming generation. It will take considerable organizational fortitude to prevent leadership and management from succumbing to the natural tensions between the two. Can one individual perform both roles successfully? Leadership and management function differently and are guided by different goals and orientations: management functions best when it seeks to establish control and predictability for the organization, while leadership is required to move an organization and position it for success in a dynamic environment (Kotter, 2013). Rather than control, leadership relies more on tools of persuasion and influence. Rather than striving for permanence and stability, leadership focuses on change and adaptability. These seemingly contradictory orientations are synthesized, integrated, and unified in the concept of *master leader*.

Master leaders are capable of establishing a balance between the forces of certainty and transformation. Healthcare institutions will not be able to sustain themselves if excessive emphasis is placed on the former. Conversely, too much change, or change that is not designed and implemented effectively, can prove destabilizing to an institution that must carry out its duties with precision and care. We posit that in the upcoming era, healthcare organizations will transition successfully when they are led by individuals who can define, embrace, and execute their roles in the context of this delicate balance.

Target Audience

This book can help executives master the leadership skills essential for performance credibility, high reliability, and commitment to the value of quality care.

The book is geared toward educators and students of healthcare management; senior healthcare executives, CIOs, CMOs, and clinicians who wish to expand their skills and knowledge of healthcare leadership; and board members interested in identifying the core competencies of senior managers and executives.

The book has two goals: (1) define and clarify the extraordinary challenges that leaders in the healthcare industry are facing and will continue to confront in the coming years, and (2) advance a model of leadership that enables executives to steer their organizations through the quagmire of uncertainty created by legislative, economic, demographic, clinical, information management, and political change. Our approach demonstrates how the transformational demands of leadership can be effectively integrated with the transactional and operational necessities of managing. We employ the CVF as the fundamental structure for guiding leaders toward an aptitude for assimilating vision development, strategic planning, and operational management.

More specifically, this book will help executives, professionals, and learners to do the following:

- ► Map out important stakeholders in four critical domains of healthcare environments
- ► Acquire knowledge, skills, and abilities in the four domains of leadership
- ► Learn to align the leadership roles and competencies with organizational goals and strategies
- ► Assess personal strengths and weaknesses through understanding of gaps between where our skills are and where they need to be
- ► Identify areas for self-improvement and further development
- ► Develop skills that have a seemingly paradoxical relationship yet are essential for effective performance
- ► Learn to realign leadership profiles during transitions and with future organizational goals
- ► Use strategies and apply new knowledge and skills to maximize leadership effectiveness

You have embarked on a journey of learning and continuous improvement that will take you through the intricacies of healthcare organizations and their transition toward a value-based organization. We hope that this book will stimulate innovative thinking and new ways of doing business based on collaboration and transparency, quality of care, and accountability for outcomes.

Competing Values Framework

The CVF serves as the theoretical basis for the approach and structure of this book as it describes the paradoxes leaders encounter and the delicate balance they must maintain. The integrative nature of this framework allows us to chart internal and external stakeholders, map out their needs and interests, and help executives choose the right set of roles and type of responses for effective management. As a **development tool**, the CVF helps executives to identify strengths and weaknesses and align their competency profile with organizational goals and strategic objectives (Belasen, 2012). As a **diagnostic tool**, the CVF helps executives to see the competing tensions that exist in the complex environment of healthcare organizations and expand the repertoire of their strategic responses. In other words, the CVF helps executives increase their managerial effectiveness and at the same time improve organizational performance. As such, the CVF **creates value** at both the personal leadership competency level and the organizational capability level. A version of this framework developed specifically for this book is offered in **Figure I.1**. Note how the framework provides a roadmap for identifying the main topics of this book while at the same time it charts the critical domains of healthcare organizations.

Organization of the Book

The CVF comprises four quadrants formed by the transactional and transformational roles that leaders must play in order to deliver results today and prepare for an uncertain future tomorrow. In Chapter 1, we describe this framework in detail, examining its roots in organizational theory, and discussing its application

Figure I.1 Leadership in Healthcare Organizations: Constraints and Opportunities

to contemporary healthcare management. We also provide context for the CVF and the demand for *master leaders* as we summarize some of the trends that are shaping the environment for healthcare organizations today.

The remainder of the book is structured in four parts, corresponding to the four domains of action (quadrants) in Figure I.1, and each part contains two chapters. Together, the eight chapters parallel the eight CVF leadership roles. While these roles and their relationship to organizational success are elaborated in Chapter 1, the remaining chapters represent the values identified with the domains of action: communication and collaboration, coordination and compliance, competition and commitment, and community and credibility.

A synoptic view of the topics covered in each chapter is provided below.

Chapter 1: Becoming Master Leaders in Healthcare Organizations

The healthcare system is in a state of substantial change, and the need for transformational and transactional skills to meet the challenges for effective organizational transitions is explored in this chapter. But what is the right balance between management and leadership? The CVF is employed as the theoretical model for explaining and identifying how tensions between transactional and transformational leadership may be reconciled. The concept of *master leader* represents an integration of the roles and functions associated with preserving order, stability, and control on the one hand, and constructing a vision, directing change, and inspiring a workforce on the other. Master leaders possess the capability, flexibility, and dexterity to implement a broad range of communication options to achieve organizational goals. This chapter provides a detailed review of the landscape of change confronting healthcare leaders and the implications for leadership roles. It identifies communication orientations and message construction strategies associated with the responsibilities of the master leader in healthcare organizations.

PART A: COMMUNICATION AND COLLABORATION

Part A, *Communication and Collaboration*, covers the upper left quadrant of the CVF. The values associated with this quadrant (or domain of action) are associated with integrity and identity. Creating a culture of interprofessional collaboration and cross-functional synergies requires participative forms of leadership and communication, empowerment and self-management, and the use of motivational strategies that match the needs of employees and the complexity of the task environment. While Chapter 2 focuses on the critical role of middle managers in designing and leading teams and work units in healthcare organizations, Chapter 3 examines the importance of situational motivation for incentivizing employees in complex healthcare organizations.

Chapter 2: Leading from the Middle Out

Historically, the forces that fostered employee identification with the unit or department were considerably more potent than those that encouraged identification with the organization as a whole. After all, healthcare organizations are made up of individuals with very specific and typically very intensive training and who work in departments that perform only those tasks for which such training applies. Thus, organizational integration and teamwork at the cross-functional and interdepartmental levels, though highly desired and holding considerable benefit, often appear elusive. Studies indicate that the failure to mobilize teamwork has considerable costs and that it contributes to inefficient and wasteful resource consumption, excessive lengths of stay for patients, and diminished quality of decision making. In Chapter 2, we discuss the critical communication roles middle managers play in healthcare organizations. Although these individuals work in units or departments that historically operated as more or less isolated silos, they can prove invaluable in efforts to improve organizational integration and teamwork at the cross-functional and interdepartmental levels, which is increasingly important for healthcare organizations trying to adapt to new demands. This chapter identifies the constraints and barriers to teamwork in healthcare organizations, articulates the benefits and advantages of establishing an environment in which teamwork can flourish, and advances strategies for promoting teamwork on both lateral and vertical bases. This chapter also covers competencies associated with facilitating cross-functional and multidisciplinary teams, empowerment, self-management, and motivation.

Chapter 3: Understanding and Motivating Healthcare Employees

Some healthcare organizations experience high levels of employee satisfaction, retention, and productivity, while others contend with dispiritedness, lack of consistently acceptable performance, and turnover problems. Not surprisingly, environments characterized by the former tend to experience higher levels of patient satisfaction and loyalty, a less pronounced consumer predisposition toward litigiousness, and enhanced organizational efficiency. Instituting and sustaining such an environment requires leaders capable of helping employees develop positive associations with colleagues in both their particular areas of professional specialty as well as with the organization as a whole. Striking the right balance can be baffling for and feel beyond the reach of organizational managers. Leaders capable of achieving identity alignment at both functional and organizational levels understand the relationship of culture and motivation, and create what we term a *patient-centered* approach in the construction of systems by which standards of performance are defined, monitored, evaluated, and rewarded. This chapter focuses on competencies associated with emotional intelligence, supportive communication, mentoring, and resolving conflicts as well as the relationship of such competencies to organizational culture and human resources policy.

PART B: COORDINATION AND COMPLIANCE

Part B, *Coordination and Compliance*, covers the lower left quadrant of the CVF. The values associated with this quadrant are associated with security and stability. Effective healthcare leaders complement the adaptive culture (discussed in Chapter 1) with a highly reliable culture that supports integration of processes, efficiency of program delivery, and security and stability. While Chapter 4 focuses on technical processes and human systems and the execution of strategies aimed at promoting excellence of care; Chapter 5 examines the drivers of healthcare quality improvement, utilization of data-driven measurement programs, and compliance with Centers for Medicare and Medicaid Services (CMS) regulatory requirements and value-based purchasing. The importance of patient protection and evidence-based leadership is highlighted as well as the need to synchronize the sociotechnical systems in healthcare organizations.

Chapter 4: Becoming a Highly Reliable Healthcare Provider: The Role of Leadership

The definition of reliability with respect to health care is on the precipice of a fourth generation of change. Historically, the notion of reliability was characterized by "do no harm." As medicine modernized in the late part of the 18th century, reliability came to be characterized more by adherence to defined processes for administering care. Quality was assured or controlled to the extent that an organization could demonstrate that established protocols were followed in the administration of care. Toward the latter part of the 20th century, a new movement to define reliability began to take shape. Rather than focusing almost exclusively on procedures, the industry was encouraged to also focus on clinical outcomes. Today we are witnessing a paradigmatic shift in which evidence will play a more vital role in determining reliability. But most critically, evidence is unlikely to be related exclusively to assessments of the patient's condition in the confines of the healthcare organization, but on a longitudinal basis and in the patient's environment. This chapter reviews this phenomenon and identifies the implications and management obligations associated with provider organizations assuming a broader and more externally focused role in the continuum of care. Competencies examined in this chapter relate to performance evaluation, quality management, planning and coordination, and managing health information and informatics.

Chapter 5: Leading the Value-Based Organization: Championing Quality and Improving Safety

The concept of *quality* tends to be characterized most notably by the degree to which care is delivered properly and effectively. Yet quality has profound associations with operational soundness, financial and resource utilization, legal and compliance activity, stakeholder relations, and human resource management. Quality is at the center of an institution's principles. Among the most significant challenges healthcare organizations face is establishing a definition of quality that is integrative and that defines a common institutional ethic. Healthcare organizations are experiencing mounting pressure to abide by stringent regulatory and financial rules and constraints. This chapter describes the emerging and more comprehensive approaches to defining quality and identifies how strategic planning can integrate quality with operational management. Competencies discussed in this chapter relate to ethics and integrity, health policy and law, compliance, and healthcare cost control.

PART C: COMPETITION AND COMMITMENT

Part C, *Competition and Commitment,* covers the upper right quadrant of the CVF. The values associated with this quadrant are associated with goals and innovation. The external environment of healthcare organizations is rapidly changing, with a level of competition that requires leaders to act strategically and proactively. Effective healthcare leaders align resources and capabilities with external needs to ensure that the organization operates optimally. Chapter 6 identifies strategic objectives and marketing strategies that help to position the organization well within the market; Chapter 7 builds on the ideas and strategies discussed in Chapter 6 by covering goal setting, strategic planning, and allocation of fiscal resources aimed at attaining the vision of the organization.

Chapter 6: Leading with Vision: Competing Successfully in Healthcare Environments

The systematic and formal management of competitive relationships in health care, as compared with other industries, is a relatively recent phenomenon. From the mid-1950s, through the advent of Medicare and Medicaid, and up to the proliferation of managed care and the decline of fee-for-service models, competition was generally a second-tier priority for healthcare leaders. As the need for defining a place in the market and shaping an identity have emerged as core functions, marketing has become centrally related to organizational success or failure. Still, it is not uncommon for healthcare organizations to conceive of marketing in relatively narrow functional terms largely synonymous with promotion and advertising rather than as a comprehensive and strategic dimension of planning. This chapter establishes a broad-based working definition of marketing; identifies its relationship to the management of competition; demonstrates the value of key tools such as market analysis and competitor analysis; and highlights the relationship of marketing to organizational mission, vision, goals, stakeholder relations, and organizational values, in addition to policy, economic, and demographic trends. Essential competencies identified in this chapter relate to strategic planning and marketing, financial management and analysis, value-based health care, and the relationship of these competencies to organizational vision and mission.

Chapter 7: Achieving Sustained Commitment to the Goals of the Healthcare Organization

Like any organization, a healthcare institution guided toward the future by clear goals while preserving the agility and flexibility to navigate through shifting environmental circumstances should be well positioned to succeed. Yet the integration of goal setting and flexibility is beset by challenges particular to the healthcare industry. For example, the needs of the moment tend to be especially demanding and draw much of the organization's brainpower, energy, and resources toward operational necessities. At the same time, the environment is changing in ways that create uncertainty and a lack of coherence with respect to predictability. Given these challenges, mobilizing the mechanisms of and resources for goal setting and goal achievement in a manner that obtains both the input and support from internal and external stakeholders can seem beyond the control of healthcare leaders. This chapter focuses on how leaders can systematically construct goals—along with a program for their achievement—that reflect and account for both the mission of the organization and the changes that bear upon the industry. Competencies treated in this chapter include stakeholder analysis, critical thinking, goal setting, and decision making.

PART D: COMMUNITY AND CREDIBILITY

Part D, *Community and Credibility,* covers the lower right quadrant of the CVF. The values associated with this quadrant are associated with internal and external constituencies and with the importance of joint accountability. Higher rates of patient satisfaction and shifting toward a community perspective through shared resources and common goals facilitate trust between healthcare providers and patients. Chapter 8 focuses on the promotion of effective community relationships as well as the risks and limitations of using a community perspective.

Chapter 9 focuses on the transformative role of the master leader in creating a patient-centered culture and in improving the effectiveness of communication processes that shape the public image of the organization. Effective internal and external communications are central for the public image and the perception of organizational credibility.

Chapter 8: Healthcare Delivery: A Community-Based Perspective

Hospitals are becoming increasingly linked to the communities in which they reside, to the larger network of healthcare providers in general, and to the wider environment, which shapes the health of consumers who come to them for care. Consider the growth of healthcare systems, the impending proliferation of electronic systems for medical record management, the expanding need to examine clinical outcomes on longitudinal bases, the trend in which environmental influences of health are increasingly examined in the context of providing care—all of these factors draw the attention of the hospital to what occurs outside its doors. This chapter identifies those trends, which, when taken together, demand a more external and community-based perspective for healthcare institutions, and focuses on how healthcare leaders can marshal their organizations as they build and leverage relationships in their environments. This chapter examines competencies relating to the role of a leader whose organization must fit into broader alliance structures that serve the health needs of communities.

Chapter 9: Patient Satisfaction and Quality Care: The Role of Leadership Communication

Prior to the 1880s, hospitals were largely avoided by those who could afford to obtain care in their homes. Shortly thereafter, with the advent of more reliable surgical procedures and antiseptic approaches to caregiving, hospitals became the desired venue for the treatment of illness and disease. It has remained this way for well over 100 years. Today we are witnessing something of a trend reversal with the development of models by which the delivery of health care is occurring in more ambulatory-based facilities in the communities in which people live and work. Considerable experimentation is under way with respect to shifting the caregiving environment from the hospital to smaller, community-based venues, for example, patient-centered medical homes, which allow for more immediate, cost-effective, and well-coordinated care. This chapter addresses the importance of patient-centered and community-based innovations and reviews how healthcare organizations can evaluate their benefits and applicability to their systems. Competencies covered in this chapter focus on patient satisfaction, physician leadership, continuum of care and community-based health delivery systems, innovation, and continuous improvement.

Chapter 10: Strategies for Maximizing Leadership Effectiveness in Healthcare Organizations

Chapter 10 is also the concluding chapter is this book. It revisits the main ideas, strategies, insights, and evidence that were presented throughout the book in a scorecard fashion to help managers, executives, professors, and students to develop a robust understanding of and to acquire skills essential for leading complex healthcare organizations.

Responding to the challenges of leading healthcare organizations through transitions that demand alterations to organizational structure and strategy involves the development of a fundamentally more sophisticated and diverse complement of skills than has traditionally been in practice. Until the current generation of leadership, the skills necessary in health care focused on organizing structures, assigning tasks, constructing systems and policies that could respond to regulatory demands, and establishing protocols for accountability. As we approached the new millennium, it became convincingly clear that a new leadership paradigm was essential—yesterday's transactional leadership skills have become obsolete, even archaic. It is no longer enough for a healthcare manager to be a good technocrat, an efficient supervisor, and a proficient engineer of operational activity.

Today, the skills needed to direct healthcare organizations are more complex, more interdependent, and more multidimensional. In this regard, it is not surprising that such skill sets house elements that hold the potential for incompatibility and even conflict. For example, if we focus too heavily on the needs of the moment we risk losing sight of the instability and uncertainty in the terrain of the healthcare system; after all, the dynamics of healthcare economics, policy, and technology are tremendously fluid. If our gaze is too outward, we risk losing sight of the myriad of detail that keeps our operation in proper running order. In short, the demands on healthcare organizations require an approach to leading that unifies transactional and transformational emphases, and that successfully shifts these from an either/or to a both/and framework.

As guided by the CVF, the master leader—the focus of this chapter—possesses a skill composite characterized by flexibility and balance. The master leader encompasses the humanistic orientation necessary to galvanize a workforce toward a common goal, the environmental perspective essential for determining where and how the organization may fit into the context of a market and a future, the operational skills critical for achieving organizational efficiencies in an era increasingly characterized by resource limitations, and an understanding of how productive capacity can be maximized. This chapter will center on the importance of acquiring paradoxical skills and on the need to dynamically integrate the competencies described throughout the book into a capacity that encourages master leaders to manage the complexity of healthcare environments with courage, constancy, and confidence.

References

Belasen, A. T. (2012). *Developing women leaders in corporate America: Balancing competing demands, transcending traditional boundaries.* Santa Barbara, CA: Praeger.

Kotter, J. (2013, January 9). Management is (still) not leadership. *Harvard Business Review* [Web log]. Retrieved from http://blogs.hbr.org/2013/01/management-is-still -not-leadership/

CHAPTER 1 ▶

Becoming Master Leaders in Healthcare Organizations

LEARNING OBJECTIVES

Students will be able to:

- Contextualize and compare the cost-driven environment of the US healthcare system to other developed countries
- Recognize the economic pressure for reform and the need for a master leader in healthcare organizations
- Understand that the skills needed to manage a healthcare organization are complex, interdependent, and multidimensional
- Identify executive roles and competencies and how they are integrated into important managerial leadership responsibilities
- Analyze the conditions for building strong culture and crafting appropriate message orientations
- Distinguish effective communication strategies for handling internal and external stakeholders

Introduction

Healthcare leaders face unprecedented challenges: a shortage of key workers; millions of first-time recipients of health insurance; an aging population; a need to fortify evidence-based quality systems; technological changes that dramatically influence the nature and exchange of information; emerging treatment modalities that alter how and where medical care is administered, and pressures to contain costs and develop strategic alliances. Healthcare organizations require leaders to have one foot planted in an uncertain future and the other in a present that requires maintenance of operations.

Leadership and management function differently. Management strives for control and predictability. Leadership relies on influence to position the organization for success in a dynamic environment. Rather than striving for permanence and stability, leadership focuses on change and adaptability. Considerable organizational fortitude is required to prevent leadership and management from succumbing to natural tensions between them, particularly as such tensions manifest in healthcare organizations.

These seemingly contradictory orientations are unified in the world of the master leader. The concept of *master leader* represents an integration of the roles and functions associated with preserving order, stability, and control on the one hand, and constructing a vision, directing change, and inspiring a work force on the other. Master leaders possess the capability, flexibility, and dexterity to implement a broad range of communication options to achieve organizational goals. Herein, we identify communication orientations and message construction strategies associated with the responsibilities of the master leader in healthcare organizations.

The competing values framework (CVF) provides the theoretical basis for defining how paradoxically related roles can become compatible in order to address the complex, unprecedented challenges healthcare organizations face.

Changes and Trends in Health Care

Prior to World War II, just 10% of the nation's workers were covered by health insurance provided by their employers. At the time, health insurance was inexpensive, and with wage controls in place during the war, employers began to offer health insurance as a means of enticing prospective employees to join their organizations. By 1950, the number of workers receiving this benefit jumped five fold, to 50%. In 1965, the federal government implemented Medicare and Medicaid, which extended health coverage to the elderly and the poor, respectively. So, in a relatively brief period (less than 20 years), systems were implemented and programs were enacted such that sizable segments of the population—workers, those hovering at or below the poverty line, and senior citizens—would have their healthcare needs paid for by third parties. We became a nation of people covered by health insurance. Not surprisingly, the healthcare industry grew, and it grew at almost exponential velocity during the following decades; indeed, in 1960, national health spending accounted for 5.2% of GDP and escalated to approximately 17% by 2010 (Highlight Health, n.d.).

Interestingly, and in retrospect, we might even say *amazingly*, the insurance system remained largely cost-based for decades to come, just up to the very latter part of the 20th century (Shi & Singh, 2008). Under this arrangement, whatever it cost healthcare providers to take care of people's health needs was reimbursed by a third party. Payers placed little pressure on providers to keep costs down. Not that healthcare organizations or individual practitioners strove to be inefficient, but being inefficient didn't carry the same penalties as in other industries. The cost of inefficiency was simply built into the expense base and passed along to a willing payer.

Moreover, the push to outpatient care did not begin in earnest until the 1990s so competition for patients did not become as intense an issue until then.

The brakes were first applied to the system in 1983 when the federal government instituted prospective payment in the Medicare system (Levine & Abdellah, 1984). For the first time on a large-scale basis, fixed fees were assigned for the treatment of hundreds of diagnoses. In the 1990s, health maintenance organizations (HMOs) and other managed care companies followed suit, determining in advance the amount they would pay to providers for caring for their subscribers. Other trends were taking shape at the same time, in particular, a massive shift to outpatient care that was fueled by a combination of new surgical procedures such as laparoscopy and arthroscopy, as well as by insurance companies that began demanding that care be provided in the least expensive clinical venue possible (Danzon & Pauly, 2001). In short, the world of health care was changing in dramatic fashion.

Prior to the 1990s, we may view the execution of leadership in health care as occurring largely within transactional parameters. Establishing systems of governance, ensuring compliance in a rule-laden industry, and building hierarchical organizational structures to achieve clarity of role and function—these were the hallmarks of leadership for much of the period from the 1960s through the 1990s. Systems were not particularly open; hospitals tended to function cooperatively, though not necessarily interdependently. Leadership in the arena of brokering tended to occur with the medical staff; after all, this was the one stakeholder group that could exercise the most sway with respect to the policies and direction of the hospital. Innovation communication; conceiving and introducing fundamental change—was a commodity that received less organizational emphasis than operational management (Belasen & Rufer, 2014). Capital acquisition, however, was important. It was here that hospitals had no choice—a hospital caught off guard by failing to remain clinically current with the most up-to-date x-ray machine or rehabilitation equipment, risked losing its medical staff to facilities that stayed closer to the leading edge.

A particular synchronicity typified the relationship between leadership and management during these many years. Hierarchies in hospitals were spawned, and with adherence to rules and procedures dominating organizational activity, monitoring and coordinating constituted principal functions.

As we moved into the 1990s, the emerging set of environmental conditions and demands collided with, and made easy dispatch of, the relative simplicity of prior decades. The change had a tsunami-like ferocity and swiftness: reimbursement was now determined as much by the payer as by the provider, hospitals watched as large segments of their customer base migrated to outpatient facilities, and patients were getting older and sicker, consuming more resources and requiring progressively advanced levels of clinical expertise. A dual assault on revenue was unleashed: competition for patients was increasing while payments for providing care were shrinking. The role of leadership was quickly changing, but the rule-governed nature of the industry was not; in fact, the regulatory emphasis was expanding. Moreover, as advances were altering the nature of how care was being provided, it was also altering the nature of how information was acquired, stored, exchanged, and managed.

Leaders who were unable to reposition their role from transactional system administrators to that of transformational change architects were ill equipped to guide their organizations into the complex future that was already whooshing through the entrances of their hospitals. Now open, the system required relationship management across a range of fronts, and leadership needs began to take on the appearance of multiple and interlocking chessboards. Hospital leaders now needed to devote more time to the quest of outmaneuvering rivals in competitive mode while engaging them cooperatively to advance mutual and industry interests. Creative and bold approaches to workforce management involved questioning assumptions about normative workweek patterns and role structures. Bringing their organizations to the attention of the public through channels of advertising demanded new ways of thinking about how communication could be employed in the service of identifying and reaching customer bases. Negotiating contracts with managed care organizations was pivotal in determining revenue flow into the hospital, which panels of physicians could practice at the hospital, and which patients could be served by the institution. Envisioning a service mix that addressed the emerging and future healthcare needs of the communities they served demanded expertise in market analysis and forecasting.

Moreover, the dimensions of the healthcare organization—its very status as an independent organizational entity—were no longer guaranteed. Pooling resources in the quest to achieve economy of scale meant joining forces with others. Who wins in this game? Who determines the culture of the emergent organization? Leaders suddenly found themselves having to confront challenges that seemed distant from the galaxy they recently inhabited. Responding to the interests of the community while simultaneously integrating into a system that served the needs of multiple communities, often with discrepant cultural characteristics and clinical needs, required leadership acumen capable of unifying mutually exclusive forces. A rapid and aggressive shift from transactional to transformational leadership roles was in order. Success now demanded an ability to innovate, to broker, to mentor, and to facilitate.

All the while that demand for paradigmatic change was being foisted on organizational leaders in health care, the need for the institution to maintain operations—to take care of patients and pass muster in the face of intense regulatory scrutiny—was not abating. Managers were fixed in hierarchies that had to remain defined and stable to ensure orderliness in accomplishing the work of the organization. On the other hand, the organization around them was afloat in uncharted waters that, by definition, demanded flexibility and agility.

The Complex and Dynamic Nature of Healthcare Environments

The challenges facing the healthcare industry are unprecedented in scope, number, and magnitude. Organizational realignments have changed the provider landscape and have made the *healthcare system*, rather than the individual hospital, the dominant entity in the provider industry. Uncertainty about the course and impact of legislation stifles the progress of provider institutions or introduces uncomfortable levels of guesswork into their strategic planning. An aging population calls for clinical protocols and resource configurations that address increasingly acute and prolonged states of illness. Information management technologies are evolving rapidly, increasing diagnostic and clinical capabilities, but also requiring huge investments of capital and, analogous to the electrical grid, linking provider organizations to one another through patient data.

Pressure to establish reliable systems of quality management as well as outcome- and evidence-driven models of care delivery require hospitals to monitor the effects of their work well after patients walk out the door, and demand that hospitals ready themselves for a progressively expansive role in the continuum of care. Similarly, the trend of identifying the impact of environment on health and connecting such knowledge to the provision of patient care is taking root. Clinical advancements are occurring at a rapid rate, changing the skill mix in ways that require human resources forecasting expertise not traditionally common in healthcare organizations. Projected shortages of critical caregivers, especially the key clinical positions of physician and nurse, are expected to continue. Administrative demands are increasing at a rate such that management ranks are expected to require considerable expansion.

As hospitals and other provider institutions continue to coalesce into larger systems, far more integrative and systematic approaches to planning and market development will be necessary to fill beds with patients whose health needs are highly compatible with the mission and orientation of the facility. That means coordinating and collaborating with other facilities in strategic partnerships. It also means reaching into the community and having a well-conceived approach to managing relationships with key stakeholder groups, including physicians, payers and patients. New patients are entering the system through reform, creating both opportunities and challenges. This phenomenon could mean new sources of revenue and market share, but it is not likely to occur without the proper forethought, including the recognition that many of the newly covered patients have little experience with how to engage the system effectively.

While all these trends are occurring, it is still necessary for the institution to be managed properly. This involves ensuring that the appropriate resources are available for patients entering the facility, that those resources are deployed efficiently, and that responsibilities are carried out effectively.

The future is filled with uncertainty, challenge, and change. It is also filled with promise and opportunity. This future is on our doorstep.

Master Leaders: Balancing Act

What is the right balance between management and leadership? How do we evaluate the tradeoffs between behaviors and roles that are both mutually exclusive and collectively exhaustive? How do we account for shifts in behaviors when organizational leaders and managers grapple with a changing environment? How do we group and differentiate roles and behaviors across hierarchical levels and organizational lines to facilitate internal and external communications?

As discussed in the next section, both transformational qualities and transactional rigor are needed for effective managerial leadership. Master leaders help inspire and energize people to think onward and outward (outside-in) in addition to directing and focusing organizational resources and capabilities inwardly (inside-out) to achieve organizational goals. Master leaders combine vision-setting and high risk tolerance, task-oriented and hands-on coaching, and analyzer and sensitivity skills, which results in energizing employees and setting higher performance targets. They ask "how," not just "why"—they guide rather than find fault. They convert the process of doing into an opportunity for learning. Master leaders are more successful in handling novel or exceptional situations and generally exhibit greater behavioral and cognitive complexity than less effective managers (Belasen & Frank, 2008; Denison, Hooijberg, & Quinn, 1995; Hart & Quinn, 1993).

Competing Values Leadership

The competing values framework (**Figure 1.1**), a tool made of integrated, inevitably bonded paradoxes, helps us understand the triggers and implications of a balanced managerial leadership. The CVF is highlighted in the literature as one of the 40 most important frameworks in the history of business, and the framework

Figure 1.1 Competing Values Framework (CVF): Leadership Roles

Modified from: Quinn, R. E. (1988). *Beyond rational management: Mastering the paradoxes and competing demands of high performance* (p. 48). San Francisco, CA: Jossey Bass. Reproduced with permission of John Wiley & Sons Inc.

has been studied and tested in organizations for more than 25 years (Cameron, Quinn, DeGraff, & Thakor, 2006).

Originated by Quinn and Rohrbaugh (1983) and Quinn (1988), the CVF highlights the contradictory nature inherent in organizational environments and the complexity of choices faced by managers when responding to competing tensions. These responses include a variety of managerial roles differentiated by situational contingencies. The CVF displays the repertoire of leadership roles by aligning pairs of roles with specific domains of action (**Figure 1.2**).

The innovator and broker roles rely on creativity and communication skills to bring about change and to acquire the resources necessary for change management. The monitor and coordinator roles are more relevant for system maintenance and integration and require project management and supervision skills. While the director and producer roles are geared toward goal achievement, the facilitator and mentor roles are aimed at generating a motivated work force driven by commitment and involvement. The upper part of the framework contains transformational roles while the lower part includes transactional roles (Belasen, 2000).

Transformational leadership qualities contribute to greater follower motivation, satisfaction, and results. Transformational leaders are deemed to be altruism oriented and grounded in caring based on benevolence. These factors compel followers to go beyond their self-interest and focus on the organization and

Figure 1.2 Competing Values Framework: Leadership Roles (Top Managers)

Modified from: Hart, S. L., & Quinn R. E. (1993). Roles executives play: CEOs, behavioral complexity, and firm performance. *Human Relations, 46*, 543–574.

the greater community. This generates good will and provides a propensity for positive results. Thus, the transformational leader sparks both an interpersonal dependence with followers and an empowering independence that encourages identification with the organization and its environment.

Transactional managers focus on the orderly accomplishment of tasks and work activities, largely with an immediate or short-term focus. They provide correction when necessary and offer rewards for positive behavior. Compliance, sometimes by coercion, is stressed while creativity and innovation are deemphasized and discouraged because these phenomena represent departures from the status quo. Power is unequal between managers and followers, and communication, when negatively established, is often blocked by uncertainty, fear of reprisal, and mistrust. Simply put, what is most important to the transactional manager is getting things done, whereas the transformational leader focuses on the people who perform the work and the relationship of those people to the work environment.

The key to successful mastery is recognizing the contradictory pressures on the managerial role. Master leaders know how to navigate these roles to balance contradictory demands from diverse constituencies. They are also perceived by others as displaying the eight CVF roles more often than less effective managers (Denison et al., 1995). Gender differences do not change this conclusion: men and women are regarded as equally competent (or incompetent) leaders when assessed objectively by their supervisors, peers, or staff in terms of how well they display the CVF roles (Vilkinas, 2000; Belasen & Frank, 2012).

Master leaders display behavioral complexity that allows them to master contradictory behaviors while maintaining some measure of behavioral integrity and credibility. The concept of paradox reinforces the idea that the structure of this behavioral complexity is not neat, linear, or bipolar, but is instead a more complicated form (Denison et al., 1995). This finding was also supported by other studies that used full-circle assessments to measure the perceptions of leadership roles and their effects on managerial behavior across levels (Belasen, 1998; Hooijberg & Choi, 2000).

Successful organizations benefit from the effective blending of the eight leadership roles—the essence of great *managerial leadership*. Using contemporary management theory, our goal is to demonstrate the organizational benefits of leaders functioning as architects of inspirational change, communicating the vision for their organization, and mobilizing support for that vision while also ensuring that tasks are accomplished, resources are managed effectively, and performance goals are obtained successfully. When leadership and management function interdependently, organizational goals are infinitely more attainable. By tracing the evolving leadership and managerial challenges in the healthcare industry, we provide a window into the critical attributes of master leaders.

Hart and Quinn (1993) developed a model of four archetypal leadership roles that correspond with four domains of action to test the efficacy of the CVF. They also investigated the importance of cognitive and behavioral complexity as the condition for superior leadership performance. These roles (and domains) are depicted in the inner circle of Figure 1.2: taskmaster (performance), vision-setter (direction), analyzer (conformance), and motivator (inspiration). The outer circle includes the leadership challenges expected of healthcare CEOs. Executives in healthcare organizations are challenged to clarify the strategic vision for their organizations; inspire employees to transform their ways of thinking about patient care and the culture of the organization; employ evidence-based best practices to improve patient quality and safety; and improve the overall efficiency and productivity of the organization.

The results of Hart and Quinn's study (1993) specifically underscored the importance of the vision-setter and motivator roles (which overlap the transformational roles) for business performance. The findings also indicated that the unbalanced playing of the taskmaster and analyzer (which overlap the transactional roles) appears to be detrimental to business performance and organizational effectiveness. Superior performance was achieved by organizations with executives who played all four roles concomitantly. Master leaders spent more time focusing on broad visions for the future while evaluating performance plans. They also paid attention to relational issues while simultaneously addressing tasks and action plans. When managers overemphasize one set of values (or play certain roles extensively without considering the other roles) the organization may become dysfunctional. This sentiment was echoed by Quinn (1988) who labeled this imbalance "the negative zone." The single-minded pursuit of one set of values without paying needed attention to the other values or roles creates conditions of suboptimization that often lead to organizational failure.

Personality Traits and Roles

When a manager plays a particular role, the choice of that role is influenced by personality traits or characteristics. Personality traits and their interrelationships have been documented to affect managerial goals, values, and needs (Herringer, 1998; Sharp & Ramanaiah, 1999) as well as leadership behavior (Hogan, Curphy, & Hogan, 1994). For example, the five factor model (FFM) (Costa, McCrae, & Dembroski, 1989; Digman, 1997) consists of four emotionally stable traits: agreeableness, extroversion, conscientiousness, and openness (Costa & McCrae, 1992) and a fifth trait, emotional stability (at the low end of neuroticism) was found to be related to effective transformation and transactional role behaviors (Belasen & Frank, 2008; Bono & Judge, 2004; Leung & Bozionelos, 2004).

In addition to the relationship between the first four FFM traits, low levels of emotional stability, the fifth trait, would seem to be associated with behavioral extremes indicated by Quinn's (1988) negative zone. Responding appropriately to competing demands requires balanced role strengths along with high levels of emotional stability, whereas lower levels of emotional stability combined with weaker, unbalanced role behaviors, give rise to reactionary, extreme behaviors that often result in ineffective outcomes. Less effective managers who engage in restricted, inflexible modes of thinking find themselves confined to the negative zone, whereas effective managers, who are able to detect and respond to contradictory signals, reside within the positive zone.

Managers who are able to master the paradoxical behaviors and skills associated with all of the roles have the capacity to use a set of adaptive responses to deal with complexity in a variety of situations. The concept of paradox underscores the importance of developing behavioral flexibility and considering the dynamic interplay across the various roles. By observing the roles and types of messages used by managers across hierarchical levels, we can also obtain a clearer picture of shifts in emphasis in how each level appreciates its roles and expectations in terms of responses to changes in the task environment (Belasen & Frank, 2010).

The CVF is particularly helpful in clarifying expectations during organizational transitions and shifts in importance of organizational goals. Knowing in advance what senior managers communicate and detecting the tone of the messages should also help managers avoid second guessing and, instead, focus attention on messages that are consistent with the expectations of higher-level managers.

Leadership and Management: Not Necessarily Yin and Yang

There is no question that both leadership and management are demanding, challenging, and vital to the successful operation of organizations. But management and leadership have different centralities: management is job centered, whereas leadership is employee centered. Management is responsible for the attainment of organizational goals in an effective and efficient manner through planning, organizing, staffing, directing, and controlling organizational resources. A key word in that definition is *control*. Managers use centralized authority for *controlling* and *directing* the behavior of employees to ensure that organizational stability is maintained. In management, the executive serves an operational role; he or she formally possesses *power*, that is, the *control* over resources and the responsibility for the outcome of the employees' actions. Leadership, on the other hand, is not bound by the hierarchical relations that govern managerial roles and serve as the source for organizational authority. Rather, leadership is a process of influence. While managers use explicit sources of administrative power (e.g., reward, legal action, punishment) to structure the situation, leaders use implicit sources of power to structure attitudes and shape the identity of followers through persuasion and inspiration.

Leadership and management function in dissimilar ways to ensure organizational livelihood; however, because they aim for distinct outcomes it can be very difficult for one to succeed at both leading and managing. Management relies heavily on control, whereas leadership relies on shared authority and the empowerment of subordinates. It is difficult for people to successfully practice management and leadership simultaneously because management and leadership hold the potential for conflicting agendas and outcomes. Management maintains stability, predictability, and order through a desired *culture of efficiency*; leadership creates change within a *culture of integrity* that helps the organization thrive over the long haul by promoting openness and honesty, positive relationships, and long-term innovation. While management strives for productivity, leadership strives for change (Belasen, 2000). It can be argued that management follows homeostatic processes geared toward equilibrium while leadership employs the forces of morphogenesis, adaptation, and frame breaking. Leadership cannot replace management. In fact, in order for a company or organization to succeed, leadership and management must go hand in hand. The challenge for success in both functions lies in balancing management duties with leadership utilities—the attributes of master leaders.

Although manager and leader are typically considered contrasting roles, and because leadership is not bound by position, in theory anyone in an organization can have a leadership presence, including a manager. The term *manager* indicates a transactional, authoritative position derived from the organizational hierarchy that is concerned with internal consistency, procedures and policies, setting goals for employees, and emphasizing tasks and duties. Conversely, a leader functions transformationally and informally, and the role is often assumed organically, not assigned. Leadership is based on interacting with others to create a shared organizational purpose and reality, influencing and structuring attitudes, helping followers to identify their value systems, and emphasizing people rather than tasks. A transformational leader exhibits behaviors that communicate the mission and vision of the organization, examines new perspectives and creative ideas for solving problems, and develops and mentors employees. One of the main differences between managers and leaders is that managers have subordinates and leaders have followers. However, because of the fluidity of many forms of organizational structure, managers are often leaders and leaders are often managers. This is especially true in healthcare organizations.

The Role of Communication

Communication is the vibrant thread that ties together employee vitality, clarity of direction and purpose, and results and progress. Master leaders use communication as a tool to achieve organizational goals. However, this tool must be used strategically, laser focused to produce results, not merely to fill the airwaves. A plethora of communication does not guarantee vital and engaged employees who are aligned to produce results. In fact, over-communicating can be as destructive as under-communicating. The former can cause confusion, misunderstandings, loss of productivity, and can overwhelm those on the receiving end. The latter can lead to distrust, uncertainty, low morale, and a lack of alignment.

Communication from a transactional perspective is a largely information-based and downward (management to workforce) exchange of information through formal and informal channels. Clear, concise, targeted instructions to subordinates lead to the accomplishment of tasks that fuel results. On the other hand, communication from a transformational perspective is largely vision based and is multidirectional—upward and downward as well as horizontal.

An important question is how managers select the right role in which to communicate different tasks and goals and use the most effective message orientation, or right approach, for each task or goal they encounter. Often managers at different levels see themselves as members of separate constituencies in the same organization rather than as members of the same team. The common language offered by the CVF ameliorates the separateness because it is essentially an organizational language that identifies performance criteria that are common across the hierarchy. Clarifying managerial roles and expectations can help minimize role ambiguity as well as reduce the potential for role conflict. Likewise, interpersonal conflicts associated with turf issues, status, and power can be avoided in favor of developing a constructive dialogue and encouraging positive communication.

Rogers and Hildebrandt (1993) and Belasen (2008) suggested that each quadrant in the CVF represents a different message orientation with significant parallels and polar opposites: relational, hierarchical, promotional, and transformational (**Figure 1.3**). When managers use the mentor and facilitator roles, for example, they use a relational approach to communication, which places emphasis on the insights and feedback of the receivers. A promotional orientation fits the behaviors displayed by the director and producer roles that rely on

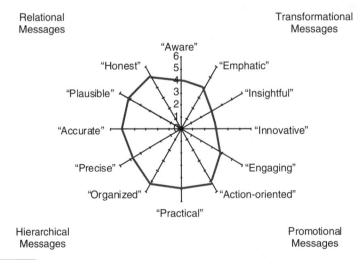

Figure 1.3 Competing Values Framework: Message Orientations and Styles

Modified from: Belasen, A. T. (2008). *The theory and practice of corporate communication: A Competing values perspective* (p. 114). Thousand Oaks, CA: Sage.

persuasion strategies to meet functional objectives. A transformational orientation matches the styles and behaviors of the innovator and broker roles that are geared toward selling ideas effectively and meeting future organizational and adaptation goals. Hierarchical message orientations, on the other hand, align with the monitor and coordinator roles, which focus on integrating individuals and groups through work processes and systems of control. Transformational-based messages are aimed at sustaining the ability of the organization to adapt to change. There is a focus on adaptation and change, branding, and reputation management to address interests of external stakeholders (Gotsi & Wilson, 2001). Success is determined by the extent to which the framing of communication is insightful, mind stretching, and visionary.

Promotional messages relate to the mission of the organization to meet external expectations for products, to perform productively to maximize owners' returns on equity, and to enhance performance credibility and organizational accountability (Belasen, 2008). Success is determined by the extent to which the communication is framed in a conclusive, decisive, and action-oriented manner. Hierarchical messages reflect rules of behavior and codified decisions aimed at regularizing interactions between managers and employees. Hierarchical messages characterize the flow and dissemination of formal communications across organizational lines. Success is determined by whether the communication frame seems realistic, practical, and informative. There is a focus on organizational identity, coordination, symbolic convergence, compliance, uniformity, and control (Belasen, 2008; Fairhurst & Putnam, 2004).

Relational messages are aimed at personal relationships, informal interactions, peer communications, and maintaining an awareness of the importance of the role of the individual in completing the organization's mission. There is a focus on social identity, common understanding, commitment, and concerns for human development. These messages maintain the circle of interactions within the organization and stimulate opportunities for revising and realigning social networks with the mission and goals of the organization. Members who constantly seek to improve relationships through constructive cycles of feedback and positive communication are discerning and perceptive of the needs of individuals and groups as important organizational stakeholders.

Competing Frames

Recognizing the existence of competing frames can be used as a personal roadmap for self-improvement (i.e., diagramming personal profiles) or as a tool to help managers understand how well they need to balance the different orientations across the quadrants and the steps they can take for improving oral and written communication. One application (which emphasizes style over content) is diagrammed in Figure 1.3.

In this real-life example, the manager seems to place more weight on relational and hierarchical message styles than on transformational and promotional, suggesting a preference toward working with individuals within boundaries of trust, structures, and rules. This manager's profile, however, seems to deflect the need for placing importance of equal value on the right side of the framework where messages are aimed at energizing people toward new ideas and commitment to engage in new tasks. When subordinates, peers, and supervisors provide their inputs (often referred to as 360 assessments), this framework can become a powerful tool for guiding improvement efforts based on expectations from others (Belasen, 2008). Under normal conditions the four message orientations or approaches are reflections of administrative responsibilities, with top executives communicating strategic priorities and managers and supervisors translating them into concrete and more practical objectives and tasks that employees accomplish.

The Advantage of Creating Appropriate Messages

Managers reporting to higher levels can gain a number of advantages by using the model of message orientations described in this chapter. Having a strong understanding of the frequency (amount of content), flow (who the message is directed to), and the intensity of the message (power of the message or the source of the message) can help mitigate communication roadblocks as well as clarify organizational directions and expectations. The model is particularly helpful in clarifying expectations during organizational transitions and shifts. This model is relevant for explaining communications and message orientations in healthcare organizations undergoing transition. Knowing in advance what managers communicate, as well as detecting the tone of the messages, should also help managers avoid second guessing objectives and instructions; instead, it will allow them to focus attention on messages that are consistent with the expectations of higher-level managers.

When the lines of communication are clear and the messages reach their target audiences with appropriate orientation, the consistency of organizational communication increases. Creating appropriate messages and choosing the right communication channels to deliver messages can help managers align their goals with the expectations of higher- and lower-level managers, thus increasing vertical alignment across administrative lines. This should also help reduce the opportunity for miscommunication and the potential for conflict between senders and receivers. Knowing that managers at all levels of the organization demonstrate an awareness of the four orientations also provides an additional tool in developing a common language for sharing expectations across administrative levels. Awareness of these differences could help ameliorate unnecessary frustrations and misunderstandings among the managerial levels especially during organizational transitions (Belasen & Frank, 2010).

When paired with the role quadrants of the CVF these message orientations provide an avenue for engaging employees in such a way that optimal performance becomes possible. The ultimate goal of a for-profit enterprise is to maximize value and profitability for the shareholder, and is accomplished by integrating the transformational and transactional aspects of managerial leadership. Similarly, nonprofit and governmental organizations, whose aim is service in its many facets, rely on a blend of transformational and transactional approaches. As discussed in the following section, the arena of health care provides key insights into the application of high performance leadership and the roles and message orientations used by master leaders.

The Healthcare Industry: A Divergence of Leadership and Management

The healthcare industry has been twisted and turned by a whirlwind of forces since the middle of the 20th century. Finding a balance, that state of homeostasis in which leadership and management cohabit so that healthcare organizations can move forward, has become an increasingly daunting challenge. It is no wonder that since the early part of the 1990s organizational realignments—mergers, acquisitions, reductions in size, expansions, wholesale changes in service offerings, diversifications, and closures—have occurred with resounding speed and frequency (Galloro, 2011). A glimpse into the window of the challenges healthcare managers have faced can help us appreciate the uneasiness of transformational–transactional dynamics and how the balance between them needs to shift as environmental conditions change. The implications for the roles, functions, and definitions of leadership are profound, and shades of these implications are evident in all healthcare institutions across the spectrum of the industry.

The Paradoxical Nature of Change and Stability

What had been for years a relatively noncontentious relationship between the roles and functions of leadership and management, suddenly became a struggle with agendas and purposes that diverged. Leaders had to enter into unfamiliar territory using new tools of navigation; managers, on the other hand, needed to work within the confines of predictable boundaries and reliable processes using tools that had served their needs for quite some time. Strains and stresses between leadership and management are not unique to health care. All industries ebb and flow, and shifts between maintaining stability and envisioning change take place in ways that defy predictability. Moreover, organizations benefit when they have leaders who have the skill and incentive to imagine ways of positioning their organizations for success in the future and managers who are skilled at ensuring that vital processes are followed effectively and efficiently.

Is it inevitable that leading and managing are destined to be bound by a mutually exclusive governing dynamic? Hardly. The competing values framework offers insight into strategies for achieving the right balance between transformational and transactional leadership roles. The concept of *alignment* provides a starting point. We posit that the more alignment that exists in four sets of organizational relationships, the more proximal and synchronous leadership and management will be and the more likely that the integrated force of transformational and transactional roles will be achieved.

Grove Memorial Hospital

Mission and function. A small community hospital of 200 beds, Grove Memorial Hospital has served a working class community just outside of a large metropolitan area for the past 50 years. The hospital recently determined that it could not sustain itself as an independent institution in light of constricted revenue streams. After exploring relationship opportunities, the hospital made a strategic decision to merge into a system comprised of six hospitals (we'll call the system Midwest Elite), all of which were larger than Grove Memorial; the flagship was a state-of-the-art, 550-bed hospital with over 700 physicians on its medical staff. Grove Memorial took pride in being a center of health education for the community and for providing "high touch" acute care basic services. It was homey. Grove Memorial was the type of hospital in which patients and employees were neighbors. The board was composed of local business owners and community residents. Once absorbed into Midwest Elite, Grove Memorial's service menu was forced to change in order to facilitate Midwest Elite's achievement of broader, system-wide goals. The board of Midwest Elite determined that Grove Memorial should focus on specialty care, and in particular on orthopedic surgery (e.g., knee and hip replacements, joint repair). A struggle ensued between the boards of Grove Memorial and Midwest Elite over the mission and function of Grove Memorial. The local board won the battle, but the larger board won the war: the mission of the hospital remained community care, but the function shifted to specialty care. No longer would Grove Memorial serve only residents of the community. Instead, patients from a wider geographical area would be directed there for orthopedic care. The gap between the mission of the organization and the function of the organization created confusion for core stakeholders: employees, consumers, the community, physicians, suppliers of products, and third-party payers. Leadership was exercised on a more transactional than transformational basis. Whether the shift away from a community hospital orientation was good policy and a sound business decision is fodder for debate. But leadership was required to recast the mission of Grove Memorial and to move it in a fundamentally different direction. As such, transformational leadership was essential in order to persuade the array of stakeholders to move in the same direction.

Message orientation and organizational direction. Grove Memorial was caught in a paradox: it sought to capture and communicate two ostensibly contradictory themes in its message orientation. On one hand, it desired to reassure its constituencies, internal and external, that it was not changing. On the other hand, the organization needed to communicate a new direction. Achieving success with one message, by definition, negated the second. Transformational-based messages steer stakeholders to envision opportunities and possibilities for the organization, and such possibilities represent a departure from the status quo. Success is dependent on the extent to which such messages resonate, hold credibility, are motivational, and point the way with clarity. Energizing and mobilizing followers is a hallmark of transformational leadership and communication. On the other hand, hierarchical message orientation is of value in facilitating stakeholder appreciation for steadiness and constancy; it may be employed to provide an understanding of status rather than to chart a new course. Grove Memorial could hardly brand itself as a community hospital when it was now serving the needs of a region. It was disinclined to be perceived exclusively as a "center of excellence"—known principally for a particular medical specialty—for fear of alienating what had always been its core community.

Facing a dilemma of the sort Grove Memorial confronted is not uncommon for organizations. How can communication be organized strategically so that it projects reassurance and, at the same time, newness—comfort *and* enthusiasm— security *and* anticipation—permanence *and* change? All organizations face such challenges. Some fail because of an inability to find a healthy balance—going too far in an attempt to satisfy one drive creates the risk of communicating either staleness or, on the other extreme, instability. The related danger is trying to have it both ways and failing to present them as compatible.

The key is aligning communication strategy and orientation with organizational direction. Grove Memorial could not embark on a successful communication campaign until it resolved the question of its identity and direction. Once accomplished, it could construct messages that could help it explain why and how it was transitioning from what it was to what it planned to be, and why this course of action was desirable or necessary or both. Grove Memorial could employ multiple and highly coordinated message orientations as part of a comprehensive strategy in which its future direction logically evolved from a successful and well-known past.

Culture and external environment. Not surprisingly, organizational culture is resistant to change. Adapting culture to environmental change demands that leaders perform on transformational levels. Cameron and Quinn (1999) developed a model for assisting managers and other change agents to make sense of their organization's culture. The model allows for a comprehensive assessment that maps the cultural profile of the target organization along the lines of four culture types: hierarchy, market, clan, and adhocracy. The predominant cultural type of an organization is identified by surveying employees' attitudes toward organizational dominant characteristics, leadership, management of employees, core values, strategic emphasis, and criteria for success. Their methodology, which includes a theoretical framework and a validated instrument, allows for the systematic diagnosis of an organization's predominant current and preferred cultures. Systematic cultural diagnosis is a necessary precursor to implementing effective change efforts. Assessments of organizational culture are useful because they help managers and organizations adapt to the demands of external environments and enhance organizational performance. These four types of cultures are consistent with the dimensions and quadrants of the CVF and are depicted in **Figure 1.4**.

The *hierarchy* culture is characterized by a formalized and structured workplace. Rules and procedures govern organization members' actions. Leaders are good coordinators and organizers who help to maintain a smooth running operation. Value is placed on stability, predictability, and efficiency. The organization is oriented toward internal concerns and is kept together by formal rules and policies. The *market* culture is characterized by a focus on the external environment and transactions with external constituencies including investors, business partners, and regulators. The organization is a results-oriented workplace. Leaders are hard-driving producers and competitors. Value is placed on competitive actions and meeting goals and targets. The glue that holds the organization together is an emphasis on winning.

Figure 1.4 Four Types of Cultures

Modified from: Cameron, K.S., & Quinn, R.E. (2011). *Diagnosing and changing organizational culture*. John Wiley & Sons.

The *clan* culture is characterized by a workplace that is supportive and interactive. The organization dominated by a clan culture is like an extended family to its members. Leaders act as and are thought of as mentors and even parental figures. The glue that holds the organization together is loyalty and tradition. Individual development, high cohesion, positive morale, teamwork, and consensus are valued. Success is defined in terms of the internal climate and concern for organizational members. Finally, the *adhocracy* culture is characterized by a dynamic, entrepreneurial, and creative workplace. Organizational members are risk takers. Effective leadership in an adhocracy culture is visionary, innovative, and risk oriented. Commitment to innovation is the glue that holds the organization together. Value is placed on being on the leading edge of knowledge, products and services, being poised for change, and meeting challenges. Success means producing new and original products and services.

Grove Memorial, for the better part of its history, had a predominantly clan–hierarchy culture (**Figure 1.5**). This was quite serviceable because the hospital was highly integrated into the community, and internal communications reaffirmed a particular fraternal orientation in the workforce. The decades-long approach to cost-based reimbursement meant that the financial woes rarely rose to a threshold where job security was threatened. Employment longevity was high. Supervisors, managers, and employees all shopped in the same stores and their children attended the same schools. Work life was an extension of family and community life for the employees of Grove Memorial.

Now, however, a new dynamic was stubbornly chafing at the clan culture that had been deeply entrenched in the social fabric of the hospital. This was the

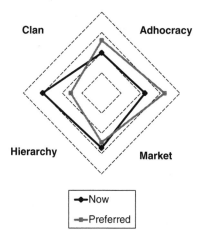

Grove Memorial: From Clan and Hierarchy Innovation and Performance

Figure 1.5 Culture in Grove Memorial Hospital

need to become more entrepreneurial, and it was getting increasingly difficult for Grove Memorial to resist its encroachment. More and more, patients were being encouraged to seek treatment in outpatient locations, HMOs and PPOs were becoming stingier when developing payment schedules, and employers were doing all they could to reduce exposure to high premiums, including curtailing the once generous nature of their benefit programs. Hospital administrators began to think about reinvigorating the culture and shifting it from the left to the right side of the CVF (see Figure 1.5).

The hospital had no choice but to examine things like departmental efficiency, employee productivity, and return on investment for its programs and services. Lifetime employment was no longer a guarantee. If the clinical program in which an employee worked closed down, there may not be another place in the hospital for that person. If an employee was less than satisfactorily productive, perhaps the hospital would need to replace that person with someone more capable. This was all new to Grove Memorial, and the impact on culture was swift and startling. When change is inevitable, leaders who remain fixed in transactional approaches to their role are likely to find themselves engaged in damage control. Leaders who seek to align culture with environmental trends are far more likely to help their organizations transition and transform successfully.

Skills and roles. As roles evolve, so too should the skills that enable those roles to mature and actualize with proficiency. Grove Memorial, like thousands of other hospitals across the country, prided itself on a staff with proven technical and clinical skills. Many employees, in fact, had received formal training as a precondition for employment. Hospitals are regimented, hierarchical, and paternalistic environments and, as such, standards of performance tend to be uniform and decision-making latitude is fairly narrow (Longest & Darr, 2008). However, the changes that took root in the 1990s began to dismantle the relatively narrowly defined skill orientation. As reimbursement programs shrank and competition for patients increased, the need for efficiency and a more focused and bold approach to customer service increased.

Many hospitals examined ways to flatten hierarchies to reduce the number of layers through which problems and decisions needed to be communicated. This brought decision-making responsibility closer to the level of the rank-and-file employee as well as reduced the time between problem identification and solution implementation. Moreover, there was a need for customer relations skills, brought about largely by competition, but also by the aging of the population; older patients are often sicker and have reduced capacities for absorbing, processing, and retaining information (McPhee, Winkler, Rabow, Pantilat & Markowitz, 2011). Thus, today we see increasing numbers of employees who possess not only the capabilities required for technical responsibilities, but also increased aptitudes for flexibility, communication, decision making, and teamwork.

The experience of Grove Memorial highlights the need for another skill: tolerance of ambiguity. The more uncertain and unpredictable the organizational future, the greater the need is for employees who can navigate their way through change with minimal stress and burnout. As roles change, organizations are well advised to plan for the impact of that change on employees' skill sets. Employees who do not possess or develop the necessary skills are likely to fail; and if many employees fail, the likelihood is greater that the organization will fail as well.

Leadership in Healthcare Organizations: Transcending Boundaries

We may substitute any industry for the healthcare industry and identify fluid and emerging patterns of needs that call for varying levels and emphases of transformational and transactional orientations. We have examined the healthcare industry not because of its distinctiveness but because of its representativeness. Environmental and organizational forces cause companies in all industries to evolve and adjust in order to succeed. Not all organizations do. The manner by which transformational leadership blends with and complements transactional management will go a long way in determining whether the organization can prosper or fail. Too much of the wrong emphasis at the wrong time will either prevent the organization from moving forward in a changing world or pay short shrift to all of the vital processes that enable the organization to function efficiently.

The CVF offers guidance on the relationship among the critical roles in an organization. The tension to achieve alignment between transactional and transformational roles holds rich potential for energizing an organization in a positive direction or miring an organization in a stuck position or a state of chaos. Master leaders who envision a future filled with possibilities are well served by recognizing the value of managers who oversee vital processes; an organization without order and structure cannot accomplish its work regardless of the genius of its visionaries. On the other hand, an organization lacking an aptitude for adaptation and maturation can fall behind its competitors and lag in its market. After all, processes need to be managed, monitored, and controlled and employees must be inspired if their energy, skill, and dedication are to be maximized and their adaptive potential realized. Alignments function much like a fulcrum, creating balance between transactional and transformational organizational tendencies. Leaders capable of reframing transformational and transactional roles from either/or to both/and—to transcend the boundaries between the two—can employ that reframed perspective to move their organizations forward in a strategic direction. This is the realm of the master leader.

Conclusion

In her book *From Management to Leadership: Strategies for Transforming Health*, Jo Manion (2011) suggested that the study of leadership in healthcare organizations is nonlinear in actual applications because leaders assume nontraditional roles that demand mastery of new and different competencies that match the need to manage complex systems with multiple stakeholders and high levels of interdependence. Manion cites a study by the American Hospital Association (AHA) that identifies administrative pitfalls driving the emerging paradigm of leadership in healthcare organizations. These pitfalls are listed with their parallel CVF quadrants (see **Figure 1.6**):

1. Little or no sense of shared vision and mission within healthcare organizations (*lower right quadrant*)
2. Ineffective communication skills, especially at the executive level (*upper left quadrant*)
3. Unwillingness to abandon hierarchical control structures, particularly at the executive and board levels (*lower left quadrant*)
4. Refusal to let go of the hospital mentality and traditional modes of service (*upper right quadrant*)

Not only does our model (Figure 1.6) address these pitfalls by elaborating on the leadership roles and competencies needed to sustain the goals and capabilities

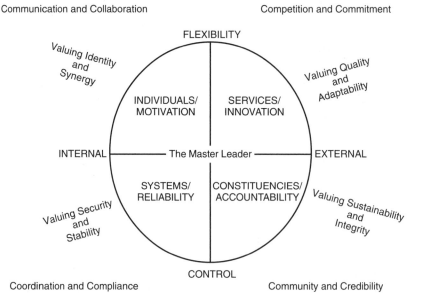

Figure 1.6 Leadership in Healthcare Organizations: Constraints and Opportunities

of healthcare organizations, it also captures the essence of healthcare organizations as complex systems that require transactional and transformational roles along with paradoxical skills essential for effective performance. Note how the framework provides a road map for identifying the main topics of this text and at the same time it charts the critical domains of healthcare organizations and leadership challenges.

In the larger sense, responding to the challenges of leading healthcare organizations through transitions that demand alterations to organizational structure and strategy involves the development of a fundamentally more sophisticated and diverse complement of skills than has previously been in practice. For the majority of the past half century, the skills necessary in health care focused on getting the day's work accomplished. Organizing structures, assigning tasks, constructing systems and policies that could respond to regulatory demands, establishing protocols for accountability—these occupied the bulk of managers' attention. Doing all this within a confined and defined set of means was secondary as long as a willing third-party payer existed.

This context began to change as the last century came to an end. In a sense, the bill came due for the extraordinary expansion of the healthcare system, which occurred in the latter half of the 20th century. For many years, expenses were simply passed along to consumers in the form of higher deductibles, larger co-pays, and decreased choice of providers. Employers struggled to find ways to contain the rate of premium escalation. Government programs were pressed to contain spending. At the same time, patients continued to get older and sicker, consumers became more adept at discovering information about their health, and technology changed how care was delivered and information was managed. As consumer needs and expectations grew, the ability to pay for it all emerged as an issue of considerable national attention.

For healthcare organizations, yesterday's transactional leadership skills quickly became obsolete, even archaic. Simply, it is no longer enough for a healthcare manager to be a good technocrat, an efficient supervisor, a proficient engineer of operational activity. This is not to suggest that the skills associated with such functions are unimportant or irrelevant, quite the contrary. But they no longer occupy the domain of prominence they did when transactional responsibilities were the hallmark of the administrators' work. Leadership roles can no longer be differentiated along transactional and transformational responsibilities because both are needed. In this chapter we argued in favor of replacing this dichotomy with the more holistic and integrative skill sets represented by the master leader. We contend that this skill composite and the master leader concept represent a fertile area for future study, particularly as it applies to the challenges of the healthcare industry.

Case Study: The Acquisition of Abbott Hospital

Sister Mary Theresa, head of Mt. Mercy Hospital, a 372-bed facility, had received notification of acceptance of her offer to purchase Abbott Hospital, a 108-bed short-term acute general care facility located in a growing city in the Midwest. Abbott was owned by MEDICO, a professional hospital management company and operated as a not-for-profit corporation with no sectarian affiliations.

The eight civilian and military hospitals in the city have a combined bed capacity of 1,500. There are approximately 338 physicians, surgeons, dentists, and dental surgeons operating from these hospitals. The chamber of commerce and the medical community predict that this level of care will not be adequate to service the expansion of the city's population and projected economic growth.

During her tenure as chief administrator of Mt. Mercy, Sister Mary Theresa has become a controversial figure. Her supporters describe her as a strong-willed, articulate, well-organized woman who deserves credit for developing Mt. Mercy into a regional force in both medical care and basic research. Her opponents in the lay and medical communities contend that she is a cold, calculating opportunist who works only for the interests and gains of Mt. Mercy Hospital. Sister Mary Theresa describes herself as a hard worker with little patience for incompetence. Over the years she built a solid core of well-trained, capable physicians who admit primarily to Mt. Mercy Hospital. Both supporters and detractors agree she is persuasive, intelligent, unafraid of confrontation, and a tough competitor.

During Abbott's first year of operation, MEDICO lost over $2 million. Later, MEDICO management fired the administrative staff at Abbott and offered Dr. John Coletti the position of chief administrator. Coletti had been with MEDICO while completing his doctorate in hospital administration. His reputation in the company was based on his experience in several difficult administrative situations. MEDICO management viewed Coletti as a strong, decisive, and self-confident administrator. Coletti spent much of his time during his first months at Abbott staffing departments with people he characterized as strong leaders. Coletti revised the wage and benefits program for employees in order to stabilize what had become an excessive turnover rate. He was extremely pleased when, within 14 months, Abbott was operating at break-even. MEDICO management consequently viewed him as one of their successful administrators.

Both Sister Mary Joseph, director of nursing at Mt. Mercy, and Dr. John Cassler, the Mt. Mercy medical chief of staff, have been strong supporters of Sister Mary Theresa. The three mutually agreed that contacting MEDICO

Courtesy of: Shockley-Zalabak, P. (1994). The acquisition of Abbott Hospital. In *Understanding organizational communication: cases, commentaries, and conversations*. New York: Longman Publishing Group (p. 11–21). Reprinted with permission.

regarding the intent to purchase Abbott might be timely after MEDICO's initial financial losses. Sister Mary Theresa felt that acquisition of Abbott was the best way to pursue the satellite hospital concept outlined in Mt. Mercy's long-range plan. Sister Mary Theresa contacted only select members of the board of directors of Mt. Mercy regarding her decision to approach MEDICO.

Sister Mary Theresa was frustrated when MEDICO management refused to answer her telephone calls. Both Cassler and Sister Mary Joseph also received no response. MEDICO seemingly would not communicate directly with anyone at Mt. Mercy. Sister Mary Theresa, once again with only informal approval of selected board members, hired a consulting firm to act as an intermediary for discussing the purchase of Abbott with MEDICO.

The consultants notified Sister Mary Theresa that MEDICO would entertain an offer somewhere in the vicinity of $30 million. Sister Mary Theresa and Sister Mary Joseph met with financial advisors to the Sisters of the Sacred Heart and determined that an offer of $28 million was in order. The verbal acceptance of the offer by MEDICO made headlines in local newspapers.

Sister Mary Theresa called a board of directors meeting immediately after the story broke and obtained unanimous approval to proceed with the necessary steps to finalize the purchase. Although some members of the Mt. Mercy board felt she was again operating autocratically, they could not fault the results of her efforts. Mt. Mercy staff did not take issue with Sister Mary Theresa's rationale of the multihospital concept, instead their line of questioning centered on determination of the purchase price. They were concerned about the lack of formal assessment of the value of Abbott Hospital. Sister Mary Joseph responded that assessors qualified to evaluate the worth of a hospital were extremely rare, and in any case, MEDICO and Mt. Mercy had mutually agreed on the price. At this point, the staff recommended approval of Sister Mary Theresa's plans.

In order to finalize the Abbott purchase, Sister Mary Theresa began the formal application process for a certificate of public necessity. The state law requires that transfer of ownership of an acute care facility be preceded by obtaining a state certificate of public necessity for construction or modification of acute care facilities from the city's project review board. The procedure to obtain state consent for transfer of ownership involves formal documentation of projected benefits to the community and clients within the service area of the facility. Part of this documentation includes public testimony from hearings held in the local community and at the state level. Mt. Mercy personnel were expected to present and defend their position with regard to the Abbott purchase. Any interested parties from the community or health service field were invited to present information relevant to the proposed transfer of ownership. Timing of the hearings was important to Sister Mary Theresa because the purchase agreement between Mt. Mercy and MEDICO called for an additional $100,000 per month if closing and transfer of ownership did not occur by the agreed upon date.

At the public hearings, Sister Mary Theresa began her formal statement to the group by indicating the significance of changing from a single autonomous institution to a multihospital system. The multihospital system was defined as a

(Continues)

combination of distinctly operating institutions under the single ownership and operation of one management unit. Sister Mary Theresa proposed that a multi-hospital system would achieve economies that could possibly contain or even reduce cost of patient care. She proposed that economies of scale are possible through central management and judicious consolidation of services, equipment, and personnel. She further argued that the smaller institution (Abbott) could improve care by its linkage to the larger comprehensive institution with its greater technology and scope of resources and services. The multihospital system would still be locally operated while effecting cost containments that could not be achieved by the duplication of services necessary for single unit care facilities. Her final argument centered on the advantages of a combined medical staff and administrative services. Sister Mary Theresa submitted a detailed plan of the proposed economies that would substantiate Mt. Mercy's claims of debt service capability through the combined operating revenues of Mt. Mercy and Abbott.

Sister Mary Theresa's written statement confirmed publicly the purchase price of $28 million. An initial $2 million was available from the operating reserves of Mt. Mercy Hospital. The hospital's operating budget would assume associated expenses for acquisition estimated at $500,000. The Monroe Foundation of St. Louis had made a $2 million donation to be applied directly to the purchase price. The balance of $24 million was to be obtained through the issuance of tax-exempt bonds.

Sister Mary Theresa estimated consolidation savings during the first year of acquisition at $673,000. These savings would result from the elimination of the Abbott management contract with MEDICO, using Mt. Mercy's data-processing capabilities, and the combination of maintenance contracts with Mt. Mercy's existing suppliers. Additional revenue economies were projected in laboratory services, purchasing, nursing administration, admitting, and electrocardiography.

Meanwhile, many local doctors went on record opposing the purchase. Among the most vocal was Dr. Martin Leeham, a powerful member of the "old guard" of the medical society. Leeham, noted for having a hot temper and being very outspoken, was considered a fine doctor and surgeon by his colleagues. He was one of the first doctors in the city to perform legalized abortions. During the past 16 years he has not exercised his admitting privileges at Mt. Mercy Hospital, even for cases not expected to run afoul of the Ethical and Religious Directives (ERD) for Catholic Healthcare Organizations (written by the American Conference of Bishops). Leeham also led a group of doctors and businesspersons in the community to approach the city council with a certificate of public necessity to build a 200-bed hospital in the northwest section of Auston. The hospital was to be doctor-owned and administered with no religious affiliation. Sister Mary Theresa and her board were very vocal in their opposition to such a plan and attended all public hearings to voice their objections. The plan for the doctor-owned hospital was defeated and left Leeham with a bitter attitude toward Sister Mary Theresa.

Soon afterward, the second public hearing for approval of the certificate of public necessity was scheduled with the project review board of the Auston

Council of Governments. Publicity from the county medical society meeting had aroused broad community interests. The ERD and the subject of abortions and sterilizations received widespread press coverage.

Abortions and sterilizations constituted 25% of the surgical revenues at Abbott. The ERD prohibits abortions or sterilizations in hospitals under Catholic ownership and operation. Opponents of the acquisition claimed that many of the new doctors locating their offices near Abbott intended to utilize the surgical facility at Abbott for abortions and sterilizations.

Sister Mary Theresa expected the project review board meeting to be emotional with strong opposition to approval of the certificate. During the meeting she refused to answer any questions relating to a description of the ERD. She stated the code would be operational at Abbott and consistently confined her comments to advantages from the multihospital concept and cost economies. The public opposition from the lay and medical community was not well organized and failed to mount any significant counterarguments. The project review board voted to approve the certificate of public necessity, thus clearing the way for a final hearing to be held with the State Department of Health Facilities Advisory Council. Sister Mary Theresa felt pressure to obtain immediate approval to avoid activating the price escalation clause. A delay could cost Mt. Mercy at least $100,000.

Sister Mary Theresa, Dr. John Cassler, Sister Mary Joseph, and Dwight Morris, attorney for Mt. Mercy, attended the meeting. Unlike the previous hearings, Mt. Mercy representatives expected staff of the health facilities advisory council to be well prepared. Sister Mary Theresa repeated her basic remarks about the multihospital concept. The health facilities advisory council staff immediately challenged the validity of her projected economies and raised the issue of closing emergency room services at Abbott. Sister Mary Theresa countered with a flat refusal to consider closing emergency room services without a thorough needs analysis. She supported her figures by asking council staff to specifically indicate areas of possible error in her projections. The council attorney, Jim Redden, launched into a lengthy statement about the power and influence of Mt. Mercy. He questioned community willingness to allow further expansion of that influence, citing newspaper articles following the county medical society meeting. The representatives from Mt. Mercy were somewhat alarmed at what they considered Redden's lack of objectivity. Several days later, a certificate of public necessity was granted by the state to Mt. Mercy for the acquisition of Abbott Hospital. Sister Mary Theresa had won her battle over the opponents of Mt. Mercy's expanding influence in the medical community.

Upon receipt of the certificate, Mt. Mercy retained Kidder, Kidder, and Company to handle a private placement of tax-exempt bonds to finalize the $28 million purchase. Bonds were quickly placed, and combined with operating reserve and foundation monies, the acquisition was completed.

Sister Mary Theresa contacted Dr. John Coletti, Abbott administrator under MEDICO, and asked him to remain. Coletti agreed, feeling the progress he had made at Abbott would continue.

(Continues)

Early in January 1991, Sister Mary Theresa requested that the Mt. Mercy personnel department interview all Abbott staff members. Staff members were promised continued employment for a three-month probationary period, at the end of which permanent placement would be discussed. Staffs of both hospitals were informed they could be transferred between hospitals at administrative discretion. No seniority and accrued benefits from Abbott would transfer to Mt. Mercy/Abbott staff status. Coletti was not consulted or notified of these actions by the Mt. Mercy personnel department. He complained directly to Sister Mary Theresa and expressed concern that these actions would seriously undermine morale.

Sister Mary Theresa nevertheless directed the personnel department to continue with the interviews. Sister Mary Joseph was instructed by Sister Mary Theresa to advise all Abbott department heads that they were to report directly to their counterparts at Mt. Mercy. Abbott department heads thus became assistant department heads. Coletti was furious and threatened to resign his position immediately unless this policy was altered. Sister Mary Theresa held to her basic reorganization plan, and Coletti submitted his resignation letter immediately. Five department heads from Abbott also resigned.

Amidst turbulent conditions, Abbott Hospital became an operating satellite of Mt. Mercy Hospital. The ERD became the governing code on the Abbott on the same day.

Within two weeks of the Mt. Mercy takeover, six doctors had resigned from the staff of Mt. Mercy at Abbott. They transferred their staff privileges to Memorial, a local hospital that permitted abortions and sterilizations in its surgical facilities.

Sister Mary Theresa took over John Coletti's responsibilities and hired Adam Sampson to become assistant administrator for Mt. Mercy at Abbott. Sister Mary Theresa asked him for monthly reports summarizing the general operating and financial status of the satellite. At his previous position, the hospital's financial problems were dramatically turned around. Sampson had taken the credit for the progress, although reliable sources considered the hospital's staff to be the major change factor. Sampson considered himself an idea man who will work to avoid confrontation if possible. Observers generally described him as a nice person who takes orders well.

During the same month, Sister Mary Theresa formed a Mt. Mercy at Abbott Operational Review Committee comprising Sister Mary Joseph, Dr. John Cassler, and Adam Sampson. The committee was to meet monthly to review all phases of the Abbott operations. Sister Mary Theresa had set a goal for Abbott to break even within 13 months. She intended to make whatever adjustments necessary to facilitate the goal.

During the first few months after the acquisition, revenues for Abbott ran 15% to 20% below projected levels. Revenues from surgery and associated patient care days were the hardest hit, with a decline of 62%. The pediatrics occupancy rate was an unacceptably low 21%. Mt. Mercy staff doctors were not admitting patients to Abbott at a greater rate than before the purchase. Administrative costs were up 6% to 8%, within the anticipated range for the change to Mt. Mercy procedures. Sister Mary Theresa expressed concern about Abbott revenues to Cassler.

She reminded him that cost economies from consolidation were meaningless if she could not keep her operating revenues at a level necessary to service the acquisition debt. Sister Mary Theresa then instructed the operational review committee to look for possible consolidation of services, which would revise the operating structure of Mt. Mercy in order to strongly encourage Mt. Mercy staff doctors to utilize Abbott for all pediatrics and related cases. The beds vacated by pediatrics at Mt. Mercy could accommodate a planned surgical ward expansion.

In a management committee meeting, a somewhat frustrated Sampson indicated he was not getting cooperation from the Abbott staff. Sampson's specific analysis of doctor admissions confirmed Mt. Mercy staff doctors were not increasing their utilization of Abbott facilities. Sampson asked Sister Mary Theresa and the other committee members to consider transfer of Mt. Mercy personnel to Abbott to give him a staff that might be more responsive to his needs for operating information. Furthermore, he was finding it difficult to fill the administrative vacancies that had followed Coletti's resignation. Sampson indicated that while he was impressed with the competency of the Abbott staff he did not feel he was getting helpful input to facilitate correcting the bleak revenue picture. Sister Mary Theresa was opposed to transferring personnel between the two facilities. She proposed immediate reinstatement of accrued benefits from Abbott tenure to all Abbott staff members remaining on the combined staffs. Sister Mary Joseph strongly concurred, emphasizing the linkage between overall staff morale and the high quality of staff–patient relations for which Mt. Mercy and Abbott had been known. Sampson seemed hesitant about their proposal but did not challenge it. Cassler proposed initiation of formal conversations with a number of his colleagues to determine what types of services might attract both new doctors and increased admissions to Abbott from doctors currently exercising staff privileges at Mt. Mercy.

During the meeting, Cassler confirmed Coletti's appointment as director of planning for Memorial Hospital. He further reported Leeham's latest efforts to persuade several new doctors to move their practices to Memorial. Committee members were aware that Memorial had applied for a certificate of public necessity to add 26 additional beds. All committee members agreed a public response to Leeham was inappropriate.

Six months after the acquisition, accrued benefits were reinstated for the original Abbott staff members. Sister Mary Theresa and Sister Mary Joseph had begun plans to relocate all pediatrics services from Mt. Mercy to Abbott. Several staff doctors had expressed mild displeasure to Cassler but did not seem to be contemplating any serious opposition. Cassler also reported success in forming a group of staff doctors to study service needs that could be accommodated specifically at Abbott.

Sister Mary Theresa, without committee or board knowledge, began seeking additional foundation monies for debt service in the event revenues were not sufficient within 13 months to meet the debt service schedule. As she looked ahead, Sister Mary Theresa saw many difficulties but was exhilarated by the challenges of making a multihospital concept work.

(Continues)

Case Study Review Questions

1. What are the major change issues in this case?

    Organizational change management theory centers on the models developed by Kurt Lewin, who suggested a three-step theory, and John Kotter, who developed a more detailed eight-step theory using Lewin's initial framework. These theories can be mapped to the CVF and the leadership profiles and communication orientation components specifically (see **Table 1.1**). Organizations in transition can be thought of as moving through the CVF framework in a counterclockwise direction keeping an external to internal to external focus. First, a new vision for the organization is established (external), then buy-in is needed from all people involved (internal) and new systems are developed and monitored against goals/vision (internal). Finally, the organization moves back to an external focus based on productivity and long-term planning with an eye toward the competition and marketplace. Likewise, the communication orientations can be mapped to this same sequence, moving from transformational to relational through hierarchical

Table 1.1 Stakeholders and CVF Roles

Lewin's Three-Step Model	Kotter's Eight-Step Model	CVF	Leadership Roles	Message Orientation
Unfreezing—overcome the pressures of individual and group resistance	1. Establish compelling reason for change	Upper right (external)	Innovator Broker	Transformational
	2. Form a powerful coalition to lead change	Upper left (internal)	Mentor Facilitator	Relational
	3. Create a new vision			
	4. Communicate the vision			
Movement—promote driving forces (positives) and restrict restraining forces (negatives)	5. Empower others to act on vision	Lower left (internal)	Monitor Coordinator	Hierarchical
	6. Create and reward short-term "wins"			
	7. Consolidate improvements			
Refreezing—stabilize new environment by balancing driving and restraining forces	8. Reinforce change by demonstrating relationship between new environment and organizational success	Lower right (external)	Director Producer	Promotional

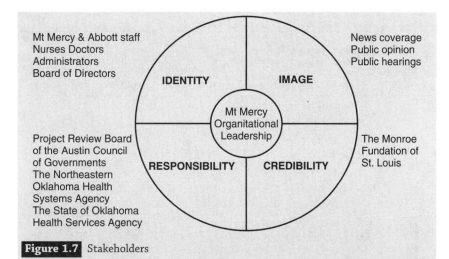

Mt Mercy & Abbott staff
Nurses Doctors
Administrators
Board of Directors

News coverage
Public opinion
Public hearings

IDENTITY

IMAGE

Mt Mercy
Organitational
Leadership

Project Review Board
of the Austin Council
of Governments
The Northeastern
Oklahoma Health
Systems Agency
The State of Oklahoma
Health Services Agency

RESPONSIBILITY

CREDIBILITY

The Monroe
Fundation of
St. Louis

Figure 1.7 Stakeholders

and finally promotional. The communication mapping is less rigid and less precise, because it is important to implement message orientation according to the situation/environment, the audience, and the communication goal rather than a predetermined path.

2. Map out the key players in the environment of Mt. Mercy.

The case presented is an opportunity to explore this mapping process and identify the opportunities for effective message orientation based on the importance of the key players and their level of impact on the organization. It also clearly illustrates the communication breakdowns that can occur when a leader refuses to adopt different messages in order to adapt to changing environments and respond effectively to organizational stakeholders. We used the process suggested in Belasen (2008) to identify the stakeholders (**Figure 1.7**) and their relative importance (**Table 1.2**).

3. Evaluate the types of communication used by Sister Mary Theresa.

It is clear from the way Sister Mary Theresa operates that her managerial style can be found on the lower half of the CVF diagram. She is strongly control focused and competitive and does not venture much into the collaborate (upper left) or create (upper right) quadrants. The words that her supporters use to describe Sister Mary Theresa, "strong-willed, articulate, well-organized," and "unafraid of confrontation and a tough competitor," are the same terms associated with the control quadrant. Thus it is not surprising that Sister Mary Theresa's predominant communication orientation also lies on the lower half of the CVF. The type of messages that Sister Mary Theresa offers are hierarchical and promotional and can be expressed as organized, practical, and action oriented. As **Figure 1.8** shows, Sister Mary Theresa displays strong preference for hierarchical messages in her communications with her staff, the board, and the regulators.

(Continues)

Table 1.2 Importance and Influence of Stakeholders

	Importance of Stakeholders				
Acquisition Period	**Stakeholders**	**Unknown**	**Little or No Importance**	**Some Importance**	**Significant Importance**
Influence of Stakeholders	Sisters of the Sacred Heart				X
	Sister Mary Theresa				X
	Sister Mary Joseph and Dr. John Cassler				X
	Mt. Mercy Hospital board of directors			X	
	MEDICO management and shareholders				X
	Area residents (public and customers)			X	X
	Dr. John Coletti				
	City Council of Governments		X	X	
	Community			X	X
	Dr. Martin Leeham		X		
	Abbott's department managers		X		
	Abbott's physicians and staff	X			
	Media			X	

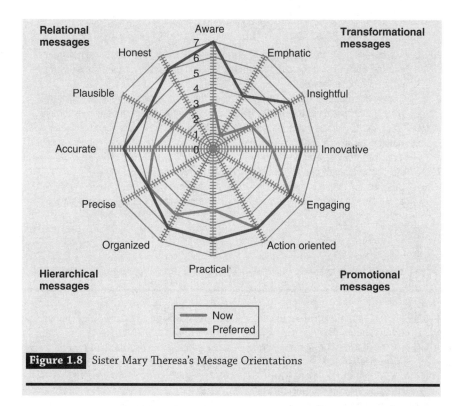

Figure 1.8 Sister Mary Theresa's Message Orientations

Review Questions

1. Discuss current and emerging challenges faced by healthcare leaders.
2. What are the major differences between transactional and transformational forms of leadership? Are these differences reconcilable?
3. What are the tenets of the CVF? How does this framework provide an integrated view of organizational environments?
4. A key to successful mastery is recognizing the contradictory pressures on the managerial job. Explain.
5. What are the strengths of the master leader?
6. Discuss the different types of message orientations, then illustrate each type with examples using a managerial situation.

7. What is the special role of the CVF in facilitating understanding across hierarchical lines?
8. Assume you are a consultant hired by Grove Memorial to help the hospital administrators develop ways to shift the culture from the left side of the CVF to the right side. What do you propose they do?
9. Review the model in Figure 1.8 and discuss the relationships among its quadrants. What tradeoffs should the master leader consider when balancing these quadrants?
10. Trace the leadership roles played by Sister Mary Theresa in the various situations. How effective was she? Should members of her board support her actions without more information? Why or why not?
11. Identity sources of conflict as leaders of Mt. Mercy acquire Abbott.
12. Describe the differing values, interests, and influences in the medical community and at Mt. Mercy. Determine how past events have contributed to the present situation.

References

Belasen, A. T. (1998). Paradoxes and leadership roles: Assessing and developing managerial competencies. *Management Development Forum, 1*(2), 73–98.

Belasen, A. T. (2000). *Leading the learning organization: Communication and competencies for managing change.* Albany, NY: SUNY Press.

Belasen, A. T. (2008). *The theory and practice of corporate communication: A competing values perspective.* Thousand Oaks, CA: Sage.

Belasen, A. T., & Frank, N. M. (2008). Competing values leadership: Quadrant roles and personality traits. *Leadership and Organizational Development Journal, 29*(2), 127–143.

Belasen, A. T., & Frank, N. M. (2010). A peek through the lens of the competing values framework: What managers communicate and how. *The Atlantic Journal of Communication, 18,* 280–296.

Belasen, A. T., & Frank, N. M. (2012). Women's leadership: Using the competing values framework to evaluate the interactive effects of gender and personality traits on leadership roles. *International Journal of Leadership Studies, 7*(2), 192–215.

Bono, J. E., & Judge, T. A. (2004). Personality and transformational and transactional leadership: A meta-analysis. *Journal of Applied Psychology, 89*(5), 901–910.

Cameron, K. S., & Quinn, R. E. (1999). *Diagnosing and changing organizational culture.* New York, NY: Addison-Wesley.

Cameron, K. S., Quinn, R. E., DeGraff, J., & Thakor, A. (2006). *Competing values leadership: Creating value in organizations.* London, United Kingdom: Elgar.

Costa, P. Jr., & McCrae, R. (1992). *NEO-PR-R Professional Manual.* Odessa, FL: Psychological Assessment Resources.

Costa, P., Jr., McCrae, R., & Dembroski, T. M. (1989). Agreeableness vs. antagonism: Explication of a potential risk factor for CHD. In A. Siegman & T. M. Dembroski (Eds.),

In search of coronary-prone behavior: Beyond type A (pp. 41–63). Hillsdale, NJ: Lawrence Erlbaum.

Danzon, P., & Pauly, M. (2001). From hospital to drugstore: Insurance and the shift to outpatient care. *LDI Issue Brief, 7,* 1–4.

Denison, D. R., Hooijberg, R., & Quinn, R. E. (1995). Paradox and performance: Toward a theory of behavioral complexity in managerial leadership. *Organization Science, 6,* 524–540.

Digman, J. M. (1997). Higher-order factors of the big five. *Journal of Personality and Social Psychology, 73*(6), 1246–1256. doi : 10.1037/0022-3514.73.6.1246

Fairhurst, G. T., & Putnam, L. L. (2004). Organizations as discursive constructions. *Communication Theory, 14*(1), 5–26.

Galloro, V. (2011). Picking up speed: Health reform among the drivers cited for recent mergers and acquisitions. *Modern Healthcare, 41,* 22–26.

Gotsi, M., & Wilson, A. M. (2001). Corporate reputation management: "Living the brand." *Management Decision, 39*(2), 99–104.

Hart, S. L., & Quinn R. E. (1993). Roles executives play: CEOs, behavioral complexity, and firm performance. *Human Relations, 46*(1993), 543–574.

Herringer, L. G. (1998). Relating values and personality traits. *Psychological Reports, 83*(3), 953–954.

Highlight Health. (n.d.). *Discover the science of health.* Retrieved from http://highlighthealth .com

Hogan, R. T., Curphy, G. J., & Hogan, J. (1994). What we know about leadership: Effectiveness and personality. *American Psychologist, 49*(6), 493–504.

Hooijberg, R., & Choi, J. (2000). Which leadership roles matter to whom? An examination of rater effects on perceptions of effectiveness. *The Leadership Quarterly, 11*(3), 341–364.

The Joint Commission. (n.d.). *Accreditation, health care, certification.* Retrieved from http://jointcommission.org

Levine, E., & Abdellah, F. (1984). DRGs: a recent refinement to an old method. *Inquiry: A Journal of Medical Care Organization, Provision and Financing, 21,* 105–112.

Longest, B., Jr., & Darr, K. (2008). *Managing health services organizations and systems (5th ed.).* Baltimore, MD: Health Professionals Press.

Leung, L. L., & Bozionelos, N. (2004). Five-factor model traits and the prototypical image of the effective leader in the Confucian culture. *Employee Relations, 26*(1), 62–71.

Manion, J. (2011). *From management to leadership: Strategies for transforming health.* San Francisco, CA: Jossey-Bass.

McPhee, S., Winkler, M., Rabow, M., Pantilat, S., & Markowitz, A. (2011). *Care at the close of life: Evidence and experience.* New York, NY: McGraw-Hill Medical.

Quinn, R. E. (1988). *Beyond rational management: Mastering the paradoxes and competing demands of high performance.* San Francisco, CA: Jossey-Bass.

Quinn, R. E., & Rohrbaugh, J. (1983). A spatial model of effectiveness criteria: Towards a competing values approach to organizational analysis. *Management Science, 29,* 363–377.

Rogers, P. S., & Hildebrandt, H. W. (1993). Competing values instruments for analyzing written and spoken management messages. *Human Resource Management Journal, 32*(1), 121–142.

Sharp, J. P., & Ramanaiah, J. P. (1999). Materials in the five-factor theory of personality. *Psychology Reports, 85*(1), 327–330.

Shi, L., & Singh, D. (2008). *Delivering healthcare in America: A systems approach.* Sudbury, MA: Jones & Bartlett.

Shockley-Zalabak, P. (1994). *Understanding organizational communication: Cases, commentaries, and conversations.* New York, NY: Longman.

Vilkinas, T. (2000). The gender factor in management: How significant others perceive effectiveness. *Women in Management, 15*(5/6), 261–271.

PART A ▶

Communication and Collaboration

The upper left quadrant of the competing values framework (CVF) focuses on interpersonal relationships, cross-functional synergy, teamwork, motivation, and cohesion. The master leader is an inspirational and supportive figurehead devoted to developing team members who are committed to the values of quality care and patient satisfaction. Healthcare leaders need to balance the requirements of the tasks with the responsibilities toward employees' motivation and personal goals. Effectiveness in this quadrant is a function of the ability of the leader to initiate and sustain interprofessional collaboration and effective interpersonal communication. While this quadrant or domain of action includes dynamics and processes that require applications of inward-bound leadership (e.g., internal focus, flexibility, people orientation), an overemphasis on this quadrant might create a dent in the skill profile of the leader as the span of attention of the leader must also include aspects from the other three quadrants. For example, excessive emphasis on the upper left quadrant might give less weight to the need to respond to external stakeholders or negate the need to develop a community perspective, as discussed in Part D, *Community and Credibility*. This apparent paradox is essential for learning and self-improvement. Organizational leaders

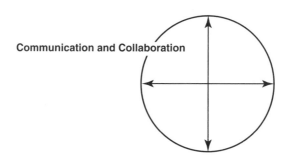

Communication and Collaboration

and healthcare executives must increase their behavioral flexibility to become effective master leaders—leaders who embrace paradoxes and recognize the inherent tension that exists between opposite quadrants. Hence the two chapters in Part A focus on the shifting role of middle managers in designing and leading teams and examining the importance of situational motivation for incentivizing activities that also support the external image and credibility of the organization.

CHAPTER 2 ▶

Leading from the Middle Out

LEARNING OBJECTIVES

Students will be able to:

- Use a diagnostic tool to help differentiate and group roles assumed by middle managers in healthcare organizations
- Identify where and how middle management in healthcare organizations creates the greatest value
- Explore ways to avert the potential for leadership failure in healthcare organizations through attention to leadership development and effective succession planning
- Understand the critical role of middle managers in designing and leading cross-functional teams
- Recognize the complementary skills associated with effective functioning of teams in healthcare organizations

Introduction

In this book we lay out the premise that leadership and management are both essential and that the master leader integrates the behaviors and competencies of both. Top-down leadership that champions strategic initiatives and management from the middle out that implements these initiatives create opportunities for highly reliable organizations. In those organizations in which middle managers are seen principally as a liability on the balance sheet, and their reduction or elimination is sought, the span of control for senior managers becomes broader. By extension, this will force senior managers to focus more intently on operational aspects of the organization. In an era of stability, this may be more acceptable (or at least less harmful). However, given the magnitude of transitions in health

---

Patricia's Dilemma

Patricia works at University Medical Center as administrative manager of a department in the faculty practice group. Senior management of the medical center told the department to merge with another group to share administrative costs, and Patricia was given the job of implementing the combined structure.

Right away, she began working on the project—planning the merger, working out staffing, integrating financials, preparing a new budget, and expanding the space to accommodate a new larger group. Though it was a huge project, she welcomed the challenge, knowing that it would provide excellent experience as well as increasing her visibility among the physicians and administrators with whom she would work. A successful implementation would capture people's attention and would definitely advance her career.

Everything was moving along smoothly, and her project passed the halfway point. Then the bombshell hit: the expansion space had been promised to another department, and the COO forgot to tell her. Now she had to scramble to find a suitable space for the merged department; the timetable did not change, the budget remained the same, and everyone expected success. Oh, and she was still accountable for results.

These situations generate added anxiety to middle managers and cause immense frustration. Add to this the typical constraints middle managers experience in healthcare organizations, including silos, shortages of staff, cost pressures, and unclear direction, and you can see why this is one of the toughest jobs. In this case, senior management made the decision to merge two small units to save money, a move that makes all the sense in the world, and they delegated the implementation to the middle manager, Patricia. But some other individual made a decision that squeezed her ability to succeed on a project she had regarded as a great career opportunity, and now she faces the real possibility of failure. The specialty nature of a healthcare environment fuels this silo mentality, reflecting and reinforcing narrowness of decision-making latitude. In such a climate, middle managers may perceive they lack freedom to exercise creativity and autonomy when identifying decision-making options.

Patricia began thinking about leaving the Medical Center and looking for another job.

---

care, a middle management downsizing strategy will tilt senior managers' attention too much toward operational issues and too far from strategizing, planning, visioning, and helping the organization adapt to an environment in flux. In all likelihood, excessive reduction in middle management may crimp the ability of the organization to develop master leaders. The key is to reframe the role of middle managers from a liability to an asset. But this will occur only if senior managers understand the value proposition of middle management and help develop it as strategic asset.

Recently, many scholars have pondered whether or not middle managers are necessary within an organizational structure. According to Federico and Bonacum (2010), not especially—most middle managers earn their promotions based on clinical and technical skills and, in that advancement process, have not been evaluated for their ability to successfully lead improvement efforts. Unlike other successful industries, health care has not invested adequate resources in preparing new middle managers for their role. For example, a variety of healthcare occupations bring with them different cultures and communication practices that must be bridged and mobilized from the middle out for optimal operations using quality management skills (Leathard, 2003; D'Amour, Ferrada-Videla, Rodriguez, & Beaulieu, 2005).

Many middle managers, reporting feeling underappreciated, have pointed to the lack of information or poor communication that they receive from upper level executives. For example, recent studies showed that senior executives perceived them to be motivated by extrinsic rewards, not intrinsic, and that they perform their jobs primarily because of external regulation and, to a lesser degree, internal motivation (Belasen & Fortunato, 2013). Other studies showed that middle managers operate within the spectrum of difficult and demoralizing policies, procedures, and guidelines established by senior management (Morris & Upchurch, 2012) and oftentimes they are unsure of the tasks they are given and more importantly, what is required of them in that role. For example, Currie (2000, 2006) described middle managers in healthcare settings as reluctant but resourceful managers operating at the junction of top-down and bottom-up predicaments with the constant need to revalidate their worth to the organization. Middle managers have been perceived as intermediaries that slow organizational efficiency without adding much measurable value (Embertson, 2006).

Have middle managers been deskilled as top executives rationalize resources and capabilities? Are they suffering from mistaken identity? Are they secure in their positions? Are they well regarded and targeted for upward mobility? Indeed, there is a large gap between the perceptions and mindset of top executives with regard to the amount of communication that they share with middle managers, versus the actual communication reported by those same middle managers (Belasen, 2008). How do healthcare organizations improve if middle managers, responsible for knowledge transfer and innovation implementation, are removed from the decision-making process or circumvented?

In this chapter we (1) discuss the dynamics associated with traditional and transitional roles of middle managers in healthcare organizations; (2) provide a diagnostic framework to help differentiate and group roles assumed by middle managers in healthcare organizations; (3) identify where and how middle management in healthcare organizations creates the greatest value; and (4) explore ways and offer strategies to avert the potential for leadership failure in healthcare organizations.

Between a Rock and a Hard Place

"Middle management" is a term associated with relentless downsizing, corporate drudgery, and career dead-ends. Bashed by management gurus, dismissed by social scientists, and painted as victims by the media, middle managers seem permanently relegated to the sidelines of corporate power. But is this popular picture accurate? Are middle managers really no longer valued by today's performance-driven organizations? While managers have maintained their commitment to their tasks and to their colleagues, they are increasingly cynical and distant from their organizations. They are confused about their future and how to manage their careers. This comes at a time when the value of middle management is much greater than ever before (Osterman, 2009).

The value of middle managers in an era characterized by uncertainty and interdependence is under attack. Middle managers are viewed as an expendable commodity that adds complexity and hinders top managers' ability to understand what's really going on at the front line. Evidence suggests that executives increasingly prefer to get closer to their operating core. How do healthcare organizations improve if middle managers, responsible for knowledge transfer and best practices implementation, are removed or circumvented? Given the complexity of healthcare systems and compliance requirements, failure can occur when processes become disjointed and when middle managers are disempowered to pursue continuous improvement.

Positioned centrally within the chain of command, middle managers handle multiple, often contradictory, roles and deal with diverse sets of internal and external stakeholders. They engage in dual lines of reporting with top-down implementation roles and bottom-up championing roles. Functioning as intermediaries across hierarchical levels, middle managers must strike a delicate balance between creativity and efficiency, and transformational and transactional roles. In fact, many scholars would liken the middle manager's responsibilities to those of a strategist, change architect, or a communication conduit between corporate thought, action, and results (Belasen, 2000; Haneburg, 2010; Wooldridge, Schmid, & Floyd, 2008). Others argue that allowing middle managers to play a more active role in decision making and in the execution of strategies contributes to dynamic organizational enrichment (Beck & Plowman, 2009). Indeed, middle managers with active involvement in the strategy process have been found to demonstrate higher levels of commitment to organizational goals and contribute to the success of strategic initiatives (Huy, 2001; Vilà & Canales, 2008).

An organization that empowers its middle managers allows for greater diversity of viewpoints. Middle managers can draw ideas, perspectives, and impressions from their direct reports and utilize them in their communications with top executives. In fact, evidence shows that middle managers' upward leadership and downward influence affect the alignment of organizational activities with the strategic context (Balogun & Johnson, 2004; Floyd & Lane, 2000; Rouleau & Balogun, 2011). They help facilitate the need for change in communications with executives and help implement change in interactions with lower levels (Belasen, 2000; Belasen & Frank, 2010; Kuyvenhoven & Buss, 2011).

In the healthcare industry, middle managers are an important part of the organizational resources and capabilities. They support the organization through their vital know-how, experience, and internal and external networks and help strengthen the social identity and culture of the organization (Valentino, 2004). In hospitals, for example, middle managers translate strategic-level goals into actionable improvement plans at the department or work unit level, engage employees in safety and quality assurance efforts, and identify and improve processes over time. In that sense, they differ significantly from senior managers, who are more concerned with the overall direction of the organization, strategic objectives, and resource allocation. Looking at **Figure 2.1**, as transmitters of communication with much responsibility for day-to-day operations and internal processes, middle managers act more as negotiators and ambassadors to first line supervisors and peer managers and are often on the lookout for tradeoffs that often escape the attention of senior managers and that are central for the performance of the organization (Osterman, 2009). Effective middle managers know how to relate to lower levels and use appropriate channels of communication to respond to employees' questions or need for feedback.

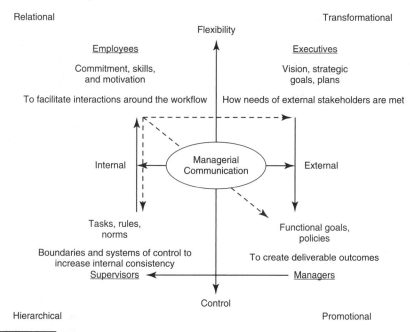

Figure 2.1 The Central Position of Middle Managers in Organizational Communication

Belasen, A. T., & Frank, N. M. (2010). A peek through the lens of the competing values framework: What managers communicate and how. *Atlantic Journal of Communication*, 18, 280–296. Reprinted by permission of The New Jersey Communication Association (http://www.njca.rutgers.edu) and The New York State Communication Association (http://www.nyscanet.org).

Middle managers work in many ways to accomplish core tasks and ensure continuity, keep the organization going, and attain positive organizational outcomes. They implement strategy, translate goals from executive level to smaller subunits, create local relevance, interpret shifting contexts, clarify words and actions of executives, and promote organizational discourse, thus assimilating current and new employees into organizational practices and perceptions. Middle managers' central location within the hierarchy also reinforces their mediation roles in interpreting critical events and in creating shared meaning (Beck & Plowman, 2009; Belasen & Frank, 2010). While senior managers are too distant, middle managers are closer to frontline employees, can leverage informal networks, and let employees feel valued and not alienated. Evidence suggests that middle managers in healthcare services support their employees by stimulating their commitment to the organization and by facilitating their careers (Carlström, 2012).

A Crack in the Armor

In healthcare organizations, which currently undergo massive transitions, reliance on interprofessional collaboration and distributed leadership has given rise to a general call to enact micro forms of leadership (Alvesson & Sveningsson, 2003a, 2003b; Carroll, Levy, & Richmond, 2008; Larsson & Lundholm, 2010) primarily due to integration challenges that must be met at the operational, not institutional, level (Gilmartin & D'Aunno, 2007). At the same time, healthcare units and teams operate in environments that are largely influenced by broader organizational and institutional goals (Finn, Currie, & Martin, 2010). If so, who other than middle managers with their cross-hierarchical, cross-boundary roles can better perform these roles? Yet, detractors of middle management have continued to disregard the value proposition and, therefore, advocated the removal of unnecessary layers of middle management during transitions. For example, Hamel (2011) saw middle management as inefficient and the multilayered organization as ineffective and challenged organizational designers and senior managers to achieve high levels of coordination without relying on a supervisory superstructure that included middle managers.

During the 1990s, rightsizing and reengineering, the prime strategies for creating a lean and efficient organization, were used by senior executives across many industries to create structures and processes that are agile and flexible, organic and adaptive (Belasen, 2000; Hammer & Champy, 1993). As hierarchies have been flattened through delayering and the implementation of horizontal management and as empowerment and team-based structures have become more common, there has also been a growing emphasis on self-management, interprofessional collaboration, and distributed forms of leadership (Avolio, Walumbwa, & Weber, 2009; Pearce, 2004). Distributed leadership in healthcare organizations and other contexts is well documented in the research literature (Buchanan, Addicott, Fitzgerald, Ferlie, & Baeza, 2007; Chreim, Williams, Janz, & Dastmalchian, 2010; Currie, Lockett, & Subomlinova, 2009; Denis, Langley, & Rouleau, 2010; Raelin, 2011).

Delayering, or the process by which senior executives become more directly connected with lower levels, has led to an increase in executive *span* and at the same time to a reduction in *depth* through the elimination of intermediate positions, typically middle managers (Rajan & Wulf, 2006). Evidence shows that the number of lower managers reporting to the CEO has increased (span of control) steadily over time, from an average (median) of 4.4 (4) in 1986 to 8.2 (7) in 1998; at the same time, the number of positions between the CEO and department managers (or division heads), has decreased (depth) by more than 25% (Rajan & Wulf, 2006). Evidently, these two trends have continued to dominate Fortune 500 companies (Neilson & Wulf, 2012).

More recently, as technology advances and social media allow executives and senior managers to know more or interact directly with stakeholders and customers, one trend is becoming clear: the traditional job of the middle manager has begun to shift dramatically (Grafton, 2011). In today's healthcare industry, in which social media help healthcare providers to manage relationships with patients and filter or transfer important information (Kane, Fishman, Gallaugher, & Glaser, 2009), middle managers are not being judged simply on results as before. They are also being judged on process, and the process has increasingly become heavily controlled (Osterman, 2009; Valentino, 2004).

The reduction in hierarchical layers creates spillover effects with a larger span of control to executives but with added responsibilities to the remaining middle managers, who are expected to deal with tactical, operational issues. The combination of greater span with less depth creates a dual effect of narrowing expertise or de-skilling and decreased autonomy, which detracts from morale and internal motivation. Surviving middle managers work more and produce more while receiving the same pay, often without recognition. Other middle managers have inherited more tasks and greater variety but with routine responsibilities that require monitoring, not necessarily decision making. They feel increasingly isolated from the management team, lose confidence in their cognitive and judgmental abilities and, uncertain about their roles, often respond by shifting commitments. It is the diminished role in decision making—the freedom to determine "how to get there," the making of the decision, not the execution—that is demoralizing. So much for Vroom's (1964) expectancy theory and the strength of the linkage between choices and outcomes. Are middle managers well prepared for these challenges? Systemic barriers and stereotypical biases may inhibit or slow down their ability to act.

The Set-Up-to-Fail

In hospital settings, at times of cutback and downsizing, frustrated middle managers appear to slide out to isolated, out-of-reach positions, in effect choosing an avoidance strategy (Vivar, 2006). Unable to respond to crossover pressures, they tend to abandon their traditional responsibilities (McConville & Holden, 1999). Sliding out can be either self-initiated or forced (Farrell & Rusbult, 1992). Middle managers flee their tasks by staying away or by laying low (Carlström, 2012).

When the emotional impact of the work middle managers perform is not acknowledged, they might feel lonely and abandoned, and become frustrated and resistant to change (Kuyvenhoven & Buss, 2011). Middle managers reportedly fear missing relevant information and remaining uninformed of important projects or decisions, and they suffer from a mixture of boredom and anxiety, making it even more difficult to prioritize and move projects forward.

Meanwhile, employees at lower levels point fingers at middle managers who they believe overmanage their units or excessively monitor their performance. Top executives, on the other hand, worry about failures in meeting strategic objectives, poor financial results, stakeholder dissatisfaction, or consumer disapproval, and increasingly turn to the middle manager as a convenient scapegoat. Refusing to recognize the problem, hospital administrators, for example, may react unfavorably to this behavior, typecasting middle managers as abdicators and low performers that must be further monitored and evaluated. In turn, affected middle managers become confused and demoralized, and without trust, so essential for sustained relationship, they gradually become less committed and less involved. Indeed, in healthcare organizations middle managers are regularly viewed as "forgotten practitioners" (Hayes, 2005).

This self-reinforcing process is prime for conditions of possible failure, known also as the Pygmalion effect described in the seminal work by J. Sterling Livingston (1969) who advocated for the importance of setting up high expectations to avert failure.

Given the hardships inevitably faced by middle managers, it should come as no surprise that they are often blamed for organizational failures. This is because the organizational work they are charged with carrying out is interconnected and often too complex to evaluate. Healthcare organizations often have limited ability to learn from failures due to overemphasis on independent work units, slack resources that breed inefficiency, and removal of managers from daily work activities, which, in turn, reduces the opportunities for broader perspectives and organizational synergy.

Veteran middle managers are considered corporate dinosaurs who will always offer a reason why something cannot be achieved. They are perceived as mediocre or weak performers, who, in turn, tend to live down to the low expectations that their senior managers have set for them, in effect perpetuating a vicious cycle of perceived incompetence (Manzoni & Barsoux, 2002). The way executives relate to their middle managers is subtly influenced by what they expect of them. If their perceptions of mediocrity lead to setting low expectations or ignoring middle managers altogether, productivity of the affected middle managers is likely to be poor, which, in turn, reinforces the initial perception of uncommitted middle managers. This self-fulfilling prophecy creates exclusive clubs of winners (in-group) and losers (out-group) with members in the out-group being treated with rules, policy guidelines, and authority while the members of in-group enjoy greater feedback, interactions, and close proximity to decision makers. The sustained attack on middle management to focus on operational effectiveness away from strategic circles, putting them in a sink-or-swim predicament, suggests that middle management is an occupation where autonomy is systematically constrained (Osterman, 2009).

With rising CEO turnover rates, hospitals need to develop adequate programs to identify and train new leaders. Moreover, these programs should build a strong talent pipeline with those already working at the organization, as a recent survey found it costs hospitals less to develop and retain leadership in-house than to hire and train new managers (Caramenico, 2013). Hospitals that do not groom internal leaders spend four times more than hospitals that do. A crisis in healthcare leadership can be prevented if leadership development programs and succession planning exist along with willingness by senior managers to target successful middle managers for upward mobility, coaching, and development. These observations point to a critical area where succession planning practices can and should be improved: the CEO and the board need to initiate the selection of internal succession candidates and ensure their preparation.

Succession Planning

Succession planning involves evaluation of current organizational capabilities and future needs as well as identification of suitable candidates who could assume key positions within the organization. While many middle managers in healthcare organizations may have the skills and knowledge to become effective top executives, a survey conducted by Witt/Kieffer in early 2012 revealed that most healthcare organizations in the sample studied did not have a formal succession planning process. Healthcare CEOs, it was reported, are delaying their departure from their posts with 54% indicating that they have no plans to retire any time soon despite the fact that 73% of them are between the ages of 55 and 62 and 24% are age 63 and over. Fifty-one percent of the survey CEOs indicated that they have worked with the senior management team to identify potential successors; 39% have worked with their boards to develop a formal planning process; 34% mentored their successors; and 29% have identified a successor to step into their roles. At the same time, 63% claimed that they are too young to retire. It can be concluded that while they understand the importance of grooming the next successor, they do not see this as an urgent matter (Witt/Kieffer, 2012).

Thanks in part to changes under the Affordable Care Act, the dynamics of hospital CEOs has begun to shift. A survey by Challenger, Gray & Christmas, Inc. in mid-2013 found that of the 949 CEO changes in 2013, health care leads with 195 departures. Healthcare CEO departures hit a record high of 78 in the third quarter of 2013, with 26 changes in September alone. CEO turnover can cause even greater tensions for both internal and external stakeholders—especially if some of them are blaming the existing CEO for leading the company down the wrong path (Miles, 2009).

Effective succession planning includes four essential steps:

1. Engaging the board of directors to articulate a profile of the company's desired CEO and criteria for measuring performance. Diligent board involvement can make a big difference in the careful evaluation of current talent and mechanisms for sustaining a pool of talented candidates.
2. Assessing the cadre of middle managers against these criteria.
3. Evaluating the qualifications of possible candidates against two time frames: a short-term emergency time frame and a more planned succession in the medium or long term.
4. Providing support through coaching and mentoring, and facilitating the transition for the top position by removing unnecessary barriers and reducing stress to create a setting in which the new CEO can be most effective.

It is important to plan for the possibility that a CEO must be replaced on short notice, for example, if the individual currently in the position becomes incapacitated or is terminated by the board. Stephen Miles (2009) offers some diagnostic questions for directors to consider: First, is there an emergency candidate who can take the reins for a time if the CEO were to leave tomorrow? This is often the CFO, COO, or a board member. Second, who do we have to invest in today so that he or she will be prepared tomorrow? Third, has the organization developed a team strong enough to ease the transition to a new CEO? And finally, is there in place a seasoned chairperson or lead director who is willing to coach and mentor a new CEO?

Becoming Hypereffective

One response of middle managers who are conscious about the chances of being eliminated, demoted, or bypassed, is to perform a variety of tasks and assume a large number of roles in meeting new work expectations, in effect, becoming hypereffective. On the surface, hypereffective managers appear more efficient and have a greater desire to develop success for their organizations. On the negative side, a great deal of personal time is traded in order to maintain or achieve the goals of the organization. Downsizing, reorganization, and organizational transitions exacerbate these conditions. While managers may be making greater strides in achieving organizational goals, areas of management that were once deemed important are often neglected. There is a trade-off in that hypereffective managers clearly find few opportunities to diminish the performance of some in order to increase their attention to others (Belasen, Benke, DiPadova, & Fortunato, 1996).

While hypereffectiveness may sound good, it tends to transform middle managers into conservative and overworked managers who are pushed to the limits by the expectations of those above them who demand nothing short of better results (Belasen, 2012). The larger source of productivity gain was most likely the result of the vastly increased allocation of managerial activity from personal (non-value-maximizing) activities to activities that enhance organizational effectiveness, in some cases with little or no support from human resource systems (Belasen & Frank, 2004). Overextending the roles middle managers play might trigger unsustainable behaviors of hypereffectiveness. Consider the following situation.

You are effectively working with the team and hit a snag in delegating job tasks. You know what you want to see done and how it should be done. However, you are reluctant to pass the tasks off to team members because you believe that nobody does it as well as you or you don't trust their effectiveness. So, even though holding onto these additional tasks doubles your workload, you just can't let it go. Have you ever heard the old saying: "If the shoe fits, wear it"? Well, hypereffectiveness is almost the opposite. The shoe clearly doesn't fit, but the leader wears it anyway. You have to have the ability to regulate your time, efforts, and roles and know when to say enough is enough. Hypereffectiveness is not realistic for long periods of time. It may allow the leader to momentarily be effective due to adrenaline rush. Ultimately, however, the process is unsustainable!

Researchers found that movement toward the efficiency frontier was not singularly conclusive, but the pattern of change in the tasks and responsibilities underlying the management and leadership roles performed by the hypereffective middle managers suggested a severe loss of discretionary time and an increase in the sense of powerlessness among the managers surveyed. Increased organizational efficiencies have come about only in part due to changes in work processes and in traditional managerial roles. Pressure to increase hours at work comes from the need to better perform the dual management and leadership roles as well as from the need to pick up the slack left from those who remain uninvolved or were laid off and leads to major stress.

It takes considerable organizational fortitude to prevent leadership and management from succumbing to the natural tensions between the two. Can one individual perform both roles successfully? Leadership and management function differently and are guided by different goals and orientations: management functions best when it seeks to establish control and predictability for the organization, while leadership is required to move an organization and position it for success in a dynamic environment (Kotter, 2013). Rather than control, leadership relies more on the tools of persuasion and influence. Rather than striving for permanence and stability, it focuses on change and adaptability. These seemingly contradictory orientations are synthesized, integrated, and unified in the concept of *high-impact managerial leadership*.

Leaving Out Middle Managers

A hospital in New Jersey recently developed a 3-year capital acquisition plan to modernize it radiology program. Among other things, the plan included upgrading the MRI and special procedures equipment. The hospital's current technology had at least 5 years of acceptable clinical usefulness. However, in light of the diagnostic modernization undertaken by competitor hospitals, the hospital was concerned that some physicians would elect to bring their patients elsewhere.

But now the hospital was in a quandary. The inability to reliably predict revenue flow, HMO and PPO arrangements, and patient mix resulting from uncertainty associated with the Affordable Care Act and related health policy was causing the hospital to reconsider its approach regarding which technology to upgrade and the timeframe. For example, one option was to engage a nearby free-standing radiology center in partnership—or purchase it outright—as this could constitute a less expensive and potentially effective solution for outpatients. Another option was to extend the timeframe of or the financing mechanism for the new technology.

The bulk of the discussion regarding these options was confined to the senior management level of the hospital. Middle managers were kept out of the loop. They went about their usual business developing reports and filling in for daily gaps in staffing—the very activities they have been doing for years. Senior management quietly complained about the minimal value of such reports, especially because the data varied so little from week to week *and* because such reports seem so trite in light of the great urgency to chart a direction for the future of the radiology program.

But why shouldn't middle managers continue doing business as usual? It makes them feel productive and it has become habit. Most especially, they haven't been groomed to do anything else.

In fact, there are a great number of things middle managers could be doing. For example, they could conduct assessments of patient satisfaction throughout the hospital in the event some radiological tests were eventually outsourced; they could develop cross-training programs for staff, a project that could help with retention, succession planning, and professional development; and they could research the training needs of upgraded technologies.

Instead, the middle managers at the hospital remain fixed in a mode in which their potential is neither understood nor realized. Instead of being viewed as a vital asset, they are viewed as a cost to the institution. Middle managers are seen as having marginal value and are treated as such; accordingly, they are not given the tools, training, mandate, and respect necessary to succeed. In the worst case scenario, they are caught on the wrong end of a self-fulfilling prophecy. In the long run, it is the hospital, its employees, and most especially, the patients who go there for care who will fail to get as meaningful an experience as possible because of it.

High-Impact Middle Managers: Integrating Leadership and Management Roles

High-impact middle managers are capable of establishing a balance between the forces of certainty and transformation. Healthcare institutions will not be able to sustain themselves if excessive emphasis is placed on the former. Conversely, too much change, or change that is not managed and implemented effectively, can prove destabilizing to an institution that must carry out its duties with precision and care. We posit that in the upcoming era healthcare organizations will transition successfully when they are led and managed by individuals who can define, embrace, and execute their roles in the context of this delicate balance.

As **Figure 2.2** shows, high-impact managers are centrally located within the chain of command and typically perform or directly influence three important tasks: (1) technical tasks linked to the operating core, routines, and compliance; (2) people tasks involving leading, motivating, and developing direct reports; and (3) strategic tasks associated with financial reports, analysis, and strategic communication including direct involvement in headquarter projects and boardroom discussions (Belasen & Frank, 2010).

What is the right balance between management and leadership? How do we evaluate the tradeoffs between behaviors and roles that are both mutually exclusive and collectively exhaustive? How do we account for shifts in behaviors when organizational leaders and managers grapple with changing conditions of the environment? How do we group and differentiate roles and behaviors across hierarchical levels and organizational lines to facilitate internal and external communications?

As discussed in the next section, both transformational qualities and transactional rigor are needed for high-impact managerial leadership. Effective leaders help inspire and energize people to think onward and outward (outside-in) in addition

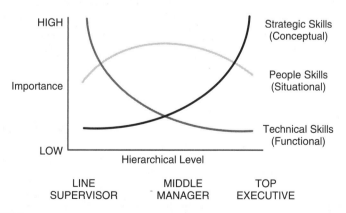

Figure 2.2 Hierarchical Levels and Requisite Skills

Communication and Collaboration   Competition and Commitment

Figure 2.3 Competing Values Leadership Roles

Modified from: Quinn, R. E. (1988). *Beyond rational management: Mastering the paradoxes and competing demands of high performance* (p. 48). San Francisco, CA: Jossey-Bass. Reproduced with permission of John Wiley & Sons Inc.

to directing and focusing organizational resources and capabilities inwardly (inside-out) to achieve organizational goals. They ask "how," not just "why"—they guide rather than find fault. They convert the process of doing into an opportunity for learning. High-impact leaders are more successful in handling novel or exceptional situations and generally exhibit greater behavioral and cognitive complexity (Denison, Hooijberg, & Quinn, 1995; Hart & Quinn, 1993) than less effective managers (Belasen & Frank, 2008). The competing values framework (**Figure 2.3**), a diagnostic tool made of integrated, inevitably bonded paradoxes, helps us understand the triggers and implications of a balanced managerial leadership.

Competing Values Leadership

The competing values framework (CVF; see Figure 2.3) displays the repertoire of leadership roles by aligning pairs of roles with specific domains of action.

The innovator and broker roles rely on creativity and communication skills to bring about change and acquire resources necessary for change management. The monitor and coordinator roles are more relevant for system maintenance and integration and require project management and supervision skills while the director and producer roles are geared toward goal achievement. The facilitator and mentor roles are aimed at generating a motivated work force driven by commitment and involvement. The upper part of the framework represents transformational roles while the lower part displays transactional roles (Belasen, 2000).

Transformational roles contribute to greater follower motivation, satisfaction, and results. Transformational roles are deemed to be altruism oriented and grounded in caring, based on benevolence. These factors compel followers to go beyond their self-interest and focus on the organization and the greater community. This generates good will and provides a propensity for positive results. Thus, the transformational leader sparks both an interpersonal dependence with followers and an empowering independence that encourages identification with the organization and its environment.

Transactional roles, however, focus on the orderly accomplishment of tasks and work activities, largely with an immediate or short-term focus. They provide correction when necessary and offer rewards for positive behavior. Compliance, sometimes by coercion, is stressed; creativity and innovation are deemphasized and discouraged because these phenomena represent departures from the status quo. Power is unequal between managers and followers, and communication, when negatively established, is often blocked by uncertainty, fear of reprisal, and mistrust. Simply put, what is most important to the transactional manager is getting things done; the transformational leader focuses on the people who perform the work and the relationship of those people to the work environment.

The key to successful high-impact middle managers is recognizing the contradictory pressures on the managerial job. High-impact leaders know how to navigate across the roles to balance the often conflicting demands from diverse constituencies. They are also perceived by others as displaying the eight CVF roles more often than less effective managers (Denison et al., 1995). Gender differences did not change this conclusion: men and women are regarded as equally competent (or incompetent) leaders when assessed objectively by their boss, peers, or staff in terms of how well they display the CVF roles (Vilkinas, 2000; Belasen & Frank, 2012).

The CVF can be used diagnostically to evaluate the relative strengths and weaknesses of managers performing the variety of leadership roles. As such, the framework helps facilitate understanding across hierarchical levels (Belasen, 2008). **Figure 2.4** illustrates the responses by middle managers and others about the choice and extent of behaviors they use to manage the workplace.

The diagram shows the reactions of direct reports (first line supervisors) and superiors (top executives) to a composite self-assessment profile of middle managers. While middle managers believe that, on balance, they perform the repertoire of roles needed to support operations, their bosses think that they need to shift their focus from external to internal operations (people, processes, structures, coordination). Meanwhile, direct reports would like to see greater emphasis on innovation, change leadership, and communication. The difference between how middle managers perceive themselves versus how others perceive them, as Huy (2011) observed in his study, is that middle managers make valuable contributions that often go unnoticed by most senior executives who frequently favor a nonaffective task focus.

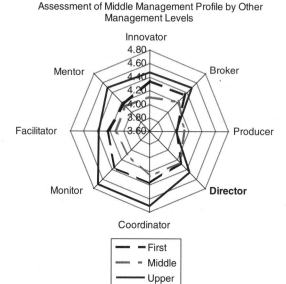

Assessment of Middle Management Profile by Other
Management Levels

Figure 2.4 Middle Managers' Leadership Profile

Belasen, A. T. (2008). *The theory and practice of corporate communication: A competing values perspective* (p. 206). Thousand Oaks, CA: Sage Publications.

   High-impact middle managers are individuals who make substantial qualitative and quantitative contributions to their organizations and move work forward with tact and velocity. They understand the complexity of their work environment and feel energized by being the conduit between corporate thought, action, and outcomes (Haneburg, 2010). As a result, they are able to provide much richer views to problem-solving communication with diverse insights. The more successful middle managers display higher education levels, better physical health, more emphasis on work performance, planning, coordination of work units, decisiveness, cooperation, and heightened intellectual efficiency. The less successful middle managers compensate for weaknesses in educational background and social skills by emphasizing job-related skills, diligence, and technical knowledge.

   Effective middle managers direct communication flow at the intersection of multiple information channels. They are responsible for communicating organizational goals and objectives, making sure executive level directives and internal processes are understood by direct reports. At the same time, they are the voice of their employees, protecting their needs and securing resources for effective execution of functional and organizational goals. For decades middle managers have been required to take tacit knowledge (personal, difficult to formalize) relating to strategic levels and convert it into explicit knowledge (codified and transmittable) for the front line levels (Beck & Plowman, 2009, p. 912). It's no wonder the front line employees prefer informal channels of communication when it comes to corporate goals and strategy. In fact, official discourse conveyed from senior management through middle management was found to be highly ineffective (Huy, 2001), causing confusion. It has been observed that "middle managers help resolve this . . . by acting as sense-makers" (Beck & Plowman, 2009). In this respect, Huy (2002) attributes the success of middle managers to balancing the competing commitments to both change and continuity by being attuned to subordinates' emotional needs for consistency, dependability, and opportunities for personal development.

Adding Strategic Value

In their study of middle managers' involvement in healthcare strategy processes, Floyd and Wooldridge (1997) proposed that middle managers' boundary-spanning position allowed them to influence top management as well as front line employees. Similarly, King and Zeithaml (2001) found that middle managers in hospitals who were privy to information regarding their organization's competitive advantage were able to convey the information to appropriate management and staff throughout the organization.

Balancing strategic awareness with operating experience requires an effective mix of leadership and management roles as well as knowledge of conflict resolution, persuasion, and problem solving communication—the forte of high-impact middle managers. Indeed, communication competence is a skill most needed by middle managers as the complexity of information and number of potential interactions is greater for middle managers than for senior managers or operating-level managers (Beck & Plowman, 2009). Another mix between leadership and management roles involves strategy implementation. High-impact middle managers optimize their functioning by facilitating adaptability while acting in the capacity of innovator and broker roles and by implementing deliberate strategy using the director and producer roles depicted by the CVF (Belasen, 2012). Facilitating adaptability requires the middle manager to relax regulations to get new projects started, to secure time for experimental programs, to locate and provide resources for trial projects, and to encourage informal discussion and information sharing (Floyd & Wooldridge, 1994). They can implement deliberate strategy by monitoring activities to support top management objectives, translate goals into action plans and work unit objectives, and sell top management's initiatives to subordinates, adding strategic value to their positions.

Brache (2004) defuses the notion that middle managers are not prepared to deal with strategic issues or do not know the strategy because they focus more on operational (e.g., selecting and training employees, purchasing, improving productivity, designing marketing programs) rather than strategic issues. These competing organizational interests place the middle manager in a difficult and stressful position because they cannot function in a strategic vacuum. According to Brache (2004), if the organization's strategy is clearly established and communicated, middle managers can use it responsibly to guide their operational decisions and link them with strategy. In fact, Mollick (2011) found that middle managers, rather than innovators or organizational strategy, were best able to explain variation in firm performance. Managers accounted for 22.3% of the variation in revenue among projects, as opposed to just over 7% explained by innovators and 21.3% explained by the organization itself—including firm strategy, leadership, and practices. Far from being interchangeable, individuals uniquely contribute to the success or failure of a firm. Additionally, even in a young industry that rewards creative and innovative products, innovative roles explain far less variation in firm performance than do managers. According to Mollick (2011), innovators can initiate change or stimulate new ideas; however, middle managers develop the logistical plan for operationalizing the innovation as well as allocating resources for monitoring and coordinating the implementation. The role of the middle manager in the strategic process is broad and complex where both formulation and implementation are well connected (Noble & Mokwa, 1999; Parsa, 1999).

As shown in **Figure 2.5**, leadership is exercised through social (broker, facilitator) and task (coordinator, monitor) behaviors (Madlock, 2008). In addition to the persuasion aspect of managerial communication and the ability to control language, gestures, and tone of voice, Shaw (2005) suggested that they must also share and respond to information in a timely manner in order to be perceived as competent communicators by their subordinates. Moreover, they should actively listen to other points of view, communicate clearly and succinctly to all levels of the organization, and utilize appropriate communication channels. Indeed, the strategic value of middle managers in healthcare organizations is in removing barriers to problem solving and in stimulating innovation and learning. By reframing

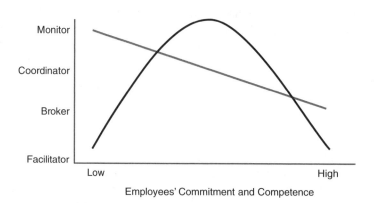

Figure 2.5 Situational Leadership

employees' perceptions of failures from sources of frustration to sources of learning, managers can engage employees in system improvement efforts that would otherwise not occur (Tucker & Edmondson, 2003).

Knowing when to provide structure and direction and when to let go through delegation and trust requires a subtle balance between transactional and transformational roles vital for running healthcare organizations effectively. Middle managers can accomplish this task through synthesizing information as well as championing and executing plans (Belasen, 2012). Synthesizing information consists of gathering intelligence on the feasibility of new programs, communicating the activities of competitors and suppliers, and assessing changes in the external environment. Championing involves justifying and defining new programs, evaluating the merits of new proposals, searching for new opportunities, and proposing programs or projects to higher-level managers (Floyd & Wooldridge, 1997; Mantere, 2008). Middle managers' duality of operating experience and proximity to decision authority centers makes their championing roles critical for sustaining competitive advantage (Hackworth & Kunz, 2011; Morrison, Roberts, & Von Hippel, 2000). This expectation is also in line with Kanter's (1982) seminal study of effective middle managers who excel in growth-oriented organizations and who share the qualities that define high-impact managers: thoroughness, persistence, discretion, persuasiveness, and comfort with change.

Middle managers perform what Sullivan (1992) called "playing coach in which the manager is a delegator and a doer, a strategist and an operator, a long-range planner as well as an immediate implementer" (p. 270). In this respect, the middle manager operates both in the arena of senior management (the coaches) and that of the staff (the players). Simply being able to communicate with both groups is not enough. Middle managers need the knowledge and skills to function effectively with both groups and the flexibility to shift from the role of a manager to the role of *team builder and team leader* as well as implement innovation.

Building Effective Teams

The silo structure of many healthcare organizations, especially hospitals, and lack of integration across disciplines and functional units create obstacles for interprofessional collaboration, sharing knowledge, and shifting workload flexibly to deal with emergent issues and unexpected bottlenecks. Ultimately, the highly specialized units, clinical and administrative, breed complexity, redundancy, and lack incentives for using broader goals and incentives for continuous improvement.

Freed (2005) suggested that a lack of proper presence of middle management in innovation implementation can stymie hospital turnarounds. Hypothesizing that middle managers are largely overlooked in extant healthcare innovation implementation, Birken, Shoou-Yih, and Weiner (2012) sought to identify the relative contribution of middle managers to healthcare organizations' achievement of innovations related outcomes. Middle managers' influence on front line employees, they concluded, was positively related to organizational outcomes such as effectiveness, competitive position, efficiency, and financial performance. Variation in healthcare quality may be related to either circumvention of middle managers or poor communication flow of key strategic and clinical information across practice sites and units. By bridging informational gaps, middle managers help to manage the demands associated with innovation implementation, align incentives, transcend professional barriers, and identify priorities to promote innovation implementation.

So how can healthcare executives strengthen their organizational capabilities to perform complex tasks that often cut across diverse units and departments while minimizing the handicaps inherent in their functional structures?

Gratton and Erickson (2007) examined 55 large teams that demonstrated high levels of cooperative behaviors despite the complexity of their structures and isolated eight best practices that correlate with team success. The eight practices were reinforced by positive executive support, good human resource practices, a strong team leader, and the group composition itself.

1. *Investing in signature relationship practices.* Executives can promote collaborative behavior through personal commitments by championing system-wide efforts and by making highly visible statements with supportive and inclusive communication processes.
2. *Modeling collaborative behavior.* In organizations where executives break the silo pattern in their organizations with collaborative behaviors and mutual support regardless the constraints of disciplinary boundaries, teams perform well.
3. *Creating a gift culture.* Creating incentives for collateral structures of communication and informal networks help support the social identity of organizational members and encourage them to collaborate.
4. *Ensuring the requisite skills.* Human resource (HR) departments that launch training and education programs aimed at teambuilding and resolving conflicts have a major impact on the success of teams.
5. *Supporting a strong sense of community.* When executives and HR directors reinforce an adaptive culture that rewards learning and transfer of best practices across functional lines, organizational members feel more confidence in reaching out to others.
6. *Assigning team leaders that are both task and relationship oriented.* These two roles are complementary and both are important for effective team functioning, especially during team transitions through various developmental cycles (e.g., forming, storming, norming, performing).
7. *Building on heritage relationships.* Team members who know each other and who develop common understanding and mutual respect over time help promote continued collaborative behavior.

8. *Understanding role clarity and task ambiguity.* When team members are familiar with the roles and their latitude on how to perform responsibilities or complete tasks, uncertainty and anxiety levels are reduced, adding to the success of team performance.

Bachiochi, O'Connor, Rogelberg, and Elder (2000) identified six important areas of mastery for team leaders. The combination of these six qualities creates a powerful model of team leadership that combines task and human skills essential for effective team leadership:

1. Background and expertise (possess job knowledge).
2. Task-oriented skills (planner/organizer, decision-maker, delegator [shares power], problem solver, facilitator, motivator).
3. Interpersonal skills (conflict management, persuasion/influence, coach/ mentor, understanding/support).
4. Communication skills (effective listener, able to communicate information and vision, provide feedback).
5. Liaison skills (networker, responsible, accountable).
6. Personal characteristics/traits (self-confidence, emotional stability, consistency/trust, flexibility).

Because teams often operate without direct supervision or through distributed (or shared) leadership, the emphasis on joint accountability is often the most important factor that shapes the outcomes of team efforts. The Albany Stratton Veterans Affairs Medical Center (VAMC) in Albany, NY, is a prime example of how collaborative teams with joint accountability were established in the 1990s and since then have changed the outlook of the VAMC for the good. Located in the capital of New York state, this medical center serves veterans in 22 counties of upstate New York, western Massachusetts, and Vermont (U.S. Department of Veterans Affairs, n.d.).

The VAMC provides specialized medical services such as cardiac catheterization, cardiac rehabilitation, nuclear medicine, radiation oncology, stereotactic radiosurgery, hospice/palliative care, adult day health care, posttraumatic stress disorder, compensated work therapy, memory clinic, geriatric assessment, nursing home, and respite care. In addition, it offers a women veteran's health program that addresses a variety of healthcare needs specific to women veterans. Services include gynecology, bone density screening, and on-site mammography. There is also extensive diagnostic laboratory medicine and radiology including computerized tomography and magnetic resonance imaging. The primary care program provides services at the medical center and at several community-based outpatient clinics.

The goal of the VAMC is to provide the highest quality healthcare services through continuous quality improvement and technical excellence. The VAMC has many internationally recognized scientists conducting medical research in areas of cancer, pneumonia, and posttraumatic stress disorder.

During 1991–1992, the VAMC was chosen as a pilot site from within the VA system to receive consulting support and resources to implement continuous quality improvement (CQI). From its inception, the CQI garnered momentum through the intellectual stimulation, enthusiastic commitment, and continuing sponsorship of the VAMC leadership team. The following traces this quality effort by briefly describing the strategic objectives, key competitive advantages, core processes, ownership, establishment of multifunctional teams, performance objectives, elimination of non-value-added activities, building core capabilities, empowerment and self-management, and training to sustain the effort.

In March 1991, the CQI steering committee was initiated by the hospital director, and included himself, the chief of staff, associate director, associate director for nursing, CQI coordinator, associate chief of staff for education, and president of the medical staff. The committee revised the mission statement to reflect the new quality objectives and also redefined the core values of the hospital to include innovation, excellence, truthfulness, teamwork, trust, quality, empowerment, dignity, and compassion. In 1992, the VAMC developed a 4-year plan that addressed three key areas: training, CQI teams, and infrastructure development. The infrastructure development was centered on the mission, vision, and values of the hospital, strategic quality planning, education, communication, and reward and recognition. In addition, an organizational assessment was developed to provide employees with opportunities to participate and be involved in CQI teams.

As part of the national VA system, the Albany VAMC has a competitive advantage because patients who are veterans receive care at a reduced cost (compared to other healthcare institutions). A second competitive advantage is the low turnover rate of the nursing staff, which saves on recruitment and training costs commonly incurred by other healthcare facilities. The "captive clients," coupled with low turnover, also promote continuity in service delivery and maintenance. Within the larger scope of the American healthcare delivery system, the Albany VAMC needed to contain healthcare costs as the trend of rising costs for inpatient hospital care continued to accelerate. Prior to implementing CQI, the VAMC demonstrated its superior performance by being the recipient of prestigious awards within the VA system. One such award was the 1993 Robert W. Carey Quality Award recognizing the VAMC for its benchmarked accomplishments and quality improvement.

The VAMC wanted to improve its organizational capabilities through the CQI process by organizing around core processes. Seven selected processes were OR cancellations, sputum cytology, emergency room (ER) waiting time, total hip replacement, discharge planning, medical records, and contract hospital. CQI teams were chartered based on the three levels: (1) projects involving large issues that concerned the entire medical center, for example, performance ratings; (2) projects that cut across functional lines or that required multidisciplinary treatments; and (3) projects with processes that were contained within a specific service or group of people, for example, laboratory specimen testing

Belasen, A. (2000). *Leading the learning organization: Communication and competencies for managing change.* Albany, NY: SUNY Press.

and service quality deployment. The teams varied structurally—sputum cytology was interdisciplinary in nature, while the ER was based on self-management principles. By April 1994, there were 20 chartered teams. Virtually all of these teams were supported by the CQI education task team, which provided the essentials needed to perform quality control training and analysis.

The steering committee did not eliminate functions or departments but rather revised the way services were provided by making them more sensitive to the needs of veterans and to the institutional goals of the medical center. For example, the contract hospital team identified a need to clarify the procedures for payment of reimbursement claims for veterans receiving care in non-VA hospitals. Steps were taken to ensure that veterans understood these procedures; the outcome was a reduction in unauthorized claims. In addition, the steering committee placed a high priority on the need for in-house and contract training in the area of quality improvement and self-management. The CQI training plan attempted to meet two objectives: (1) create and nurture a CQI environment, and (2) assist the staff with the use of process management tools and techniques. During the first phase of the training plan in 1991, the CQI steering committee held weekly meetings to review and discuss Deming and quality process control (QPC) videotapes and the information gathered by members who had attended off-site seminars. Once this information was accumulated, the committee designed a training plan for all employees.

The first step was to introduce the principles of CQI to all employees. This basic CQI training has become part of new employee orientation at a service or committee level in order to provide theory and techniques for implementation of the CQI process. The second phase of the plan involved the development of an internal CQI training team consisting of four master trainers. These trainers were responsible for conducting quality deployment workshops and training other members to lead future training sessions. Members of the CQI training team became facilitators and consultants for individual groups, so that managers and staff could utilize the tools needed for a given situation. Some of this training included:

- CQI awareness
- Tools and techniques for process improvement
- Service quality deployment
- Managing and responding to patient complaints and concerns
- Mentor training
- Cultural diversity in the workplace
- Creative leadership
- Labor/management relations
- Vision through focusing on the customer
- Interpersonal and communication skills
- Employee orientation

In addition, performance appraisal systems were modified to include elements of quality in areas such as leadership, technical competence, and coaching. Although participation in CQI was voluntary, employees were nonetheless accountable for upholding CQI principles.

Employees were encouraged to participate and be involved in the process improvement teams through team and peer recognition activities. Effective January 1995, the hospital redesigned its performance evaluation reward system. Previously, a supervisor would meet with employees, discuss their performance ratings for the past year, and then give a monetary reward. The new system, based on CQI principles, empowered the employees to recognize themselves for various achievements through individual or team efforts. These achievements must be consistent with the mission, vision, values, and critical success factors of the VAMC. All employees were qualified to receive $1000 during a fiscal year and could submit proposals as often as they wished. Recognition was noted in the following areas:

- Patient satisfaction
- Quality of work life and staff satisfaction
- Customer satisfaction
- Cost reduction
- Process improvement
- Teamwork
- Empowerment (shared responsibility)
- Quality of care
- Safety

Three of the success stories at the Albany medical center (VAMC) are the self-directed work teams, eye clinic waiting time, and the sputum cytology specimen process.

Self-directed work teams. The hospital has four services that are self-directed. Supply service developed their own plan for self-direction, whereas human resources, the eye clinic, and ward 9C received assistance from an outside consultant. Human resources had been self-directed for approximately 1 year by the end of 1995 and had projected completing the transformational cycle toward self-direction by 1998. This service was chosen as the pilot because of numerous internal and external problems. The eye clinic had been developing an implementation plan since 1995 with a goal to become self-directed. Ward 9C also began their process in 1995, but had taken longer to develop it because of the multidisciplinary nature of the group. A fifth team was also chosen for self-direction—the newly developed VISN (Veterans Integrated Services Network).

Eye clinic waiting time. A process improvement team (PIT) was initiated to review the time that patients spent waiting in the clinic. The PIT team used CQI tools and techniques to understand and analyze the process within the clinic. It was determined that a waiting time of 80 minutes total was reasonable. The flow chart and time study then indicated 28/56 patients waited an average of 1.8 hours with over half of the patients waiting in excess of 2 hours. The team decided on several improvements, including establishing a receptionist in the clinic and ensuring that the appropriate forms were available in the exam room. The average waiting time was reduced to 78 minutes with only 2 out of 22 patients waiting 2 hours or more in the clinic.

Sputum cytology specimens. The laboratory noted that 17% to 28% of specimens submitted for sputum cytology were rejected as unsatisfactory. A multidisciplinary PIT team was chartered to study the problem. Flow charts, cause-and-effect diagrams, and Pareto charts were used to identify and verify the data. Based on the analysis of the process, eight improvements were noted. Some of these improvements included establishing a centralized specimen collection center in the laboratory, providing in-service sessions to the medical and nursing staff to update them on any changes, and developing a computer ward order entry system for the needed laboratory tests.

Conclusion

The concept of sliding up (governance role) and down (advocacy role) was used by Hales (2006) to describe how middle managers drifted downward, from managerial roles to employee advocacy roles (Carlström, 2012; McConville, 2006). It is important, however, that a middle manager be confident enough to exercise upward leadership and, if necessary, challenge unethical or unreasonable decisions. Downward they should demonstrate a willingness to share power by creating meaningful opportunities for staff involvement as well as to take an active interest in staff career development (Sullivan, 1992). Regaining employees' trust after off-putting or disappointing experiences can be quite challenging. Kelly and Nadler (2007) suggest focusing on a few key factors, including becoming a transformational leader and shifting the focus to influencing processes and decisions, not controlling them.

High-impact middle managers add value to their organizations in a multitude of ways including follower development and performance and increased motivation, morality, and empowerment among the direct followers (Dvir, Eden, Avolio, & Shamir, 2002). Although a manager may primarily exhibit behaviors of transformational leadership to inspire employees, it is sometimes necessary to assert a transactional leadership style depending on the nature of the task (Aldoory & Toth, 2004). Successful strategies for high-impact middle managers include:

1. *Take responsibility for your success and your career.* Discover what you're good at and in which roles you excel. Set goals and challenges and go for them. Communicate your goals with management, and ask for feedback along the way toward achieving your goals. Identify your skills gaps and areas of weakness. Then, take ownership by seeking out the knowledge you need to perform at a higher level. Get outside your comfort zone. Steer change.

2. *Seek out a mentor.* Find someone in your organization or in your industry who can provide you with coaching or direction on how to achieve your

goals. Check in with your mentor at least once a month for feedback. Listen to the feedback and self-improve where needed.

3. *Be a self-starter.* Do you wait to be assigned projects or new responsibilities or do you seek them out? Self-starters don't wait for others to tell them how to achieve a goal. They identify opportunities, propose new projects, and improve work processes and systems. They believe in continuous improvement and constantly seek new challenges and ways to improve their work and departmental activities.

4. *Achieve more results than others.* If you are not consistently achieving more results than expected, identify one or two areas within your position or department where you can make a positive impact in a short period of time. Look for at least one improvement you can make on a weekly basis. It doesn't have to be big—small improvements done consistently will create long-term results.

5. *Know how to facilitate team interactions.* Every team is charged with particular tasks and follows certain interpersonal dynamics. This requires skills that transcend a range of leadership qualities including understanding and managing transitions, initiating structure, resolving conflict, and managing interpersonal relationships.

6. *Be a problem solver.* Every work team and department has opportunities for improvement. Set an intention to become aware of problems in your work area. Talk with people informally about the problems before you bring up the issue in a meeting. Initiate conversations with coworkers or direct reports about how the problem might be solved. Once you have some solutions, present them to management and make sure to give credit to the people contributing solutions and ideas. What are the issues that slow down workflow or get in the way of you or your team quickly responding to other departments or to customers? Bring up those areas in team meetings, and when you do, be prepared to present a few possible solutions.

7. *Become solution oriented.* High performers believe there is a solution to every problem, and are determined to find it. It's not enough to become aware of problems, you also have to believe that an easy solution is available. Hold a positive, solution-oriented focus whenever working with colleagues.

8. *Maintain a positive and enthusiastic attitude.* Successful people show high levels of energy when they approach a task. They don't dwell on problems or failures. They take a learning approach by reflecting on what they learned when they make a mistake so they can improve their performance in the future. Most importantly, high performers are highly motivated and have a passion for what they do.

9. *Think and act strategically like an executive.* Have an outside-in perspective by incorporating the goals of external stakeholders in your thinking and decisions.

It is very important that executives know how to appropriately judge the middle manager in ways that are fair and just in order to avoid undue bias. Coaching or mentoring programs have also been known to help cultivate more effective middle managers. Guttman (2012) suggested that by encouraging and facilitating self-coaching among high-potential midlevel managers, organizations can benefit from the principles of executive self-coaching while minimizing the investment they need to make. Best practices for management coaches include the following: be available and accessible; listen; use the Socratic method and allow managers to reason their way to answers; facilitate action plans as challenges arise; and encourage mentees (Haneburg, 2010). By embracing transformational leadership and supporting mentoring and self-coaching programs, organizations provide middle managers the support they need to succeed.

High-impact middle managers that are also hypereffective managers need to recognize and respect their own limits, both professionally and personally. Placing realistic boundaries on their own capabilities while continuing to strive for success might prove useful. A manager's personal life needs to have equal balance as well. Organizations that actively pursue a quality of work life often experience better results from all levels. By effectively leveraging the knowledge developed from learning about the CVF, middle managers can continue on the path of becoming high-impact managers while still achieving a high level of work-life balance.

Application Activity: 10 Benefits Resulting from Clinical Integration

In today's healthcare landscape, there are a wide range of approaches and strategies have been employed to achieve successful clinical integration (CI). Regardless of the strategy, when designed and implemented correctly, CI offers tremendous potentials for efficiencies and improvements in healthcare quality and patient satisfaction.

Here are 10 identified benefits of CI to consider when exploring your CI options and feasibility (Smith, 2013):

1. **Increased collaboration.** The use of care teams to implement a CI program addresses gaps in the care continuum while reducing ineffective or unneeded process steps. This approach allows hospitals and healthcare providers to learn to operate as a team to better align, or realign, their efforts to improve quality, patient safety, and patient and family satisfaction.

2. **Improved efficiency.** CI eliminates healthcare waste and redundancy, making it possible for hospital systems to provide patients with focused, seamless systems of care across and between healthcare providers.

3. **Integrated systems.** CI programs provide hospital systems with many more monitoring and enforcement tools than through a typical medical staff organization, including the payment of financial incentives for physicians who actively participate in the program and penalties for those who do not.

---

4. **Payer partnerships.** As CI improves the quality of patient care and clinical processes and reduces costs, hospitals are able to achieve market differentiation. This
type of differentiation is attractive to health plans and can serve as the catalyst for
payer partnerships.

5. **Improved care management.** Organizations that are successfully clinically integrated benefit from improved care management. Patients who see multiple doctors
are well aware of the fragmented and redundant services and care they receive. Case
management serves as the foundation to accomplish coordination of care across
traditional health settings. Its goal is to achieve the best clinical and cost outcomes
for both patient and provider and is most successful when case managers are able to
work within and outside organized health systems.

6. **Integrated continuum of care.** At the center of CI is teamwork among healthcare
providers who work to ensure patients get the right care at the right time in the right
setting. CI care management teams collaborate with adult daycare, independent living, assisted living, and skilled nursing facility partners. Together with infrastructure
focused on supporting caregivers and patients to efficiently assess, document,
communicate, and meet patient needs, CI enables hospital systems and healthcare
networks to achieve this core objective.

7. **Clinical data systems.** An integrated technology (IT) platform that supports continuity of care and enables access to medical history and critical patient data for all
stakeholders is imperative in CI, easing communications across the care continuum
and providing information that measures service, performance, quality, and outcomes
on an individual provider and network-wide basis.

8. **Patient-centered communication.** In many networks, communication skills training is
provided to physicians and healthcare providers with the goal of establishing clear channels of communication as a vital part of the CI program. The Joint Commission (formerly The Joint Commission on Accreditation of Health Care Organizations [JCAHO]) has
cited communication breakdown as the single greatest contributing factor to sentinel
events and delays in care in U.S. hospitals. The CI emphasis on timely and clear communication is key to influencing patient behavior, resulting in cost and quality benefits.

9. **Improved pharmaceutical management.** Most medication errors are not caused
by individual carelessness, but rather by faulty processes that lead people to make
mistakes or fail to prevent the mistakes. CI improves pharmaceutical management by
allowing hospitals to identify gaps in the medication management process and allowing them to take actions to help make patients safer.

10. **Improved health of the community.** CI emphasizes wellness initiatives such as
outreach programs and classes to empower the patient with tools, knowledge, and
practical solutions to participate actively in their care, ultimately leading to a healthier
population. Extensive research in the past 3 decades indicates that receiving wellness
and prevention advice and care from trusted local hospitals and physicians resonates
with individuals.

Review Questions

1. Assuming you are a middle manager in charge of a plan to increase interprofessional collaboration in your hospital, use the eight best practices discussed in the chapter for building a successful CI team.
2. Develop a set of milestones and activities to help facilitate the CI implementation through the transition and action phases discussed in this chapter.
3. What role(s) would you assume in this CI team?
4. Use the 10 benefits described above to evaluate the success of your CI team.

References

Aldoory, L., & Toth, E. (2004). Leadership and gender in public relations: Perceived effectiveness of transformational and transactional leadership styles. *Journal of Public Relations Research, 16*(2), 157–183. doi: 10.1207/s1532754xjprr1602_2

Alvesson, M., & Sveningsson, S. (2003a). The great disappearing act: Difficulties in doing "leadership." *Leadership Quarterly, 14*(3), 359–381. doi: 10.1016/S1048-9843(03)00031-6

Alvesson, M., & Sveningsson, S. (2003b). Managers doing leadership: The extra-ordinarization of the mundane. *Human Relations, 56*(12), 1435–1459. doi: 10.1177/00187267035612001

Avolio, B. J., Walumbwa, F. O., & Weber, T. J. (2009). Leadership: Current theories, research, and future directions. *Annual Review of Psychology, 60*, 421–449. doi: 10.1146/annurev.psych.60.110707.163621

Bachiochi, P. D., O'Connor, M. S., Rogelberg, S. G., & Elder, A. E. (2000). The qualities of an effective team leader. *Organizational Development Journal, 18*(1), 1–28.

Balogun, J., & Johnson, G. (2004). Organizational restructuring and middle manager sense making. *Academy of Management Journal, 47*(4), 523–549.

Beck, T. E., & Plowman, D. A. (2009). Experiencing rare and unusual events richly: The role of middle managers in animating and guiding organizational interpretation. *Organization Science, 20*(5), 909–924.

Belasen, A. T. (2000). *Leading the learning organization: Communication and competencies for managing change.* Albany, NY: SUNY Press.

Belasen, A. T. (2008). *The theory and practice of corporate communication: A competing values perspective.* Thousand Oaks, CA: Sage Publications.

Belasen, A. T. (2012). *Developing women leaders in corporate America: Balancing competing demands, transcending traditional boundaries.* Santa Barbara, CA: Praeger.

Belasen, A. T., Benke, M., DiPadova, L. N., & Fortunato, M. V. (1996). Downsizing and the hyper-effective manager: The shifting importance of managerial roles during organizational transformation. *Human Resource Management, 35*(1), 87–118. doi: 10.1002/(SICI)1099-050X(199621)35:1<87::AID-HRM6>3.0.CO;2-T

Belasen, A. T., & Fortunato, M. (2013). Situational motivation: Challenging the binary. In M. Paludi (Ed.), *The psychology of business success.* (p. 173–196). Santa Barbara, CA: Praeger.

Belasen, A. T., & Frank, N. M. (2004). The perceptions of human resource managers of the shifting importance of managerial roles in downsizing organizations. *International Journal of Human Resources Development and Management, 4*(2), 144–163.

Belasen, A. T., & Frank, N. M. (2008). Competing values leadership: Quadrant roles and personality traits. *Leadership and Organizational Development Journal, 29*(2), 127–143.

Belasen, A. T., & Frank, N. M. (2010). A peek through the lens of the competing values framework: What managers communicate and how. *The Atlantic Journal of Communication, 18,*(5) 280–296.

Belasen, A. T., & Frank, N. M. (2012). Women's leadership: Using the competing values framework to evaluate the interactive effects of gender and personality traits on leadership roles. *International Journal of Leadership Studies, 7*(2), 192–215.

Birken, S., Shoou-Yih, D., & Weiner, B. (2012). Uncovering middle managers' role in healthcare innovation implementation. *Implementation Science.* Retrieved from http://www.implementationscience.com/content/7/1/28

Brache, A. P. (2004). Strategy and the middle manager. *Training.* Retrieved from http://www.kepner-tregoe.com/pdfs/articles/StrategyMidMan.pdf

Buchanan, D. A., Addicott, R., Fitzgerald, L., Ferlie, E., & Baeza, J. I. (2007). Nobody in charge: Distributed change agency in healthcare. *Human Relations. 60*(7), 1065–1090. doi: 10.1177/0018726707081158

Caramenico, A. (2013, October 16). Healthcare experiences the most CEO turnover. *FierceHealthcare.* Retrieved from http://www.fiercehealthcare.com/story/healthcare-experiences-most-ceo-turnover/2013-10-16#ixzz2jJU7OH2r

Carlström, E. D. (2012). Middle managers on the slide. *Leadership in Health Services, 25*(2), 90.

Carroll, B., Levy, L., & Richmond, D. (2008). Leadership as practice: Challenging the competency paradigm. *Leadership, 4*(4), 363–379. doi: 10.1177/1742715008095186

Challenger, Gray & Christmas, Inc. (2013). 2013 September CEO report: 107 CEOs out, highest quarterly total since Q4 2008. Retrieved from http://www.challengergray.com/press/press-releases/2013-september-ceo-report-107-ceos-out-highest-quarterly-total-q4-2008

Chreim, S., Williams, B., Janz, L., & Dastmalchian, A. (2010). Change agency in a primary health care context: The case of distributed leadership. *Health Care Management Review, 35*(2), 187–199. doi: 10.1097/HMR.0b013e3181c8b1f8

Currie, G. (2000). The public manager in 2010: The role of middle managers in strategic change in the public sector. *Public Money & Management, 20* (1), 111–119. doi: 10.1111/1467-9302.00197

Currie, G. (2006). Reluctant but resourceful middle managers: The case of nurses in the NHS. *Journal of Nursing Management, 14*(1), 5–12. doi: 10.1111/j.1365-2934.2005.00613.x

Currie, G., Lockett, A., & Subomlinova, O. (2009). The institutionalization of distributed leadership: A "Catch-22" in English public services. *Human Relations, 62*(11), 1735–1761. doi: 10.1177/0018726709346378

D'Amour, D., Ferrada-Videla, M., Rodriguez, L. S., & Beaulieu, M. (2005). The conceptual basis for interprofessional collaboration: Core concepts and theoretical frameworks. *Journal of Interprofessional Care, 19 (suppl 1),* 116–131. doi: 10.1080/13561820500082529

Denis, J., Langley, A., & Rouleau, L. (2010). The practice of leadership in the messy world of organizations. *Leadership, 6*(1), 67–88. doi: 10.1177/1742715009354233

Denison, D. R., Hooijberg, R., & Quinn, R. E. (1995). Paradox and performance: Toward a theory of behavioral complexity in managerial leadership. *Organization Science, 6*(5), 524–540. doi: 10.1287/orsc.6.5.524

Dvir, T., Eden, D., Avolio, B., & Shamir, B. (2002). Impact of transformational leadership on follower development and performance: A field experiment. *The Academy of Management Journal, 45*(4), 735–744.

Embertson, K. (2006). The importance of middle managers in healthcare organizations. *Journal of Healthcare Management, 51*(4), 223–232.

Farrell, D., & Rusbult, C. E. (1992). Exploring the exit, voice, loyalty, and neglect typology: The influence of job satisfaction, quality of alternatives, and investment size. *Employee Responsibilities and Rights Journal, 5*(3), 201–218. doi: 10.1007/BF01385048

Federico, F., & Bonacum, D. (2010). Strengthening the core: Middle managers play a vital role in improving safety. *Healthcare Executive*, Jan/Feb, 68–70.

Finn, R., Currie, G., & Martin, G. (2010). Team work in context: Institutional mediation in the public service professional bureaucracy. *Organization Studies, 31*(9), 1069–1097. doi: 10.1177/0170840610376142

Floyd, S., & Lane, P. J. (2000). Strategizing throughout the organization: Managing role conflict in strategic renewal. *Academy of Management Review, 25*(1), 154–177.

Floyd, S., & Wooldridge, B. (1994). Dinosaurs or dynamos? Recognizing middle management's strategic role. *The Academy of Management Executive, 8*(4), 47–57.

Floyd, S., & Wooldridge, B. (1997). Middle management's strategic influence and organizational performance. *Journal of Management Studies, 34*(3), 465–485.

Freed, D. H. (2005). Hospital turnarounds: agents, approaches, alchemy. *Healthcare Manager, 24*(23), 96.

Gilmartin, M. J., & D'Aunno, T. A. (2007). Leadership research in healthcare. In J. Walsh & A. P. Brief (Eds.), *Academy of Management Annals* (pp. 387–438). Briarcliff Manor, NY: Academy of Management.

Grafton, L. (2011, January). Column: The End of the Middle Manager. *Harvard Business Review*. Retrieved from http://hbr.org/2011/01/column-the-end-of-the-middle-manager/ar/1

Gratton, L., & Erickson, T. J. (2007, November). Eight ways to build collaborative teams. *Harvard Business Review*. Retrieved from http://hbr.org/2007/11/eight-ways-to-build-collaborative-teams/

Guttman, H. (2012). Helping future leaders self-coach to win. *Leader to Leader, 63*, 7–12. doi: 10.1002/ltl.20003

Hackworth, B. H., & Kunz, M. B. (2011). Health care and social media: Building relationships via social networks. *Academy of Health Care Management Journal, 7*(2), 1–14.

Hales, C. (2006). Mowing down the line, the shifting boundary between middle and first-line management. *Journal of General Management, 32*(2), 31–55.

Hamel, G. (2011). Let's fire all the managers. *Harvard Business Review, 89*, 48–60.

Hammer, M., & Champy, J. (1993). *Reengineering the corporation.* New York, NY: Harper Collins.

Haneburg, L. (2010). *The high impact middle manager: Powerful strategies to thrive in the middle.* Alexandria, VA: ASTD Press.

Hart, S. L., & Quinn, R. E. (1993). Roles executives play: CEOs, behavioral complexity, and firm performance. *Human Relations, 46*(1993), 543–574. doi: 10.1177/001872679304600501

Hayes, D. (2005). New effort to boost middle manager skills is under way. *Community Care, 1559*, 1–2.

Huy, Q. N. (2001). In praise of middle managers. *Harvard Business Review, 79*(8), 72–79, 160.

Huy, Q. N. (2002). Emotional balancing of organizational continuity and radical change: The contribution of middle managers. *Administrative Science Quarterly, 47*(1), 31–69.

Huy, Q. N. (2011). How middle managers' group focus emotions and social identities influence strategy implementation. *Strategic Management Journal, 32*(13), 1387–1410.

Kane, G., Fishman, R.G., Gallaugher, J., & Glaser, J. (2009). Community relations 2.0. *Harvard Business Review, 87*(11), 45–50.

Kanter, R. M. (1982). The middle manager as innovator. *Harvard Business Review, 60*(4), 95–105.

Kelly, J., & Nadler, S. (2007, March 3). Leading from below: CEOs can't change companies on their own, the secret is to foster a leadership mentality throughout the ranks. *The Wall Street Journal.* Retrieved from http://online.wsj.com/news/articles /SB117139153010507497

King, A., & Zeithaml, C. (2001). Competencies and firm performance: Examining the causal ambiguity paradox. *Strategic Management Journal, 22*, 75–99.

Kotter, J. (2013, January 9). Management is (still) not leadership. *Harvard Business Review* [Web log]. Retrieved from http://blogs.hbr.org/2013/01/management-is-still-not-leadership/

Kuyvenhoven, R., & Buss, C. (2011). A normative view of the role of middle management in the implementation of strategic change. *Journal of Management & Marketing Research, 8*(1), 1–14.

Larsson, M., & Lundholm, S. E. (2010). Leadership as work-embedded influence: A micro-discursive analysis of an everyday interaction in a bank. *Leadership, 6*(2), 159–184.

Leathard, A. (2003). Introduction. In A. Leathard (Ed.), *Interprofessional collaboration: From policy to practice in health and social care* (pp. 3–11) New York, NY: Brunner-Routledge.

Livingston, J. S. (1969). Pygmalion in management. *Harvard Business Review*, July–August, 81–89.

Madlock, P. E. (2008). The link between leadership style, communicator competence, and employee satisfaction. *Journal of Business Communication, 45*(1), 61–78. doi: 10.1177/0021943607309351

Mantere, S. (2008). Role expectations and middle manager strategic agency. *Journal of Management Studies, 45*(2), 294–316. doi: 10.1111/j.1467-6486.2007.00744.x

Manzoni, J. F., & Barsoux, J. L. (2002). *The set-up-to-fail syndrome: How good managers cause great people to fail.* Boston, MA: Harvard Business School Press.

McConville, T. (2006). Devolved HRM responsibilties, middle managers and role dissonance. *Personnel Review, 35*(6), 637–653.

McConville, T., & Holden, L. (1999). The filling in the sandwich: HRM and middle managers in the health sector. *Personnel Review, 28*(5/6), 406–424.

Miles, S. A. (2009, July 31). Succession planning: How to do it right. *Forbes.* Retrieved from http://www.forbes.com/2009/07/31/succession-planning-right-leadership -governance-ceos.html

Mollick, E. R. (2011). People and process, suits and innovators: The role of individuals in firm performance. *Strategic Management Journal, 33*(9), 1001–1015.

Morris, J., & Upchurch, B. (2012). The practices of successful managers. Retrieved from http://www.businessknowhow.com/manage/successful-manager.htm

Morrison, P. D., Roberts, J. H., & Von Hippel, E. (2000). Determinants of user innovation and innovation sharing in a local market. *Management Science, 46*(12), 1513–1527.

Neilson, G. L., & Wulf, J. (2012). How many direct reports? *Harvard Business Review, 90*(4), 113–119.

Noble, C. H., & Mokwa, M. P. (1999). Implementing marketing strategies: Developing and trusting a managerial theory. *Journal of Marketing, 63*(4), 57–73.

Osterman, P. (2009). *The truth about middle managers: Who they are, how they work, why they matter.* Boston, MA: Harvard Business School Press.

Parsa, H. G. (1999). Interaction of strategy implementation and power perceptions in franchise systems: An empirical investigation. *Journal of Business Research, 45,* 173–185.

Pearce, C. (2004). The future of leadership: Combining vertical and shared leadership to transform knowledge work. *Academy of Management Executive, 18,* 47–57.

Quinn, R. E. (1988). *Beyond rational management: Mastering the paradoxes and competing demands of high performance.* San Francisco, CA: Jossey-Bass.

Raelin, J. (2011). From leadership-as-a-practice to leaderful practice. *Leadership, 7*(2), 195–211.

Rajan, G. R., & Wulf, J. (2006). The flattening firm: Evidence from panel data on the changing nature of corporate hierarchies. *The Review of Economics and Statistics, 88*(4), 759–773.

Rouleau, L., & Balogun, J. (2011). Middle managers, Strategic sensemaking, and discursive competence. *Journal of Management Studies, 48*(5), 953–983. doi: 10.1111/j.1467-6486.2010.00941.x

Shaw, K. (2005). Getting leaders involved in communication strategy: Breaking down the barriers to effective leadership communication. *Strategic Communication Management, 9,* 14–17.

Smith, M. (2013, December 3). *Health directions: The franchise model: An emerging strategy for clinical integration* [Web log]. Retrieved from http://info.healthdirections.com /blog/

Sullivan, M. (1992). The changing role of the middle manager in research libraries. *Library Trends, 41*(2), 269–281.

Tucker. A. L., & Edmondson, A. C. (2003). Why hospitals don't learn from failures: Organizational and psychological dynamics that inhibit system change. *California Management Review, 45*(2), 55–71.

U.S. Department of Veterans Affairs. (n.d.). *Fact Sheet: Albany Stratton VA Medical Center Albany, NY.* Retrieved from http://www.albany.va.gov/albfactsheet.asp

Valentino, C. L. (2004). The role of middle managers in the transmission and integration of organizational culture. *Journal of Healthcare Management, 49*(6), 393–404.

Vilà, J., & Canales, J. I. (2008). Can strategic planning make strategy more relevant and build commitment over time? The case of RACC. *Long Range Planning, 41*(3), 273–290. doi: 10.1016/j.lrp.2008.02.009

Vilkinas, T. (2000). The gender factor in management: How significant others perceive effectiveness. *Women in Management, 15*(5/6), 261–271. doi: 10.1108/09649420010372922

Vivar, C. G. (2006). Putting conflict management into practice: A nursing case study. *Journal of Nursing Management, 14*, 201–206. doi: 10.1111/j.1365-2934.2006.00554.x

Vroom, V. H. (1964). *Work and motivation.* New York, NY: Wiley.

Witt/Kieffer (2012). *Healthcare CEOs and the need for better succession planning.* Retrieved from http://www.wittkieffer.com/file/thought-leadership/practice/Healthcare%20CEOs%20and%20Succession%20Planning.pdf

Wooldridge, B., Schmid, T., & Floyd, S. (2008). The middle management perspective on strategy process: Contributions, synthesis, and future research. *Journal of Management, 34*, 1190–1221. doi: 10.1177/0149206308324326

CHAPTER 3 ▶

Understanding and Motivating Healthcare Employees

LEARNING OBJECTIVES

Students will be able to:

- Frame the context for understanding the challenge of motivating employees with different needs
- Understand the advantages and disadvantages of using intrinsic and extrinsic sources of motivation
- Learn about integrative theories and concepts of motivation
- Recognize the importance of situational motivation
- Relate motivation to leadership roles
- Learn about effective motivational strategies
- Analyze incidents and apply situational motivation tools to increase employee satisfaction and improve performance

Many people who work in health care have a Mrs. J in their lives . . . a parent or a brother or sister, or maybe a child who gets sick, or maybe even some chance encounter with a stranger that sends them on a path to a career in health care. When we step back from the challenges and difficulties of making certain that our institutions are properly managed, we can take comfort in knowing that the work we do is intended to help others who are sick. There is no doubt that all who work health care—no matter the job—contribute in some way to taking care of people. And there is no question that such devotion constitutes a source of inspiration and fulfillment.

Mrs. J

When I was 16 years old, I had the opportunity to spend the summer interning in a hospital that my uncle managed. I was very excited! I had never thought about working in a hospital and this felt more enticing than working in the daycamp near my home.

My uncle said we would get to the hospital every day early enough to have breakfast together and that we would meet for lunch when possible. On the first day, my uncle took me to the security office and arranged for me to be issued an ID tag. Wearing it made me feel like an official member of the hospital. I was amazed as we walked through the halls. Everyone on the staff knew my uncle and he knew them—not only their names, but little things about them. "How's your daughter doing in college this semester?" he asked one man. "Did you ever get that new car?" he asked another. Many people worked there, so I was amazed that he seemed to know all of them, but more pressing at that moment, would I ever be able to navigate the maze of hallways?

My job was to be a transporter. Mrs. Jankiewicz was my very first patient. I was to transport her, in her wheelchair, to have some tests in another area of the hospital. She kept chatting the whole way, telling me how much I reminded her of her son when he was young. Mrs. J was 87, and I vividly recall her being "very together." She confided that her body was "betraying" her. I was 16 and not yet comfortable in my own skin. I could relate! After our first excursion, I visited Mrs. J (she said to call her Clara, but Mrs. J felt more respectful to me) every chance I got. We would sit and talk about her past, her family, and she asked me about mine.

On the Tuesday of my second week working at the hospital, I brought flowers from my uncle's garden to Mrs. J. She wasn't in her room, but I found a vase and left the flowers for her. I would pop in later for one of our talks. Disappointed that someone else got to transport her that morning, I went on with my other duties. Then I saw it—there it was—all the paperwork at the nurses' station. It honestly never occurred to me that Mrs. J might die! I ran to the men's room and sobbed! It felt like I had lost a member of my own family.

Over the next few days, I went through the motions at work. My uncle understood my pain and we talked about the inevitability of death and the fact that we will all die sometime. Of course, I knew this, but one thing he said to me changed the course of my life: "David," he said, "You were an important part of her life at a time when she needed it most. You were a kind and caring friend to her during her last days and you helped her feel the value of her life."

When I got back to high school in the fall, I committed myself to my coursework, determined to get into a good college, and then medical school. I never once thought about another career path. I am now a physician in a large practice in Texas and have many patients in my care. But every morning when I walk into the hospital, I say a silent hello to my very first patient, my dear old friend, Clara Jankiewicz—Mrs. J.

But motivation is also complex. Human beings seek a range of incentives, some intangible, and some tangible. If a person is consistently asked to do too much, he or she may experience burnout, even if the patient care elements of the job are rewarding. And what if the excessive work requests are made because fellow workers are not as capable? Over time, that may evoke anger and resentment in addition to burnout. Motivating employees is a challenging and complex undertaking. The benefits of doing it effectively are significant—higher levels of productivity, employee satisfaction, retention, and quality of performance; the risks of ineffectiveness can be disastrous. The impact goes well beyond employees. The failure to establish a climate in which employees feel motivated will take its greatest toll on those who entrust their health and welfare to our institutions. This chapter identifies the critical nature of motivation in a healthcare environment, presents its multidimensional character, and advances a perspective for leaders to embrace as they expand their view of their role and responsibility relative to motivating the workforce.

Introduction

Health care is changing in ways that demand a far greater focus on motivation. The particular types of change have the potential to add considerable stress to the work environment and to the lives of employees in healthcare settings:

- ▶ Mergers and medical practice consolidation are shifting organizational identity and, potentially, the relationship of the employee to the organization.
- ▶ Consolidation is occurring at all levels and, as a result, employees are increasingly distanced from the senior levels; at the same time, continuous quality improvement (CQI), patient-centeredness, and evidence-driven principles underscore the importance of their role and intensify their participation in the work of the organization.
- ▶ Cost containment translates into less generosity with respect to adding resources; therefore, work burdens may intensify (and resource gaps may be increasingly filled by temporary or part-time workers, interfering with productivity and consistency).
- ▶ Rapid changes in diagnostic, therapeutic, and information management protocols and systems are creating changes in work assignments, skill mix, and organizational structures.
- ▶ Legislation is introducing uncertainty and, by extension, anxiety.
- ▶ The influx of new patients will require a more concerted focus on patient management skills and organizational efficiencies.

▶ The large increase in numbers of new employees and managers will require considerable strategic thinking to get it right.

▶ Increased scrutiny from regulatory bodies and from state and federal legislation places more accountability on each employee.

Some healthcare organizations experience high levels of employee satisfaction, retention, and productivity, while others contend with dispiritedness, lack of consistently acceptable performance, and turnover problems. Not surprisingly, environments characterized by the former tend to experience higher levels of patient satisfaction and loyalty, a less pronounced consumer predisposition toward litigiousness, and enhanced organizational efficiency. Instituting and sustaining such an environment requires leaders capable of helping employees develop positive associations with colleagues in both their particular areas of professional specialty as well as with the organization as a whole. Leaders that also recognize cultural diversity and individual differences can also apply different rewards to motivate employees and increase the alignment at both functional and organizational levels. An important outcome is a patient-centered approach in the construction of systems by which goals are articulated and performance outcomes are well defined, monitored, evaluated, and rewarded.

Effective healthcare leaders must be willing and able to contextualize, and sometimes individualize, their motivational strategies. However, researchers know too little about what people do to regulate their own actions and self-motivate; and even managers fail to understand the motives and values of direct reports (Murphy, 2001). We agree with Locke and Latham's (2004, p. 400) assertion that "work motivation needs to be studied from new perspectives" and their calls to develop theories of motivation that are valid, integrative, and useful to practitioners. In this chapter we suggest that motivation is situational.

It is strikingly important for managers to ensure that employees remain properly and effectively motivated. The more managers understand the principles and theories of motivation presented in this chapter, the more effective they will become. A dip in motivation will hurt retention, productivity, or both. In light of the fact that demand for workers exceeds supply, managers who fail to appreciate and effectively apply the principles of motivation risk losing their best workers. If the identity of the organization changes (e.g., during a system expansion or a shift from solo to multispecialty practices), loyalty may correspondingly diminish. Therefore, as leaders move their organizations through transformational experiences, they will put themselves at serious risk if they fail to be sufficiently mindful of principles of motivation. For example, nurses whose organizations merge may decide to leave (they can get another job relatively immediately!) if the motivational and communication efforts are weak or poorly executed. We present motivation in a way that will encourage healthcare managers and organizational leaders to understand its importance, complexity, and relevance as well as get them to reflect on their own experience and need to ramp up their attention.

The Leadership Challenge in Healthcare Organizations

While human motivation is a complex and long-studied subject, and efforts to motivate employees ranging from the rank-and-file to the CEO have been both extensive, costly, and arguably one of the most important functions of leadership, most of us fall prey to the view that motivation is a straightforward concept. After all, if we understand that people have multiple needs, they perform in proportion to financial incentives, and they need to be treated with respect, isn't that pretty much all we need to know? Well, not quite, as motivation is a complex concept with intervening variables, different work situations, and interaction effects among personal and organizational factors.

Despite the continued prominence of seminal research on motivation theory that articulated a hierarchy of needs, modern approaches to motivation in management have tended to neglect the interaction effects between different factors that affect the motivation to work (Belasen & Fortunato, 2013). At best, industrial psychologists put emphasis on the intrinsic motivational factors with the leadership challenge being that of aligning individual needs and skills with goals and means (Locke & Latham, 1990; Vroom, 1964). Economics literature, with its traditional emphasis on financial rewards, has been even more narrowly focused linking performance with outcome and utility (Marris, 1964; Ross, 1973). Finally, human resource (HR) directors and supervisors have tended to focus on *either* extrinsic *or* intrinsic factors, without sufficient attention to the differences of the task environment, employing one or the other as a matter of organizational policy rather than as the outcome of a thoughtful needs assessment analysis.

To motivate a diversified workforce, especially in complex settings such hospitals or healthcare systems that are staffed primarily by professionals and staff specialists, a capable manager must consider a number of factors including personal traits, career options, competence, personal commitment, ambition level, education, age, and gender. As the Affordable Care Act is implemented, the American Medical Association (AMA) suggests that merit increases can be distributed in addition to regular raises, and that thoughtfully planned and executed merit raises that reward good performance are more effective than standard annual increases as "younger employees may be motivated by different incentives" (Cash, 2013).

The way to energize, direct, and sustain positive behavior that advances the goals of individuals and at the same time promotes collective performance is still an experiment in progress because each person is unique, demonstrating divergent reactions to external regulation, appraisal, or monetary reward. The different reactions to contingencies of reinforcement (i.e., financial rewards, punishment, and extinction) by a diversified workforce of a complex hospital, for example, makes it essential for managers to understand how people think, feel, and behave and learn to use the best strategies to motivate them. Consider the following scenarios (Belasen & Fortunato, 2013):

▶ The hospital CEO and other senior executives are clearly far along the needs hierarchy, yet most compensation systems focus on extrinsic, financial incentives only. How would the board of directors evaluate the role that intrinsic motivators might be playing in the utility of senior executives, and how might their total compensation be improved by trading extrinsic for more valuable intrinsic opportunities? This reflects an important financial integrity goal that the board of directors adopts with the expectation that senior managers fit into this framework.

▶ Middle managers in healthcare organizations are sometimes the victims of inappropriate efforts to employ intrinsic motivators. These motivators are unproductive because middle managers, especially those in the ranks long enough to have been passed over for promotion to more senior ranks, often first need assurances of job stability prior to accepting intrinsic recognition and reward as meaningful.

▶ The minimum-wage employee needs security first, affiliation next. Human resource programs that seek to induce loyalty (e.g., to reduce shirking and turnover) are often failing to act on the former. Employees who are so unfortunate as to need improvements in first-level physiological need (e.g., reasonable work conditions) are very unlikely to respond well to "employee of the week" programs, which induce their self-esteem, when basic needs are not being met.

▶ There are times when the situation is sufficiently nuanced that an extrinsic need is palpable but leadership cannot offer it without first offering something intrinsic. This counterintuitive case is illustrated by the problem of new leadership of a hospital with a unionized workforce that has historically witnessed distrust between management and labor. The new leadership needs to first invest heavily in intrinsic rewards that build trust before it can productively turn to extrinsic rewards (such as performance pay). The performance pay may be much needed by the rank-and-file but not valued or even accepted in an atmosphere of mistrust (the pay may be seen as part of an insidious divide-and-conquer strategy, for example). Intrinsic rewards must be linked with meaningful experiences, whether employees are washing floors or taking blood pressure or replacing knees, making them feel part of the team.

Leadership Approaches and Motivation

Mounting evidence that transformational leadership contributes to increased employee motivation and performance has encouraged research into the mechanisms behind its achievements (Alimo-Metcalfe, 1995; Barker & Young, 1994; Eagly, Johannesen-Schmidt, & Van Engen, 2003; Kark, Shamir, & Chen, 2003; Rosener, 1990; Trinidad & Normore, 2005). If Benabou and Tirole (2003) are correct, this would imply the need for caution in the use of extrinsic motivators that depreciate the personal relationships between leaders and followers.

Building on the initial conceptualization of Burns (1978), Bass (1985) extended the concept of transformational leadership to describe leaders who motivate followers to do more than they originally intended to do by presenting followers with a compelling vision and encouraging them to transcend their own interests for those of the group or unit. Transformational roles have been typically categorized into four types: idealized influence, inspirational motivation, intellectual stimulation, and individual consideration. The first trait, *idealized influence*, refers to leaders who have high standards of moral and ethical conduct, who are held in high personal regard, and who engender loyalty from followers. The second, *inspirational motivation*, refers to leaders with a strong and value-centered vision of the future that generates enthusiasm, builds confidence, and inspires followers, often using symbolic actions and persuasive language. The idealized influence and inspirational motivation are highly correlated and are sometimes combined to form a measure of charisma. The third trait, *intellectual stimulation*, refers to leaders who challenge existing organizational norms, encourage divergent thinking, and who push followers to develop innovative strategies. Finally, *individual consideration*, the fourth transformational leadership trait, refers to leader behaviors aimed at recognizing the unique growth and developmental needs of followers; a strong leader here will demonstrate skill by coaching followers and consulting with them.

Transactional leaders, on the other hand, rely upon the traditional economic value of relationships with employees (i.e., exchange of performance for reward) to motivate employees to achieve desired outcomes. They are good at using principles and existing rules and policies to structure the incentive system in the organization to achieve conformance, whereas transformational leaders rely on intangible sources of motivation to energize employees.

The two types of leadership, transformational and transactional, seek to accomplish organizational goals by motivating employees on a continuum that ranges from extrinsic to intrinsic values. Despite the inclination to assume that transformational leadership and intrinsic motivation are to be lexicographically preferred, Belasen and Fortunato (2013) actually advance the thesis that intrinsic and extrinsic factors should *not* be treated as if they are dichotomous but rather represent varying degrees (i.e., hierarchy) of motivation. Unfortunately, at best, extrinsic and intrinsic motivators have been treated as opposite-equals on a continuum. Merely shifting away from extrinsic and toward intrinsic factors without due consideration for the deeper structure of motivation can potentially do harm to employee morale and performance. This approach has led to a proliferation of leadership theories and leadership effectiveness approaches differentiated by the intrinsic/extrinsic dichotomy such as autocratic/democratic leadership styles, consideration/initiating styles, and employee-centered/job-centered approaches. Even more situational approaches such as vertical dyad leadership (Dansereau, et. al., 1975), Fiedler's (1967) contingency model, and Hersey and Blanchard's situational theory (1982) followed similar differentiation.

While senior managers with the power to use extrinsic motivators should generally first improve the employee's sense of security, and only then go on to employ intrinsic motivational factors in a second stage of motivational strategy, there are also times when something intrinsic must first be offered to create the trust to go back down the hierarchy and repair extrinsic deficiencies (Belasen & Fortunato, 2013).

Motivation Is a Complex Concept

Organizations expect employees to carry out specific tasks to achieve the organizational goals. Motivation is regarded as the momentum that spurs people to behave in various ways and to seek to fulfill a variety of needs, thus employers need to know what makes their employees tick so that they can channel this energy toward certain outcomes such as patient satisfaction, high performance, and improved return on investment.

Kumar, Poornima, Abraham, and Jayashree (2003, p. 12) define motivation as "the way in which urges, drives, desires, aspirations or needs direct control or explain the behavior of human beings." Phares and Chaplin (1997, p. 434) regard motivation as "the forces within us that activate our behavior and direct it toward one goal rather than another." Daft (2011, p. 200) sees it as "the forces either internal or external to a person that arouse enthusiasm and persistence to pursue a certain course of action."

Motivation is multidimensional in nature, a complex concept with applications and outcomes that are shaped by external and internal factors. A common agreement is that intrinsic and extrinsic factors are the two primary types of motivated behavior. Intrinsically motivated behaviors are those based in the inherent satisfactions of the behaviors *per se*. Intrinsic motivation represents a prototype of self-determined activity. Intrinsic motivation is based on acquiring a sense of accomplishment and pleasure in an activity rather than working toward an external reward (Ryan & Deci, 2000).

In contrast, extrinsic motivation refers to a broad array of behaviors having in common the fact that activities are engaged in not for inherent reasons, but for instrumental reasons such as the performance of an activity for the purpose of reaching a particular outcome (Vallerand & Ratelle, 2002). Rewards such as promotions or compensation increases, or threat of punishment are the general forms of extrinsic motivation. They are externally administered or derived.

According to Pinder (2008), one of the difficulties facing researchers trying to explain and define the source of human motivation was the distinction of concepts at a high enough level of specificity to be useful, but low enough to be broad in scope and generality. In the process, social researchers have studied numerous concepts. One of the earliest concepts was simple instinct. Psychologists assumed that, like all animals, humans are born with involuntary behavioral tendencies. As early as 1923, William McDougall defined instinct as, "an innate disposition which determines the organism to perceive (or pay attention to) any object of a certain class, and to experience in its presence a certain emotional excitement and an impulse to action which find expression in a specific mode of behavior in relation to that object" (McDougall, 1923, p. 110). Unfortunately, this definition was overly broad and sweeping, allowing everything to be attributed to instinct, and as a result, providing no real value to researchers.

As an alternative to instinct theory, Robert Woodworth developed and proposed drive theory as a method for explaining human motivation. As Pinder (2008) observed, drive theory added a degree of nuance, distinguishing between primary and secondary drives. In his earlier work, Woodworth (1918) defined primary drives as those compelling one to acquire that which is necessary for physical survival (e.g., food, water) or removing that which is detrimental to survival (e.g., toxic fumes, fire). On the other hand, secondary drives are defined as learned associations between primary drives and external events, actions, or conditions. For instance, a primary drive to reduce cold could trigger the secondary drive of putting on a sweater. Although drive theory generated much research, it was also too vague to be of practical use.

To categorize needs in a manner useful to social researchers, Henry Murray (1938) articulated the theory of psychogenic needs, consisting of 27 distinct needs with corresponding emotional states. As Pinder (2008) noted, there are several key points regarding Murray's theory. First, Murray recognized that these needs were only hypothetical, and could not be directly observed or quantified, but only inferred from a person's actions. Second, he recognized that needs could be, and often were, initiated by environmental factors. Finally, Murray recognized that not all needs would be able to be met by any individual, designating those needs as *frustrated*. Of the 27 needs that Murray identified, two are particularly relevant to motivational psychology, namely the needs for achievement and power. Maslow, Alderfer, and McClelland based much of their work on the framework created by Murray. Their theories will be discussed further in this chapter.

Cultural Differences and Motivation

Although these theories are all legitimate and applicable in numerous contexts, most effective managers reject a template approach to employee motivation. As Lazenby (2008) pointed out, this is because people are different, and factors that motivate one person may discourage another. Therefore, the manager's essential problem is determining when to employ a given motivational theory. To assist managers in this process, psychologists have conducted studies in an attempt to isolate and understand those personality characteristics relevant to motivation.

According to Lazenby (2008), there are two broad categories of people. The first category consists of those individuals who enjoy challenges and learning new skills—these people can be said to have a *mastery* or *learning* orientation. For these people, intrinsic motivators work quite well. The second category consists of those individuals who seek out situations where they can excel and avoid situations where success is uncertain—they can be said to have a *performance orientation*. They tend to measure their worth in terms of how well they perform, regardless of how simple the task may be. Because these people are easily discouraged by difficult challenges, they tend to see intrinsic factors as threatening. These are the sorts of needs assessments that leaders and managers must consider when allocating tasks.

Cultural values and norms also play an important role in motivating individuals. As a road map for guiding managers in cross-cultural environments, researchers developed a model of cultural self-representation. This model evaluates culture based on the following criteria (Latham, 2012):

▶ **Individualistic or collectivistic.** This refers to the degree that people work for themselves and expect to be rewarded, or work for the common good.

▶ **High or low power distance.** Power distance refers to the distance between management and labor. High power distance cultures see this relationship as far apart and distinct, with labor very dependent upon management. Low power distance cultures see this relationship as blended, with labor and management interdependent.

These factors have significant implications in the management of personnel. For instance, cultures that recognize individual performance, and value competition and achievement of personal goals, are also characterized with a strong expectation that rewards be linked directly to performance. On the other hand, collective cultures value cooperation, affiliation, and interdependence, where a person's reward is seen in terms of the ability to benefit the whole. Similarly, managers from high power distance cultures often resent the lack of deference they receive in cultures with lower power distance indexes, while workers from low power distance cultures are often offended by management arrogance from higher power distance cultures.

To cope with these differences, the model of cross-cultural representation advises managers to consider the following principles when formulating motivational and reward systems (Latham, 2012):

1. Identify the cultural characteristics on the collectivism/individualism and power distance spectrums.
2. Understand yourself and the cultural values you represent.
3. Understand the meaning of various managerial practices (flat versus differential salary reward distribution and top-down versus two-way communication styles).

Intrinsic and Extrinsic Rewards

One of the most representative theories is two-factor theory, also known as Herzberg's motivation-hygiene theory. Herzberg's (1964) research suggested that the work characteristics associated with dissatisfaction were quite different from those pertaining to satisfaction, which facilitated the notion that two factors influence work motivation: hygiene factors and motivators. Hygiene factors include: company policy and administration, level and quality of supervision, work conditions, salary, security, reporting relationships, and promotion opportunities.

When hygiene factors are poor, employees would be dissatisfied. But when hygiene factors are improved, the sense of dissatisfaction would be reduced or removed. Motivators fulfill high-level needs with reference to these aspects: achievement, recognition, work itself, responsibility, empowerment, and personal growth.

When these motivators are administered, employees would be highly satisfied and therefore, motivated. Herzberg contended that both factors were of equal importance. However, positive hygiene would only result in average performance—preventing dissatisfaction for further deterioration. In contrast, higher-level motivators actually increased the level of employee work enthusiasm and satisfaction. Herzberg's central theory also enables us to understand the relationships between employers and employees.

Psychological Theories of Motivation

Following advancements made by Goldstein (1934), Murray (1938), Maslow (1943, 1954), Rogers (1961), McClelland (1953, 1987), Herzberg (1964, 1989), Vroom (1964), Adams (1965), Alderfer (1972) and others, psychologists reached agreement on the general contours of a theory of motivation that did not change appreciably afterward. Most of these theories fell under two broad categories (Belasen & Fortunato, 2013):

1. *Stimulation, incentive, or positive reinforcement theory,* correlating specific rewards with desired outcomes. The behavior reoccurs if the outcome is still valued. Popularized by Skinner's (1938) theory of operant conditioning, the rewards—in effect, intervening variables—ensure that the link between the behavior and the outcome remains strong. Incentive or reinforcement theory helps explain what energizes and directs the behavior. This gave rise to such theories as path-goal (House, 1971; Mitchell, Smyser, & Weed, 1975); goal-setting (Locke & Latham, 1990), in which individuals have a drive to reach a clearly defined end-state characterized by proximity, difficulty, and specificity; self-efficacy (Bandura, 1995, 1997), involving cognitive, motivational, affective, and selection processes; and expectancy-valence (Vroom, 1964) theories, in which motivation is viewed as the result of a rational choice *increasing positive net expected outcome.* Individuals are said to be engaged in value-maximizing behavior, if they seek not only to increase but also to optimize.

2. *Reduction, drive, or needs theory,* linking behaviors with a strong desire to lower or minimize socioeconomic costs or psychological effects. Individuals are engaged in behaviors aimed at *decreasing undesired negative*

outcomes. In these models, the individual is driven or motivated to reduce punishment or discomfort. Once the drive is satisfied, its strength diminishes in value and is replaced with another drive. This is akin to the theory of cognitive dissonance, which similarly posits that people have a motivational drive to decrease inconsistencies or cognitive mental gaps by changing their attitudes, beliefs, or actions.

This movement gave rise to such theories as drive (Goldstein, 1934); needs (Murray, 1938); hierarchy of needs—physiological, security, belonging, esteem, and self-actualization (Maslow, 1943, 1954); multiple need theory—achievement, affiliation, and power (McClelland, 1953, 1987); Herzberg two-factor theory (1964, 1989); and Alderfer's (1972) existence, relatedness, and growth (ERG) theory, in which it is argued that when higher levels are not met and are thought too difficult to achieve, individuals redouble their efforts to get lower needs more fully met.

At the heart of these theories is the behavioral idea that unmet needs drive individuals to take action to decrease the gap between undesired and desired levels. Unsatisfied needs influence behavior in a way that satisfied needs do not. Some needs are absolute, others relative and are understood only in a social context. In equity theory (Adams, 1965) for example, employees assess the costs and benefits they give and receive against those of others in the workplace and cope with perceived inequity by decreasing efforts or commitments to restore an equilibrium that is a form of social fairness.

Needs-Based Theory

Maslow's (1943) seminal work remains critical and is perhaps the best-known theory of motivation. In Maslow, a hierarchy of needs distinguishes lower-level physiological needs (e.g., food, shelter, and safety) from higher sociopsychological needs (e.g., relationship, self-esteem, and self-actualization). Once a deficiency in needs is recognized, a behavioral response aimed at remedying the deficiency is triggered. The hierarchy of needs theory predicts an ongoing pursuit of activities geared toward reducing the psychological stress created by the gap between the current and the desired state of affairs. Once an existing need is met, it ceases to become a motivator, and the potency of a higher-level need increases in value and the individual is motivated to achieve higher-level goals.

While Maslow's theory draws on satisfaction-progression of needs, Alderfer's ERG theory added dynamics of frustration-regression into the mix. That is, when needs in a higher category are not met, individuals may respond by reinvesting efforts in a lower-category need. For example, if a growth need such as self-esteem is not met (and efforts to meet it are frustrated), then individuals will invest more effort in a lower, relatedness need such as belonging, in the hopes of later achieving the higher need. Once higher goals are achieved, self-transcendence occurs, where these goals and needs become the baseline for higher-order needs.

Van den Broeck, Vansteenkiste, Lens, and De Witte's (2009) empirical study confirmed the frustration-regression cycle by showing that workers who were unemployed for extended periods of time or faced extreme financial hardships lowered their expectations of benefit in a given work environment. They became more flexible in their job search than those who were newly unemployed. The implications of this study were of enormous importance to hiring managers. The study clearly showed that people were willing to do a job they wouldn't normally take to fulfill their lower-level needs. These people will most likely be less committed to the organization or look to reap the short-term benefits provided.

Another needs-based theory, developed by David McClelland (1953, 1987), essentially an extrinsic motivational model, is aimed at illustrating how the needs for achievement, needs for affiliation, and needs for power influence the behaviors of people in a managerial context. People are not born with these needs, but may acquire them through lifetime experiences.

A person's need for achievement is their desire to accomplish something difficult, to master complex skills, or to reach a high standard of success and to exceed others. This need is formed by setting and meeting high standards of achievement. The need, on one hand, is affected by intrinsic drive for action, and, on the other hand, stems from the pressure given by the extrinsic expectations of others. Need for achievement is relevant to the level of difficulty of tasks that people opt to challenge. Those with a high need for achievement tend to enjoy the process of being challenged and the realization of their potential. However, those with low needs for achievement tend to use risk-averse behaviors, minimizing the importance of or avoiding highly difficult tasks altogether.

The need for affiliation depicts the individual's desire to feel a sense of involvement and belonging within a social group in order to form close personal relationships and establish friendships. Those who have a high need for affiliation prefer warm interpersonal relationships and approval from others in social interactional life. Those who have low need for affiliation tend to be either too arrogant or too indifferent.

The need for power refers to the individual's desire to control or impose their will on others, take ownership, or to establish their legal power or centralized authority. Of course, abuse of power or unethical use of personal power might lead to dissatisfaction for others, as well as conflicts and unrest in work units and social systems.

Following Belasen and Fortunato (2013), this body of literature can be characterized in brief in the following way:

1. People have *multiple needs* imbedded in a *hierarchical* structure (with lower-level needs such as the physiological and the need for security

coming first, and needs such as the need for belonging or for esteem taking prominence only once the former are fully or partially met).

2. People are motivated to expend effort to advance themselves if they believe that such effort can lead to performance, which will in turn be recognized and rewarded in meaningful ways.

3. People differ in a variety of important ways, bringing different emotional orientations and drive to bear on their work. For example, some people appear to have a need for achievement, power, or affiliation.

Self-Determination and Reciprocity

Individuals in a social system expect reciprocity in social relationships: what they invest and gain from a relationship should be proportional to the investments and gains of the other person in the relationship. Furthermore, when individuals perceive relationships as inequitable they feel distressed and are strongly motivated to restore equity either by reducing their efforts or by shifting the focus of their relationships (Ryan & Deci, 2002).

Van Yperen (1995) studied nurses working with patients who had intellectual disabilities and examined their equity perceptions with regard to turnover rate. The results showed that nurses who felt a lack of equity (giving more than they received from the organization in return) were more likely to vocalize their desire to leave the organization. They also manifested a higher burnout rate than nurses who found equilibrium in the workplace. At the opposite end of the spectrum, nurses who felt they were being overbenefited by the organization also had a high burnout rate (Disley, Hatton, & Dagnan, 2009).

The study shows that the perception of equity may have a median point, and the further employees deviate from that point in either direction, the more likely they are to quit or be unhappy in the workplace. A possible solution to this problem is to change the equity perception of the employees. In the case of the overworked nurses, managers could highlight how important their work is and all the good they are doing by serving people with intellectual disabilities. They deserve both to be recognized and treated well by their organization.

In the healthcare field, nursing turnover is a widespread problem. Galletta (2011) used self-determination theory (SDT) to analyze how job autonomy and intrinsic work motivation play a fundamental role in the relationship with affective commitment, and how it mediates their effects on turnover. According to the SDT, the extent to which the work environment sustains and promotes job autonomy is what allows employees to activate positive and autonomous work behaviors (Gagné & Deci, 2005). Galleta's findings confirmed that maintaining an autonomous, motivated, and committed workforce is essential for retention. Further research by Vilma and Egle (2007) supported the finding that empowerment and autonomy help increase the motivation of registered nurse practitioners and nurse managers as well as improved their performance level. In fact, when autonomy was absent, nurses' competencies did not reach their full potential.

The Power of Collaboration

Recent interdisciplinary work has focused on an evolutionary basis for behavior that is cooperative, positing that people may meet deeply felt needs *through collaborative relationships* (Camerer, Loewenstein, & Rabin, 2004; Henrich & Henrich, 2007). The Israeli researcher, entrepreneur, and speaker Yochai Benkler, recipient of the Ford Foundation Visionaries Award, strongly advances the view that humans have a deep predisposition to cooperate (Benkler, 2011). This view implies that instead of using variable rewards and sanctions to motivate people, supervisors should create opportunities for engagement and involvement with purposeful outcomes. This view is consistent with the finding that a motivated workforce, complemented by a supportive communication system and an adaptive culture, is a source of competitive advantage for companies (Belasen, 2000).

Behavioral Economics

Belasen and Fortunato (2013) noted that behavioral economists (Camerer et al., 2004; Ho, Lim, & Camerer, 2006; Pink, 2009; Wilkinson, 2008) have demonstrated that the long-standing focus on *extrinsic* motivation in the business world and in economic theory is substantially deficient.

Pink (2009) surveyed a broad (but selective) array of behavioral research to argue that psychologists and behavioral economists know something business does not: extrinsic motivation is often not the best motivator. Many studies have shown that people offered the highest financial reward for success often underperform those offered lower or even no financial reward. Not only are financial rewards *not* correlated positively with performance, but their mere existence at some point in the experiment can harm future performance, as in the case of subjects who were found to lose interest and productivity after extrinsic rewards were removed (while those without such extrinsic rewards remained intrinsically motivated).

Pink concluded that what matters most are autonomy, mastery, and purpose.

- ▶ **Autonomy.** People have a need to be given the freedom to work in the ways that suit them best. Supervision and control can be very counterproductive.

▶ **Mastery.** People need the support, time, and opportunity to truly master their work. Mastery is a goal with enormous appeal for most employees.

▶ **Purpose.** Employees do well with autonomy and the opportunity and support to master tasks, but they do even better if the purpose (mission) is meaningful.

According to Pink (2009), if employees have all three, they will be motivated.

A careful review of the psychological, economic, and leadership research, however, reveals that Pink's theory of motivation (with its exclusive focus on intrinsic factors) is oversimplified. It is perhaps motivated by an excessive focus on the deficiencies of the economic model of motivation. Frey (1997) for example, set out to design an economic theory of motivation that explains how extrinsic and intrinsic motivation may conflict with one another. Frey sees the principal task as one of optimizing the performance of managers who have a direct positive response to extrinsic rewards, but who may, based on the characteristics of the task environment, incur an offsetting negative effect on their intrinsic motivation that was already in place. Hence, performance pay or other extrinsic rewards ultimately lead to *ambiguous* results, depending upon whether the deterioration of intrinsic motivation partially, fully, or more than fully crowds out the direct positive effect of the reward. If an organizational leader takes away one lesson from this motivational research, it should be that intrinsic motivation needs to take a more prominent role, with a focus on giving employees more autonomy, more opportunities for mastery, and to build consensus around organizational purpose—what we usually call *mission*.

Choosing Appropriate Motivational Strategies

Belasen and Fortunato (2013) provided a list of diagnostic questions to help organizational leaders use appropriate motivational strategies. Before a leader seeks to enhance the motivation of his or her followers, he or she should ask the following groups of questions.

Sociopsychology-motivated questions:

▶ What is the nature of the task? Is it formulaic or creative? Except for the most formulaic tasks, intrinsic motivation is important.

▶ Where in the needs hierarchy is the employee?

▶ Are basic physiological needs being met?

▶ Do employees have financial and emotional security (e.g., minimum wage employees are assured of retention if clear performance goals are met)?

▶ Do employees have a sense of belonging (e.g., has the organizational culture embraced the employee and vice versa)?

▶ Are employees treated with esteem and do they derive self-esteem from their work relationships?

▶ Are employees given a chance to achieve self-actualization through a combination of autonomy in the work lives, opportunity and support in their attempts at mastery of their profession or craft, and internalization of a motivating purpose or mission?

▶ Is there social equity?

Economics-motivated questions:

▶ What is the current state of compensation and to what extent and how does it include performance-based bonuses? Do not assess the level of extrinsic motivators as too high or low independent of this basic information.

▶ Does the leader know most of what the employee knows, or is there a large gap between the two with uncertainty about effort? If there is much uncertainty about work effort and its quality, then performance-based compensation might sensibly play some role.

▶ Can the compensation of the employee be aligned with the financial performance of the firm or to his contribution to the financial performance of the firm? How correlated are the actual efforts of the employee with his contribution to the performance of the firm? How correlated is the performance of the employee and the overall performance of the firm?

▶ For middle- and lower-level employees especially, how does the firm's compensation compare with industry efficiency wages or fair wage norms?

Leadership-motivated questions:

▶ Is the leader employing a mix of transformational and transactional skills, a mix of extrinsic and intrinsic motivators, or is he or she singing a one-note tune in all situations?

▶ Is there a credible, honest relationship between the leader and his or her employees?

▶ Has the leader shown the wisdom to grant appropriate levels of autonomy to his or her team? Has the leader created opportunities to develop true mastery of craft or specialty profession?

▶ Have the organization and its leadership jointly articulated a mission (purpose) that is valuable to its members? Is it currently serving to motivate them? Can the power of purpose be improved?

Conclusion

In this chapter we argue that only by appreciating the complex nature of work motivation can we responsibly improve the motivation of organization or team members. For example, senior managers with the power to use extrinsic motivators to first improve the employee's sense of security can better employ intrinsic motivational factors in a second stage of motivational strategy, but there are also times when something intrinsic must first be offered to create the trust to go back down the hierarchy and repair extrinsic deficiencies.

What is the nature of the task? What needs are employees seeking to satisfy? Do employees feel valued and is there a sense of equity? There are many more questions to be asked, but narrowing down the general area first will help in assessing the situation. First, a leader must have the strategic goals and vision of the organization in mind and use the resources at the leader's disposal to most effectively reach those goals. Take an underperforming hospital with low ratings in patient satisfaction, for example. The internal motivation of staff may be low, causing a rise in patient dissatisfaction. If the basic needs of the staff are not being met, tangible rewards will most likely be more effective than more training on patient care. If those basic needs are being met, the workers may simply feel undervalued by the hospital. Giving the employees a feeling of job security may be the solution. Another strategy may be to give staff more autonomy in a safe way that won't endanger patients. Adaptability is key from a motivational standpoint. Quality listening is vital to diagnosing any problem. Master leaders are able to recognize the needs and desires of employees and provide those things while advancing the organization as a whole.

Motivation is situational (Guay, Vallerand, & Blanchard, 2000). Master leaders in healthcare organizations must be willing and able to contextualize and sometimes individualize their motivational strategies to be effective.

Review Questions

1. Compare and contrast different needs-based approaches for motivating employees. Which one provides greater value in complex healthcare organizations?
2. Which types of rewards, intrinsic or extrinsic, are more important in healthcare organizations?
3. Does the importance of intrinsic or extrinsic rewards vary over time as employees progress through their career upward or even laterally?
4. Which motivational strategy is more appropriate for energizing, directing, and sustaining the behaviors of cross-functional team members?
5. What would be the appropriate strategy for motivating a middle manager in a healthcare organization undergoing transitions?

Case Study: Motivation and Job Satisfaction Among Medical and Nursing Staff in a Cyprus Public General Hospital

Background

The objective of this study was to investigate how medical and nursing staff of the Nicosia General Hospital is affected by specific motivation factors, and the association between job satisfaction and motivation; furthermore, it aimed to determine the motivational drive of sociodemographic and job-related factors in terms of improving work performance.

Methods

The study used a previously developed and validated instrument addressing four work-related motivators (job attributes, remuneration, coworkers, and achievements). Two categories of healthcare professionals, medical doctors and dentists (N = 67) and nurses (N = 219), participated, and motivation and job satisfaction was compared across sociodemographic and occupational variables.

Results

The survey revealed that achievements was ranked first among the four main motivators, followed by remuneration, coworkers, and job attributes. The factor remuneration revealed statistically significant differences according to gender and hospital sector, with female doctors and nurses and accident and emergency (A+E) outpatient doctors reporting greater mean scores ($p < 0.005$). The medical staff showed statistically significant lower job satisfaction compared to the nursing staff. Surgical sector nurses and those >55 years of age reported higher job satisfaction when compared to the other groups.

Conclusions

The results are in agreement with the literature, which focuses attention toward management approaches employing both monetary and nonmonetary incentives to motivate healthcare professionals. Healthcare professionals tend to be motivated more by intrinsic factors, implying that this should be a target for effective employee motivation. Strategies based on the survey's results to enhance employee motivation are suggested.

From: Lambrou, P., Kontodimopoulos, K., & Niakas, D. (2010). *Human Resources for Health, 8*, 26. doi:10.1186/1478-4491-8-26. Retrieved from: http://www.human-resources-health .com/content/8/1/26. This is an Open Access article distributed under the terms of the Creative Commons Attribution License (http://creativecommons.org/licenses/by/2.0), which permits unrestricted use, distribution, and reproduction in any medium, provided the original work is properly cited.

Case Study Review Questions

1. Discuss how the medical and nursing staff of the Nicosia General Hospital is affected by specific motivation factors.
2. Examine the association between job satisfaction and motivation.
3. Evaluate the motivational drive of socio-demographic and job-related factors in terms of improving performance in this hospital.
4. Discuss the importance of using monetary and nonmonetary incentives to motivate healthcare professionals.

References

Adams, J. S. (1965). Inequity in social exchange. *Social Psychology, 62*, 335–343.

Alderfer, C. (1972). *Existence, relatedness, & growth.* New York, NY: Free Press.

Alimo-Metcalfe, B. (1995). An investigation of female and male constructs of leadership and empowerment. *Women in Management Review, 10*(2), 3–8.

Bandura, A. (1995). *Self-efficacy in changing societies.* New York, NY: Cambridge University Press.

Bandura, A. (1997). *Self-efficacy: The exercise of control.* New York, NY: Freeman.

Barker, A. M., & Young, C. E. (1994). Transformational leaderships: The feminist connection in postmodern organizations. *Holistic Nurse Practitioner, 9*(1), 16–25.

Bass, B. M. (1985). *Leadership and performance beyond expectation.* New York, NY: Free Press.

Belasen, A. T. (2000). *Leading the learning organization: Communication and competencies for managing change.* Albany, NY: SUNY Press.

Belasen, A. T., & Fortunato, M. (2013). Situational motivation: Challenging the binary. In Michele Paludi (Ed.), *Implementing best practices in human resources* (pp. 173–196). Santa Barbara, CA: Praeger.

Benabou, R., & Tirole, J. (2003). Intrinsic and extrinsic motivation. *Review of Economic Studies, 70*(3), 489–520.

Benkler, Y (2011). *The penguin and the leviathan: How cooperation triumphs over self-interest.* New York, NY: Crown Business.

Burns, J. M. (1978). *Leadership.* New York, NY: Harper & Row.

Camerer, C. F., Loewenstein, G., & Rabin, M. (Eds.). (2004). *Advances in behavioral economics.* New York, NY: Princeton University Press.

Cash, S. (2013, May 20). Pay that motivates your medical practice staff. *American Medical News.* Retrieved from http://www.amednews.com/article/20130520/business/130529997/4/

Daft, R. L. (2011). *Leadership* (5th ed.). Delhi, India: Cengage Learning India Private Limited.

Dansereau, F., Graen, G. G., & Haga, W. (1975). A Vertical dyad linkage approach to leadership in formal organizations. *Organizational Behavior and Human Performance, 13*, 46–78.

Disley, P., Hatton, C., & Dagnan, D. (2009). Applying equity theory to staff working with individuals with intellectual disability. *Journal of Intellectual & Developmental Disability, 34*(1), 55–66.

Eagly, A. H., Johannesen-Schmidt, M. C., & Van Engen, M. L. (2003). Transformational, transactional, and laissez-faire leadership styles: A meta-analysis comparing women and men. *Psychological Bulletin, 129*(4), 569–591.

Fiedler, F. E. (1967). *A Theory of Leadership Effectiveness,* New York: McGraw-Hill.

Frey, B. (1997) *Not just for the money: An economic theory of personal motivation.* Cheltenham, England: Edward Elgar.

Gagné, M., & Deci, E. L. (2005). Self-determination theory and work motivation. *Journal of Organizational Behavior, 26*(4), 331–362.

Galletta, M. (2011). Intrinsic motivation, job autonomy and turnover intention in the Italian healthcare: The mediating role of affective commitment. *Journal of Management Research, 3*(2), 1–19.

Goldstein, K. (1934). *The organism: A holistic approach to biology derived from pathological data in man.* New York, NY: American Book.

Guay, F., Vallerand, R. J., & Blanchard, C. (2000). On the assessment of situational intrinsic and extrinsic motivation: The situational motivation scale (SIMS). *Motivation and Emotion, 24*(3), 175–213.

Henrich, N., & Henrich, J. (2007). *Why humans cooperate?* New York, NY: Oxford University Press.

Hersey, P., & Blanchard, K. H. (1982). *Management of organizational behavior: Utilizing human resources* (4th ed.). Englewood Cliffs, NJ: Prentice-Hall.

Herzberg, F. (1964). The motivation-hygiene concept and problems of manpower. *Personnel Administration,* January–February, 3–7.

Herzberg, F. (1989). One more time: How do you motivate employees? In J.S. Ott (Ed.), *Classic readings in organizational behavior* (pp. 93–102). California: Brooks/Cole.

Ho, T. H., Lim, N., & Camerer, C. F. (2006). Modeling the psychology of consumer and firm behavior with behavioral economics. *Journal of Marketing Research, 43*(3), 307–331.

House, R. J. (1971). A path-goal theory of leader effectiveness. *Administrative Science Quarterly, 16,* 321–339.

Kark, R., Shamir, B., & Chen, G. (2003). The two faces of transformational leadership: Empowerment and dependency. *Journal of Applied Psychology, 88*(2), 246–255.

Kumar, S. A., Poornima, S. C., Abraham, M. K., & Jayashree, K. (2003). *Entrepreneurship Development.* New Delhi, India: New Age International Pvt. Ltd..

Lambrou, P., Kontodimopoulos, K., & Niakas, D. (2010). Motivation and job satisfaction among medical and nursing staff in a Cyprus general hospital. *Human Resources for Health, 8,* 26 doi: 10.1186/1478-4491-8-26. Retrieved from: http://www.human-resources-health.com/content/8/1/26

Latham, G. P. (2012). *Work motivation.* Thousand Oaks, CA: Sage Publications.

Lazenby, S. (2008). How to motivate employees: What research is telling us. *Public Management, 90*(8), 22–25.

Locke, E. A., & Latham, G. P. (1990). *A theory of goal setting and task performance.* Englewood Cliffs, NJ: Prentice Hall.

Locke, E. A., & Latham, G. P. (2004). What should we do about motivation theory? Six recommendations for the twenty-first century. *Academy of Management Review, 29*(3), 388–403.

Marris, R. (1964). *The economic theory of managerial capitalism.* London, United Kingdom: Macmillan.

Maslow, A. H. (1943). A theory of human motivation. *Psychological Review, 50*(4), 370–396.

Maslow, A. H. (1954). *Motivation and personality*. New York, NY: Harper.

McClelland, D. C. (1953). *The achievement motive*. New York, NY: Appleton-Century-Crofts.

McClelland, D. C. (1987). *Human motivation*. New York, NY: Cambridge University Press.

McDougall, W. (1923). *Outline of psychology*. New York: Scribner.

Mitchell, T., Smyser, C. M., & Weed, S. E. (1975). Locus of control: Supervision and work satisfaction. *Academy of Management Journal, 18*, 623–631.

Murphy, S. T. (2001). Feeling without thinking: Affective primary and the nonconscious processing of emotion. In J. A. Bargh & D. K. Apsley (Eds.), *Unraveling the complexities of social life: A festschrift in honor of Robert B. Zajonc* (pp. 39–53). Washington, DC: American Psychological Association.

Murray, H. A. (1938). *Explorations in personality*. New York: Oxford University Press.

Phares, J. E., & Chaplin, W. F. (1997). *Introduction to personality* (4th ed.). New York, NY: Addison Wesley Longman.

Pinder, C. C. (2008). *Work motivation in organizational behavior* (2nd ed.). New York, NY: Psychology Press.

Pink, D. H. (2009). *Drive: The surprising truth about what motivates us*. New York: Penguin Riverhead Books.

Rogers, C. (1961). *On becoming a person: A therapist's view of psychotherapy*. London, United Kingdom: Constable & Co Ltd.

Rosener, J. B. (1990). Ways women lead. *Harvard Business Review, 68*(6), 119–125.

Ross, S. (1973). The economic theory of agency: The principal's problem. *The American Economic Review, 63*(2), 134–139.

Ryan, R. M., & Deci, E. L. (2000). Intrinsic and extrinsic motivations: Classic definitions and new directions. *Contemporary Educational Psychology, 25*, 54–67.

Ryan, R. M., & Deci, E. L. (2002). Overview of self-determination theory: An organismic dialectical perspective. In E. L. Deci & R. M. Ryan (Eds.), *Handbook of self-determination research* (pp. 3–33). Rochester, NY: University of Rochester Press.

Skinner, B. F. (1938). *The Behavior of Organisms*. Appleton-Century; New York: 1938.

Trinidad, C., & Normore, A. H. (2005). Leadership and gender: A dangerous liaison? *Leadership and Organization Development Journal, 26*(7/8), 574–590.

Vallerand, R. J., & Ratelle, C. F. (2002). Intrinsic and extrinsic motivation: A hierarchical model. In E. L. Deci & R. M. Ryan (Eds.), *Handbook of self-determination research* (p. 37–63). Rochester, NY: University of Rochester Press.

Van den Broeck, A., Vansteenkiste, M., Lens, W., & De Witte, H. (2009). Unemployed individuals' work values and job flexibility: An explanation from expectancy-value theory and self-determination theory. *International Association of Applied Psychology, 59*(2), 296–317.

Van Yperen, N. W. (1995). Communal orientation and the burnout syndrome among nurses: A replication and extension. *Journal of Applied Social Psychology, 26*(4), 338–354.

Vilma, Z., & Egle, K. (2007). Improving motivation among health care workers in private health care organizations: A perspective of nursing personnel. *Baltic Journal of Management, 2*(2), 1–12.

Vroom, V. H. (1964). *Work and motivation*. New York, NY: Wiley

Wilkinson, N. (2008). *An introduction to behavioral economics*. New York, NY: Macmillan.

Woodworth, R. S. (1918). *Dynamic psychology*. New York, NY: Columbia University Press.

PART B ▶

Coordination and Compliance

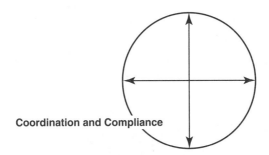

Coordination and Compliance

The lower left quadrant of the competing values framework (CVF) focuses on the technical systems and the values of stability and reliability. The master leader is a dedicated, conscientious figurehead who recognizes the importance of building a culture of reliability and responding to regulatory requirements. This quadrant shifts the focus of the leader from leading the social systems (see Part A) to managing the technical systems. Thus, coordination of functional units using control systems and measurement programs is vital for compliance with regulatory requirements and for achieving expected outcomes. Optimizing operating efficiencies and standardizing work processes can help healthcare organizations meet program and organizational goals consistently and effectively.

Healthcare leaders need to balance the requirements in Part B against the demands coming from the other quadrants, especially the opposite quadrant (competition and commitment). While this quadrant or domain of action includes systems of reliability and tools of quality control and quality measurement that require application of inward-bound leadership (i.e., internal focus, control, process orientation), an overemphasis on this quadrant might create a dent in the skill profile of the leader as the span of attention of the leader must also include aspects from the other three quadrants. For example, an overemphasis on the lower left quadrant might result in overmanagement or excessive monitoring of conformance and possibly lead to a failure to meet the broader goals of innovation and change, which are at the center of Part C. This apparent paradox is essential for learning and self-improvement.

Organizational leaders and healthcare executives must recognize the tradeoffs between polar opposites and increase the repertoire of their responses by acquiring skills and competencies associated with all of the four quadrants. Indeed, master leaders who embrace paradoxes and who see their organizations as contradictory systems encourage planning and control and the use of measurement programs to enable compliance while giving equal weight to the need to remain agile and adaptive.

Hence the two chapters in Part B, Chapters 4 and 5, focus on the need to develop a highly reliable culture that includes aspects of empowerment, efficiency, and continuous improvement, as well as to make investments in infrastructure that affect the quality of patient care services.

CHAPTER 4 ▶

Becoming a Highly Reliable Healthcare Provider: The Role of Leadership

LEARNING OBJECTIVES

Students will be able to:

- Explain how the changing landscape in healthcare is heightening the need for a more comprehensive approach to achieving high reliability
- Identify the complexity and multidimensionality of the concept of reliability
- Provide a definition for achieving high reliability as it pertains to healthcare leadership
- Understand the four interrelated underpinnings of a highly reliable culture—empowerment, ecosystem, efficiency, and effectiveness—as well as the role of leadership with respect to the achievement of such a culture
- Describe how patient care and continuous improvement constitute pillars of an organization-wide effort toward the achievement of high reliability
- Identify how provisions of the Affordable Care Act are stimulating cooperative arrangements among healthcare providers to achieve high levels of reliability

Introduction

Every industry grapples with the concept of reliability. Companies seek to promote reputations for being reliable because they understand that impressions of reliability can have a significant influence on consumer behavior. Consider the auto industry. A recent *Consumer Reports* assessment of reliability revealed some surprises, including the decision by *Consumer Reports* not to recommend two popular Toyota models because of crash test performance failures (Durbin, 2013).

But a closer look indicates that reliability ratings are more than just about safety. Respondents to the *Consumer Reports* survey indicate that ease of use of particular functions and amenities such as navigation systems also influence perceptions of reliability. Consumer satisfaction is a key factor in beliefs about reliability and may pertain to personal taste, a need for clarity, or to a failure for a product or service to meet basic expectations. For example, a lower-than-anticipated fuel economy rating could impair assessments of reliability. And then there is the dilemma about how to evaluate products or services that are very new. For example, performance criteria are not fully developed for many of the recently designed electronic engines; is it fair to subject them to the complete range of standards against which other automobiles are judged? Further, should the history of a product or service be taken into account when assessing reliability? How might prior record be factored into the reliability equation? Additionally, there is the notion of how long a model has been available. Newer auto models may benefit from not having much of a track record related to error rates, but this could be offset by not having an established reputation—how valid is a reliability rating in a case like this? These are not casual considerations since they could substantially influence purchasing decisions of thousands of automobiles.

Reliability is complicated, and many variables interlink to form an overall impression of reliability. We may take any of a few approaches to defining reliability. One clearly focuses on safety, another on consumer satisfaction achieved through engagement with the product or service and perceptions of reputation, and yet another on the efficiency and effectiveness of the processes organizations employ to accomplish their work. As we will explore in this chapter, the complexities of healthcare demand no less than a very comprehensive definition, one which takes into account all of these approaches and more. Most particularly, this chapter advances a leadership perspective on reliability for healthcare that balances attention to operational soundness, clinical quality, consumer satisfaction, and effectiveness of participation in the healthcare ecosystem.

What Is Reliability?

Mariano Rivera is widely considered to be the best relief pitcher in the history of baseball. Rivera's many accomplishments, since joining the New York Yankees in 1995, include the most wins of any relief pitcher ever. But perhaps even more amazing is his score on a relatively little known statistic called *WHIP*, which refers to the combination of walks and hits per inning pitched. Referencing the Elias Sports Bureau, Prager (2013) notes that the average WHIP among all pitchers today is 1.29; that is, for every inning pitched, a pitcher will give up, on average, a total of 1.29 hits and walks. Rivera's WHIP of 1.0035 ranks him third on the list of top 10 pitchers of all time. Adding to the astonishing nature of his feat, each of the other pitchers in the top 10 played during an era when pitchers had a more domineering presence in the sport; in fact, Rivera's most recent peer in the top 10 played his last game in 1916 (Prager, 2013).

Rivera had been remarkably steady in his control, providing his team with almost unparalleled consistency of outstanding relief pitching over the course of a career that spanned 19 seasons. Interestingly, what contributed to his greatness is not that he fooled batters with a range of pitches that kept them guessing whether a fastball, curveball, slider, changeup, or knuckleball would be coming their way. Rather, as a teammate noted, "His mechanics are perfect. And he throws only one pitch" (Prager, 2013). Batters knew that this same pitch, called a cutter, would be delivered each time. It simply didn't matter because the outcome was rarely in doubt; making a connection with a pitch thrown by Rivera that produced a hit was exceedingly difficult. Moreover, because Rivera had been so successful he seldom needed to expend the same level of energy as other relief pitchers; thus, he was able to provide late inning relief on a very frequent basis. The *quality* of his effort resulted in *efficiency* of effort.

The aura around Rivera, rooted in his dependability, is captured in the references made about him by fans, aficionados, and baseball experts:

- ▶ "Mariano Rivera, The Most Reliable Man in the World" (Cohen, 2010)
- ▶ "No other player can instill calm in his team's fans as reliably as Mariano Rivera" (Olney, 2004)
- ▶ "In terms of reliability for getting a single out, no pitcher has been more effective than Rivera in the history of the game" ("A Quick Glance," 2013)

Although Rivera had a reputation for being virtually flawless, he erred at least once per inning according to his WHIP score. That is, he gave up at least one hit or walk for each inning he pitched. Further, he also lost four games on average each year. Because he appeared in 67 games on average per season, his losing percentage was approximately 6%. Therefore, the greatest relief pitcher of all time experienced an imperfection rate of approximately 10% for each inning he pitched and he cost his team the game 6% of the time.

Naturally, reliability cannot be separated from industry or professional endeavor. For example, a 6% rate of loss due to human error would be catastrophic in the airline industry. Each day, approximately 30,000 commercial flights take off and land in the United States. If we employed Rivera's WHIP rate to calculate the number of unfortunate airline incidents and his loss rate of 6% as a measure of achieving an end result directly opposite of what is intended, planes would have some sort of problem roughly 10% of the time and, horrifyingly, 1800 flights per day would take off but not reach their destinations.

Yet, airline travel today is considered to be the safest it has ever been. According to Mouawad and Drew (2013), "In the last five years, the death risk for passengers in the United States has been one in 45 million flights." The 23 fatal crashes in 2012 would be the equivalent of a loss rate of 0.000077. How does this compare to the most reliable relief pitcher in baseball history, who lost 6 games out of every 100 in which he appeared? Mouawad and Drew offer an observation that puts this in perspective: "According to Arnold Barnett, a professor of statistics at MIT, flying has become so reliable that a traveler could fly every day for an average of 123,000 years before being in a fatal crash." This record of achievement is no accident, but instead the result of hard work and a concentration on the painstaking examination of relevant data. "Safety has improved since the late 1990s as the airline industry and regulators learned to analyze massive quantities of data for anomalies and voluntarily made changes to head off potential problems, according to Thomas Hendricks, Airlines for America's senior vice president for operations and safety" (Zajac, 2012).

Reliability Is Multifaceted

As noted, there are many ways by which we can examine the notion of reliability. For one thing, there is no question that reliability is inextricably linked to context. For example, there are great differences between baseball and the airline industry—at least if we are inclined to view the comparison through the lens of some statistical summary that, in reality, cannot serviceably capture the caliber of performance on a relative basis. A 6% failure rate would be unspeakably catastrophic in one while in the other would constitute a standard that is elusive even to its titan practitioners.

But a larger question looms: What does it mean to be reliable? The term *reliable* is part of our everyday lexicon and is bandied about easily, comfortably, and seemingly without need for qualification or definition. For example, we may think about a friend who is dependable, who is always there for us. We count on the friend to protect our interests, to have our welfare in mind as he or she decides how to act in a given situation, particularly if we count on that person to help us. In this way, we conceive of reliability as something of a predictor—we *anticipate* that the friend will behave in a manner beneficial to us because this is how the person behaved in the past. It all seems so simple, and on this level of interpersonal conduct, most of us would profess to know reliability when we see it.

But perhaps even in the realm of social relations there is more complexity than meets the eye. Consider these questions: Just how dedicated is that friend, that is, are there limits to his or her reliability? Does the friend's reliability involve some personal sacrifice and, if so, how much sacrifice is the friend willing to endure? What happens if our needs exceed his or her capability to satisfy them? What if the wrong advice is provided, no matter how well intentioned? Will we recognize poor advice when it comes our way? What mechanisms do we possess for seeing it?

How do we sort out bad advice from good advice? Suppose we reject the advice because it somehow does not feel right? Do we inform the friend, knowing full well that failure to do so means that he or she would not learn and, therefore, could reissue similarly unhelpful advice in the future? On the other hand, we recognize that the friend took the time to help and, thus, might we experience even some reluctance to inform him or her that the advice was bad? Suppose we yield to that reluctance and withhold feedback—might we place some distance between ourselves and this friend, thereby limiting the closeness of the relationship?

Finally, suppose we did tell the friend that we thought the advice was not to our liking. Did we present it in a way that the person could understand and grow from the experience and, hopefully, give us better advice next time? As a result of the discussion, is our relationship closer? If we assess our friend's advice as ineffective on multiple occasions, how much of the friend's failure to provide good advice comes from his or her poor judgment, lackluster effort in accumulating the right information to make an informed judgment, or the execution of an agenda that may be at variance with ours? Or, most tellingly, perhaps the problem wasn't caused by our friend at all, but rather with our own failure to provide sufficient and helpful feedback, which may have allowed the friend to make a mid-course correction in his or her advice giving? Do we have enough self-awareness to recognize that our feedback influences our friend's ability to be helpful? These are all normal human dilemmas that most of us experience at one time or another.

Reliability is a more complex concept than a first glance would suggest, and it has been treated in a wide variety of ways. So what exactly is it? For example, is it a function of containing errors? Is it a measure of quality? Though these are surely related, they are not the same. Is reliability related to repeatability as in the research realm of methodology? Or perhaps a function of consistency of ratings across those charged with monitoring, measuring, interpreting, or evaluating some phenomenon? Is reliability, like beauty, in the eye of the beholder, or some trait or quality inherent in the thing or phenomenon we observe or monitor? Should we think of reliability as relating more to process or to outcome?

If a patient leaves a hospital and the hospital can document that it did everything correctly, but the patient fails to abide by care directives postdischarge because he did not adequately comprehend those directives, did the hospital perform in a way that can still be characterized as reliable? To complicate matters slightly, suppose the discharged patient understood the directive, say, to take a particular medication, but elected not to because he did not understand the consequences of not taking the medication, can the hospital declare that it acted reliably? That it acted responsibly? If the hospital could demonstrate that it committed no errors, but its failure to maintain an efficient operation resulted in an excessive length of stay for that patient, could it still wear the mantle of reliability? How would the answer change if the patient showed no sign of a problematic outcome upon discharge, but had to be readmitted on what was subsequently determined to have been an avoidable basis?

The healthcare system is moving closer to providing an answer to the last question. In late 2012, the government began penalizing hospitals that experienced excessive readmissions following hospital stays. All told, over 2200 hospitals received such penalties resulting in a cumulative forfeiture of $280 million in Medicare funds (Rau, 2012).

Toward a Leadership Perspective

Health care has made important strides over the past 100 years with respect to reliability. Most encouraging, reliability has never been taken for granted. Without interruption, sharpening our understanding of the complexity, vital nature, and place of reliability in health care has been a vibrant pursuit. Much like the progress that has been made with patient care—continuously refining our understanding of and capability for treating illness and injury—we have continued to strengthen our definition and understanding of reliability and the tools for measuring it.

We may conceive of reliability as residing on multiple levels. Unquestionably, reliability is inextricably linked to safety and effectiveness of patient care. For example, Reinersten and Clancy (2006) suggest as a "convenient" definition "defect-free operations over time" (p. 1536). Others have extended this approach by operationalizing it; for example, Pronovost et al. (2006) observe that reliability has often been "presented as a defect rate in units of 10 and generally represents the number of defects per opportunity for that defect. In health care, an opportunity for defect usually translates to a population of patients at risk for the medical error or adverse effect" (p. 1600). Healthcare organizations are also generally considered to belong to that particular category called *high reliability organizations* (HROs), which "exist in such hazardous environments where the consequences of errors are high, but the occurrence of error is extremely low" (Baker, Day, & Salas, 2006, p. 1576).

Definitions that focus on safety are critical. The consequences of error in a healthcare environment can be perilous, even fatal. Despite ongoing and concerted efforts to make inroads in safety, the healthcare industry still has a long way to go. According to Packer-Tursman (2014), Senator Bernie Sanders, chair of the Senate Health, Education, Labor & Pensions Subcommittee on Primary Health and Aging, indicated at a recent hearing that the issue of preventable medical errors "has not received anywhere near the attention it deserves," and that only heart disease and cancer kill more Americans.

In a similar vein, Landrigan et al. (2010), reported in *The New England Journal of Medicine* that substantial progress had not been made in the decade following the Institute of Medicine's landmark report indicating that up to 98,000 deaths and over 1 million injuries occur each year as a result of medical errors

(Kohn, Corrigan, & Donaldson, 1999). Likewise, O'Reilly (2011) estimates that one in three patients is harmed during a hospital stay.

Those who lead healthcare organizations have a special responsibility to place safety within a broader context of reliability. When a patient enters the healthcare organization, how can the organization feel confident that all that takes place with the patient is proper, produces error-free results to the extent possible, and leads to the best possible health outcome for the patient? All departments, functions, and staff play a role in the processes involved in these pursuits. And while reliability may evoke common beliefs relative to such goals as dependability and quality—or, perhaps, dependability *or* quality—each profession and employee may be guided by different agendas to satisfy particular requirements associated with the goals. For example, the management of infection rates is linked to length of stay; after all, the higher the latter, the greater the opportunity for the former (Chant, Smith, Marshall, & Friedrich, 2011; Dulworth & Pyenson, 2004; Lilly et al., 2011; Vincent et al., 2009). Yet, the processes of ensuring low infection rates and the protocols for producing operational efficiencies that minimize the likelihood of a protracted length of stay differ and tend to be treated as discrete. While it is essential for those charged with responsibility for such functions to engage in continuous improvement, a climate for fostering teamwork is essential in order to establish collaborative efforts.

Moreover, our healthcare system is changing in ways that have a profound impact on the notion of reliability. We have a far greater ability to monitor a patient's health when he or she departs from a healthcare organization than ever before. Not only are the means of communicating with the patient exceedingly more advanced than even a few years ago, but the continuing progress toward electronic medical and health records makes possible the sharing of important patient-related data. This phenomenon will continue to inform our beliefs about reliability, requiring us to extend our responsibilities with respect to reliability beyond the boundaries of our institutions. Such a shift should force us to adapt and to design a next phase of reliability, one in which the institution is part of a continuum of care and in which the patient, including his or her health experience prior to the patient's arrival at the institution and after discharge from it, increasingly occupies a more central place in how we view reliability.

The tools for tracking the patient's health status and changes thereto are growing more sophisticated. As observed, these apply not only to the period when the patient is in the hospital (or any other healthcare facility) but also to a protracted and perhaps ongoing period after the patient leaves as well as before he or she arrives. Changes on this order of magnitude always produce accompanying refinements of process, even of a paradigmatic order. For example, as it became evident that measuring compliance with standards was not a sufficient barometer of quality because it did not provide enough focus on the systems and protocols of delivering care, the concept of *quality improvement* was developed. This brought attention to the *processes* of care delivery and, perhaps most significantly, inspired the mindset that enhancing such processes is ongoing. The landscape of healthcare is changing dramatically—and at an aggressive pace—calling for leaders to imagine and institute ways of conceiving reliability more broadly. As such, while containing error is a vital component of reliability, the demands of leadership warrant a perspective that goes further.

Reliability as an Integrated Construct

The purpose of this chapter is to present a unified and comprehensive approach to reliability, one that is inclusive and reflective of the broad challenges healthcare leaders must be prepared to address in an era of transformation. A leadership perspective on reliability must reach beyond the goals, monitoring systems, and measures employed by each of the various caregiving functions and programs that compose a health delivery organization or system. It must accommodate the range of these goals and unify them such that quality *as well as* proficiency, process *as well as* outcome, and perceptions of reliability *as well as* evidence of headway toward progressively improved levels are brought together. Leadership functions to assimilate the pieces into a whole and create an ethos by which all employees can appreciate the connection between their specific work and the larger purpose of the organization.

The scope of practice and activity in the majority of departments and functions in healthcare organizations are significantly influenced, if not outright mandated, by requirements and standards established by regulatory, licensing, and/or accrediting bodies. Particular measures of such activity, along with the data produced by those measures, may translate into a reliability assessment. Such measures are critical. Much like the WHIP score in baseball and, more generally, win–loss records across all sports, they offer guideposts on the dependability of the services, constitute a baseline for continuous improvement, and allow for comparisons with other organizations.

But organizational leadership must take a broader perspective. Leadership in health care has a special responsibility with respect to reliability in at least four ways:

- ► First, it is the distinct obligation of leadership to set the tone for reliability and to establish its priority status in the organization. No one would argue against reliability being important, but there is a difference between giving lip service to a goal and mobilizing an organization toward achieving it.
- ► Second, leadership bridges the various and seemingly discrete departmental orientations toward and protocols for reliability into a coherent organizational framework; that is, leaders focus the organization's attention on the alignment of reliability at the departmental level with organizational mission, purpose, and values. It must be emphasized that this does not

suggest that leaders behave autocratically; in fact, quite the opposite—effective leaders create a culture in which all stakeholders contribute to this process.

▶ Third, leaders must view their organizations as part of the larger healthcare system and, therefore, must work in concert with others to ensure their organization's capability to adapt to change. In this way, successful leaders frame their organizations as a component in a wider context and help their organizations establish links to others in ways that serve the interests of the organization and its consumers.

▶ Fourth, and it may be argued most critically, leaders channel and articulate an organizing principle by which the other three are achievable—that is, reliability is established as an institutional priority, linkages between each function's orientation toward reliability and the organization as a whole are understood, and internal and external environmental foci are assimilated. This organizing principle—that is, the common bond foundational to the model of reliability most relevant to healthcare leaders—is bidimensional: the welfare of the patient and an unwavering commitment to continuous improvement.

Taken together, these four propositions for leadership define the achievement of a highly reliable culture as involving the establishment of a patient-centered environment and the execution of a corresponding and integrated set of strategies that promotes and maintains excellence of care, efficiency of resources, productive engagement with continuum of care partners, and processes that ensure continuous improvement.

The definition is grounded in the premise that all activities flow from the common commitment to serve patients in the most dependable and high-quality manner. While obvious on face value, this is not easy to achieve. The competing values framework (CVF) highlights the natural tensions that emerge in any organization. Absent effective leadership, the various functions retreat to agendas that tend to be self-protective, self-advancing, or both. This does not necessarily emanate from a poor intention, but more likely from an inability to easily align a given department's agenda with the larger organizational mission.

Take a common, everyday example: staff members of a rehabilitation service and a nutrition planning department who fail to effectively coordinate their schedules may easily feel exasperated if the time set aside to counsel a patient could not be used as planned because a clinician from the other department got there first. Resolving the problem at the moment of its occurrence could be achieved with an on-the-spot scheduling adjustment—for example, one employee could return in a few minutes, perhaps after visiting another patient. And yet, what has the appearance of being a quick and easy fix could have profound implications for all involved—for the clinicians, for their departments, for the nurse who coordinates care activities for the patient, for the hospital as a whole, and, most disturbingly, for the patient. Seemingly inconsequential scheduling adjustments, as they accumulate, possess the potential to contribute to a patient's overall length of stay. They reinforce, even subtly (and often not so subtly), differences between and among departments, which could, in turn, contribute to a fractured or silo-dominated organizational culture. The charge nurse is now unable to be definitive with the patient with respect to when a clinical visit will occur. The patient will not have a clear picture about the schedule of activity related to his or her care. Then there is the ripple effect. Another patient, who may have thought the visit from the nutritionist would take place at 11:00 AM, is interrupted from a conversation with a friend at 10:30 AM by the nutritionist.

Does this one relatively insignificant scheduling problem rise to the level of organizational calamity? Of course not. But what if it occurs 10 times a day, or 50, or 100, or 1000? What is the cost of solving a problem that need not have occurred in the first place? Suppose both clinicians earn $20 per hour, and the time associated with adjusting schedules for each episode of overlapping patient visits involved 15 minutes each. If this problem arose eight times per day, the cost to the hospital would be $80 each day. On an annualized basis the cost would be $29,200. And if this *little* problem is occurring with these two departments, undoubtedly it is occurring on a more widespread basis. If this sort of problem adds even a small increment to the length of stay, the cost could escalate to potentially hundreds of thousands of dollars. In addition, what might be the costs that are less tangible, for example, the introduction of some confusion to the patient? Does it chip away at the patient's inclination to recommend the hospital to others or to return if another hospitalization is necessary? Further, is it possible that any staffing shortages could be addressed, even partially, by ensuring that effective coordination of scheduling occurs?

If we isolate and examine the indices of reliability from the departments involved—rehab services and nutrition planning—we may discover they are doing an impeccable job. The quality of their work may be judged to be suitable and commendable, particularly if we define reliability exclusively as a function of error. We may find that patient satisfaction levels are reasonably high. By all accounts, whether based on The Joint Commission (TJC) standards, Department of Health regulations, or the various standards that may be developed by professional associations or required by licensing agencies, the work performed by these departments may be quite admirable. However, woven deeply into the fabric of their relationship is an interdepartmental dynamic that may not be readily detectable by the tools and measures of reliability or quality. So while the hospital's leadership may have done an excellent job of hiring highly competent managers for these functions—professionals who are adept at instituting and maintaining programs that are efficient, perform in accordance with high quality standards, and can demonstrate good clinical results—something remains amiss. This is where we enter the domain of leadership.

A Leadership Perspective on Reliability

In the case of the rehab/nutritionist example, two aspects of leadership emerge as relevant to the broader definition of reliability. First, the concept of continuous quality improvement underscores the importance of being amenable to the notion that we can always do better. This is far more easily said than done. A natural inclination is to protect vulnerabilities and weaknesses from becoming exposed. Such self-protection is a powerful human drive (Gass & Seiter, 2010). Therefore, it requires a particularly effective leader to create a context of trust such that defensiveness does not constitute an insurmountable trait. It follows, then, that one of the most vital elements of leadership with respect to reliability is the creation of a culture in which openness to change supersedes—and, in fact, neutralizes—defensiveness.

Second, fostering a collaborative environment is central to making progress toward the achievement of high levels of reliability. If rehab services and nutritional planning fail to coordinate, and instead begin to view the other as the party responsible for the glitch, an impasse may develop. Left unaddressed, the impasse may intensify and, at some point, mistrust is likely to settle in. Working relationships may be cordial on the surface, but an unspoken wariness may prevail beneath the surface. It may not be acutely harmful and may not detract from the fine work performed by both departments. And in all probability, this tacit relationship problem could go on for quite some time without being captured by measures of reliability.

Further, the departments involved may elect to simply live with the situation because it does not seem excessively problematic and because an expedient solution is not apparent. Furthermore, the department managers may have many other matters demanding their attention, including ensuring an adequate staffing complement on any given day. So this seemingly minor problem—and perhaps hundreds just like it—remain buried in the labyrinth of activity that goes on every single day in the hospital.

Achieving a very reliable service or function in a healthcare organization may be feasible even as other services in the organization cope with obstacles to the achievement of reliability and may not perform as strongly. Yet, achieving a highly reliable healthcare organization as a whole cannot occur without considerable and focused leadership attention. "The organization must commit to the goal of high reliability," according to the Fifth International High Reliability Conference hosted by The Joint Commission, formerly the Joint Commission on Accreditation of Health Care Organizations [JCAHO, 2012]). The definition of achieving a highly reliable healthcare organization presented above is built on the premise that leadership must attend to—and most significantly, must integrate—four dimensions of organizational performance (**Figure 4.1**).

These four dimensions, which assimilate through the shared bonds of patient care and continuous improvement, involve empowerment, ecosystem, effectiveness, and efficiency. An examination of each follows.

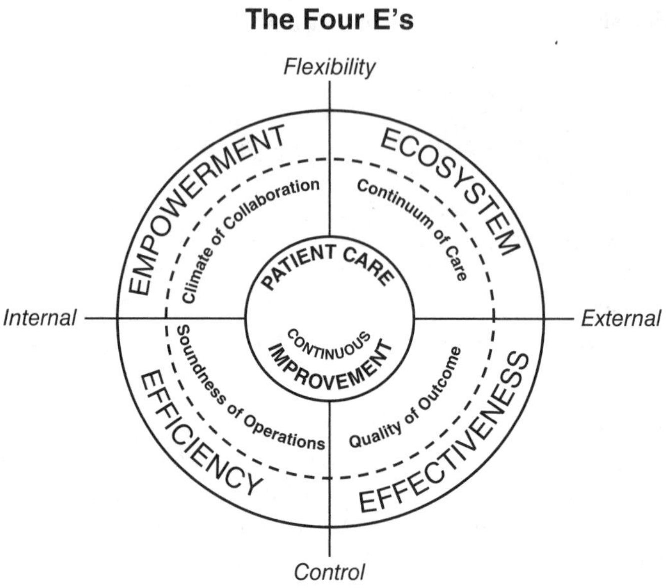

The Four E's

Figure 4.1 Dimensions of Reliability

Empowerment

Joseph Martin, the administrator of a 400-bed hospital in Florida, recalled an incident in which an elderly patient, accompanied by his wife, came to see him about a month following his discharge. The patient was admitted for bursitis and was doing well from the treatment and aftercare. Nonetheless, the patient and the wife seemed angry. Joseph invited them to sit and explain the reason for their discontent. The patient indicated that he had received a bill for durable medical equipment—including a walker, cane, and toilet safety rails—that were supplied to him at discharge. He assumed the charges would be completely covered by his insurance. Instead, only a portion was covered and the patient was responsible for $97. The patient expressed confusion about why, after receiving over $9,000 for his care, the hospital could not absorb the $97 expense.

The patient proceeded to describe a series of interactions with various hospital personnel in his efforts to have the charge waived. The first call to the billing department resulted in a representative explaining that the $97 was the responsibility of the patient, not the hospital. The representative attempted to ease the patient's mind by informing him that the full charge for the equipment was, in fact, $845. Then the representative indicated that he lacked the authority to make an exception.

The patient asked the representative to check with his supervisor. The representative indicated that the supervisor had gone for the day, but would check with her tomorrow and call him back. The following afternoon, the supervisor called the patient and reiterated the representative's position that the hospital would not pay for a charge that properly belongs to the patient. Pressed by the patient, she also stated that she would not be able to authorize an exception. The patient insisted on speaking with the manager of the billing department and was informed that this would have to wait for the following day because the manager was tied up in meetings. The same discussion occurred the following day with the manager insisting he did not possess the authority to approve a waiver of charges.

"Well, who can?" demanded the patient.

"I can put in a request to my administrator," the manager responded.

"How long will that take?" asked the patient.

"I can't guarantee a specific time, but I will label the message a priority," replied the manager.

After 2 days of not hearing back from anyone at the hospital, the patient and his wife elected to visit instead and insisted on seeing Martin.

Notwithstanding whether the hospital should accede to the patient's request, this patient's irascibility had three interrelated bases. First, the patient's expectation that he would not have an out-of-pocket expense went unfulfilled. Second, he could not understand why the hospital would not support him; after all, the hospital received a great deal of money for taking care of him, and the amount in question was, by comparison, very small. Third, he could not gain easy and immediate access to someone who possessed the organizational leverage to fully resolve the matter. This may have proven to be the most serious of the problems. The hospital may have been forgiven for not waiving the charge if the relationship between the patient and the hospital was grounded in trust.

Research on persuasion suggests that the hospital could pay a price for the patient's experience, and specifically with respect to its credibility. The pioneering work of Hovland, Janis, and Kelly (1953) on the relationship of senders and receivers of messages determined that credibility resides on multiple dimensions. Today, it is generally accepted that there are three primary underlying dimensions of credibility: expertise, trustworthiness, and dynamism (Larsen, 2010; Pornpitakpan, 2004; Reinard, 1988). The failure of the various employees to respond in a manner perceived by the patient as knowledgeable could tarnish the patient's impression of their expertise and, by extension, that of the hospital and those who work there. But, more significantly, their lack of willingness to commit to an answer could mar perceptions of trustworthiness. Again, this is not to suggest that the hospital should bear responsibility for the patient's charge; that is up to the hospital. The patient resides in a world in which responses to consumer questions are generally provided more quickly and without requiring the consumer to navigate tedious and ostensibly impotent chains of command structures. At each stage of the sequence of interactions, the patient's frustration was heightened further, more by the lack of authoritativeness than by the failure to receive the waiver of the fee.

Joseph elected to absorb the patient's share of the expense, but the damage was already done. In this case, no employee was performing in a manner contrary to the hospital's best interests or, for that matter, the patient's. However, each employee was bound by a set of constraints that prevented him or her from moving beyond a limited scope of decision making, making it difficult to address the range of concerns presented by the patient. The rules governing employee conduct, both tacit and explicit, may provide clarity with respect to performance expectations, but simultaneously function as restraints on behavior and the perceived latitude for decision making. The challenge for leaders of healthcare institutions involves striking a more effective balance between restraint and flexibility, between empowering employees in a way that allows them to strengthen their effectiveness while operating under a common set of guidelines to preserve consistency of decision making across the organization.

Hospitals have had less success than other industries in pushing decision making downward. This is not surprising in light of five characteristics that, when taken together, constitute a formidable obstacle to the goal of achieving empowerment.

- ► First, jobs in hospitals tend to be highly specialized. As a result, the scope of practice and responsibility tend to be relatively limited.
- ► Second, healthcare environments are highly rule-governed. In this respect, healthcare organizations have extensive reporting responsibility internally and to agencies at the local, state, and federal levels as well as to accrediting bodies. Accordingly, a climate in which behavior is relatively prescribed renders it challenging to conduct oneself with the flexibility for a broad range of problem solving.
- ► Third, healthcare organizations tend to have relatively centralized decision-making structures. Moving problem resolution closer to the time and place of the problem's occurrence, though generally desired, runs counter to the history of management practice in the industry.
- ► Fourth, the trend toward coalescing into larger systems via mergers and acquisitions means that policy development occurs on an increasingly remote basis relative to each employee in the healthcare system.
- ► Fifth, adding what might be construed as additional decision making responsibilities, including the need to confer with others, may be perceived as burdensome to staff who already have demanding schedules (Apker, 2001).

A core element in overcoming the barriers is the promotion of teamwork. Collaboration may occur under certain circumstances, despite the failure of leadership to promote such an organizational dynamic. However, it will not occur routinely and systemically in the absence of a concerted and ongoing effort to promote it. Consider this account from a writer whose mother became ill at Disney World:

When we made our way out, a cast member immediately spotted us and asked if we needed assistance. We had made our way out of the building so my mom could sit in her ECV, and the cast member popped back inside to call for help and then made sure to stay with us until help arrived. First on the scene was a security guard who took down some basic information and asked me if her condition was "ride induced." Since we had only done the Tiki Room and two minutes of Country Bears, it was safe to say that this was not a reaction to a ride. An area manager came next and talked to us briefly, conferred with the other cast members, and hung around to oversee the situation. She couldn't have been nicer...EMTs were quickly on the scene to attend to the patient. Even though we were pretty sure she was having a flair up [sic] from her ulcer problem, the paramedics took no chances. They evaluated the situation and decided she needed to be moved backstage and probably be taken to the hospital. The security cast member and other attraction cast members were sure to keep other guests away from the area to allow the EMTs to work and keep my mom as comfortable as possible.

Reproduced from Touringplans.com, Helmstetter, Kristen, What Happens During a Medical Emergency at Disney World? http://blog.touringplans.com/2012/03/14/what-happens-during-a-medical-emergency-at-disney-world

The kind of orchestrated attention given to the Disney patron, which was executed collaboratively, is well-planned, encouraged, monitored, and employed by management as a basis of evaluating and rewarding staff conduct.

Collaboration is essential to overcoming the barriers to empowerment. To the extent that employees function in highly specialized roles, multiple perspectives must be combined in order to solve problems that go beyond the particular specialty. Problems that go undetected or unreported are problems that cannot get solved. Problem identification and problem resolution are fundamental to the achievement of a high reliability organization. Constructing and maintaining a culture that promotes high reliability cannot occur without an emphasis on teamwork. Baker et al. (2006) emphasize that "teamwork is an important component of HROs" (p. 1578). The authors distinguish teamwork from "taskwork," which focuses on the "knowledge and skill" necessary for the assignment, by indicating that teamwork has a considerably more expansive set of responsibilities: "Teamwork depends on each team member being able to anticipate the needs of others, adjust to each other's actions, and have a shared understanding of how a procedure should happen" (p. 1579).

Teams engaged in clinical activity (for example, responding to a cardiac arrest code) typically have a more defined understanding of each member's role than teams engaged in nonclinical work, such as organizing interdepartmental work processes. In carrying out a specific caregiving assignment such as a surgical procedure, the roles, responsibilities, and interrelatedness of the surgeon, anesthesiologist, nurses, surgical assistants, and aides are generally understood; parameters of conduct are well-established in these circumstances and adapting to one another's actions and roles occurs fluidly. In other contexts, such as organizing a central-ized scheduling system, the outcome, the process for achieving it, and the roles and responsibilities of those contributing to the process, all have more variability. The challenge for leaders is how to convert that variability from an obstacle to an asset. An understanding of the defining elements of an HRO can prove helpful in this regard. Roberts and Rousseau (1989) suggest that HROs are characterized by systemic complexity and interdependence of elements across the system, each with systems of control; a high volume of individuals involved in decision-making processes; considerable accountability with considerable penalties for poor perfor-mance; rapid response to decision making; and a need to focus on multiple, press-ing, and interrelated goals. Similarly, Belasen's (2008) summary of the hallmarks of an HRO—"preoccupation with failure; reluctance to simplify interpretations, sensitivity to operations, commitment to resilience, and deference to expertise" (p. 19)—is instructive because of the priority placed on the alignment of operations and decision-making structures to achieve error avoidance.

Empowerment cannot be effectively achieved without collaboration. Given the highly specialized training and roles of healthcare workers, putting the pieces of the puzzle together to solve a problem requires input from others. Therefore, leaders are encouraged to study the principles of teamwork that prevail in clinical contexts for their application to managerial planning and decision-making contexts. Salas, DiazGranados, Weaver, and King (2008) provide a framework that leaders may employ as they seek to introduce and continuously reinforce a teamwork mentality and corresponding skills training into their organizations. They argue that a highly func-tioning HRO team environment must have clearly defined leadership, performance monitoring systems, the capacity to provide back-up support, flexibility to adjust to shifting circumstances, a collective willingness to subjugate individual goals for the greater good, a climate of trust, and systems for feedback. While these competencies are pertinent to all organizations, they are particularly critical to an HRO's ability for achieving goals related to safety, quality, and continuous improvement of work pro-cesses. Studies show that training based on the framework produces cognitive, affec-tive, and performance improvements (DiazGranados et al., 2008; Klein et al., 2008).

In 2011, the American Hospital Association convened healthcare leaders to explore the future of the primary care model as influenced by the Affordable Care Act. Among the principles advanced by the group: "The workforce must change how it functions on multiple levels. Care must be provided by inter-professional teams where work is role-based, not task-based, and the team must be empowered to create effective approaches for delivering care" (American Hospital Association, 2011). For organizations to achieve high levels of reliability, the same principle must hold true at the system level.

Ecosystem

Traditionally, when a patient entered a healthcare facility, the patient's condi-tion was evaluated; caregivers applied their knowledge, skills, and experience in considering treatment options; and with the patient's (or surrogate's) approval, caregivers selected and executed a treatment approach. The patient was also advised by the caregivers as to what should occur next and a feedback loop was established which, over the past few decades, placed the primary care practitioner in a central place in that loop. Undoubtedly, this will continue. But this model is likely to prove too confining in the future. Each hospital, and in fact each practitioner, will be connected through its patients to the broader system of care management. And as this new model takes shape, what it means to be reliable will, by necessity, also evolve.

It may be argued that we are on the precipice of conceiving of *outcome* differently. Referencing the work of Moskowitz and Bodenheimer (2011), the Cooley Dickinson Health Care System asserts that "there is an emerging recognition that focusing only on the prescription of care through the doctor's office or hospital is woefully inadequate to integrating real change in the lives of patients. Evidence-based health broadens our perspective, making the patient the center, surrounded by teams of medical professionals, community-based services, support systems for behavior change, and programs of navigation, transportation, and cultural change" (Cooley-Dickinson, 2013). The American Hospital Association issues a prescription for the future and notes the consequence of failure: "Hospitals should evolve from traditional 'hospitals' to 'health systems,' partnering with community organizations and patients in order to advance the community's wellness and health needs. [It is] recognized that efforts have been made in the past to configure a new system. However, this recommendation is different in that it emphasizes that without effective linkage with the community, this evolution will not be successful" (American Hospital Association, 2011).

Healthcare organizations have always interacted with and responded to the activities of other caregiving institutions and practitioners with respect to the care needs of their patients. Physicians in medical practice direct their patients to specialists and hospitals when their health needs warrant such attention. Hospitals refer patients to rehabilitation clinics and skilled nursing facilities, and so on. In this way, all healthcare organizations have been part of and have always connected with others in the healthcare system. Yet, all too often, transitions by patients from one element of the system to the next often feel like starting from scratch. Feedback systems have been relatively meager, in part because each entity in the system maintained its own database, and the capacity to exchange and employ data from other parts of the system has been limited. The more constrained this ability, the less capably the parts of the system work together to anticipate health issues and work with the patient to prevent health problems. Moreover, until recently, incentives and pressures to exchange information and bolster its portability have not been particularly powerful.

Aside from the lack of tools to facilitate coordination, there has been a tendency in health care for departments, services, and professions to remain relatively segregated. This is far from surprising in light of the great differences in training and skill requirements of the multitude of professions in every healthcare organization. Until now, the silo culture present in many healthcare organizations was microcosmically representative of the healthcare industry more generally. Concerted efforts have been undertaken to change course, to adapt to the evolving need for interdisciplinarity on both horizontal and vertical bases.

It may be argued that four developments, and particularly their cumulative impact, are accounting for the trend, and the impact on reliability will be substantial. First, pressures to reduce costs have forced a renewal of "merger mania" (Creswell & Abelson, 2013). In light of expectations that systems are likely to continue to expand, it is expected that reliability—measures of performance—will continue to undergo standardization. Second, incentives for the institution of electronic medical records are broadening as are disincentives for failure to do so. The patient, including all of the data about his or her health and information that bears upon it, will constitute a vital link among an increasingly expansive chain of providers. The intelligibility, adaptability, and common use of such data will, over time, produce similarities of data collection, storage, retrieval, exchange, and, invariably, interpretive practices. Assessments of reliability both across and within systems will be far more possible. Third, the increasing availability of information that will help consumers make informed choices about the quality of care they can expect will heighten the attention toward and, in all likelihood, competition among facilities to demonstrate positive outcomes. As this occurs, consumer demands for comparing apples to apples should produce more user-friendly, accessible, and common measures of performance. And fourth, as our understanding of biology, physiology, genetics, and disease management continue to advance, the ability to predict one's health status will increase. As such, the notion of an outcome, which has been typically confined to relatively brief periods following a medical intervention, should expand. The relationship between a clinical experience and longer term health and wellness will assume an increasingly longitudinal character. As such, measures of reliability should correspondingly expand.

Leaders who have the capacity to move their organizations into the wider context of continua of care will have an edge in positioning these organizations for success. Managing in a vacuum is rapidly becoming a thing of the past. The upper right quadrant of the CVF draws our attention to the importance of building partnerships, managing relationships with other provider organizations, and negotiating system-wide principles and measures of reliability that benefit the whole while also serving the interests of their individual organizations. By keeping patients' needs at the center of their efforts, they increase their chances of success quite considerably.

Effectiveness

Historically, quality tended to be a function of limiting errors rather than producing good work on a consistent basis. For example, prior to 1970, The Joint Commission standards focused on minimum or baseline levels of performance and outcomes; at that time a shift commenced and standards began to reflect "optimal achievable levels of quality" (The Joint Commission, 2013a). And yet, there is a long way to go, and ensuring unwavering attention to reliability does not occur without difficulty. After all, health care is in a relatively constant state of change and there is no time, proverbially, to close shop for renovations; accordingly, one can never claim, "Now is an opportune time to devote to reliability."

The achievements of Owensboro Medical Health System (OMHS) in Kentucky are a case in point. In 2005, OMHS established quality as the single most important institutional priority. Over the next several years, OMHS's mortality rate diminished, reaching a point of 20% below the average for hospitals across the country. The achievement, according to Linda K. Jones, vice president of clinical services, rests on steadfast commitment to avoid being distracted. In light of seemingly never-ending change in healthcare environments, remaining focused on a particular goal requires a concerted institution-wide effort that starts with the board and permeates the entire organization. Jones states: "In 2012 alone we implemented our first EMR and prepared to move into a new replacement facility. In the face of two monumental changes like this, it would be easy to become distracted from our HRO work and tackle it later. . . . But we have very intentionally incorporated high reliability into everything we do. It's not just a 'strategy'—it is the prevailing, defining attitude in our organization" (May, 2013).

The Joint Commission has steadily shifted its focus on quality over the years to ensure that reliability is integrated into, and does not remain distinct from, operational processes and caregiving activities. In its most recent broad initiative, the Center for Transforming Healthcare (2013), The Joint Commission acknowledges the complex and typically systemic-oriented underpinnings of departures from providing high-quality care by encouraging the use of sophisticated tools, such as Lean Six Sigma (George, 2002), to address the need for evidence-driven and data-based approaches to achieving high reliability.

Moreover, in recognition that reliability is best accomplished from collaborative efforts, much like our principle of ecology would indicate, the Center for Transforming Healthcare organized project teams comprising multiple healthcare organizations to develop specific reliability protocols for various problems common to a healthcare environment, including hand hygiene, hand-off communications, wrong site surgery, surgical site infections, preventing avoidable heart failure hospitalizations, safety culture, preventing falls with injury, sepsis, and insulin safety. The goal is to strengthen our understanding about underlying causes of error and develop specific plans for improvement as well as monitoring and measuring systems.

The Joint Commission has not only encouraged partnerships across its accredited members, but has encouraged reliability initiatives though partnerships with other entities, for example, state hospital associations. Consider the extensive partnership with the South Carolina Hospital Association.

The core effort is a commitment to institute processes that occur on an error-free basis. The participants in these projects recognize that such reliability goals cannot be achieved without the development of very specific protocols, standards of performance, proven methods of measuring reliability, teamwork, and leadership responsible for motivating all stakeholders toward the goal. South Carolina has taken a leadership role in fostering high reliability in the recent past. For example, "In the management of heart attack care, the average door-to-balloon time across the state dropped from 93 minutes to 49 during a five year period (2006–2011). Central line infections decreased by 67% statewide in two years (2010–2011)" (May, 2013, p. 26).

These models are certain to be replicated across states, healthcare systems, and other collections of providers. The core goal is to realize soundness of quality. The aggressiveness with which health care will embark on the quest to achieve quality will intensify. After all, the tools and processes employed to achieve higher levels of quality continue to be refined, consumer expectations for quality are strengthening, and access to consumer-friendly information regarding outcomes is broadening. Yet, there is recognition that the road ahead is relatively uncharted and that the quest for delivering consistently high quality care will occur through the adoption of proven tools as well as inventiveness. "There's nothing in the high reliability literature that demonstrates how to move a hospital or health system from low to high reliability in the real world," says Mark R. Chassin, MD, FACP, president of The Joint Commission and the Joint Commission Center for Transforming Healthcare. "That has great implications for what we need to do in health care. We must create our own roadmaps. That's what The Joint Commission has done. We have charted a pathway that takes into account where health care is today and describes specific next incremental steps. The findings of the South Carolina Safe Care Commitment will go far in demonstrating to the field what exactly it takes to become a highly reliable healthcare organization" (May, 2013, p. 26).

Case Study: TJC/South Carolina

Hospital Association Partnership

Center for Transforming Healthcare, SCHA Team Up to Make Health Care More Reliable (OAKBROOK TERRACE, Ill. – February 25, 2013).

The Joint Commission Center for Transforming Healthcare and the South Carolina Hospital Association (SCHA) today announced the South Carolina Safe Care Commitment, a multi-year engagement that will strengthen participating

---

The Joint Commission. (2013b, February). Center for transforming healthcare, SCHA team up to make health care more reliable. Retrieved from http://www.centerfortransforminghealthcare.org/cth_scha_team_up_to_make_health_care_more_reliable/

hospitals' processes, systems, and structures, resulting in patient care that is consistently excellent and consistently safe.

The initiative, which is the first of its kind for the Center, includes 20 hospitals from seven health systems located throughout the state. CEOs and other executives from participating South Carolina hospitals will meet regularly to collaborate on processes to move health care toward the same highly reliable performance seen in industries such as aviation and nuclear power.

Success will be measured through the results of safety culture survey assessments, evidence that improvement activities have produced significant reductions in patient harm, and associated cost savings. In addition, the South Carolina hospitals will utilize a Web-based electronic application created by the Center to identify critical practices leading to high reliability in health care and help hospitals assess their performance in these areas.

The collaboration between SCHA and the Center is part of the Center's efforts to solve health care's most critical safety and quality problems by creating solutions for progressing toward high reliability in health care. High reliability is defined as consistent performance at high levels of safety over long periods of time. In other words, highly reliable health care is care that is dependably excellent, every time, for every patient.

"South Carolina hospitals are already involved to great effect in a number of projects that target individual safety issues such as preventable infections. This engagement is different because it offers the potential to transform hospitals into far safer providers of health care in a permanent way," says Mark R. Chassin, MD, FACP, MPP, MPH, president, The Joint Commission and Joint Commission Center for Transforming Healthcare. "We applaud the courage of the South Carolina Hospital Association and its participating hospitals for daring to strive for high reliability and aiming to achieve the ultimate goal of zero patient harm."

"We at SCHA are very proud of our member hospitals' exemplary collaborative work in the realm of quality improvement," says Thornton Kirby, president and CEO, The South Carolina Hospital Association. "With the launch of South Carolina Safe Care Commitment, we are ready to move to the next level of patient safety. We look forward to working closely with the Joint Commission Center for Transforming Health Care along this exciting journey to achieve high reliability."

Beyond the hospitals initially participating in the project, the collaboration between the Center and SCHA is designed to improve safety and quality in health care organizations across the state. The lessons learned about identifying the underlying causes of specific breakdowns in care and creating targeted solutions at participating hospitals will be spread to other health care organizations. This focus on offering targeted, tested solutions has been a hallmark of the Center, which has through its Targeted Solutions Tool™ provided a step-by-step process to assist accredited health care organizations in measuring performance, identifying barriers to excellent performance, and implementing the Center's proven solutions that are customized to address specific barriers (The Joint Commission, 2013b).

Efficiency

The relationship between efficiency and reliability is considerable and multifaceted. The greater the control over and understanding of operational processes, the greater the likelihood that (1) the process can be replicated, (2) each activity that contributes to the process can be measured and evaluated for its contribution to the process, (3) transitions between the various activities in the process can be managed more adeptly, (4) continuous improvement practices can be executed more capably and with greater exactitude, (5) the resources necessary for a given set of processes can be more capably defined and managed and their contribution more precisely known, and (6) the relationship of the process to the outcome can be ascertained.

It has been many years since the once-pervasive cost-based reimbursement model has significantly shrunk. The introduction of the diagnosis related group (DRG) model in 1983 and resource-based relative value scale (RBRVS) later that decade, followed by the broad rollout of prospective payment systems throughout the 1990s, and the ubiquitous growth of HMOs and PPOs—these all assured that increasing attention would be paid to the cost of care delivery and, by extension, operational efficiencies. All these had the effect of shifting responsibility, at least in part, for determining payment amounts from the provider to the payer. As it became more and more challenging to pass along the costs for inefficiency, healthcare organizations had to discover ways of instituting processes in which activity and resource utilization that did not favorably contribute to caregiving or operational expedience could be eliminated. Yet, the barriers to efficiency are formidable. Healthcare had a long tradition of passing costs along to third parties, and despite facing mounting constraints to inefficiency, healthcare organizations adapted slowly. The availability of cost shifting, outlier provisions, flexibility with respect to coding diagnoses, and other strategies reinforced the notion that providers could exercise some control over the inflow of reimbursement.

The majority of efforts through the 1980s and 1990s did not go especially far in linking efficiency to quality. This is not to suggest that quality was ignored; for example, excessive readmission rates would not go unnoticed, and providers responsible for such excesses could have had their participation in HMO panels revoked. But the preponderance of effort was to gain some control over costs that were spiraling upward in a relatively uncontained manner.

A new phase of efficiency is dawning. Technology and legislation are aligning in such a manner by which efficiency is becoming reframed from expense reduction to a fundamental strategy for achieving both organizational objectives and care goals. As our definition of achieving high reliability suggests, this can occur only in the context of a collaborative, partnership-driven effort that focuses on quality of care.

The Accountable Care Organization (ACO) provision of the Affordable Care Act is one of the least publicly discussed yet most important elements of the legislation. If provider organizations cluster into an ACO, they reap benefits for keeping patients well and delivering care economically and efficiently. Under the terms of the Affordable Care Act, an ACO must manage the care of at least 5000 Medicare recipients for a period of no less than three years. The more an ACO can demonstrate that the care it provided satisfied particular quality and efficiency criteria, the more bonus incentives they receive. ACOs can consist of a range of providers, including medical practices, rehabilitation facilities, hospitals, and so on. Financial incentives for eliminating test and procedural redundancy will be secured to the extent that cooperation manifests across the spectrum of providers in an ACO. System-wide information management technologies, including electronic medical record programs, make possible the sharing of all relevant data and help to root out needless or redundant tests and procedures.

There are potential adverse side effects of ACOs. First, and most significant, the more robust the incentives for forming systems, the larger the systems will be that invariably emerge. As this occurs, competition among providers could diminish which, in turn, could fuel price increases. Such a situation would accomplish the very opposite of what was intended. Moreover, as an ACO becomes very large, it could gain leverage in negotiations with third-party payers. At the same time, the individual parts of the system could be constrained from policy development and building their own cultures while stifling creativity and individuality. Given the potential drawbacks, many argue that the ACO concept will undergo revision or that a more effective model will replace it. According to Gold (2013): "ACOs are already becoming pervasive, but they may be just an interim step on the way to a more efficient American healthcare system. 'ACOs aren't the end game,' says Chas Roades, chief research officer at The Advisory Board Company in Washington, DC."

Yet, the larger point prevails. Despite the downsides, the development of ACOs represents a step toward melding quality and efficiency. The CVF highlights the potential for organizational tensions to exist between the lower quadrants, suggesting that different parts of the organization may see their rewards more fully associated with the achievement of high-quality results while other parts prosper to the extent they effectively exercise control over tasks and processes. ACOs blur the lines, suggesting that organizations will benefit only when they strive for and achieve both. Moreover, because ACOs, by definition, relate to the common efforts of entities within systems, results can occur only through collaboration. The more consistent the set of procedures, the more likely they can be replicated, and the more known the outcome. This is fundamental to the achievement of high reliability. The area for risk relates to the reliability dimension of empowerment. As systems enlarge and as standardization, by necessity, becomes increasingly widespread, decision-making freedoms at local levels could narrow. Thus, healthcare leaders are encouraged to find ways to ensure that empowerment and efficiency do not manifest in a zero-sum relationship. To the extent this occurs, the organization could prevail with respect to task efficiencies, but it is all the more likely that these will be short-lived and the organization will fail to grow and will lose its edge on productivity.

The literature on continuous quality improvement (CQI) is instructive. CQI evolved from the total quality management movement by underscoring the ongoing nature of improvement processes. Sollecito and Johnson (2013) contend that

Continuous Quality Improvement: Process and People

In health care, CQI is defined as a structured, organizational process involving personnel in planning and executing a continuous flow of improvements to provide quality health care that meets or exceeds expectations. CQI usually involves a common set of characteristics, which include the following:

- A link to key elements of the organization's strategic plan
- A quality council made of up the institution's top leadership
- Training programs for personnel
- Mechanisms for selecting improvement opportunities
- Formation of process improvement teams
- Staff support for process analysis and redesign
- Personnel policies that motivate and support staff participation in process improvement
- Application of the most current and rigorous techniques of the scientific method and statistical process control

---

Data from Sollecito, W., and Johnson, K. (2013). *McLaughlin and Kaluzny's Continuous Quality Improvement in Health Care* (3rd. Ed.). Burlington, MA: Jones & Bartlett Learning.

process improvement cannot be viewed as distinct from the input, efforts, and direct involvement of all levels of staff:

The formation of ACOs comes with additional layers of challenges because the processes cut across various organizations. Differences in culture, organizational complexity, purpose, scope of service, personnel, community served, and history will require considerable leadership attention and creativity to ensure that staff participation serves the goals of empowerment. The guidelines given in the *Continuous Quality Improvement: Process and People* textbox constitute a valuable framework. Creative leaders may employ the establishment of an ACO as an opportunity to organize a common purpose while permitting the individual organizational entities to retain some measure of cultural distinction. This enables the implementation of mechanisms to define, measure, and manage reliability parameters while not choking off the creativity and energy of each entity, the ingredients necessary for organizational motivation.

Conclusion

Many years ago, as the era of modern medicine began—during the transition from the 19th to the 20th century—reliability was loosely associated with a low rate of error, that is, the avoidance of mistakes. Indeed, over the coming decades, as quality assurance became an important guide for hospitals, measures of performance tended to focus on what went wrong. To the extent that providers performed in accordance with standards and protocols, they could claim they were reliable. As time marched on, the limitations of this approach became clear—the avoidance of error does not automatically translate into quality of outcome. Thus, during the period of the 1970s and 1980s, health care began to redefine standards and began to focus more on the particular processes of delivering care. Today, an emerging emphasis on linking quality of outcome to all of the various processes involved in the delivery of care is taking shape. Moreover, as has been demonstrated in this chapter, such links cannot be separated from the broader environment in which care is delivered. If the quality of care is as strong as the weakest link in the chain of providers, then providers must find ways to come together and coordinate efforts more fully than ever before. Technologies such as electronic medical records and health policies such as ACO legislation provide both the means and the impetus, respectively, to foster such cooperation. And yet, the road ahead is uncharted. Leaders of healthcare organizations have a special responsibility for creating a vision for achieving high levels of reliability by harnessing the creativity and productivity of all those who work in their organizations and empowering them to search for ways to enhance quality and efficiency. But they must also look outward, working in tandem with other organizations that provide care and collaborating with them to ensure that they all contribute to the health outcomes that patients deserve. Only by taking a comprehensive and holistic approach to achieving reliability will organizations effectively serve the public trust and be able to take pride in their dedicated efforts to become truly reliable.

Case Study: Process-of-Care Measures

Improvement Strategies of Top-Performing Hospitals

The following synthesis of performance improvement strategies is based on a case study series published on The Commonwealth Fund website, WhyNotTheBest. org. The hospitals profiled in this series were identified based on their performance on the process-of-care measures, or "core measures," reported to the Centers for Medicare and Medicaid Services (CMS). Please see the case studies for a full description of the selection methodology.

The case studies describe the strategies and factors that appear to contribute to performance improvement on the core measures. It is based on information obtained from interviews with key hospital personnel and materials provided by the hospitals.

The hospitals profiled in the case study series are:

▶ Luther Midelfort Mayo Health System, Eau Claire, Wisconsin
▶ Flowers Hospital, Dothan, Alabama
▶ Gaston Memorial Hospital, Gastonia, North Carolina
▶ Oklahoma Heart Hospital, Oklahoma City, Oklahoma
▶ St. Mary's Health Center, Jefferson City, Missouri
▶ NorthShore University Heath System, Evanston, Illinois

(Continues)

"Case Study Series on Process-of-Care Measures: Improvement Strategies of Top-Performing Hospitals", Commonwealth Fund. Reprinted with permission.

Management and culture	Leadership	Dedicate staff time to quality improvement	• 20% of staff time is protected from other responsibilities to develop and test new ideas, supporting a culture of experimentation (Luther Midelfort Mayo Health System).
		Conduct strategic planning	• Strategic planning takes place every 180 days, supported by ongoing data collection, monitoring progress toward goals, and adoption of plans that support the goals (Luther Midelfort Mayo Health System).
		Devote time at board meetings	• 20% of board meetings is reserved for discussions of quality among the whole board, not just a quality subcommittee (Gaston Memorial Hospital).
		Derive momentum from national campaigns	• Participate in a national improvement collaborative, such as those sponsored by the Institute for Healthcare Improvement and the Centers for Medicare and Medicaid Services (Gaston Memorial Hospital).
		Commit resources based on potential to affect quality	• Explicit prioritization of spending based on expectation about the impact on the patient (Oklahoma Heart Hospital).
	Physician engagement	Establish peer-to-peer counseling	• Physicians discuss quality data and performance with peers whose performance does not meet standards (Gaston Memorial Hospital; Flowers Hospital; St. Mary's Health Center). • Reinforcement of performance goals through personal feedback (Flowers Hospital).
		Review variances at a high level	• Medical staff has a peer review committee to review variation from practice standards and present findings to all physicians (St. Mary's Health Center).

		Urge adoption of practice standards	• The president and the board provide direction to the entire medical staff about the importance of adopting standards of practice related to core measures (St. Mary's Health Center).
		Make core measures part of physician credentialing	• As one of the criteria for physician credentialing, performance on core measures is assessed (St. Mary's Health Center).
		Facilitate communication between physicians and CMS	• Doctors address questions about the quality measures and receive responses directly from CMS through the QualityNet website (NorthShore University Health System).
		Appoint physicians to lead improvement committees	• Using physicians to lead teams not only provides clinical expertise, but helps build support for implementing needed changes (St. Mary's Health Center). • Involve hospitalists in care map and order set design to ensure physician buy-in (Gaston Memorial Hospital).
Clinical staff engagement		Designate case managers to attend to discharge measures	• Designated discharge care managers focus on getting each patient the correct discharge instructions and follow-up appointments (NorthShore University Health System).
		Establish pharmacist review of drug-related protocols	• Pharmacists review prescribing decisions throughout patients' hospitalizations to address problems or deviations from standards directly with doctors (NorthShore University Health System).
		Create interdisciplinary teams of caregivers	• With doctors, nurses, pharmacists, and others involved in the care process at the table, it is possible to avoid surprises or slips later (Gaston Memorial Hospital).

(Continues)

		Appoint process improvement team to coordinate changes	• A designated process improvement team can provide the expertise in process redesign, complementing the work of the clinical performance improvement team (Luther Midelfort Mayo Health System). The team can also coordinate the staging of all improvement efforts so as not to overload any particular area (Luther Midelfort Mayo Health System).
		Provide quality improvement education to clinical staff	• Nurses, doctors, and pharmacists are trained in ways to improve care (NorthShore University Health System).
		Support favorable nurse–patient ratios	• Most hospitals agree adequate staffing is important to quality care. Oklahoma Heart Hospital makes it one of its core strategies (Oklahoma Heart Hospital).
	Motivating staff	System and regional benchmarking	• Hospitals compare their performance with other hospitals in their system, region, or peer group to instigate competition and motivate improvement (Luther Midelfort Mayo Health System; St. Mary's Health Center; Gaston Memorial Hospital). • Use of performance data to highlight practice variations within the hospital (Gaston Memorial Hospital).
		Discuss performance data	• Display and discuss data throughout the hospital to create transparency and accountability (St. Mary's Health Center). • Discuss and display data weekly, even for a small number of patients, to focus staff attention (Luther Midelfort Mayo Health System).

		Celebrate successes	• Use newsletters, meetings, and positive feedback to recognize good results (Flowers Hospital).
Monitoring and Measurement	**Monitoring adherence to standards**	Perform a daily audit or concurrent review of care	• Every hospital in this series has a method of auditing the achievement of care standards on a daily basis—giving them time to intervene if they find deficiencies (For example, see Flowers Hospital; St. Mary's Health Center; NorthShore University Health System; Luther Midelfort Mayo Health System). • Bed management rounding is a process during which care is monitored and the status of patients is recorded (NorthShore University Health System).
	Electronic monitoring systems	Feed data from electronic health records into real-time census tracker	• One hospital has simplified the daily audit by using a data feed out of the electronic health record as a real-time census tracker, with all the core measures included (NorthShore University Health System).
		Reconcile medication	• To discharge the patient with the correct medications, one hospital performs daily medication reconciliation to ensure a complete record is available whenever discharge is scheduled (Flowers Hospital).
	Use of data to benchmark and motivate	System and regional benchmarking	• Hospitals compare their performance with other hospitals in their system, region, or peer group to instigate competition and motivate improvement (Luther Midelfort Mayo Health System; St. Mary's Health Center; Gaston Memorial Hospital).

(Continues)

		Discuss performance data	• Display and discuss data throughout the hospital to create transparency and accountability (St. Mary's Health Center). • Provide individualized feedback to physicians with scores compared with benchmarks (St. Mary's Health Center). • Discuss and display data weekly, even for a small number of patients, to focus staff attention (Luther Midelfort Mayo Health System).
Problem Identification and Solving	**improvement infrastructure**	Support staff with a central quality department	• Every hospital in this series has staff with expertise in quality measurement and improvement. Centralized quality departments can play an important role in supporting teams (Luther Midelfort Mayo Health System).
	Improvement methods	Use the plan-do-check-act cycle	• Hospitals have adopted similar quality improvement methods. The Plan-Do-Check-Act strategy is a favorite at Luther Midelfort Mayo Health System.
		Support continuous quality improvement	• Ongoing examination and improvement of care processes (Oklahoma Heart Hospital).
Practice Improvements	**Standardizing care**	Have physicians create care maps	• Physician involvement in the design of care maps ensures buy-in and clinical relevance (NorthShore University Health System, Gaston Memorial Hospital).
		Explore the evidence base	• Even if physicians don't write the care map themselves, showing them the medical evidence in support of it increases buy-in (St. Mary's Health Center.

		Place care map in medical record	• Having the care map in the medical record has helped physicians adhere to the plan (NorthShore University Health System).
		Use care map to define what data are collected	• Measures should be closely aligned with processes in order to affect the outcomes desired (Luther Midelfort Mayo Health System).
		Align order sheets with care map	• Designing order sets so that the easy approach is the right approach is a core tenet of human factors engineering (Luther Midelfort Mayo Health System).
		Align progress notes with care map	• Physician-designed progress notes with check-offs of relevant criteria provide physicians with a useful reminder of the decisions embedded in the care map; pre-printed orders complement this tool (Flowers Hospital; St. Mary's Health Center; Oklahoma Heart Hospital).
		Use color-coded nursing materials	• Each of the four HQA conditions is given a color; care plans, file labels, and educational materials are color- coded to make them easy to find and use (Flowers Hospital).
	Electronic support systems	Use computerized physician order entry	• When a physician orders care not aligned with the care map, a prompt lets him/her know. The prompt can educate and lead to immediate improvement in care (Oklahoma Heart Hospital; NorthShore).

(Continues)

		Use Web-based decision tools	• Nurses respond to a series of questions to guide them toward a decision about whether to order a vaccination (NorthShore University Health System).
		Build electronic checklists	• An electronic checklist can generate a flowchart to guide care decisions (NorthShore University Health System).
		Create opportunities for feedback	• Information can flow from clinician to administration electronically, giving frontline staff the opportunity to express quality-related concerns that will be addressed quickly by quality improvement staff (Oklahoma Heart Hospital).

This study was based on publicly available information and self-reported data provided by the study institution(s). The Commonwealth Fund is not an accreditor of healthcare organizations or systems, and the inclusion of an institution in the Fund's case studies series is not an endorsement by the Fund for receipt of health care from the institution.

The aim of Commonwealth Fund sponsored case studies of this type is to identify institutions that have achieved results indicating high performance in a particular area of interest, have undertaken innovations designed to reach higher performance, or exemplify attributes that can foster high performance. The studies are intended to enable other institutions to draw lessons from the studied institutions' experience that will be helpful in their own efforts to become high performers. It is important to note, however, that even the best-performing organizations may fall short in some areas; doing well in one dimension of quality does not necessarily mean that the same level of quality will be achieved in other dimensions. Similarly, performance may vary from one year to the next. Thus, it is critical to adopt systematic approaches for improving quality and preventing harm to patients and staff.

Source: Meyer, 2008.

Review Questions

Many hospitals have undertaken comprehensive approaches in their quest to achieve high levels of reliability. As you review the chapter, consider these questions:

1. If you were to generate a report card for your organization, how would you rate its performance in each of the areas? Identify strengths and areas for improvement.
2. How effective is your organization with respect to empowering staff, measuring quality, evaluating efficiency, and managing relations with other providers and stakeholders? What gaps exist between where your organization is and where you would like it to be? What is the responsibility of leadership with respect to narrowing those gaps?
3. Which of the activities identified in the case study on process-of-care measures can be pursued most quickly by your organization? What are the obstacles to getting started? How can those obstacles be overcome?
4. In becoming a highly reliable organization, how capable is your organization in resolving any tensions between providing quality care and achieving organizational efficiencies?

References

A quick glance at Mariano Rivera's awesome start to the season. (2013, May 13). Retrieved from http://itsaboutthemoney.net/archives/2013/05/20/a-quick-glance-at-mariano-riveras-awesome-start-to-the-season/

American Hospital Association. (2011). *Workforce roles in a redesigned primary care model* [White paper]. Retrieved from http://www.aha.org/content/13/13-0110-wf-primary-care.pdf

Apker, J. (2001). Role development in the managed care era: A case in hospital-based nursing. *Journal of Applied Communication Research, 29*(2), 117–136.

Baker, D. P., Day, R., & Salas, E. (2006). Teamwork as an essential component of high-reliability organizations. *Health Services Research, 41*(4 Part 2), 1576–1598.

Belasen, A. T. (2008). *The theory and practice of corporate communication: A competing values perspective.* Thousand Oaks, CA: Sage.

Chant, C., Smith, O. M., Marshall, J. C., & Friedrich, J. O. (2011). Relationship of catheter-associated urinary tract infection to mortality and length of stay in critically ill patients: A systematic review and meta-analysis of observational studies. *Critical Care Medicine, 39*(5), 1167–1173.

Center for Transforming Healthcare (2013). *Facts about the joint commission center for transforming healthcare.* Retrieved from http://www.centerfortransforminghealthcare.org/about/default.aspx

Cohen, B. (2010, June 18) *Mariano Rivera, the most reliable man in the world.* Retrieved from http://www.pinstripedbible.com/2010/6/18/1524029/mariano-rivera-the-most-reliable

Cooley-Dickinson. (2013). Evidence-based health: The new paradigm? [Web log] Retrieved from http://www.cooley-dickinson.org/main/cmoblog/evidencebased_health_the_new_paradigm_236.aspx

Creswell, J., & Abelson, R. (2013, August 13). New laws and rising costs create a surge of supersizing hospitals. *The New York Times*, D1.

DiazGranados, D., Klein, C., Salas, E., Le, H., Burke, C., Lyons, R., & Goodwin, G. (2008). *Does team building work?* Paper presented at the 23rd Annual Conference of the Society for Industrial and Organizational Psychology, San Francisco, CA, April 2008.

Dulworth, S., & Pyenson, B. (2004). Healthcare-associated infections and length of hospital stay in the Medicare population. *American Journal of Medical Quality*, *19*(3), 121–127.

Durbin, D. (2013, October 28). Lexus, Toyota top auto reliability survey. *Associated Press*. Retrieved from http://bigstory.ap.org/article/audi-gmc-volvo-crack-reliability-survey-top-10

Gass, R., & Seiter, J. (2010). *Persuasion, social influence, and compliance gaining* (4th ed.). Boston, MA: Pearson.

George, M., (2002). *Lean Six Sigma: Combining six sigma quality with lean production speed*. New York, NY: McGraw-Hill.

Gold, J. (2013). FAQ on ACOs: Accountable care organizations, explained. *Kaiser Health News*. Retrieved from http://www.kaiserhealthnews.org/stories/2011/january/13/aco-accountable-care-organization-faq.aspx

Helmstetter, K. (2012). What happens during a medical emergency at Disney World? *Touring Plans.com* [Web log]. Retrieved from http://blog.touringplans.com/2012/03/14/what-happens-during-a-medical-emergency-at-disney-world/

Hovland, C., Janis, I., & Kelly, H. (1953). *Communication and persuasion*. New Haven, CT: Yale University Press.

JCAHO (2012). Proceedings of the 5th International High Reliability Conference. Hosted by The Joint Commission, Chicago, IL, May 21–23, 2012. Retrieved from http://www.jointcommission.org/assets/1/18/HRO_Conf_Proceedings_6_27_12.pdf

The Joint Commission (2013a, February). *The Joint Commission history*. Retrieved from http://www.jointcommission.org/assets/1/6/Joint_Commission_History.pdf

The Joint Commission (2013b, February). *Center for transforming healthcare, SCHA team up to make health care more reliable*. Retrieved from http://www.pwrnewmedia.com/2013/joint_commission/south_carolina_safe_care/

Klein, C., Salas, E., DiazGranados D., Burke, C. S., Stagl, K. C., & Goodwin, G. F. (2008). *Do team training interventions enhance valued team outcomes? A meta-analytic initiative*. Paper presented at the 23rd Annual Conference of the Society for Industrial and Organizational Psychology, San Francisco, CA, April 2008.

Kohn, L. T., Corrigan, J. M., & Donaldson, M. S. (Eds.). (1999). *To err is human: Building a safer health system*. Committee on Quality of Health Care in America, Institute of Medicine. Washington, DC: National Academy Press. Retrieved from http://wps.pearsoneducation.nl/wps/media/objects/13902/14236351/H%2007_To%20Err%20Is%20Human.pdf

Landrigan, C. P., Parry, G. J., Bones, C. B., Hackbarth, A. D., Goldmann, D. A., & Sharek, P. J. (2010). Temporal trends in rates of patient harm resulting from medical care. *New England Journal of Medicine*, *363*(22), 2124–2134.

Larsen, C. U. (2010). *Persuasion: Reception and responsibility* (12th ed.). Boston, MA: Wadsworth, Cengage.

Lilly, C. M., Cody, S., Huifang, Z., Landry, K., Baker, S. P., McIlwaine, J., . . . Irwin, R. S. (2011). Hospital mortality, length of stay, and preventable complications among critically ill patients before and after tele-icu reengineering of critical care processes. *Journal of the American Medical Association, 305*(21), 2175–2183.

May, E. L. (2013). The power of zero: Steps toward high reliability healthcare. *Healthcare Executive, 28*(2), 16–26.

Meyer, J. (2008, December). Gaston Memorial Hospital: Driving quality improvement with data, guidelines, and real-time feedback. *Commonwealth Fund, 1195*(3). Retrieved from http://whynotthebest.org/contents/view/38

Moskowitz, D., & Bodenheimer, T. (2011). Moving from evidence-based medicine to evidence-based health. *Journal of General Internal Medicine, 26*(6), 658–660.

Mouawad, J., & Drew, C. (2013, February 11). Airline industry at its safest since the dawn of the jet age. *The New York Times*, A1.

Olney, B. (2004, June 28). The confidence man: Inside the mind of baseball's greatest closer, Mariano Rivera. *New York Magazine*. Retrieved from http://nymag.com/nymetro/news/sports/features/9375/

O'Reilly, K. B. (2011, April 18). One in 3 patients harmed in hospital stay. *American Medical News*. Retrieved from http://www.amednews.com/article/20110418/profession/304189940/2/

Packer-Tursman, J. (2014, July 18). 1,000 deaths a day: Senate hearing blasts hospitals for unsafe care. Healthcare DIVE. Retrieved from http://www.healthcaredive.com/news/1000-deaths-a-day-senate-hearing-blasts-hospitals-for-unsafe-care/287694/

Pornpitakpan, C. (2004). The persuasiveness of source credibility: A critical review of five decades' evidence. *Journal of Applied Social Psychology, 34*(2), 243–281.

Prager, J. (2013, June 30). A singular pitcher. *New York Times*, SS1.

Pronovost, P. J., Berenholtz, S. M., Goeschel, C. A., Needham, D. M., Sexton, J. B., Thompson, D. A., . . . Hunt, E. (2006). Creating high reliability in health care organizations. *Health Services Research, 41*(4 Part 2), 1599–1617.

Rau, J. (2012). Medicare to penalize 2,217 hospitals for excess readmissions. *Kaiser Health News*. Retrieved from http://www.kaiserhealthnews.org/Stories/2012/August/13/medicare-hospitals-readmissions-penalties.aspx

Reinard, J. C. (1988). The empirical study of the persuasive effects of evidence: The status after fifty years of research. *Human Communication Research, 15*(1), 3–59.

Reinersten, J. L., & Clancy, C. (2006). Foreword to 'keeping our promises: research, practice, and policy issues in health care reliability.' *Health Services Research, 41*(4 Part 2), 1535–1538.

Roberts, K. H., & Rousseau, D. M. (1989). Research in nearly failure-free, high-reliability organizations: Having the bubble. *IEEE Transactions on Engineering Management, 36*(2), 132–139.

Salas, E., DiazGranados, D., Weaver, S.J., & King, H. (2008). Does team training work? Principles for health care. *Academic Emergency Medicine, 15*(11), 1002–1009.

Sollecito, W., & Johnson, K. (2013). *McLaughlin and Kaluzny's continuous quality improvement in health care*. Burlington, MA: Jones & Bartlett.

Vincent, J-L., Rello, J., Marshall, J., Silva, E., Anzueto, A., Martin, C. D., . . . Reinhart, K. (2009). International study of the prevalence and outcomes of infection in intensive care units. *Journal of the American Medical Association, 302*(21), 2323–2329.

Zajac, A. (2012). Airline crash deaths too few to make new safety rules pay. *Bloomberg News.* Retrieved from http://www.bloomberg.com/news/2012-06-25/airline-crash-deaths-too-few-to-make-new-safety-rules-pay.html

CHAPTER 5 ▶

Leading the Value-Based Organization: Championing Quality and Improving Safety

LEARNING OBJECTIVES

Students will be able to:

- Identify and describe drivers of healthcare quality improvements
- Understand the importance of data and measurements in monitoring quality care
- Learn about the new CMS regulatory requirements and scoring systems
- Identify clinical processes and patient experiences as indicators for hospital compliance
- Describe the links between quality, efficiency, and financial outcomes
- Identify tools of quality control and quality management
- Understand the role of leadership in championing quality care processes and patient safety initiatives

How Quickly the World Has Changed

Dr. Joseph Martin, Sr. beamed as his son, Dr. Joseph Martin, Jr., shared the news that he was joining a highly regarded internal medicine practice. This was his first position following a 2-year residency in a large Los Angeles hospital. Joe Sr. lived in the Midwest and had been practicing internal medicine for 35 years.

Jr. indulged his father as he began to reminisce about his early days as a physician. "They really were the 'good old days,'" he insisted. "You got to know your patients.

Practices were smaller, usually with just one physician. Paperwork wasn't so complicated. Patients could see specialists when they needed to without all the red tape. I did rounds at the hospital and ordered tests without having to persuade a third party that it was necessary. It was better for everybody."

Jr. jumped in: "Yes, but how do you know that each test was necessary? And how did you know how each patient's outcome fared against a population of patients with the same diagnosis and same treatment?"

"Because I got to know all my patients very well. I knew their habits, their families, their jobs, their lives. If they had a problem with the hospital or their treatment, they told me about it," Sr. replied.

Jr. shared his views: "I agree about the importance of the patient–physician relationship, but don't you think it is important to hold all practitioners accountable for their work? There are close to a million physicians in the country. How can we develop best practice models if we don't have benchmarks and a huge database of outcomes? And shouldn't we ask patients themselves about their experience with their providers? Won't this help each organization improve?"

"Of course," Sr. responded. "But accountability should not come at the expense of the physician's role."

Jr. observed, "I agree. And the physician's role and the hospital's role will be stronger if it can be demonstrated that the work contributed to a good outcome *and* that the patient had a favorable experience. If that happens, the patient will be more likely to comply with treatment plans. Accumulating data about the physician's work and the patient's impressions of his care doesn't interfere with the good practice. It helps us all understand what good practice is. I don't think this is any different from when you entered medicine. You were far more accountable than the previous generation of physicians. Even something like needing a referral for a specialist, however imperfect the system, was a step toward making us all more accountable. And patient surveys were getting routine even back then. Now the HCAHPS are adding incentives. And value-based purchasing means that hospitals will have to show they do quality work, and not just get paid based on the quantity of tests and procedures."

"Lots of changes, and for reasons that make sense. I just hope the implementation of all this doesn't add more bureaucracy," Sr. noted.

"I agree," Jr. said. "There is a lot to adjust to. How do we make it all work so that it is meaningful and not just more red tape?"

"I have to give credit to the leadership of the hospital where I first started," Sr. recalled. "She got everyone involved in quality initiatives and formed a physician council to make sure our input was included. She also made sure to get input from every person who worked in the hospital. The program belonged to everyone, not just her."

"Implementing these changes will require strong leadership. But if we see something we think can be improved, then we have an obligation to add our voice," Jr. said.

"I guess there has to be a 'leader' in all of us if this movement toward accountability and value-based medicine is going to work," Sr. concluded.

Introduction

Healthcare organizations must change the way care is delivered. The traditional separation between clinical practices and administrative functions has given rise to silos, miscommunications, lack of integration, and rewards for inefficiency. Financially, the reimbursement program by which hospitals get paid based on quantity, diagnosis, and intervention procedures has given hospitals incentives to render services and receive payments, often regardless of quality. Technologically, most hospitals in the United States are challenged to acquire and install electronic health record (EHR) systems (Charles, King, Patel, & Furukawa, 2013). These information systems, also called electronic medical record (EMR) systems, are used by by hospitals and healthcare providers to track clinical records of patients. However, infrastructure cost and the challenges associated with installing, maintaining, and updating them as well as concerns about the privacy and security of electronic health information prevent many hospitals from optimizing their EHR or EMR systems (Nass, Levit, & Gostin, 2009). Many medical boards do not accept responsibilities over adverse or preventable events. Physicians, too, are not aware that they need to report an event—even when there has been no serious harm to the patient. Typically, they fix the problem and move on, unable to realize that they have the responsibility to monitor quality of care or establish standards (Dlugacz, 2010).

Safety seems to have low priority when volume and bottom line are pressing. In 1999, a seminal study sponsored by the Institute of Medicine estimated that medical errors contributed to 44,000 to 98,000 deaths of hospitalized patients annually, and that deaths resulting from medical errors surpassed the number of deaths related to breast cancer, the eighth leading cause of death in the United States (Institute of Medicine, 2001). Furthermore, 90% of errors were due to mishaps caused by broken systems and, to a lesser degree, human error. Malpractice lawsuits due to errors in the process of care continue to escalate (Studdert, Mello, & Brennan, 2004).

In a review of more than 350 trial, appellate, and Supreme Court case summaries between 1995 and 2001 (253 cases were included in the actual investigation), Croke (2003) identified six key areas for nursing negligence or failure. The greatest frequency of reported cases of negligence occurred in acute care hospitals (60%). These areas included:

1. **Not following standards of care.** Standards of care are derived from sources such as state boards of nursing, professional nursing associations, hospital policies and procedures, and the guidelines of federal organizations and the Centers for Medicare and Medicaid Services.
2. **Misuse of equipment.** Nurses must know the safety features, capabilities, and limitations of any equipment they use, as well as its hazards. Nurses must follow the manufacturers' usage recommendations and refrain from modifying the equipment.

3. **Inadequate communication.** Vital aspects of communication besides timeliness in reporting the change include persistence in notifying the physician of the change and accuracy in communicating the nature and degree of the change.

4. **Poor documentation.** Documentation, the purpose of which is primarily to communicate patient information among providers, must accurately reflect the nursing process, showing evidence of nursing assessment and diagnosis, planning for nursing intervention, implementation and evaluation of planned interventions, and patient response.

5. **Insufficient assessment and monitoring.** A nurse's accuracy in assessing and monitoring and timely reporting of changes in health status to a physician can often mean the difference between life and death.

6. **Not acting as a patient advocate.** Nurses are compelled to strive for excellent care of patients and the inclusion of their rights in today's healthcare system.

Transforming Health Care and Barriers to Change

Healthcare organizations are in the midst of a major transformation, and healthcare leaders must act quickly on the issue of quality care and patient safety. The traditional tension between cost and quality as mutually exclusive categories is quickly dissipating. Quality care is increasingly linked to, not separate from, efficiency, cost reduction, and optimal utilization of resources. Healthcare quality care programs and metrics are increasingly influenced by financial incentives and measured by state-of-the-art scientific tools and sophisticated methodologies. Moreover, quality programs increasingly influence the way healthcare institutions organize, coordinate, and control workflow processes, and such programs are prompting them to strengthen the participatory nature of the work environment, integrate consumer feedback in quality indices, establish zero-error-rate goals, and foster a commitment to continuous improvement. The broad exposure to quality and safety metrics, implementation of standardized clinical processes, immediate feedback via EMR and patient surveys that track performance outcomes, periodic feedback to clinicians about compliance, continuing training and education, and transparency in communication build a foundation in the art and science of quality and safety that goes beyond measuring and reporting. As patients demand higher quality and more accountability, healthcare organizations are being transformed to ingrain a culture of delivering quality care.

The implications for those who lead healthcare organizations are dramatic. Increasingly, continuous quality improvement programs in hospitals have been demonstrating that improved quality and lower costs go hand in hand, mainly because inefficiency leads to both higher costs and to poor health outcomes. Idiosyncratic practices, however, are often to blame. For example, the Clinical Quality and Patient Safety Survey that was conducted by the HealthLeaders Media Council in April 2013 reveals that only 60% of the respondents cite significant or moderate improvement due to implementation of EMRs. Moreover, only 47%

expect to increase spending on clinical decision support as part of their investment in quality and safety. The stumbling blocks mentioned most frequently as standing in the way of effective patient safety programs were fear of punishment for self-reporting errors (35%) and fear of retaliation for reporting the errors of others (also 35%). The survey included 339 healthcare providers across the United States with 35% senior leaders, 32% operations leaders, 26% clinical leaders, 6% finance leaders, and 1% information leaders with hospitals and health systems consisting of the majority (73%) of the type of organizations surveyed (HealthLeaders Media, 2013).

Accountable Care Organizations (ACOs) are taking both clinical effectiveness and resource efficiency into account. ACOs are networks of coordinated healthcare organizations characterized by a payment and care delivery model (e.g., capitation, fee-for-service) that seeks to tie provider reimbursements to quality metrics and reductions in the total cost of patient care. The ACO is accountable to the patients and the third-party payer for the quality, suitability, and efficiency of the health care provided. According to the Centers for Medicare and Medicaid Services (CMS), an ACO is "an organization of healthcare providers that agrees to be accountable for the quality, cost, and overall care of Medicare beneficiaries who are enrolled in the traditional fee-for-service program who are assigned to it" (Centers for Medicare and Medicaid Services [CMS], n.d.a).

The next sections in this chapter reinforce principles and practices described in previous chapters of this text along a central theme—successful healthcare organizations embrace the emerging quality mindset through the following:

- ▶ A paradigm shift from historically top-down and silo structures to continuous learning organizations
- ▶ The critical role played by responsible middle managers as communication conduits and important intermediaries between a more involved workforce and senior-level decision makers
- ▶ An understanding by leadership that the perspectives of multiple stakeholders (e.g., patients, staff, regulators) must be integrated in executive decision processes
- ▶ The notion that work processes will be evaluated by ever-improving IT systems and sophisticated sets of decision support systems (DSS)
- ▶ The idea that decision making will increasingly incorporate evidence and comparative effectiveness data
- ▶ Recognition that constructive engagement of care partners will become more and more vital
- ▶ An awareness of the importance of quality and safety outside hospitals, including outpatient and ambulatory care, to ensure compliance
- ▶ The relationship between quality metrics and patient satisfaction measures such as HCAHPS
- ▶ The importance of quality to marketing and reputation, given that consumers recognize quality (and the lack thereof), and quality scorecards will soon become more available to consumers

Strategy for Reinventing the System

In March 2001, the Institute of Medicine (IOM), an arm of the National Academy of Sciences, released its report entitled *Crossing the Quality Chasm: A New Health System for the 21st Century*. The IOM's Committee on Quality of Health Care in America, which authored the report, concluded that merely making incremental improvements in current systems of care would not suffice (Institute of Medicine, 2001). The report focuses more broadly on how the health system can be reinvented to foster innovation and improve the delivery of care. Toward this goal, the committee identified six aims for improvement in the quality of care:

- ▶ **Safe.** Avoiding injuries to patients from the care that is meant to help them
- ▶ **Effective.** Providing services based on scientific knowledge to all who could benefit, and refraining from providing services to those not likely to benefit
- ▶ **Patient-centered.** Providing care that is respectful of and responsive to individual patient preferences, needs, and values, and ensuring that patient values guide all clinical decisions
- ▶ **Timely.** Reducing waits and potentially harmful delays both for those who receive and those who give care
- ▶ **Efficient.** Avoiding waste, including waste of equipment, supplies, ideas, and energy
- ▶ **Equitable.** Providing care that does not vary in quality because of personal characteristics such as gender, ethnicity, geographic location, and socio-economic status

A healthcare system that achieves major gains in these six areas would be far better at meeting patient needs. Patients would experience care that is safer, more reliable, more responsive to their needs, more integrated, and more available, and they could count on receiving the full array of preventive, acute, and chronic services that are likely to prove beneficial. Clinicians and other health workers also would benefit through their increased satisfaction at being better able to do their jobs and thereby bring improved health, greater longevity, less pain and suffering, and increased personal productivity to those who receive their care.

Why Can't We Just Make Health Care Better?

Everyone recognizes that the healthcare system in the United States is not as safe, effective, patient-centered, timely, efficient, and equitable as we would like. So why can't we just change it? Why has it been so hard to make healthcare organizations better, to have them achieve these goals, despite everybody's desire to do so?

Many observers—doctors, administrators, researchers, and scholars—have wondered the same thing, and they all come to the same conclusions: the system works exactly as it has been designed to work, and the players in the system have little incentive to change. Here are some common themes among the discussions about these problems:

▶ **Fee-for-service.** As one hospital CEO put it, "If you pay for clicks, you get clicks." Rewards go to those who produce higher patient volumes. From a business perspective, this means competing more effectively for patients, growing your practice or hospital, and increasing market share. From a quality perspective, there is a valid argument that the more procedures a doctor performs every year, the better the quality and the more favorable the outcomes. So strong incentives exist to build volumes.

▶ **Silo mentality.** Health care is delivered by physicians who work as specialists, seeing the patients who present with conditions they are trained to understand and to treat. For example, gastroenterologists treat patients with swallowing difficulty, stomach pain, bowel obstructions, and a range of other conditions that affect their digestive systems, and they are experts at it. Often, their patients' symptoms are difficult to diagnose, and it takes a great deal of specialized expertise to figure out what is wrong and what to do about it. Christensen, Grossman, and Hwang (2009) term this a *solution shop* activity, meaning that the efforts of the specialty organization focus around determining the problem (diagnosis) and prescribing a solution. Once a doctor has effectively treated a patient, the job is finished because the problem is solved. However, one specialist treating one patient for one condition at one point in time seldom solves the problem. As Porter and Lee (2013) note, due to medical progress, many previously untreatable diseases are now treatable, and patients show up with multiple conditions that require different types of clinicians to work together to deliver state-of-the-art care. Diabetes is a classic example, because these patients might need care from physicians trained in endocrinology, nephrology, cardiology, vascular surgery, ophthalmology, podiatry, and primary care.

▶ **Lack of teamwork.** Despite the need to work together as a team for the good of the patient, the silo mentality has perpetuated a cultural tradition that revolves around the individual, independent doctor acting pretty much alone. According to the Institute of Medicine (2001, p. 1):

> The healthcare delivery system . . . is poorly organized to meet the challenges at hand. The delivery of care often is overly complex and uncoordinated, requiring steps and patient 'hand-offs' that slow down care and decrease rather than improve safety. These cumbersome processes waste resources; leave unaccountable voids in coverage; lead to loss of information; and fail to build on the strengths of all health professionals involved to ensure that care is appropriate, timely, and safe. Organizational problems are particularly apparent regarding chronic conditions. The fact that more than 40% of people with chronic conditions have more than one such condition argues strongly for more sophisticated mechanisms to coordinate care. Yet healthcare organizations, hospitals, and physician groups typically

operate as separate silos, acting without the benefit of complete information about the patient's condition, medical history, services provided in other settings, or medications provided by other clinicians.

In his address to the 2011 graduating class at Harvard Medical School entitled "Cowboys and Pit Crews," Atul Gawande (2011) likened traditional medical practice to the American cowboy culture, with the heroic cowboy taking center stage. In contrast, Gawande used the example of a pit crew, which operates as a highly coordinated team, each with specialized functions, working as quickly and efficiently as possible to achieve a common goal. Furthermore, many physicians perceive themselves as independent business owners whose responsibilities include achieving a positive return each year. They are not paid to coordinate and integrate patient care, so they see little advantage to cooperating with others. This makes it very difficult to integrate patient care across specialties or disciplines.

► **Cross-subsidies in reimbursement.** Many hospitals lose money on at least some of the services they provide, so they must make losses up somewhere else. Some services are lucrative, while others are losers. Lucrative services such as orthopedic surgery, cardiology, bariatric surgery, radiology, and oncology subsidize services whose revenues fall below their costs. The latter group includes mental health, which usually tops the list of unprofitable services. This has resulted in overinvestment in the lucrative services, as well as kicking off fierce competition for patients as overcapacity has resulted in many markets. While some health systems use high-margin services to cross-subsidize the money-losers, others simply shut down service lines that are not well reimbursed, leaving those patients to fend for themselves. Of course, the overcapacity that results from overbuilding the lucrative service lines means that many (if not most) providers do not achieve enough patient volume to achieve scale at a level that allows them to provide highest quality and lowest cost care (Christensen et al., 2009).

► **Outcomes and cost-effectiveness data.** Providers, payers, and administrators lack good information about patient outcomes relative to the cost of care. As Porter and Lee (2013, p. 3) observe, "There is also a near complete absence of data on the true costs of care for a patient with a particular condition over the full care cycle, crippling efforts to improve value." Despite many calls for doctors to use evidence-based medicine to make treatment decisions, there is insufficient information on the cost side of the equation. Those involved in patient care do not know how much things cost, nor how those costs relate to the patient outcomes. Thus, it is impossible to develop estimates of cost-effectiveness or to allocate resources to the most effective options.

These problems are deeply entrenched in the system, and because they benefit important constituencies who are reluctant to see things change, the goals of safe, effective, patient-centered, timely, efficient, and equitable care will likely prove elusive for some time.

The Centers for Medicare and Medicaid Services

Healthcare leaders and decision makers know what to do to bring about change and improve the quality of care and patient safety. However, as Dlugacz (2010) observed, they are faced with systemic barriers (i.e., cultural, structural, technological, financial) or lack the knowledge of how to operationalize improvements. Safe working environments and quality care are built on open communication, joint accountability, trained capacity, adequate resources, and optimal infrastructure that allow clinicians to provide care successfully and consistently. The aviation industry, for example, has created a culture of safety by closely monitoring the number of hours logged by pilots, redesigning systems, and promoting interprofessional collaboration to prevent errors. Because self-regulation provides insufficient oversight within hospitals, external regulation was needed as a driver of change to promote quality and safety and guard against suboptimization. Determined to improve how patient care services are rendered, government agencies have taken an increased role in monitoring, evaluating, and rewarding hospitals.

Recently, the CMS, an agency within the US Department of Health and Human Services responsible for reimbursing hospitals, has shifted its focus to rewarding value and penalizing poor care. With the passage of the Health Information Technology for Economic and Clinical Health (HITECH) Act on February 17, 2009, the CMS has been charged with several key tasks for advancing health information technology, including implementation of EHR incentive programs, providing a definition for the meaningful use of certified EHR technology, drafting standards for the certification of EHR technology, and updating the health information privacy and security regulations under the Health Insurance Portability and Accountability Act of 1996 (HIPAA). Much of this work is being done in conjunction with the Office of the National Coordinator for Health IT (ONC).

The HITECH Act was created to stimulate the adoption of EHRs and supporting technology in the United States. President Obama signed the HITECH Act into law as part of the American Recovery and Reinvestment Act of 2009 (ARRA), an economic stimulus bill ("What Is HITECH Act?" 2009). An EHR or EMR (electronic medical record) is an official health record for an individual that is shared among multiple facilities and agencies. Digitized health information systems are expected to improve efficiency and quality of care and, ultimately, reduce costs ("What Is Electronic Health Record?" 2011).

In 2011, healthcare providers were offered financial incentives for demonstrating meaningful use of EHRs. The Act also established grants for training centers for the personnel required to support a health IT infrastructure (Bostick, Crayton, Fishman, Peters, & Smith, 2011). Achieving meaningful use also helps determine whether an organization will receive payments from the federal government under either the Medicare EHR Incentive Program or the Medicaid EMR Incentive Program. Incentives will be offered until 2015, after which time penalties may be levied for failing to demonstrate such use. To receive the maximum reimbursement, physicians and hospitals needed to achieve stage 1 of meaningful use of standardized EHR for at least a 90-day period during the 2011 or 2012 federal fiscal year and then for the entire year thereafter. Healthcare providers must demonstrate meaningful use of a certified EHR system by 2016 in order to qualify for financial incentives under the HITECH Act.

The CMS collaborates with the ONC and other units of the Department of Health and Human Services (HHS) to establish regulations for stage 1 of the meaningful use incentive program. In 2012, the criteria for stage 2 (which will begin in 2014) and stage 3 of meaningful use were established (Centers for Medicare and Medicaid Services, 2013a).

Office of the National Coordinator for Health Information Technology

The ONC is a function within the HHS. It was created by Executive Order in 2004 and written into legislation by the HITECH Act. The ONC's mission is to promote a national health IT infrastructure and oversee its development including policy coordination, strategic planning for the adoption of health IT and health information exchanges (HIE), and establishing governance for the Nationwide Health Information Network ("What is health information exchange?" 2010). The objectives are to improve the quality of health care while reducing costs; improve the coordination of care and information among hospitals, labs, physicians, and other healthcare organizations; ensure that personal health records (PHR) remain secure; and promote the early detection, prevention, and management of chronic illness ("What is personal health record?" 2010).

Linking financial rewards to compliance with quality indicators reinforces the vitality of quality control, increases efficiency, improves patient safety, and reduces the costs of unnecessary errors. Furthermore, if poor performance and errors are reduced, the costs of detection, rework, and unnecessary complexity are also reduced, giving greater attention to investments in patient care and patient safety. Healthcare providers will also benefit from positive public image, favorable stakeholder evaluation, better performance credibility, and, ultimately, increased patient satisfaction, trust, and organizational reputation. Quality management is also helpful in educating the board and organizational leadership in understanding public scorecards and in providing reliable and valid information to stakeholders.

Additionally, in response to the HITECH Act, the ONC is reviewing proposals for the formation of up to 70 Regional Extension Centers (RECs) that will receive federal funding to help hospitals and community clinics transition from paper-based to EMR systems.

The Patient Protection and Affordable Care Act

The Patient Protection and Affordable Care Act of 2010 gave CMS the power to base a portion of hospital reimbursement payments on how well hospitals perform in 20 core measures. The law requires CMS to establish a value-based purchasing (VBP) program that rewards hospitals for quality of care based on their "achievement" or "improvement" on indicators of care quality (CMS, 2013b).

Starting October 2012, CMS rewards hospitals that provide high-quality care through the VBP program (called "pay for performance" or "evidence-based medicine"). Essentially, the program is designed to take money from low performers and redistribute it to the best performers. Value-based purchasing allows CMS to transform itself from a passive payer of volume-based claims of care to an active purchaser of care based on the quality of services for patients (CMS, n.d.b).

By making an impact on the finances of hospitals, CMS expects them to develop best practices to reduce errors and control cost. Hospitals, too, are being transformed into accountable healthcare systems with quality methods and balanced scorecards that are not defined by the credentials of the physicians and expensive equipment that they purchase but by the delivery of efficient and effective services—performing the right patient care right!

When Perception and Reality Misalign

Hospital administrators recognize the importance of implementing effective continuous improvement programs, streamlining systems and processes, and achieving greater operating efficiencies and higher levels of quality care. However, Quint Studer, founder of the Studer Group, claims that a significant obstacle for many hospitals and health systems is that their view of their organization's preparation for reform doesn't necessarily align with reality, as indicated by objective measures. In a study of more than 17,000 healthcare leaders in 44 states that examined how healthcare leaders rated the care provided at their organization and cross referenced this information with the organization's performance on the HCAHPS survey and CMS's process of care measures, he found that leaders' perceptions didn't always match the data, and many hospital leaders overrated the performance of their organization (Dunn, 2012).

For example, at hospitals where 75% to 100% of leaders reported "quality of care" was something their hospital "did well," patients responding to the HCAHPS survey didn't always agree. These hospitals scored in the 43rd percentile, on average, for the measure "Patients who gave their hospital a rating of 9 or 10 on a scale from 0 (lowest) to 10 (highest)." These same hospitals had an average score of 88.2 on CMS's clinical process of care measures. Hospitals with slightly less confident leadership, in which 50% to 74% of leaders reported "doing well," performed better on core measures (94.0 average score). According to Studer, the gap between perception and reality highlights the importance of using objective data to drive and monitor performance improvement, rather than relying on perception. This may require a cultural transformation within organizations because, historically, hospitals have been slow to embrace transparency and joint accountability (Dunn, 2012).

Evidence-Based Leadership

Healthcare leaders and hospital administrators will have to become adept at understanding variables and measures of quality care and patient safety. Leadership should be using evidence-based decisions to understand factors that increase unnecessary cost. Lowering operating costs and optimizing utilization of resources is a good business practice that can affect the bottom line positively. There is no way to monitor care and cost without data (Dlugacz, 2010). When healthcare leadership links information about processes with clinical and financial outcomes, it also creates value. Clinically, providing appropriate and timely intervention eliminates risk and potential malpractice claims. Organizationally, linking process and outcome help to move the organization from detection (retrospective control) to prevention (introspective control). Financial pressure and the possibility of losing reimbursement dollars due to poor performance can encourage healthcare leaders to proactively initiate programs to prevent, monitor, and improve the quality of indicators established by CMS.

With VBP, each hospital will have the chance to earn incentive payments tied to patient safety and quality of care. To fund the payments, each hospital will have a 1% reduction in the base operating Medicare diagnosis related group (DRG) payment. This began with discharges in October 2012. The reduction escalates by 0.25 of 1% for each of the next four years, resulting in an overall reduction of 2%.

Hospitals will be rated on indicators they report under the Hospital Inpatient Quality Reporting (Hospital IQR) program. The Hospital IQR program was originally mandated by Section 501(b) of the Medicare Prescription Drug, Improvement, and Modernization Act (MMA) of 2003. This section of the MMA authorized CMS to pay hospitals that successfully report designated quality indicators a higher annual update to their payment rates. Initially, the MMA provided for a 0.4 percentage point reduction in the annual market basket (the measure of inflation in costs of goods and services used by hospitals in treating Medicare patients) update for hospitals that did not successfully report. The Deficit Reduction Act of 2005 increased that reduction to 2.0 percentage points (CMS, 2013c).

Measurement Program: Clinical Processes

The Hospital IQR will require hospitals to be scored in the domains of "clinical process of care" and "patient experience of care." The clinical indicators will account for 70% of a hospital's value-based purchasing score, and the HCAHPS survey for 30%. As an example, each of the clinical process of care indicators is derived from best practices associated with acute myocardial infarction (AMI), heart failure (HF), community-acquired pneumonia (PN), and the Surgical Care Improvement Project (SCIP). The 12 clinical processes of care indicators and 8 patient experiences are listed below (Bombard, n.d.; The Joint Commission, n.d.):

- ► **Fibrinolytic therapy received within 30 minutes of hospital arrival (AMI).** Time to fibrinolytic therapy is a strong predictor of outcome in patients with an AMI. National guidelines recommend that fibrinolytic therapy be given within 30 minutes of hospital arrival in patients with ST-elevation myocardial infarction.
- ► **Primary percutaneous coronary intervention (PCI) received within 90 minutes of hospital arrival (AMI).** The early use of primary angioplasty in patients with ST-segment MI significantly reduces mortality and morbidity. The earlier primary coronary intervention is provided, the more effective it is.
- ► **Patients discharged with written instructions or materials (HF).** Patient nonadherence with diet and medications can significantly affect clinical status. Clinicians should ensure that patients and families understand diet restrictions, activity recommendations, medications, and the signs and symptoms of worsening heart failure.
- ► **Blood culture performed in the ED before the receipt of the initial antibiotic (PN).** Obtaining blood cultures before starting antibiotics reveals the antibiotic sensitivity patterns used to determine the best medication to treat the disease.
- ► **Appropriate initial antibiotic selection for immune competent community-acquired pneumonia patients (PN).** The North American antibiotic guidelines for community-acquired pneumonia in immune competent patients are from the CDC, Infectious Diseases Society of America, Canadian Infectious Disease Society/Canadian Thoracic Society, and American Thoracic Society. The antibiotics recommended are effective against *Streptococcus* pneumonia, the most common cause of community-acquired pneumonia.
- ► **Prophylactic antibiotic received within 1 hour before surgical incision (SCIP).** A goal is to establish bactericidal tissue and serum levels at the time of skin incision. Giving the antibiotic too early or too late increases the incidence of postoperative infection.
- ► **Appropriate prophylactic antibiotic selection for surgical patients (SCIP).** A goal of prophylaxis with antibiotics is to use an agent that is safe and cost-effective and has a spectrum of action that covers most of the probable intraoperative contaminants for the operation. First- or second-generation cephalosporins satisfy these criteria for most operations, although anaerobic coverage is needed for colon surgery.
- ► **Prophylactic antibiotic discontinued within 24 hours after surgical end time (SCIP).** Another goal of prophylaxis with antibiotics is to provide benefit to patients with as little risk as possible. Therapeutic serum and tissue levels

should be maintained throughout surgery. Intraoperative redosing may be needed for long operations. But administration of antibiotics for more than a few hours after the incision is closed offers no additional benefit. Prolonged administration does increase the risk of *Clostridium difficile* infection and antimicrobial-resistant pathogens.

► **Cardiac surgery patients with controlled 6 a.m. postoperative blood glucose (SCIP).** Hyperglycemia is associated with increased in-hospital morbidity and mortality for multiple medical and surgical conditions. Keeping postoperative blood glucose levels under control helps minimize adverse outcomes for cardiac surgical patients.

► **Surgery patients on a beta blocker before arrival who received a beta blocker during the perioperative period (SCIP).** Continuous beta blocker use in the perioperative period reduces mortality, and mortality increases when beta blockers are not used.

► **Surgery patients with recommended venous thromboembolism (VTE) prophylaxis ordered (SCIP).** Despite evidence that VTE is one of the most common postoperative complications and that prophylaxis is the most effective strategy to reduce morbidity and mortality, prophylaxis is underused. Appropriate thromboprophylaxis has a positive risk–benefit ratio and is cost-effective.

► **Surgery patients who received appropriate VTE prophylaxis within 24 hours before surgery to 24 hours after surgery (SCIP).** The timing of prophylaxis is based on the type of procedure, prophylaxis selection, and clinical judgment regarding the impact of patient risk factors. The optimal start of pharmacologic prophylaxis in surgical patients varies and must be balanced with the efficacy versus bleeding potential. Because of the inherent variability related to the initiation of prophylaxis for surgical procedures, the SCIP recommended 24 hours before surgery to 24 hours after surgery to establish a time frame to encompass most procedures.

Measurement Program: Patient Experience

The eight patient experience-of-care indicators with their associated questions are listed and discussed below. The experience-of-care measures are derived from the HCAHPS program, a patient satisfaction survey that hospitals receiving Medicare/Medicaid reimbursement must undertake. The questions from the domains (e.g., "nurse communication," "physician communication," and so on) are aggregated into a total score for the domain. There are four options for patients to select: "always," "usually," "sometimes," or "never," but only "always" counts. No score is given for any of the other three options. The patient experience-of-care domain score is the sum of a hospital's HCAHPS base score and that hospital's HCAHPS consistency score (see the following).

Survey

1. **Nurse communication.** During this hospital stay, how often did nurses treat you with courtesy and respect? How often did nurses listen carefully to you? How often did nurses explain things in a way you could understand? After you pressed the call button, how often did you get help as soon as you wanted it?

2. **Physician communication.** During this hospital stay, how often did physicians treat you with courtesy and respect? How often did physicians listen carefully to you? How often did physicians explain things in a way you could understand?

3. **Cleanliness and quietness.** During this hospital stay, how often was your room and bathroom kept clean? How often was the area around your room quiet at night?

4. **Responsiveness of hospital staff.** How often did you get help in getting to the bathroom or in using a bedpan as soon as you wanted? (Patients answer question only if they needed help with these activities.)

5. **Pain management.** During this hospital stay, how often was your pain well controlled? How often did the staff do everything they could to help you with your pain? (Patients answer questions only if they needed medication for pain.)

6. **Communication about medications.** Before giving you any new medicine, how often did staff tell you what the medicine was for? Before you were given any new medicine, how often did staff describe possible adverse effects in a way you could understand? (Patients answer questions only if they received new medications.)

7. **Discharge information.** During this hospital stay, did physicians, nurses, and other hospital staff talk with you about whether you would have the help you needed when you left the hospital? Did you get information in writing about what symptoms or health problems to look out for after you left the hospital?

8. **Overall rating.** Using a number from 0 to 10, where 0 is the worst hospital possible and 10 the best, how would you rate this hospital during your stay? (The only rating that counts in scoring is 9 or 10.) Medicare will make incentive payments to hospitals beginning in fiscal year 2013 based on how well they perform on each measure or how much they improve their performance. Hospitals will receive points on each measure based on the higher of (1) their level of achievement relative to an established standard, or, (2) their improvement in performance during a baseline period. Their combined scores on all the indicators will be translated into "value-based incentive payments" for discharges on or after October 1, 2012.

Scoring

Achievement points are awarded by comparing a hospital's rates during the performance period with all hospitals' rates from a baseline period:

- ▶ Hospital rates at or above benchmark = 10 achievement points
- ▶ Hospital rates below the achievement threshold = 0 achievement points
- ▶ If the rate is equal to or greater than the achievement threshold and less than the benchmark = 1–10 or variable achievement points

Improvement points are awarded by comparing a hospital's rates during the performance period to that same hospital's rates from a baseline period:

- ▶ Hospital rates at or above benchmark = 9 improvement points
- ▶ Hospital rates at or below baseline period rate = 0 improvement points
- ▶ If the hospital's rate is between the baseline period rate and the benchmark = 0–9 variable improvement points

Consistency points are awarded by comparing a hospital's patient experience-of-care dimension rates during the performance period with all hospitals' patient experience-of-care rates from a baseline period:

- ▶ If all dimension rates are at or above achievement threshold = 20 consistency points
- ▶ If any dimension rate is at or below worst-performing hospital dimension baseline period rate = 0 consistency points
- ▶ If the lowest dimension rate is greater than the worst-performing hospital's rate but less than the achievement threshold = 0–20 variable consistency points

CMS calculates a hospital's *total performance score* by:

- ▶ Combining the greater of either the hospital's achievement or improvement points for each measure to determine a score for each domain
- ▶ Multiplying each domain score by a specified weight (percentage)
- ▶ Adding together the weighted domain scores (CMS, 2013b).

See **Table 5.1** for a sample of domains showing weighted values.

Tools

Effective quality management programs are patient centered and linked with key CMS indicators, improvement processes, and financial outcomes. Articulating questions based on meaningful data helps to identify the variables associated with poor performance outcomes. These variables may involve equipment, people, communications, policies, procedures, and so on.

Table 5.1 Weighted Value of Each Domain, FY 2013–2015 Domain

	FY 2013 Weight	FY 2014 Weight	FY 2015 Weight
Clinical process of care	70%	45%	20%
Patient experience of care	30%	30%	30%
Outcome	n/a	25%	30%
Efficiency	n/a	n/a	20%

Data from Centers for Medicare and Medicaid Services. (2013a, February). The Medicare and Medicaid electronic health record (EHR) incentive programs: Stage 2 toolkit. Retrieved from http://www.cms.gov/Regulations-and-Guidance/Legislation/ EHRIncentivePrograms /Downloads/Stage2_Toolkit_EHR_0313.pdf; Centers for Medicare & Medicaid Services. (2013b, March). Hospital value-based purchasing program. Retrieved from http://www.cms .gov/Outreach-and-Education/Medicare-Learning-Network-MLN/MLNProducts/ downloads/Hospital_VBPurchasing_Fact_Sheet_ICN907664.pdf; Centers for Medicare and Medicaid Services. (2013c, September). Hospital inpatient quality reporting program. Retrieved from https://www.cms.gov/Medicare/Quality-Initiatives-Patient-Assessment-Instruments/HospitalQualityInits/HospitalRHQDAPU.html

Root cause analysis (RCA) is a systematic method aimed at identifying and correcting the root causes of events, as opposed to simply addressing their symptoms. By focusing correction on root causes, problem recurrence can be prevented. A typical RCA uses a fishbone diagram to highlight cause-and-effect relationships. A simple example is provided in **Figure 5.1**.

A Pareto chart contains both bars and a line graph, where individual values are represented in descending order by bars, and the line represents the cumulative total. The left vertical axis represents the frequency of occurrence while the right vertical axis is the cumulative percentage of the total number of occurrences

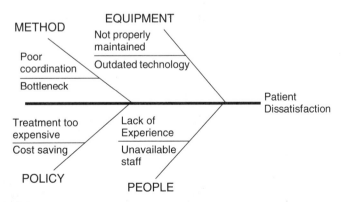

Figure 5.1 Simple Fishbone Diagram

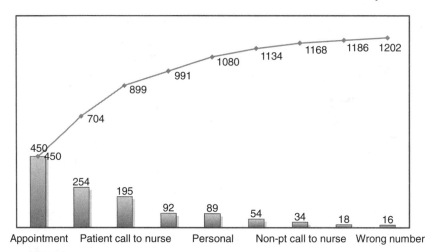

Figure 5.2 Pareto Analysis of Incoming Calls

(e.g., costs, number of calls). Because the reasons are in decreasing order, the cumulative function is a concave function. The purpose of the Pareto chart is to highlight the most important set of factors (often called *vital few* or the common sources of defects) that cause a problem (as opposed to focusing on the *trivial many*) to reduce opportunity costs and increase the potential for solving the problem relatively efficiently (**Figure 5.2**).

A run chart is simple analytical tool that allows healthcare professionals to learn from variation over time. With this information, healthcare leaders can make decisions about appropriate staffing or functional deployment of equipment during high demand for services (**Figure 5.3**).

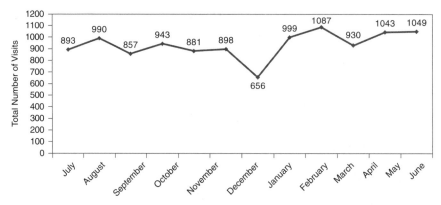

Figure 5.3 Run Chart (Flu-Related Visits)

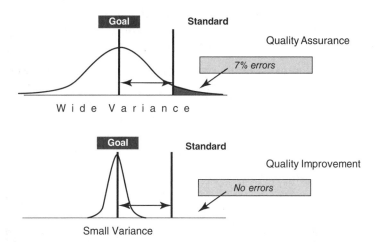

Figure 5.4 Quality Assurance and Quality Improvement

Quality assurance and quality improvement use data analysis in order to reduce faulty processes and increase patient safety. The steps include the assessment or evaluation of the quality of care; identification of problems or shortcomings in the delivery of care; designing activities to overcome these deficiencies; and monitoring to ensure effectiveness of corrective measures (**Figure 5.4**).

Control charts are used to monitor the stability of a process. In **Figure 5.5**, the chart highlights the number of occurrences in which fluctuations from the mean (= standard) toward the lower control limits or the upper control limits occurred. For example, if the control chart represents too many deviations from the expected norm of emergency room wait times, hospital administrators can take steps to review the causes to improve service quality.

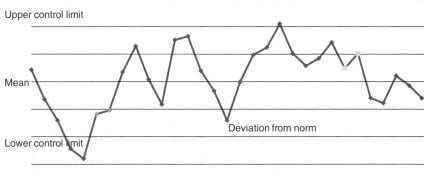

Figure 5.5 Control Chart

The Role of Healthcare CIOs in Effectively Managing Value-Based Reimbursement

To help their organizations thrive in the transition to value-based reimbursement, healthcare CIOs will need to drive the use of data analysis in decision making and begin to deploy innovative technology. This includes setting up sophisticated data analysis capabilities and deploying IT solutions to support what amounts to a fundamentally new way of operating. CIOs will also have to identify and provide the technology innovations that can help their companies profit and grow in this new environment, while educating their business colleagues on how to use these innovations to create value.

Harry Greenspun, MD, senior advisor for Health Care Transformation and Technology at the Deloitte Center for Health Solutions (DCHS), discusses ways healthcare CIOs can turn these challenges into opportunities. Named by *Modern Healthcare* in 2010 as one of the "50 Most Powerful Physician Executives in Health Care," Dr. Greenspun has advised the Obama administration and Congress on healthcare reform. He is coauthor of the bestselling book, *Reengineering Health Care: A Manifesto for Radically Rethinking Health Care Delivery* (FT Press, 2010).

The healthcare industry is moving from a volume-based business model to one based on value. What challenges face providers as they make this transition?

The industry is currently straddling the line between the old fee-for-service, volume-based world and the new and evolving value-based world. Many companies are struggling to understand the potential impact to their bottom lines of providing services at high quality and low cost while they are still operating in a volume-based world.

Which priorities should top the list for organizations making this transition?

Delivering high-value health care may depend largely on each organization's ability to collect, share, analyze, and manage health information throughout the healthcare value chain. Providers will need information from pharmaceutical organizations, payers will need information from providers, and so on. On top of that, they'll likely need access to data on outcomes not directly related to health care. For example, some research suggests that a good predictor for hospital readmittance is a patient's financial history. No healthcare company has that data.

How far along in the transition are most provider organizations?

According to recent interviews, the DCHS conducted with CIOs from major US health systems, many are at the beginning stage. They are taking foundational steps such as adopting electronic health records, building data warehouses, and setting up health information exchanges. Creating a data-driven business using advanced analytics and investing in new IT platforms may still be 3 to 5 years away.

Making this shift entails changing the culture as much as it involves embracing new technologies. Companies will have to adopt a different way of doing business—one based on collaboration and transparency. They will need to share information, working with other organizations inside and outside of health care, and engaging consumers in new ways using innovative technologies and healthcare platforms such as mobile health (mHealth). Moreover, many states are now publishing quality outcomes and rankings, so their results with these efforts will be out there for all to see.

How can healthcare CIOs help their organizations make this transformation?

First, CIOs can serve as trusted advisors, sharing how health IT can be used to support evolving service lines, develop collaborative business relationships, and engage consumers with innovative technology approaches.

Second, CIOs should be asking, "How can we cost-effectively apply technology innovations to the tasks of transforming into a data-driven business and operating under a pay-for-value system?" That means evaluating and prioritizing investments using a fundamentally different business case than in the past. Take investments in mHealth as an example. The technology to support mHealth has been around for decades; however, there was little incentive to invest in it under the fee-for-service business model. In a system that rewards service quality and value, the business case—and related ROI—for adopting innovative mHealth technologies changes drastically.

How can healthcare CIOs identify the right innovations for their companies and understand whether they are worth the investment?

Setting up a process to vet innovations and assess their ROI is a huge challenge for many. CIOs should aggressively evaluate a new technology in the context of the company's service lines, and ask: "Does it help us?" "Does it integrate with what we need?" "Is it scalable?"

One leading practice we saw through our interviews is to set up an innovation governance process. Step one entails articulating where the organization wants to go, setting up a roadmap to get there, and determining which technology innovations can help. An effective governance process will likely require active involvement by the CFO, CIO, chief medical officer (CMO), and CHRO—with each understanding the perspectives of the others.

I previously served as CMO for two large companies. When evaluating business cases for potential investments, I needed to understand the financial side in addition to the scientific and clinical sides. The same is true for CIOs. They need to make a point of understanding what is going on across the entire system and how it may be affected by proposed innovation investments. Given the disruptive nature of the transition to value-based reimbursements, blind spots are especially dangerous. CIOs should worry obsessively about what they don't know.

Case Study: Night Shift "Quietly" Rocks!!

"Night Shift 'Quietly' Rocks!!" is what the monthly hospital employee newsletter headline read in November 2012 after years of struggling to move the HCAHPS patient satisfaction scores (CMS, 2013) at Olympia Medical Center in Los Angeles, California. This 203-bed community hospital was struggling with a number of the HCAHPS survey questions. The HCAHPS survey question, "How often was the area around your room quiet at night?" scored lowest. For the first hospital pay-for-performance (CMS, 2011) period, July 2011 to March 2012, the percent of patients who answered "always" was lower than the baseline period. During the second quarter 2011, "quiet at night" scores were in the 22nd percentile.

In January 2012, leadership moved its day shift patient rounding to night shift. Leaders interviewed patients between 7:00 and 8:30 p.m. Televisions were loud, linen cart wheels were noisy, and doors that squeaked when opened were just a few of the issues leadership observed firsthand that were contributing to low scores. Instead of leadership fixing the problems, a decision was made to place the solution in the hands of the charge nurses who work at night. The charge nurses were tasked with coming up with an action plan to improve the "quiet at night" scores. The staff hung posters outside patient rooms, the Original Yacker Tracker (2013) (**Figure 5.CS1**) was implemented in one area to alert staff to high-volume noise levels, and other staff reminded employees to be quiet. The scores inched up slowly.

At the Avatar International Annual Symposium in Orlando, Florida, at the end of May, 2012, the Community Hospital of San Bernardino took away four of the "most improved" awards for HCAHPS composite scores. Michelle Bowman, Six Sigma Master Black Belt, Director of Transformation, was instrumental in that accomplishment. The plane barely came to a stop in Los Angeles when the Service Excellence Director at Olympia Medical Center was on the phone making an appointment to talk with Michelle to find out how she did it. The common thread in their journeys was involving frontline employees.

In July, the Olympia Medical Center Service Excellence Director woke to thoughts of HCAHPS struggles and decided to surprise the night shift staff and hold a meeting at night. The charge nurses were notified to send a nurse or certified nurse assistant to the 4 West conference room in 10 minutes. They were shocked. A promise was made to keep the team members for no more than 30 minutes. Respiratory therapy, security, environmental services, lab, radiology and even the emergency department were expected to send representatives as well.

Source: Bayless, J. (2013). Case study: "Night shift 'quietly' rocks!!" *Journal of the Society for Healthcare Improvement Professionals.* Retrieved from http://www.jship.org/articles /vol-2-articles-march-2013/case-study-night-shift-quietly-rocks/

Figure 5.CS1 Yacker Tracker, a Device Designed to Sound an Alert When the Noise Level Exceeds Defined Limits

Courtesy of: AGI™ Attention Getters, Inc.

There was one stipulation: *no supervisors were allowed.* It was time for the frontline, point-of-service employees to be given a chance to solve a problem on their own. Those who showed up were informed of the purpose of the meeting. The hospital stood to lose healthcare dollars if patient satisfaction scores did not improve. They reviewed the HCAHPS scores for each individual unit at the hospital. They were asked, "What gets in the way of keeping the areas around the patient rooms quiet at night?" The issues were: monitors beeping; loud patient vents; agitated patients screaming; staff entering rooms to empty trash, linen, and sharps containers after 9 p.m.; and noise made by carts, gurneys and bed wheels in corridors. Some new issues were raised: the ER staff bringing admissions to the floors and disturbing sleeping patients, patients being disturbed by nursing staff, and noise from engineering and security radios (**Figure 5.CS2**).

Next, they were asked for ideas to solve the issues. One nurse suggested not putting vented patients in the area that leads to the telemetry floor because the sound carries down the hallway. Someone else asked if environmental service workers could empty trash in patient rooms before 9 p.m. Thirty minutes into the meeting they agreed to take what they discussed back to their night shift team for additional suggestions. They were told they could not hand this off to their supervisors. As a team, they set a deadline of 1 week to return additional ideas to the Service Excellence Director. Within 30 minutes after the meeting, each

(Continues)

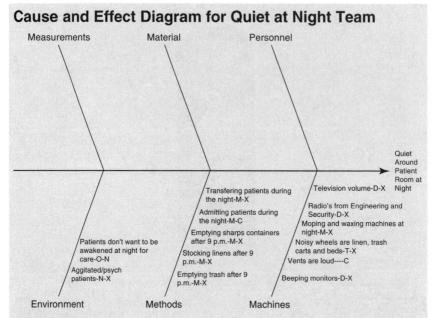

Figure 5.CS2 Fishbone Diagram of Barriers to Area Around the Patient Room Being Quiet at Night

Courtesy of: *Journal of the Society for Healthcare Improvement Professionals.*

team member had a copy of the list of barriers and ideas they had generated. Many team members followed through on their commitment to submit additional suggestions within 1 week. After one of the nursing directors attempted to submit additional suggestions she was informed the suggestions needed to come from the night shift.

One month later the Service Excellence Director showed up at 4 a.m. unannounced. A new set of frontline employees attended the meeting. They were briefed on why they were there, what their fellow team members accomplished the previous month, and they brainstormed one more time about additional barriers and solutions.

In September, something started to happening to the scores. They were on a steady incline although they had not finished the Six Sigma DMAIC process. For the period January 2011 to September 2012, the trend was statistically significant (**Figure 5.CS3**). No one could believe what had happened. This night shift team had taken all the ideas they generated and implemented them throughout the hospital. When these results were presented at the Community Board in December one of the members requested an example of the solutions. Examples included greasing hinges on noisy doors, greasing the wheels on the linen carts, and moving noisy patients away from alert patients. The board member added,

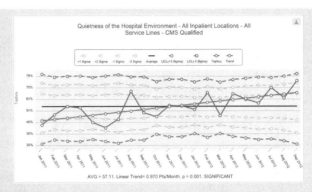

AVG = 57.11. Linear Trend= 0.970 Pts/Month. p = 0.001. SIGNIFICANT

Figure 5.CS3 Quiet at Night Avatar scores through September 2012

Courtesy of: Avatar International. (2012). Retrieved from https://www.improvingcare.com/results.php?focus=org&detail=hcahps

"Nothing that costs the hospital a lot of money." She was right. Rather than prioritizing the issues the night shift found and solutions were implemented to all of the problems independently.

During the next unannounced 4 a.m. visit, the Service Excellence Director brought chocolates for everyone to celebrate the significant results. The director was advised that her heels were making too much noise and she needed to tiptoe. The teams whispered through the celebrations on the individual units.

The team charter (**Figure 5.CS4**), Pareto charts (**Figures 5.CS5** and **5.CS6**), and individual moving range charts (**Figures 5.CS7**, **5.CS8**, and **5.CS9**) provide

Figure 5.CS4 Quiet at Night Team Charter

Courtesy of: *Journal of the Society for Healthcare Improvement Professionals.*

(*Continues*)

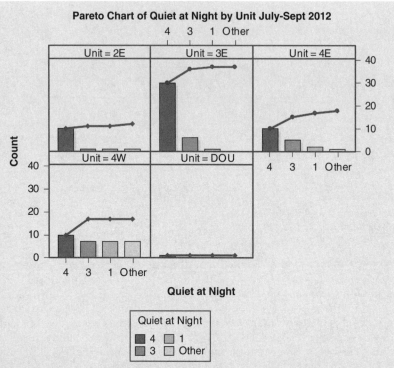

Figure 5.CS5 Pareto Chart Prior to Frontline Employee Improvement Team

Courtesy of: *Journal of the Society for Healthcare Improvement Professionals*

evidence the results were significant. The frequency of patients answering "never" and "sometimes" decreased. The lower control limits (LCL) started to move as well. In the 1st quarter of 2012 the LCL was 1.480, second quarter 1.754 and third quarter 2.072. In November, the third quarter scores ranked Olympia Medical Center in the 86th percentile based on the Avatar International database (2012). For the month of September, when the Olympia Times was printed, the night shift "quiet at night" score ranked at the 95th percentile.

Six Sigma refers to a process that produces only 3.4 defects per mission opportunities. The "quiet at night" or defects per million opportunities (DPMO) went from 452,703 to 344,828. The sigma score improved from 1.62 to 1.9. Most businesses operate at a 3 Sigma level; the goal is 6 or higher. As of Monday, February 11, 2012, the control chart is still trending upward for the fourth quarter of 2012. The percent of patients who answered "always" to the "quiet at night" question is at 73% and this ranks Olympia Medical Center at the 91st percentile in the Avatar International database.

The night shift went from giving all the reasons their scores would never improve in February 2012 to blowing the socks off everyone, including Avatar

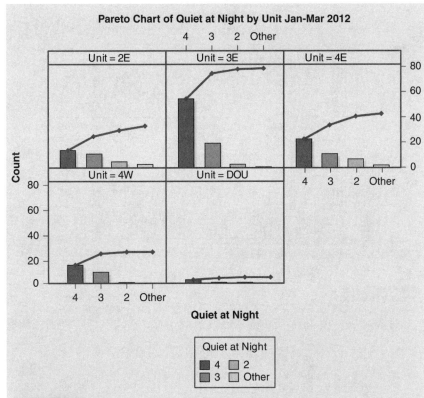

Figure 5.CS6 Pareto Chart After the Implementation of the Frontline Employee Improvement Team

Courtesy of: *Journal of the Society for Healthcare Improvement Professionals.*

International 8 months later (**Figure 5.CS10**). In November a representative from Avatar International called asking what they had done. What matrix did they adopt? What methodology was it that they could correlate to the marked improvements? They initially seemed disappointed to hear how the night shift heroes didn't require any sophisticated analysis. That the amazing night shift team took the information and the ideas they generated and made it happen. They made it look easy.

There are many theories regarding what it will require to thrive in the changing environment faced by health care today. Porter-O'Grady and Malloch in their book, *Quantum Leadership: Advancing Innovation, Transforming Health Care*, repeatedly cite engaging point-of-service workers as one of the most important

(Continues)

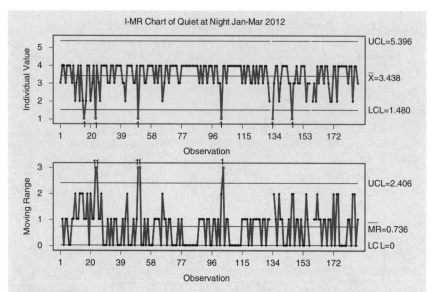

Figure 5.CS7 Individuals-Moving Range Charts January–March 2012, Displays Observations in Chronological Order (Left to Right) and Plots Control Limits of 3 Standard Deviations Above and Below the Mean/Median

Courtesy of: *Journal of the Society for Healthcare Improvement Professionals.*

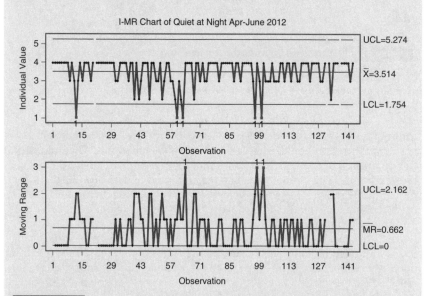

Figure 5.CS8 Individuals-Moving Range Charts April–June 2012, Displays Observations in Chronological Order (Left to Right) and Plots Control Limits of 3 Standard Deviations Above and Below the Mean/Median

Courtesy of: *Journal of the Society for Healthcare Improvement Professionals.*

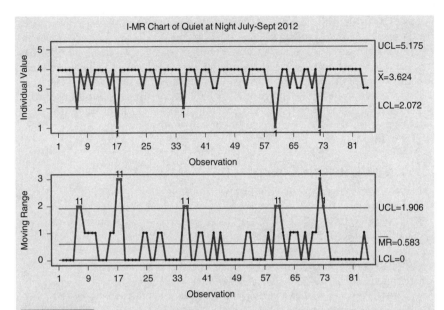

Figure 5.CS9 Individuals-Moving Range Charts July–September 2012, Displays Observations in Chronological Order (Left to Right) and Plots Control Limits of 3 Standard Deviations Above and Below the Mean/Median

Courtesy of: *Journal of the Society for Healthcare Improvement Professionals.*

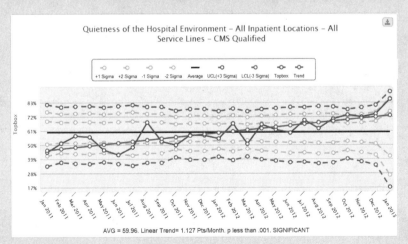

Figure 5.CS10 Quiet at Night Results as of February 11, 2013

Courtesy of: Avatar International. (2012). Retrieved February 11, 2013 from https://www.improvingcare.com/results.php?focus=org&detail=hcahps

(Continues)

steps to assure health care thrives in uncertain times. The questions for leaders today are: Why are we taking so long to adopt this leadership style? Why do we continue to insist that leaders have all the answers? Why do healthcare leaders continue to hold meetings and exclude frontline employees rationalizing that they cannot spare point-of-service workers from productivity standards in exchange for results like those achieved by the night shift team? It makes sense that during the Industrial Age leaders relied on traditional methods to improve outcomes, it was all that was known. Health care is changing and so must leaders in order to thrive in this new age.

Case Study Review Questions

1. What were the causes for the low scores on patient satisfaction?
2. How effective were the suggestions to solve the problems?
3. Go over Figures 5CS-3 to 5CS10 and explain their usefulness in tracking activities and improvement plans.

Case References

Avatar International. (2012). Technical help—Intelligent surveys online. Retrieved from https://www.improvingcare.com/results.php?focus=org&detail=hcahps

Centers for Medicare and Medicaid Services (CMS). (2011, November). Fact sheet: Hospital value-based purchasing program. Retrieved from http://www.cms.gov/Outreach-and-Education/Medicare-Learning-Network-MLN/MLNProducts/downloads/Hospital_VBPurchasing_Fact_Sheet_ICN907664.pdf

Centers for Medicare and Medicaid Services.(2013, January 9). HCAHPS: Patients' perspectives for care survey. Retrieved from http://www.cms.gov/Medicare/Quality-Initiatives-Patient-Assessment-Instruments/HospitalQualityInits/HospitalHCAHPS.html

I Six Sigma. (2013, February 14). Process sigma calculator. Retrieved from http://www.isixsigma.com/process-sigma-calculator

The Original Yacker Tracker: AGI Attention Getters Inc. (2013). Retrieved from http://www.yackertracker.com/

Porter-O'Grady, T., & Malloch, K. (2011). *Quantum leadership: Advancing innovation, transforming health care.* Sudbury, MA: Jones & Bartlett.

Conclusion

Healthcare leaders that link cost management with patient safety and quality control are also in a position to guard against suboptimization, reduce errors and complexity, maximize operating efficiencies, and influence stakeholder perceptions of organizational reputation. The role of the board in hospitals is to provide effective checks and balances and promote accountability and transparency in recording and reporting errors and failures. Senior leaders and board directors alike need to embrace evidence-based practices and measures to achieve positive and consistent organizational and clinical improvements. Understanding the connection between cost, safety, quality, outcomes, and financial success is essential for sustaining excellence.

Integrating evidence-based medicine into standardized care processes reduces errors and the cost of reworks and leads to enhanced consistency. Eliminating unnecessary variations introspectively (using a prevention approach) helps remove subjective decisions in favor of objective standards and treats patients in compliance with evidence-based indicators of consistent clinical processes and good patient practices.

The CMS method for achieving compliance by incentivizing high performers and sanctioning low performers encourages healthcare leaders to pursue quality care proactively and continuously. Once the CEO, with the constant support of visionary board members, champions the process of improvement, other parts of the organization might follow with quality care initiatives that gradually could become a well synchronized, organization-wide effort. These efforts shape the sociotechnical system of the organization by influencing members' social identity and ingrained culture of commitment on one hand, and by embracing the value of quality care and continuous improvement on the other.

Quality management is a data-driven and patient-centered initiative that must be sustained through interprofessional collaboration and interdisciplinary communication. A culture that fosters parity in quality and safety outcomes creates a continuous learning organization, an ACO that takes both clinical effectiveness and resource efficiency into account. The master leader with skills in transactional management (stabilizing processes) and transformational leadership (creating a compelling vision of success) is essential for the success of quality care and healthcare organization sustainability.

Review Questions

1. What challenges do healthcare providers face as they transition toward value-based purchasing VBP environments?
2. How do executives balance the need for high regulation with the need for flexibility in managing quality care?
3. Discuss the measurement programs for collecting and analyzing data to help optimize healthcare operations.
4. What is the role of CMS in ensuring compliance with the Affordable Care Act?
5. Do you think that VBP value-based purchasing will reinforce the need for greater accountability and greater use of evidence-based decision-making in healthcare organizations?

References

Bayless, J. (2013). Case study: Night shift "quietly" rocks!! *Journal of the Society for Healthcare Improvement Professionals.* Retrieved from http://www.jship.org/articles/vol-2-articles-march-2013/case-study-night-shift-quietly-rocks/

Bombard, C. F. (n.d.). Value-based purchasing, CE663 content. *Gannett.* Retrieved from http://ce.nurse.com/content/ce663/value-based-purchasing

Bostick, M. R., Crayton, G., Fishman, E., Peters, E., & Smith, V. (2011, March). *Sustaining state health information exchange: A state toolkit.* Retrieved from http://www.nga.org/files/live/sites/NGA/files/pdf/1103SUSTAININGHIETOOLKIT.PDF

Charles, D., King, J., Patel, V., & Furukawa, M. (2013, March). *Adoption of electronic health record systems among U.S. non-federal acute care hospitals: 2008–2012.* ONC Data Brief, no 9. Washington, DC: Office of the National Coordinator for Health Information Technology. Retrieved from http://www.healthit.gov/sites/default/files/oncdatabrief9final.pdf

Christensen, C. M., Grossman, J. H., & Hwang, J. (2009). *The innovator's prescription: A disruptive solution for healthcare.* New York, NY: McGraw-Hill.

Centers for Medicare and Medicaid Services (n.d.a). *Medicare—Accountable care organizations shared savings program—New section 1899 of Title XVIII, preliminary questions & answers* [Files]. The American Association of Clinical Endocrinologists. Retrieved from https://www.aace.com/files/cmspremlimqa.pdf

Centers for Medicare and Medicaid Services (n.d.b). *Roadmap for implementing value driven healthcare in the traditional medicare fee-for-service program.* Centers for Medicare and Medicaid Services, U.S. Department of Health and Human Services. Retrieved from http://www.cms.gov/Medicare/Quality-Initiatives-Patient-Assessment-Instruments/QualityInitiativesGenInfo/downloads/vbproadmap_oea_1-16_508.pdf

Centers for Medicare and Medicaid Services. (2013a, February). *The Medicare and Medicaid electronic health record (EHR) incentive programs: Stage 2 toolkit.* Retrieved from http://www.cms.gov/Regulations-and-Guidance/Legislation/ EHRIncentivePrograms/Downloads/Stage2_Toolkit_EHR_0313.pdf

Centers for Medicare and Medicaid Services. (2013b, March). *Hospital value-based purchasing program.* Retrieved from http://www.cms.gov/Outreach-and-Education/Medicare-Learning-Network-MLN/MLNProducts/downloads/Hospital_VBPurchasing_Fact_Sheet_ICN907664.pdf

Centers for Medicare and Medicaid Services. (2013c, September). *Hospital inpatient quality reporting program.* Retrieved from https://www.cms.gov/Medicare/Quality-Initiatives-Patient-Assessment-Instruments/HospitalQualityInits/HospitalRHQDAPU.html

Croke, E. M. (2003). Nurses, negligence, and malpractice: An analysis based on more than 250 cases against nurses. *American Journal of Nursing, 103*(9), 54–63.

Deloitte Center for Health Solutions. (2013, July). How health care CIOs can support value-based reimbursement. *The Wall Street Journal, CIO Journal.* Retrieved from http://deloitte.wsj.com/cio/2013/07/23/how-health-care-cios-can-support-value-based-reimbursement/?goback=%2Egde_35964_member_26033

Dlugacz, Y. D. (2010). *Value-based health care: Linking finance and quality.* San Francisco, CA: Jossey-Bass.

Dunn, L. (2012, August 17). 6 characteristics of high-performing healthcare organizations. *Becker's Hospital Review*. Retrieved from http://www.beckershospitalreview.com /hospital-management-administration/6-characteristics-of-high-performing -healthcare-organizations.html

Gawande, A. (2011, May 26). Cowboys and pit crews. *The New Yorker*. Retrieved from http:// www.newyorker.com/news/news-desk/cowboys-and-pit-crews

HealthLeaders Media. (2013, July). *Advancing clinical quality from data to decisions* [Report]. Retrieved from http://www.healthleadersmedia.com/intelligence/detail .cfm?content_id=293611&year=2013

Institute of Medicine (2001, March). *Crossing the quality chasm: A new health system for the 21st century* [Online]. Retrieved from http://www.iom.edu/~/media/Files /Report%20Files/2001/Crossing-the-Quality-Chasm/Quality%20Chasm%202001%20 %20report%20brief.pdf

The Joint Commission. (n.d.) *Performance measurement*. Retrieved from http://www .jointcommission.org/performance_measurement.aspx

Nass, S. J., Levit, L. A., & Gostin, L. O. (Eds.). (2009). *The value and importance of health information privacy*. Retrieved from http://www.ncbi.nlm.nih.gov/books/NBK9579/

Porter, M. E., & Lee, T. H. (2013). *Why health care is stuck—and how to fix it* [Web log]. Retrieved from http://blogs.hbr.org/2013/09/why-health-care-is-stuck-and-how -to-fix-it/?goback=%2Egde_2979291_member_276125499#%21.

Studdert, D. M., Mello, M. M., & Brennan, T. A. (2004). Medical malpractice. *New England Journal of Medicine, 350*(3), 283–292.

What is electronic health record (EHR)? (2011). *WhatIs.com*. Retrieved from http://whatis .techtarget.com/definition/electronic-health-record-i

What is health information exchange (HIE)? (2010). *WhatIs.com*. Retrieved from http:// searchhealthit.techtarget.com/definition/Health-information-exchange-HIE

What is Health Information Technology for Economic and Clinical Health Act (HITECH Act)? (2009). *WhatIs.com*. Retrieved from http://searchhealthit.techtarget.com /definition/HITECH-Act

What is personal health record (PHR)? (2010). *WhatIs.com*. Retrieved from http:// searchcompliance.techtarget.com/definition/personal-health-record-PHR

PART C ▶

Competition and Commitment

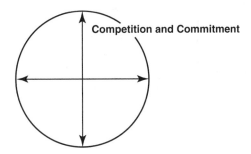

The upper right quadrant of the CVF draws our attention to the external environment and emerging issues that healthcare organizations face as they contend with rapidly changing circumstances and new sources of competition. Among the many roles leaders must play, positioning the organization for future success ranks among the most important. As noted previously, the day-to-day pressures of operating a complex healthcare organization require a great deal of attention, and because the "competition and commitment" aspects of leadership focus on external forces as well as the future, many managers find it easy to defer action until more pressing internal problems are resolved. However, a dent or underemphasis on this quadrant of the CVF could result in a highly reliable, well-functioning operation that withers because its competitors have managed to innovate and create new market opportunities.

Thus, this quadrant shifts the leader's focus from leading the social systems (Part A) and technical systems (Part B), to the external environment (Part C). Thus, just as leading the internal culture and coordinating functional units to manage control systems and measurement programs are important to ensure the optimal functioning of the organization through cultural integrity and operational outcomes, it is imperative that leaders attend to the future as well as the present.

The chapters in Part C focus on the outward-facing and forward-facing aspects of leadership, encouraging innovation, and bringing new ideas to the market. In Chapter 6, we discuss external markets and the importance of understanding customer (patient) needs. It is important to note that the leader is not—and should not—be solely responsible for innovation. The master leader recognizes that innovation and inspiration can come from all corners of the organization, as well as from outside. Inspiration often results from mundane sources—people's daily observations of operations, talking with patients and staff, analysis of market data, scrutiny of competitors, and openness to new ideas from other industries. The challenge is to put the pieces together into a comprehensible plan and develop a goal that can be communicated to the organization.

In Chapter 7, we discuss how to bring about change through goal setting, which is more complex than it first appears. Goals can serve as powerful tools for motivating employee performance, but they can also prove counterproductive when individual employees work to achieve their individual goals at the expense of the team. These nuances are discussed in light of the need for the organization to achieve its mission, and the leadership challenges of creating organizational commitment become apparent.

CHAPTER 6 ►

Leading with Vision: Competing Successfully in Healthcare Environments

LEARNING OBJECTIVES

Students will be able to:

- Understand the competitive environment in which healthcare organizations operate
- Recognize the need for marketing as a means to compete effectively in an increasingly complex business
- Appreciate that the foundation of marketing rests on understanding customers' needs and meeting them through goods and services tailored to those needs
- Define marketing in terms relevant to health care
- Define the Four Ps and describe how leaders can apply them to compete effectively
- Understand the interplay between marketers' subjective intuition and objective analysis of data, and how this relates to the innovator and coordinator roles within the competing values framework (CVF)
- Understand the fundamentals of competitive analysis and how they relate to strategy and planning

A Hospital Faces New Challenges

Deborah Whitson, the new president and CEO of Regional Medical Center (RMC), was ready for a challenge. Recently appointed to lead this nonprofit hospital health system in a growing suburban region of a metropolitan market, she saw that the organization faced challenges that few others had recognized. Although for the past four years the numbers all pointed in the right direction, growth had begun to slow. Patient volume, which had been steadily increasing, was leveling off. Having become accustomed to increased volume year after year, the administrators and staff spent their days working on operational issues like finding beds for patient overflow, trying to keep from diverting ambulances from the ER, scheduling OR time, maintaining FTE levels to required minimums, and implementing the new EHR system. Margins were healthy, so although the service line mix was probably not optimal for an institution of this size, they had more important things to worry about, and they were fulfilling their mission every day providing care for their community.

In truth, RMC's growth mirrored the expansion of the population of the area. It was located in a highly desirable residential area, and many companies had built their offices in corporate parks nearby, resulting in an influx of population that needed health care. RMC was ideally located to provide it. As a result, RMC's service area was highly desirable—a growing suburban area with a high proportion of commercially insured patients. However, their market share in the lucrative cardiac care service line had slipped—a fact that had not gone unnoticed, but with the growth of the market, cardiac care volume had still increased every year, and the unit remained busy.

The reputation of RMC had begun to slide as volume growth strained existing resources, but the staff did their absolute best to care for patients, and they took pride in their work. Nonetheless, the Hospital Consumer Assessment of Healthcare Providers and Systems (HCAHPS) scores slipped below the statewide average. This concerned Whitson, but the management team did not want to ask to take on any more big initiatives to fix it, given the workload they already had.

A few weeks into Whitson's tenure, St. Regis, the region's other large nonprofit hospital, announced that they would build a new urgent care/emergency center less than 2 miles away from RMC, in a highly visible location off the expressway, easily accessible, open 24 hours, with onsite imaging, lab, and all the services of a hospital emergency department, but no inpatient beds. In the press conference, the St. Regis CEO noted that patients needing inpatient care could be stabilized and transferred to St. Regis by ambulance within 15 minutes, saying: "If someone has a heart attack, state-of-the-art care is minutes away."

While cardiac care is highly competitive, this announcement raised the stakes, and Whitson and her colleagues were extremely concerned about the new competition. In addition, they learned that St. Regis had approached a cardiology practice that was responsible for the greatest number of inpatient admissions to RMC's cardiac service line, asking the doctors whether they would provide specialist services at the new facility.

All of a sudden, the market became a lot more competitive. And Whitson's leadership challenges became more formidable.

Introduction

For most of the healthcare industry's history, competition has not been a factor, primarily because the United States has faced a scarcity of health care. As the industry developed and grew rapidly over the past 50 years, more facilities and services have become available, and competition for business has heated up. From the perspective of classical economic theory, competition is a good thing, because it leads to higher quality and lower prices for customers. In health care, it does not always work this way, but competition has dramatic and important effects on organizations, requiring changes to the traditional mindset of their leaders. Leadership means looking externally as well as leading internally.

As Whitson and her colleagues at RMC discovered, it is easy for healthcare organizations to be lulled into complacency about external threats. To those working every day in health care, the flow of patients never stops, and they must keep focused on providing good care in an efficient and effective manner. But the world outside the institution is filled with all kinds of competitors who want a share of those patients and the revenue they represent. Marketing is the means by which the participants in a market seek to gain sustainable competitive advantage.

Still, it is not uncommon for healthcare organizations to conceive of marketing in relatively narrow terms, largely synonymous with promotion and advertising, rather than a comprehensive and strategic dimension of planning. This chapter establishes a broad-based working definition of marketing, identifies its relationship to the management of competition, demonstrates the value of key tools such as market analysis and competitor analysis, and highlights the relationship of marketing to organizational mission, vision, goals, stakeholder relations, and organizational values, in addition to policy, economic, and demographic trends.

In this chapter we will examine the role that marketing plays in helping the healthcare organization to engage in a highly competitive environment where rival institutions try to succeed by capturing market share from others. A master leader must organize resources and deploy them efficiently in order to defend the organization's current position and advance its mission relative to competitors, and the CVF can help leaders to identify and use appropriate aspects of leadership to look externally, analyze opportunities, and innovate to achieve competitive advantage.

Competition in Health Care

Free economies thrive on competition. As business organizations, healthcare institutions in the United States must compete for revenue, employees, physicians, and other scarce resources. Competition is everywhere in health care.

Competition for market share takes place to the extent that an oversupply exists in the marketplace. Under these circumstances, consumers have the luxury of choosing from among multiple providers, who are forced to compete for their business. If we faced a shortage of health care, less competition would exist because consumers would have little or no choice over which provider to use. In the case of RMC, the management team had little need for marketing because their patient volumes had grown, and they had all they could do to serve the patients coming at them. But what they did not realize was that their volume growth masked erosion in market share in their key cardiac service line, and their competitors were positioning themselves to take even more.

In the United States, for the most part, we have an abundance of healthcare services, and healthcare leaders must use marketing to gain and hold a share of the total business volume in their service areas, and growing market share has emerged as an important means of achieving a strategic competitive advantage. Note that not all healthcare services are uniformly abundant: specialties that are highly profitable for both doctors and hospitals (e.g., cardiac surgery, interventional cardiology, orthopedic surgery, CT scanning, MRI, birthing centers, and others) attract many competitors who vie for patients through enhanced facilities, special services, and advertising. Other less profitable healthcare services garner far less attention and little marketing; these include psychiatric care, substance abuse treatment, AIDS services, emergency room, trauma center, obstetrics, and others (Horwitz, 2005). Often, healthcare executives argue that they must compete vigorously for volume in profitable service lines in order to absorb losses from unprofitable services that they must provide to the community in order to fulfill their organization's mission—in essence, subsidizing the unprofitable (yet needed) services by successfully marketing the profitable ones (Evans, 2012).

Competition among healthcare organizations has often meant vying for the newest and most advanced equipment and facilities, a practice that some commentators label *the medical arms race*, likening it to the cold war era rivalry between superpowers to achieve military superiority. The strategy involves creating the most attractive, best-equipped facilities for doctors to practice in, because the more physicians a hospital or health system can attract, the more referrals they generate, and the more patient volume increases. Critics maintain that this practice has tended to produce overexpansion of facilities and duplication of expensive equipment, so payers and policymakers have tried to put the brakes on this kind of capital spending through managed care and local health system planning, but with mixed success. Even in locations where a certificate of need (CON) is required, the arms race continues (see the case of the hospitals in the Washington, DC area).

In addition, to achieve competitive advantage, healthcare organizations have shifted the search for revenue from purchasing advanced technology to adding services in geographic areas with high proportions of insured patients (Rosenthal, 2012). This has resulted in significant increases in the number of imaging studies, for instance, as the availability of equipment to provide these services has grown. In the United States, the number of computed tomography (CT) scanners and magnetic resonance imaging (MRI) units is more than twice

Proton Beam Therapy Heats Up Hospital Arms Race

Despite efforts to get healthcare spending under control, hospitals are still racing to build expensive new technology—even when the devices don't necessarily work better than the cheaper kind. Case in point: proton beam therapy, a high-tech radiation treatment for cancer.

Washington, DC, is on the verge of approving two proton treatment facilities at a total cost of $153 million. They would be built and owned by the two dominant hospital systems in the region: Johns Hopkins Medicine and MedStar Health. At the same time, the Maryland Proton Treatment Center is already under construction in Baltimore, 40 miles away.

Hopkins and MedStar have been pleading their cases before a local health department agency that grants hospitals the right to build new buildings and add services. Both health systems argue that the nearest proton therapy centers are too far away for Washington residents to use.

"We believe that this therapy is absolutely necessary, but we also think that it's appropriate to be applied to certain types of cancer with certain treatments and not everything," says Chip Davis, president of Sibley Memorial Hospital in an upscale neighborhood of Washington, where the Hopkins proton center would be built. The center would open in 2017 and is projected to generate $15.8 million in profits in 2019.

The Sibley and MedStar Georgetown plans are controversial.

"Neither should be building," says Dr. Ezekiel Emanuel, a former healthcare adviser to the Obama administration who is now at the University of Pennsylvania. "We don't have evidence that there's a need for them in terms of medical care. They are simply done to generate profits."

"It's hard to bend the cost curve when you're spending a lot of money," says Emanuel. "These are tens if not hundreds of thousands of dollars in treatment for interventions that do not improve survival, improve quality of life, decrease side effects, or save money."

The 90-Ton Cyclotron. There are already 11 proton therapy centers in the U.S., and the Maryland Proton Treatment Center is one of 17 more being developed.

The Baltimore facility is a giant cement-encased building the size of a football field, with a price tag of more than $200 million, funded by for-profit developer Advanced Particle Therapy. At its heart sits a 90-ton piece of equipment called a cyclotron, which accelerates protons until they're whizzing around at two-thirds the speed of light. The stream of protons is then directed at a tumor site, delivering a high-dose blast of radiation. The hope is that the proton beam is so focused that only the tumor gets irradiated, causing fewer side effects.

The treatment center will be staffed by physicians from the University of Maryland. Radiation oncologist Dr. Minesh Mehta, who will direct the center, says he's hopeful that the technology could be used to treat up to a quarter of all cancers. Studies suggest that proton therapy is promising for children who have brain and spinal tumors, protecting the

Source: "Proton Beam Therapy Heats Up Hospital Arms Race" by Jenny Gold, *Kaiser Health News*, May 31, 2013. *Kaiser Health News* is an editorially independent program of the Henry J. Kaiser Family Foundation, a nonprofit, nonpartisan health policy research and communication organization not affiliated with Kaiser Permanente. Reprinted with permission.

fragile developing organs near the cancer and preventing future developmental delays and secondary tumors. But childhood cancers are rare, and there's not much clinical evidence that proton therapy is better than standard radiation for most other cancers.

The particular "spot scanning" proton technology used at the Maryland center has not undergone any randomized clinical trials at all, Mehta acknowledges. A study published in the *Journal of the National Cancer Institute* in December found that prostate cancer patients who received proton therapy had no fewer side effects than those treated with standard radiation, despite it being substantially more costly.

Mehta argues that studies that show disappointing results for prostate cancer are based on flawed data sets and do not reflect the true value of proton therapy.

Doctors at the University of Maryland say their proton center is more than enough for all patients in the Washington-Maryland region. They have even invited radiologists at both Hopkins and MedStar to practice there.

That is unlikely to happen. A committee of Washington's State Health Planning and Development Agency has recommended that both proposed centers be allowed to move forward. A final decision from the agency director is expected soon.

---

that of most other Organisation for Economic Co-operation and Development (OECD) countries. These developments have induced greater demand for the services, as both doctors and patients want more and more of the newest and latest, a trend that some commentators have labeled "supply-driven demand" (Wennberg, 2004).

The nature and scope of competition has changed, as payers, policymakers, companies, and individuals have begun to resist increases in healthcare costs that seem to go unchecked year in and year out. A good example of this shift comes from the Centers for Medicare and Medicaid Services (CMS), which has initiated the hospital value-based purchasing (VBP) program (Centers for Medicare and Medicaid Services, 2011). Under this initiative, hospitals must achieve certain targets for clinical quality and patient experience, or else face cuts to their Medicare reimbursements. Because the VBP program adds no new funds for hospitals' performance on these metrics, administrators find they must compete for scarce resources, setting off intense efforts to improve quality and patient experience (Nelson, 2011). At the same time, there has been recognition that more health care is not always better health care. For example, guidelines developed by the National Committee for Quality Assurance's (NCQA) Healthcare Effectiveness Data and Information Set (HEDIS) guidelines suggest that there is a problem with the overuse of MRI and other imaging studies for low back pain in adults. The group declared that greater use of imaging studies by providers is a *negative* indicator of quality, and the NCQA benchmark for the appropriate treatment of low back pain is "the percentage of members with a primary diagnosis of low back pain who did not have an imaging study (x-ray, MRI, CT scan) within 28 days of the diagnosis" (National Committee for Quality Assurance, 2012).

To the extent that providing healthcare services remains a commercial enterprise in a free market economy, managers and executives must compete effectively for market share of services that they can provide efficiently and profitably. Marketing involves the process of aligning and organizing resources to position the organization for success, and it is the job of the master leader to ensure that this function operates optimally and aligns with the institution's mission and strategic goals.

Marketing

The essence of marketing lies in meeting people's needs, which has become the heart of marketing's definition. According to the American Marketing Association (2008), "Marketing is the activity, set of institutions, and processes for creating, communicating, delivering, and exchanging offerings that have value for customers, clients, partners, and society at large."

The notion that *offerings*—that is, goods and services—provide value to customers to the extent that they are willing, often eager, to pay for them with their hard-earned money suggests that such offerings meet people's needs. Consumers want to buy them because they derive value from their use, resulting in satisfaction and a favorable impression of the brand (Oliver, 2009). However, marketers often describe health care as a *negative service*, meaning that people do not want to buy it, but from time to time, they have to. The value derived from the purchase of health care comes from the fact that it removes or alleviates an unpleasant condition, rather than providing good feelings or pleasure. When it comes to buying services, people would much rather spend their money to purchase a vacation, or theater performance, or automobile detailing, or a massage—just about anything other than health care. This is one of the factors that distinguishes health care from other goods and services that are bought and sold in the marketplace.

Of course, because of employer-provided insurance coverage and government-sponsored healthcare payment programs like Medicare and Medicaid, most US residents are insulated from the true cost of health care, so they do not pay the full cost of these goods and services by themselves (Berkowitz, 2010). This fact, along with other unique features of medical care, has led some to maintain that health care should not be considered a product that is exchanged in market transactions (Relman, 2005). Nevertheless, curing an ailment or healing an injury is a service of enormous value to the vast majority of people, who have been willing to pay significant sums—either directly out-of-pocket or through third-party payers—to receive it. As noted earlier in this text, the United States spends the most on health care of any nation, and in doing so, its citizens are making a statement about the value they place on their health. To the extent that multiple competitors are available to provide healthcare-related goods and services, marketing enters the picture.

Marketing involves a unique mix of creative and analytical skills. Throughout history, the greatest products came from inspiration that arose from recognizing ordinary people's needs, and then coming up with a product to meet those needs.

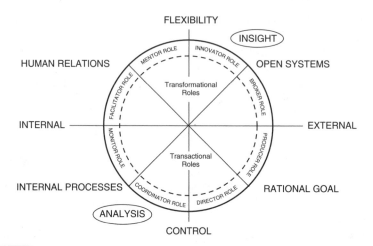

Figure 6.1 Competing Values Framework, Coordinator and Innovator Roles in Marketing

Modified from: Quinn, R. E. (1988). *Beyond rational management: Mastering the paradoxes and competing demands of high performance* (p. 48). San Francisco, CA: Jossey-Bass. Reproduced with permission of John Wiley & Sons, Inc.

Successful marketing takes more than just coming up with great ideas—many people have ideas for new products and services that they are convinced will make them rich someday, only to find that no one wants to buy them (or at least not enough people). There is also an analytical component to marketing leadership, which serves as a critically important counterweight to the intuitive insight required for innovation.

In the CVF chart depicted in **Figure 6.1**, the innovator and coordinator roles balance each other, and we will focus on this in a marketing context, examining the balance between the analysis and inspiration in healthcare organizations. Both roles are needed. The coordinator role demands that the leader organize functions so that data about the market, the patients, and the capabilities of the institution can inform management about potential problems and opportunities that could impact the organization's performance. The innovator role requires the leader to have insight into the needs of the market, to identify promising opportunities, and to devise creative methods for fulfilling those opportunities.

The Innovator Role: Insight from Experience

> Senior managers have to be prospectors. They have to continually pan for gold, turning over rocks, sifting through a lot of dirt to find worthwhile ideas. (CEO of Health System)

Ideas are the lifeblood of marketing. But where do ideas for new products and services come from? The inspiration often comes from experience—the inventor sees a need, understands the problems that arise because of the need, and solves the problem to satisfy the need. Thus, every innovation is a marketing innovation. True inspiration is less likely to come from formal marketing research such as focus groups, surveys, competitive analysis, gap analysis, or brainstorming. While these techniques can help inform the process and document the demand, insight usually comes from people who become prospectors for ideas, and they spot opportunities that others overlook.

Take the iconic Band-Aid® Brand bandages that have been used for generations of consumers for all kinds of cuts and sores. The idea came from Johnson & Johnson cotton buyer Earle Dickson, whose job did not include coming up with new ideas for wound closure products. He simply observed a need that occurred in daily life—in this case, he watched his wife accidentally cut herself while trying to prepare meals at home. The difficulty of using the then-current methods for binding wounds became apparent because of the frequency of minor injuries that his wife suffered while doing chores around the house, and his problem-solving turned into an innovation that not only helped millions of people but also created vast opportunity and value for his employer (see "Band-Aid Brand Adhesive Bandages: A Story of Innovation").

There is no simple formula for identifying needs and recognizing the opportunities that lie within. In their innovator role, the best leaders can spot the promising trends and appreciate the potential value they contain. Sometimes insight results from observation, experience, and conversation with others. The leader sees something and wonders if it could be done better or more efficiently. Often things are done because they have always been done in a certain way, people have become used to it, and no one has ever questioned the process or practice. How many times have you stood waiting in line for service and thought, "If they only changed the way they do their work, this would go a lot quicker and more smoothly"?

Note that marketing insights and innovations are not reserved solely for top management. Anyone in an organization can recognize problems, see things that need to change, and come up with creative ideas for solving problems. Witness the success of crowdsourcing that some organizations have tried, where they post a challenge in online forums along with data, and let everyone take a crack at solving the problem (Leclerc & Moldoveneanu, 2013). Internally, some larger business and technology firms have instituted crowdsourcing contests among their employees, and leaders have been surprised at the creativity and innovation that has resulted (Stieger, Matzler, Ladstaetter-Fussenegger, & Chatterjee, 2012). There is a great deal of talent and capability within organizations that conventional managers often overlook. Master leaders use the innovator role to seek out ideas from others who can see what happens on the front lines and have insights into the needs of patients as they encounter the system. In this way everyone in the organization can become a leader. In a well-led, thriving organization, no one is prevented from seeing ways to improve things, and they are encouraged to suggest ways to implement their ideas.

BAND-AID® Brand Adhesive Bandages: A Story of Innovation

BAND-AID® Brand Adhesive Bandages were invented in 1920 by a Johnson & Johnson employee named Earle Dickson, who worked as a cotton buyer. According to Johnson & Johnson's chief historian, Margaret Gurowitz, Earle's wife Josephine was prone to kitchen accidents, and whenever she cut herself, Earle had to cut a piece of adhesive tape, then cut a piece of gauze, then bandage the cut. When Earle was home, he could take care of it, but when she was by herself, she had a problem. Earle wanted a bandage his wife could apply herself, so he took those two products—adhesive tape and gauze, products made by Johnson & Johnson—and combined them by laying out a long piece of surgical tape and placing a strip of gauze down the middle. To keep the adhesive from sticking, he covered it with crinoline fabric. So now, whenever his wife cut herself, she cut a piece of the combined tape and gauze pad and used it as a bandage.

Dickson mentioned his invention at work, and a new product was born. BAND-AID® Brand Adhesive Bandages went on the market in 1921—the first ready-made adhesive bandages that consumers could apply themselves. The first BAND-AID® Brand Adhesive Bandages were just as Earle had invented them—a long strip of adhesive tape 18 inches long and 2.5 inches wide, with a 1-inch-wide strip of gauze down the middle, covered in crinoline fabric to protect it and keep it clean. You would just cut off the width you needed, depending on the size of the cut or scrape you wanted to cover, peel off the fabric backing, and stick it on. The product was a great success. In 1924, the company began manufacturing BAND-AID® Brand Adhesive Bandages pre-cut, which made using them even easier. Earle Dickson was made a vice president at Johnson & Johnson, where he stayed until his retirement. BAND-AID® Brand Adhesive Bandages became an iconic product used by millions around the world every day. It is not an overstatement to say that BAND-AID® Brand Adhesive Bandages improved people's lives, and they resulted from the insight of an observant and creative individual.

Author interview with M. Gurowitz, Johnson & Johnson Company Historian.

Meeting the needs of patients is challenging. Regardless of the setting—acute care hospital, primary care provider's office, retail clinic, outpatient surgery center, or elsewhere—the patient wants to get better and feel better. That is the benefit of *core* services delivered by the clinical care provider, and providing them is largely dictated by the treatment protocols of the provider's specialty. However, there are noncore or peripheral services as well, which affect the patient's perception of the care, and there is a great deal of room for innovation that can improve people's experiences in the healthcare system.

For example, the emergency department (ED) almost always tops the list of complaints about hospitals' service. Long waits, crowded and uncomfortable conditions, impersonal interactions with the staff, and high costs are among the persistent problems that patients experience. Conventional wisdom says there is little that administrators can do about it, because demand levels are unpredictable, and more serious cases need to be taken care of first. But recently, hospitals have been creating new ways of handling the patient flow, resulting in shorter wait times and better experiences. In one instance, an administrator decided to pose as a patient to see what it was like to visit the emergency room in his hospital. He saw that many people did not have medical emergencies, but had come in because they had no primary care provider or because their provider could not see them that day. He saw that the emergency room (ER) doctors, nurses, technicians, and other support staff did not want to keep these people waiting, but they had to take care of those with real emergencies, and they would get to the other patients when they found the time. He combined this insight with the results of an analysis that showed the hospital was experiencing a declining percentage of ED patients being admitted to the hospital—a confirmation that larger numbers of less seriously ill patients were being seen in the ER.

This insight provided the impetus to not only change procedures in triage of patients but also to locate a primary care office next to the ED, where less acute patients could be seen right away. Medical services were provided by a primary care practice owned by the hospital, staffed by employed physicians, who used the hospital's ancillary services (lab, imaging, pharmacy, etc.). The wait times in the ED dropped from over 2 hours to less than 1 hour, and the hospital's primary care practice gained new patients as well as increased revenue. Patient satisfaction increased dramatically, and the hospital began to advertise its short waiting time on billboards throughout the market area.

The fresh look at problems of patient flow in the ED turned into a business opportunity as well as a means of solving the dilemma of backlogs and long waits in the ER. The innovator role was necessary to capture the insight and create the idea for an alternative pathway to care for less acute patients. But the coordinator role was just as essential for success. Additional resources were needed to create the new primary care service—the administrator had to reallocate space, arrange for physician and nursing coverage, ensure that ancillary services would be available and sufficient, and provide for billing and administrative support. These resources needed to be justified by a business case that demonstrated the feasibility of the primary care venture, which required the administrator to quantify the demand and then to coordinate the resources of the hospital to make it a reality. By performing both roles, the administrator in this case turned into a master leader.

The Coordinator Role: Insight from Analysis

As noted above, every day people get ideas for new products that they believe will catch on, because they see an unfilled need in the marketplace and believe they have the solution. However, most new products fail within a year of introduction. Sometimes, the inventor's idea was not so great after all, and consumers did not buy the product. At other times, the idea was valid, but the product that resulted was too costly, of doubtful quality, or not sufficiently available due to poor distribution, so it failed. Often, the idea is good and the product is of high quality, but the market is not sufficient to support it. Or, the market may be large enough, but the competition is too strong. Market analysis is required to determine whether a leader's great idea can produce financial returns if he or she decides to introduce it.

Analysis Can Produce Innovation

Inspiration sometimes begins by growing out of data analysis, through an insight gained from either internal or external information, especially when compared with existing benchmarks. For example, the University of California Los Angeles (UCLA) Health System discovered that its patient satisfaction scores were significantly below the national average, hovering around the 30th to the 40th percentile (Michelli, 2011). This level of performance on critical metrics raised concerns among the leaders of the UCLA Health System. While academic medical centers often score lower than nonteaching community or general hospitals on patient experience surveys, people do not alter their service and care expectations because they are being treated in an academic medical center—they may not even know that they have been admitted to a teaching facility. They are not going to cut the hospital any slack, even if they are aware that the facility is a world-renowned hospital. They expect to be treated well.

The findings from the analysis rang the alarm, and the UCLA Health System responded by diving deeper into the issue to understand the problem from the patients' point of view. Teams of clinicians, managers, and support staff worked together to understand the patient's experience intimately, and they subsequently initiated a customer experience program designed to personalize the patient's experience. The result was significant improvement in patient satisfaction scores, and the UCLA Health System is now held out as an example of excellent patient service as well as top-notch medical care.

Similarly, the Cleveland Clinic examined its patient satisfaction scores as measured by the HCAHPS survey. It involves a set of 27 questions that measure patient experience in several domains, including communication with doctors and nurses, responsiveness of the staff, pain management, room environment, discharge instructions, and others (CMS, 2013). The HCAHPS survey benchmarks the experiences of randomly selected inpatients against other hospitals in the state and the nation. An important overall measure in the survey is the overall rating of the care received at the hospital, and CMS tabulates and reports the percentage of patients giving the hospital a 9 or 10 rating. On this key metric in the HCAHPS survey, the Cleveland Clinic ranked in the 52nd percentile, indicating that while the quality of care and outcomes may have been first-rate, the patient experience was not. The survey data prompted action by management. While these findings served as the signal that something needed attention, further study was required to diagnose the nature of the problem. By conducting observational studies of doctor–patient interactions, the leadership team derived insight into how to improve patient experience and consequent satisfaction by personalizing the communication and improving the patient's understanding of all that is going on at the bedside and throughout the hospital. As a result, HCAHPS scores rose dramatically, and in 2012 the Cleveland Clinic's overall rating ranked in the 92nd percentile after scoring near the median in 2008 (Merlino & Rahman, 2013).

In this case, the leaders of the Cleveland Clinic engaged in the coordinator role, obtaining appropriate data and comparing to benchmarks, mostly through managing the individuals responsible for this information. The leaders continued in the coordinator role, funding and organizing the effort to explore the issue of patient experience. However, with that data in hand, insight and creativity were required to devise effective methods for solving the problem, requiring leaders to engage in the innovator role.

In both of these examples, the improvements rest on a set of simple related premises: a patient wants to be treated like a person; that the patient's comfort matters to the people responsible for caregiving; and what the patient thinks actually matters to the multitude of doctors, nurses, and other caregivers that the patient encounters during a hospital stay. In these two instances, data analysis provided an impetus that resulted in further investigation, which created an insight, which then led to innovation and improvement in the metrics whose analysis alerted management to the existence of the problem in the first place. The insight would probably not have occurred had the analysis not been conducted.

Benchmarks and Key Performance Indicators

An enormous amount of information resides in healthcare organizations, and it increases every day. Leaders need analytical abilities to know what data to examine and how to interpret it. Comparing key data against benchmarks is the first step, and it frequently provides the initial signal that something needs attention. The second step is to figure out what exactly can be done about it. For both steps, a series of critical questions can form the context needed to frame the analyses, and then predictive models can answer the questions. The questions come from key performance indicators (known as KPIs), and they include:

- ▶ How can we improve efficiency of patient flow?
- ▶ How can we lower average length of stay?
- ▶ What can be done to improve patient experience and satisfaction?
- ▶ How can we become more efficient?
- ▶ How can we lower costs?

Using analytical models applied to the datasets available to healthcare leaders, answers to these questions may lurk beneath the surface, and talented analysts can uncover them with advanced modeling. Leaders do not necessarily need to know how to perform these analyses, but they do need to know how to perform the coordinator role, asking the right questions, and then understanding and using the results. Insight comes from the data, but only if the leader knows how to use it.

Marketing Actions: The Four Ps

The activities in which marketers engage to meet customer needs and take advantage of competitive opportunities have been summarized in a classic framework known as the *Four Ps* (Kotler & Keller, 2012):

- ▶ Product
- ▶ Price
- ▶ Promotion
- ▶ Place

Product refers to the activity of creating products that customers want to buy. This sounds easy enough, but the job of understanding customers' desires and preferences is anything but simple, and producing a product that is ideally suited for them often proves quite challenging. Note that the term *product* can be applied not only to tangible goods but to intangible services as well. In health care, many goods are produced to meet the needs of patients, some of which are used by the patients themselves while others are used by providers to deliver health care. These goods include items such as pacemakers, wheelchairs, hospital beds, stethoscopes, telemonitoring devices, medicines, drug-delivery devices, bandages, and many others. Services are products, too, and designing services to meet the needs of patients requires important work to understand how the patient will interact with the provider.

If anything, services are more complex products because they require *coproduction*, meaning that the customer must participate in the provision of the service (Lovelock & Wirtz, 2010). In health care, for example, the patient must show up for an appointment, present an accurate description of the problem, comply with directions that will help the doctor with an examination, undergo tests, and comply with instructions for treatment. Unless the medical condition of the patient renders him or her unable to respond (e.g., patient is unconscious), the patient almost invariably must participate in the process of delivering care.

Just as tangible goods are designed around customer needs, intangible services are also formulated to meet the expectations and desires of the consumers who will buy them. Take the encounter with a doctor in the examination room of an ED. Let's say you woke up one night with severe stomach pain that you had never felt before, and called your doctor, and the doctor told you to go straight to the ER. A person who looks like a doctor comes into the examination room, stands over you while he asks some questions, makes some notes, speaks to another person who looks like a nurse, uses unintelligible terms, and leaves. Far from being reassuring, the experience causes more distress, and it falls to the nurse to explain what is happening and what will occur next. In this case, the emergency physician may have ordered additional tests and made a referral to the gastrointestinal specialist, in order to provide a diagnosis and plan for treatment. The clinical actions performed by the doctor may have met all the requirements for good medical care, but the experience made you anxious and upset.

Both administrators and physicians have begun to realize that traditional methods of providing medical care often resulted in treating patients as objects. The approach was designed around the provider's needs, not the patient's, and everything was geared toward getting information from the patient to the doctor so that appropriate diagnosis and treatment would result. In the eyes of the provider, as long as the outcome was positive, this process defined quality care.

Until fairly recently, no one thought much about patient experience, nor did anyone define "quality care" to include the patient's feelings or satisfaction with the encounter. Recognizing that the service experience could be greatly improved, leaders have begun to consider the patient's point of view in designing the service encounter across the care continuum. For instance, the Studer Group, a consulting firm specializing in improving patient experience, has introduced a communication tool called A-I-D-E-T (Studer, 2003), which stands for acknowledge, introduce, duration, explain, and thank you (**Figure 6.2**). The A-I-D-E-T method puts people at ease during a stressful time in their lives, and encourages them to relate information more comfortably to their providers. The A-I-D-E-T model is an example of designing service delivery around the patient's needs rather than the provider's convenience.

Price has long been assumed to be fairly irrelevant in health care. For most people in the United States and Europe, third-party payers take care of the bills, and individual consumers have barely taken notice of the costs. However, as healthcare costs continued to escalate, payers have required patients to pick up more of the bill through larger premium contributions, copays and deductibles, and limitations

A stands for "Acknowledge the patient." You want to acknowledge them by their last name if possible.

I is for "Introduce." Introduce yourself, your skill set, your professional certification, and your training. "Hello, Mr. Clark. My name is Jackie and I'm a medical technologist. I will be taking your X-ray today. I have been a medical technologist for 10 years. In fact, I've done this procedure hundreds of times and I go back for additional training each year. I also have certification from the *American Registry of Radiologic Technologists*."

D is for "Duration." Describe the test: how long it's going to take; how long they're going to be there; and how long they'll have to wait on the results.

E stands for "Explanation." Explain the tests, the pain involved (be very honest), and what happens next. Explain you are going to be looking at their wrist band and why. Connect key words with patient safety and excellent care.

T stands for "Thank-you." "Thank you for choosing our hospital."

Figure 6.2 A-I-D-E-T® Communication Tool

AIDET® is a registered trademark of Studer Group. Used with permission Studer, Q. (2003). *Hardwiring excellence*. Gulf Breeze, FL: Fire Starter Publishing.

on coverage. Many employers have initiated high-deductible health plans (also known as consumer-directed health plans [CDHP]), where plan members are responsible for paying a significant deductible toward their healthcare expenses before the plan begins to pick up the costs. The allowable deductibles are indexed for inflation annually and announced by the US Treasury Department. Almost all high-deductible plans cover preventive services such as check-ups, immunizations, screenings (e.g., mammography, colonoscopy), as well as some wellness and health promotion programs (e.g., smoking cessation counseling, diabetes and nutrition education), though the extent of coverage varies significantly by plan.

This has prompted more cost-consciousness on the part of healthcare consumers, because they can no longer rely on the expectation that bills would be paid by someone else.

Consequently, price has become more important in health care. Recent studies have shown that pricing for common medical services varies widely across the United States and across different providers, with no significant differences in quality or outcomes. Consumers are being encouraged to shop around for the best price, and providers have been encouraged (or perhaps, forced) to become more transparent about the pricing of services. For example, many pharmacies now post pricing for commonly prescribed medications, allowing consumers to spend their discretionary healthcare deductible dollars more wisely. In highly competitive markets, some urgent care centers have posted prices for walk-in visits. Many health reformers regard consumers' newfound price sensitivity as a positive development that will spur higher-cost providers to more carefully manage their pricing for their markets and to become more cost-competitive.

Place refers to the location of health services within a community, and managers have looked to planners for guidance with regard to determining the optimal location for a service that the organization needs to market. The saying, "all healthcare is local" indicates the importance of place, because people look first for care in their local community when they become ill or get injured.

Most healthcare providers try to locate facilities in areas where they can find a favorable payer mix—that is, one where a high proportion of residents have private health insurance coverage, usually through their employers. One is more likely to find new hospitals, surgery centers, physician office buildings, urgent care clinics, and ancillary services (e.g., laboratory services and imaging) in growing regions of major metropolitan areas, typically suburbs with a low proportion of Medicaid beneficiaries. Planners seek out locations where investments in new facilities and equipment can be recouped in a short time frame, thus future cash flow determines where to locate facilities. In some respects the medical arms race described has shifted from competition for the latest and most advanced medical devices to competition for locations where well-insured patients live (Rosenthal, 2012).

Of course, competition also influences place decisions, and careful competitive assessment is critical to this aspect of marketing. Most leaders wish to avoid locations where multiple competitors are vying for the same market, and they will either look for another location or attempt to customize the product offering to serve a niche that competitors may have overlooked or failed to serve adequately. The latter instance takes us back to the product discussion, where the leader identifies unmet customer needs in the market and creates products (goods or services) to meet them.

When analyzing the competition, it is useful to compare data to average benchmarks in the market for a particular service. For example, if a health system is considering opening a new orthopedic facility in a particular area, it is essential to evaluate the number of orthopedic specialists already practicing in that area, and to analyze the number of patients currently being served. Benchmarks exist on the national level, and they allow the health system's planners to determine whether the area can support more doctors in this specialty. For example, the US Department of Health and Human Services has prepared projections of expected demand for physicians in various specialty categories, which can be used to evaluate the market saturation in regions or markets within United States (**Table 6.1**). Demand is expressed as the ratio of the number of physicians needed to serve 100,000 people, and planners can use this data to estimate the need for various specialists in a given geographic region or market by comparing the number in their market to the national average.

Another example where place has emerged as an increasingly important aspect of healthcare marketing has been the trend toward locating care in lower cost settings such as retail clinics and urgent care centers. The retail clinic model involves offering a limited menu of mainly routine medical services in retail outlets such as chain drugstores, supermarkets, or mass merchandise stores. The concept is to locate healthcare services outside traditional medical care settings such as physicians' offices, clinics, and hospital emergency rooms, and to use trained midlevel providers (e.g., nurse practitioners, physician assistants) to provide care for less serious illnesses and injuries. The services and procedures that these practitioners are allowed to provide (scope of practice) vary by state, as does the regulation of these clinics. In some states, retail clinics' staff must practice under the direct supervision of a licensed physician.

Patients can walk in without an appointment, be seen and treated, and receive prescriptions that can often be filled onsite. The largest such operation, Minute Clinic, is owned by the CVS drugstore chain, and it currently operates approximately 650 locations in 25 states (see http://www.minuteclinic.com).

While the retail clinic payment model has largely been "cash on the barrel"—meaning that consumers pay out of pocket for the visit at time of service—health plans have begun to cover their members for visits to these clinics. The payers recognize that if their customers went to an ER for a healthcare problem, especially during nights or weekends, they would have to pay a large bill, even with a steep copay required of the patient. The same visit to a retail clinic costs a fraction of the ER charges, so a number of plans have added incentives to use the clinics over more expensive alternatives. Furthermore, it has been estimated that of the approximately 129 million annual ER visits, most of them are for nonemergencies (Gold, 2013).

In addition, urgent care centers have been established to take care of patients in a setting that usually provides higher levels of care than that available through

Table 6.1   Physician Demand Projections per 100,000 Population, United States

Specialty	2005	2010	2015	2020	% Change
Total patient care	245.3	260.9	278.7	298.5	22%
Primary care	91.3	96.4	102.4	109.3	20
General family practice	36.9	39.1	41.4	44.0	19
General internal medicine	37.2	40.0	43.0	46.5	25
Pediatrics	17.1	17.3	18.0	18.8	9
Nonprimary care	154.0	164.5	176.3	189.2	23
Medical Specialties	30.1	32.6	35.6	38.8	29
Cardiology	7.2	7.8	8.6	9.6	33
Other internal medicine	22.9	24.8	26.9	29.2	27
Surgical Specialties	54.7	58.3	62.2	66.4	21
General surgery	13.5	14.5	15.7	16.9	25
OB/GYN	14.0	14.5	14.9	15.3	10
Ophthalmology	6.4	6.9	7.5	8.2	28
Orthopedic surgery	8.3	8.8	9.5	10.2	23
Other surgery	5.6	6.1	6.6	7.1	26
Otolaryngology	3.3	3.6	3.8	4.0	20
Urology	3.6	3.9	4.3	4.7	30
Other Specialties	69.2	73.6	78.5	84.0	21
Anesthesiology	13.0	13.9	15.1	16.3	25
Emergency medicine	8.9	9.4	9.8	10.3	15
Pathology	6.0	6.4	6.9	7.3	23
Psychiatry	13.2	13.9	14.6	15.4	16
Radiology	10.7	11.4	12.3	13.3	25
Other specialties	17.4	18.6	19.9	21.3	23

Data from: U.S. Department of Health and Human Services, Health Resources and Services Administration, Bureau of Health Professions. (2008, December). The *physician workforce: Projections and research into current issues affecting supply and demand*. Retrieved from http://bhpr.hrsa.gov/healthworkforce/reports/physwfissues.pdf; U.S. Census data.

a retail clinic, but outside traditional physician offices or ERs. Typically, urgent care centers employ providers who can treat problems that are more complex than those that a retail clinic could handle, but do not rise to the level of care available at an ER. Payers often reimburse plan members for urgent care visits, and they try to guide patients to the most cost-efficient setting depending on the problem (Blue Cross Blue Shield, 2013).

Promotion refers to the marketing communications that healthcare organizations create and send out to both internal and external constituencies, with the objective of building business. This is an intentionally broad definition, because marketing communication encompasses a great many methods beyond advertising, which is what most people think of when they hear the term *promotion*. In addition to advertising, this "P" includes public relations, outreach to physicians, internal communications to staff, special events like health fairs and community promotions, and social media. However, advertising is the most costly, the most visible, and often the most controversial aspect of promotion, because many physicians, nurses, employees, and supporters question whether allocating funds to advertising takes resources away from patient care and devotes them to branding and marketing purposes whose value remains uncertain (McCabe, 2012). The decision to invest scarce resources in advertising is one of the most difficult—and public—decisions that leaders must make.

Although direct-to-consumer (DTC) advertising by pharmaceutical companies captures the greatest share of all healthcare advertising expenditures in the United States, spending by hospitals, medical clinics, and medical providers has been increasing steadily, and now exceeds $1 billion annually (**Table 6.2**). Healthcare leaders maintain that such investments reap rewards in market share through consumer preference, as individuals take on more responsibility for deciding where to seek the best medical advice and which hospital they should choose for procedures (Newman, 2011).

While advertising for hospitals and health systems has met resistance from some internal constituencies, the need to compete for market share is so strong that leaders feel compelled to invest in this form of promotion. They are reluctant to sit back and watch their competitors assertively and publicly advertise for patients, even though there may be only anecdotal evidence that consumer-directed advertising results in increased market share. Nevertheless, there is broad agreement that patients are becoming more involved in decisions about where to go for health care, and many hospitals have determined that they must reach those consumers directly, rather than relying on physicians to refer them to their

Table 6.2 Estimated US Healthcare Advertising Expenditures, 2012

	Cost (billions)
Pharmaceuticals, direct-to-consumer	$4.16
Hospitals and medical centers, including physician practices and clinics	1.2

Data from: PharmaGuy. (2012, December 31). Some interesting pharma predictions for 2013 [Web log]. Retrieved from http://pharmamkting.blogspot.com/2012/12/some-interesting-pharma-predictions-for.html hospital. Furthermore, if the health system can attract a patient into its network of services and provide exceptional service and medical care, the patient will become loyal to the system and recommend it to friends and relatives, thus justifying the investment in consumer advertising (Cellucci, Wiggins, & Farnsworth, 2013).

The Marketing Mix

The Four Ps formulation is sometimes known as the marketing mix because marketing strategy involves some combination of these four elements, and leaders must make decisions about how and where to invest scarce budget resources for the greatest profit impact. Furthermore, not all "Ps" can receive equal support.

Healthcare leaders understand the need for marketing and choose the most appropriate methods to accomplish the organization's mission. While this requires a good deal of analysis and data, necessitating the coordinator role, for the most part the innovator role takes on greater importance here. The leader is required to integrate the competing points of view, make good judgments about the marketing strategies that he or she believes will work for the organization, and then convince others that the plan will be effective.

Partnering with Outside Organizations

Every organization faces the problem of allocating limited marketing resources, and the list of needs always seems to greatly exceed the means for accomplishing them. In many industries, marketing managers have sought to extend their resources by working collaboratively with other companies that serve the same customers in their markets. For example, a brand manufacturer and a distributor may collaborate on a joint program to develop new business for the manufacturer's product, with both partners sharing in the cost of a display at a professional conference and related promotional literature. In consumer marketing, brand marketers and retailers jointly advertise a featured product within the store's advertising and the marketer pays a portion of the cost of the ad. This is known as cooperative advertising, and it has become commonplace in the marketing of consumer packaged goods.

As healthcare becomes increasingly integrated across the care continuum, cooperative advertising opportunities will arise. Healthcare providers, especially hospitals, have traditionally functioned as standalone units, though many have begun to operate as both relatively independent entities as well as parts of systems (vertical and horizontal). As many observers have noted, in order to deliver quality care as well as to compete more effectively, hospitals must integrate with physicians, community clinics, providers of social services, long-term care facilities, and many others (Sultz & Young, 2011). Leaders must recognize the need to engage partners in collaborative approaches to marketing, especially in light of the trend to create seamless movement of patients through systems. This is likely to emerge as a crucial marketing need in the coming years, and successful healthcare organizations will adopt effective strategies for implementing cooperative marketing programs, which will not only extend limited marketing resources but also improve the organizations' ability to serve their constituencies and fulfill their missions.

Some readers might wonder why a discussion of collaboration and cooperation appears in a chapter devoted to competition and marketing. It is important to note that collaborating with partners will become essential for competing effectively in the market. In the new dynamic world of healthcare competition, cooperation may become one of the most effective strategic tools a leader can employ.

Case Study: Market Analysis

In a medium-sized US city, a prominent pediatrician and the administrator of an academic medical center dreamed of building a children's hospital that would help establish the medical center as a regional (or someday a national) destination for excellence in pediatric care. Interest in the idea began building as they shared their vision with other physicians, community leaders, and the media.

However, they also knew that they needed more than the ability to sell their vision if they wanted the project to succeed. They had to document the need for a new facility, which would require significant capital to build and equip, as well as recruit, support, and develop medical staff to care for the patients who would use it.

The medical staff, especially the pediatricians and pediatric specialists, strongly supported the project. While they had no firm data, anecdotally they told of having to refer patients out of the area because of a lack of local resources to care for them, and they vowed to refer patients to the new facility if it were built. The doctors were convinced that there was enough demand for more pediatric specialists, maintaining that families had been going out of town for care and that they had been losing patients who could not be accommodated locally. On the other hand, the population of the region, though stable, was not growing, and the demographic projections for the area suggested that the number of children ages 0 to 14 would remain flat or decline slightly over the next 20 years. The project would require a major community fundraising effort and funding from state and federal government sources, as well as taking on bond debt.

Competition from local hospitals is also a factor. While the market was served by six hospitals (five community hospitals and an academic medical center), two of the community hospitals had significant pediatric service lines and they opposed the project, warning that it would create an oversupply of pediatric inpatient beds that the community did not need.

The administrator ordered a market analysis to be conducted, to determine whether sufficient demand existed for the new facility. Although she felt sure that the hospital would succeed, much more than gut feeling was needed.

An analysis of the annual market share of pediatric patients who lived in the medical center's three-county service area was conducted by the medical

Table 6.CS1 Annual Inpatient Discharges of Pediatric Patients Residing in Service Area

	Pediatric Inpatient Discharges	Market Share (percent)
Academic Medical Center	1986	24.3%
Community Hospital #1	1871	22.9
Community Hospital #2	82	1.0
Community Hospital #3	8	0.1
Community Hospital #4	507	6.2
Community Hospital #5	1013	12.4

Data from New York State Health Department, http://www.health.ny .gov/statistics/sparcs/

center's planning department (**Table 6.CS1**). Note that the analysis was conducted on children residing in the service area, rather than the total number of inpatient discharges from area hospitals.

What do you see in the data? First, the medical center has the largest market share, but by no means does it dominate the market; the next closest competitor, Community Hospital #1, could potentially overtake the medical center if it could acquire or attract a large pediatric practice from the medical center. Indeed, the threat of this development lay in the back of the administrators' minds, and some critics suggested that the idea of building a children's hospital was merely the medical center's expensive strategy for retaining those physicians.

However, when adding up the market shares of all the hospitals in Table 6.1, you will see that the total does not add up to 100%, suggesting that the six hospitals serving the community are not treating all of the children who need acute care. The doctors were right: almost 33% of inpatient pediatric patients are going outside the area for treatment. The case for building a new children's hospital was much stronger as a result of this analysis.

Of course, many other factors must be considered before deciding to move forward with such an expensive and complex undertaking. Indeed, this analysis considered only the competitors that operate in the service area; children's hospitals in other major metropolitan locations have been receiving referrals, and they are unlikely to cease their efforts to maintain this patient volume. Further marketing research was conducted to assess the likelihood of patient referrals continuing to flow outside the market, and administrators discovered that the local pediatricians were not thrilled with the communication and feedback from the out-of-market children's hospitals, and they expressed the desire to handle more acute care patients locally. The point of this example is that the intuition that the leaders felt about the need for a new facility and the analyses conducted to assess its viability were equally important. The innovator and coordinator roles complemented one another.

Conclusion

The marketplace does not stand still, particularly in the contemporary health-care industry. Change occurs at a rapid pace, and new skills are required of those who lead healthcare organizations. Leaders must continually identify, explore, and take advantage of new opportunities in the market before competitors beat them to it.

This is a relatively new challenge for healthcare administrators, many of whom joined the profession expecting that the industry would be devoted to a more or less collaborative effort to provide patient care in a community-oriented mission. However, the fact that healthcare is a commercial business enterprise necessitates a competitive orientation by leaders, and survival depends on their ability to adapt and change rapidly to constant innovation and new demands.

In this chapter, we explored the role of marketing in this competitive environment, focusing on the competing values roles of innovator and coordinator in the CVF framework. Both roles are important for leaders, who must have insight into the marketplace, understand the needs of patients, and consider new and innovative ways of meeting those needs. At the same time, they must perform the coordinator role to manage data gathering and analysis that will both inform decisions about their insights and provide insight by bringing problems and opportunities to the attention of the leadership team.

Review Questions

1. One of the most frequent complaints heard from patients involves waiting to see a healthcare provider. No one likes to wait, yet even the most efficient scheduling systems cannot prevent waiting time once the patient arrives for an appointment. On your next visit to see your primary care or specialty care provider, take note of the waiting room. What could make the waiting experience better? What improvements can you see right in front of you? Here is the catch: the ideas you come up with cannot cost more than $100 in total.

2. Ask your friends, family members, or coworkers this simple question: Within the past year, have you bought a product or service that you were really excited about? Make a list of the answers. How many are healthcare related?

3. Go to a doctor-search website for your county. Choose a specialty, like obstetrics and gynecology or pediatrics. Find the number of doctors in that specialty who serve your county. Then, go to the US Census (http://www.census.gov/acs/www/) and find the population for your county. Calculate the ratio of physicians in that specialty per 100,000 people in your county. How does this number compare with the ratio for that specialty in Table 6.1? What does it tell you? What conclusions can you draw from this analysis?

References

American Community Survey. (n.d.). *U.S. Census Bureau*. Retrieved from http://www.census.gov/acs/www/

American Marketing Association. (2008). *The American marketing association releases new definition for marketing*. Retrieved from http://www.marketingpower.com/AboutAMA/Documents/American%20Marketing%20Association%20Releases%20New%20Definition%20for%20Marketing.pdf

Berkowitz, E. (2010). *Essentials of health care marketing* (3rd ed.). Sudbury, MA: Jones & Bartlett.

Blue Cross Blue Shield. (2013). *Deciding where to go*. Retrieved from http://www.bcbs.com/why-bcbs/immediate-medical-care/deciding-immediate-care.pdf

Cellucci, C., Wiggins, C., & Farnsworth, T. (2013). *Essential techniques for healthcare marketing professionals*. Chicago, IL: Health Administration Press.

Centers for Medicare and Medicaid Services. (2011). *Hospital value-based purchasing program*. Retrieved from http://www.cms.gov/Outreach-and-Education/Medicare-Learning-Network-MLN/MLNProducts/downloads/Hospital_VBPurchasing_Fact_Sheet_ICN907664.pdf

Centers for Medicare and Medicaid Services. (2013). *HCAHPS: Hospital care from the consumer perspective*. Retrieved from http://www.hcahpsonline.org/home.aspx

Evans, M. (2012, January 14). Juggling the lineup. *Modern Healthcare*. Retrieved from http://www.modernhealthcare.com/article/20120114/MAGAZINE/301149993

Gold, A. (2013). 70% of ER visits unnecessary for patients with employer-sponsored insurance. *Fierce Healthcare*. Retrieved from http://www.fiercehealthcare.com/story/70-er-visits-patients-employer-sponsored-insurance-deemed-unnecessary/2013-04-29

Gold, J. (2013, May 31). Proton beam therapy sparks hospital arms race. *Kaiser Health News*. Retrieved from http://www.npr.org/blogs/health/2013/05/31/187350802/proton-beam-therapy-sparks-hospital-arms-race

Gurowitz, M. (2006, July 20). BAND-AID® brand adhesive bandages. *Kilmer House*. Retrieved from http://www.kilmerhouse.com/2006/07/band-aid-brand-adhesive-bandages/

Horwitz, J. R. (2005). Making profits and providing care: Comparing nonprofit, for-profit, and government hospitals. *Health Affairs, 24*(3), 790–801.

Kotler, P., & Keller, K. L. (2012). *Marketing management* (14th ed.). Upper Saddle River, NJ: Prentice Hall.

Leclerc, O., & Moldoveneanu, M. (2013, April). Five routes to more innovative problem solving. *McKinsey Quarterly*. Retrieved from http://www.mckinsey.com/insights/strategy/five_routes_to_more_innovative_problem_solving

Lovelock, C., & Wirtz, J. (2010). *Services marketing* (7th ed.). Upper Saddle River, NJ: Prentice Hall.

McCabe, J. (2012). *Hospital advertising and marketing* [Web log]. Retrieved from http://blogs.upstate.edu/ceo/2012/12/07/hospital-advertising-and-marketing/

Merlino, J. I., & Rahman, A. (2013). Health care's service fanatics: How the Cleveland Clinic leaped to the top of patient-satisfaction surveys. *Harvard Business Review, 91*(5), 108–116.

Michelli, J. A. (2011). *Prescription for excellence: Leadership lessons for creating a world-class customer experience from the UCLA Health System*. New York, NY: McGraw-Hill.

National Committee for Quality Assurance. (2012). *HEDIS 2013: Healthcare effectiveness data and information set* (Vol. 1). Washington, DC: National Committee for Quality Assurance.

Nelson, P. (2011, April). Value-based purchasing raises the stakes. *The Hospitalist.* Retrieved from http://www.the-hospitalist.org/details/article/1056049/Value-Based _Purchasing_Raises_the_Stakes.html

Newman, A. (2011, September 12). A healing touch from hospitals. *The New York Times.*

Oliver, R. L. (2009). *Satisfaction: A behavioral perspective on the consumer* (2nd ed.). Armonk, NY: M. E. Sharpe.

PharmaGuy. (2012, December 31). Some interesting pharma predictions for 2013 [Web log]. Retrieved from http://pharmamkting.blogspot.com/2012/12/some-interesting -pharma-predictions-for.html

Quinn, R. E. (1988). *Beyond rational management: Mastering the paradoxes and competing demands of high performance.* San Francisco, CA: Jossey-Bass.

Relman, A. S. (2005, March 7). The health of nations. *The New Republic.*

Rosenthal, M. (2012, May 1). Higher costs resulting from medical arms race. *Managed Care Executive.*

Stieger, D., Matzler, K., Ladstaetter-Fussenegger, F., & Chatterjee, S. (2012). Democratizing strategy: How crowdsourcing can be used for strategy dialogues. *California Management Review, 54*(4), 44–68.

Studer, Q. (2003). *Hardwiring excellence.* Gulf Breeze, FL: Fire Starter Publishing.

Sultz, H. A., & Young, K. M. (2011). *Health care USA: Understanding its organization and delivery* (7th ed.). Sudbury, MA: Jones & Bartlett.

U.S. Department of Health and Human Services, Health Resources and Services Administration, Bureau of Health Professions. (2008, December). *The physician workforce: Projections and research into current issues affecting supply and demand.* Retrieved from http://bhpr.hrsa.gov/healthworkforce/reports/physwfissues.pdf

Wennberg, J. E. (2004). Practice variations and health care reform: Connecting the dots. *Health Affairs.* doi:10.1377/hlthaff.var.140.

CHAPTER 7 ►

Achieving Sustained Commitment to the Goals of the Healthcare Organization

LEARNING OBJECTIVES

Students will be able to:

- Distinguish between types of commonly used goals: organizational, individual, strategic, and operational
- Appreciate the power of goals to influence and motivate employees, managers, and teams
- Recognize the importance of setting goals that are appropriate to the team and organization, as well as to individuals
- Take into account the potential side effects and unintended consequences of improperly formulated goals
- Understand the role of goal setting in strategic planning, operational planning and project planning
- Utilize the competing values framework (CVF) to understand the relationships between the various roles that master leaders must play and goal measurement frameworks such as the balanced scorecard

A Change of Management

Mike had just taken over as CEO of the Dimas Medical Supply Company, which had been family owned and operated for almost three decades. The company had built strong relationships with hospitals and medical practices throughout their markets, but changes in the healthcare industry were having a significant impact on the medical supply business. A capital investment group decided to buy the company, and they selected Mike to succeed the retiring president and owner, a son of the original founder of the firm.

He faced some difficult challenges. The business had been successful, but mergers and consolidations among customers changed the purchasing dynamics for medical supplies at all levels of the healthcare industry. Many hospitals with which they had done business for years became a part of large health systems, and their local purchasing authority diminished. The remaining independent hospitals had increasingly turned to group purchasing organizations (GPOs) that leveraged their size to exact price concessions from all suppliers, as well as expanding the geographic region from which they sourced. In addition, competitors detected some complacency on the part of Dimas, which they exploited. Consequently the business had begun to experience declines in revenue and market share. The family members who had operated the business were reluctant to lay off any employees, so company financials had deteriorated significantly. Mike's bosses at the investment firm knew that trimming expenses would immediately improve the bottom line, however beyond this short-term goal, the company needed to regain its footing and resume its growth in order to reestablish a positive cash flow and generate a return to investors.

The first order of business was to get the company's expenses in line with revenue, which meant layoffs—for the first time in anyone's memory, people working at Dimas lost their jobs, so it was a traumatic event. This happened in the first month of Mike's joining the firm. Other expenses were reduced as well, but the psychological impact of those cost reductions paled in comparison to the layoffs that took place. The former owners expressed dismay about the staffing decisions that Mike had made, and they sympathized with the employees, but they were gone and couldn't do anything about it. To Mike, they were not being very helpful, as they implied that things would be different if they were still in control.

Ninety days into the job, Mike had begun to rebuild the management team, bringing in a few people from the outside as well as identifying some real stars within the company, who had been overlooked by the former owners. The latter group had expressed their concerns about the company's competitive position in the market and the need for change, but the former CEO and management team dismissed their concerns as pessimism. Mike saw that several of them had good ideas for solving problems and improving the business, which he embraced, encouraged, and agreed to fund.

As he reached the date that marked his first 100 days in office, Mike decided to call a company-wide meeting. He talked about achieving the short-term goals of returning the company to profitability and stabilizing the financial outlook, and he thanked the employees for their hard work, loyalty, and patience while these difficult changes were made. Then he began talking about the future, laying out a vision in which the company could compete effectively in some very promising categories while maintaining customer loyalty in the core business. These goals were clear and simple, and people began to see where the company was headed. He ended his talk by saying: "I see you in this new direction for the company. You belong here. Now, you need to see yourself in this vision, because we all need to reach these goals together." For the first time since he arrived, people began smiling and nodding.

Introduction

Mike's talk succeeded because he clearly separated the past from the future, as well as the short term from the long term. In setting goals for the company, he made it a priority to articulate them with clarity and simplicity so that everyone could comprehend them and get behind them. The goals he articulated were neither specific nor quantitative, but rather were tied to his vision of future success for the firm. People could understand them and see themselves in that vision.

Organizations cannot operate on squishy goals that lack specifics, but goals can be articulated in different ways for different audiences. Talking about goals solely as "10% compound annual growth rate" or "15% return on sales" will usually engender confusion and disinterest among most employees. However, goals do need to be specific in order to produce optimal results, thus stating them in terms that employees can understand is critical to success. For example, workers can relate to goals such as "10% improvement in sales," or "improve our customer satisfaction scores to the 90% level by the end of the year." In addition, goals must be reachable, or employees will become discouraged. For example, setting a goal to "increase patient volume by 50% in the next fiscal year" may strike the leader as a good stretch goal that he hopes will motivate employees to go above and beyond their ordinary duties to reach, but unless there is a clear and rational plan for achieving such an ambitious goal, employees will only become frustrated.

In this chapter, we will discuss the process of setting goals based on the evidence and realities of the marketplace, including market potential, anticipated growth, competition, and regulatory demands.

Goals fall into three basic categories—individual, organizational, and project based.

Individual Goals

In health care, as well as in business organizations generally, establishing individual goals plays an important managerial role. For employees, they provide definitive performance expectations that must be met, and thus provide a basis for determining whether the employees have done the job that the company needs them to do. In addition, goals allow employees to self-manage, such that managers are not required to constantly monitor and micromanage every aspect of their employees' behavior, thus helping employees prioritize tasks on the job (Shalley, 1995). In addition, goals serve the purpose of motivating people to invest effort in the desired direction of the firm (Latham & Budworth, 2006).

Management by Objectives

Peter Drucker, one of the most renowned management theorists of the 20th century, coined the term *management by objectives* (MBO) in the 1950s. The basic idea is that rather than closely supervising every activity of each employee, managers should set objectives and hold people accountable for reaching them. Thus, more responsibility would rest on the shoulders of those who are closest to the work being performed, and a different form of worker–boss interaction would result. The MBO process requires the company to set specific goals that both the employee and employer have decided upon and agreed to, and therefore workers know what is expected of them, so they can mutually agree upon performance. Done properly, both the individual's goals and the organization's goals should be aligned (Drucker, 1974).

Drucker also emphasized the importance of making the individual's goals specific, measurable, achievable, realistic, and time based–using the acronym SMART. This would help ensure that they align with the organization's goals while providing the manager with a means for evaluating employee performance. By making the goals specific, they can be measurable. For instance, instead of stating a goal like "improve quality of patient care," a healthcare leader's goal could be "reduce the 30-day readmissions rate by 75%," which is a very clear goal that all would agree is important to the organization. The goal also has to be achievable, and in this example healthcare professionals recognize that reducing 30-day readmissions by 75% is not achievable, since a great many factors lie outside the providers' control. Senior management may want to reduce readmissions by 75% but it is just not going to happen, so, the goal must also be realistic. Finally, it must be time based, a parameter that sets a realistic deadline for achieving the goal. For example, if the manager were given no deadline by which to reduce 30-day readmissions, he could still be working on it 10 years later with no end in sight. A restated goal might read like this: "Within the next 12 months, reduce the 30-day readmissions rate by 25%."

While the goal (reducing 30-day readmissions by 25% in the next 12 months) meets the SMART criteria for a good goal that can apply to both an individual manager's performance and the organization, it clearly will require a comprehensive set of interrelated goals and strategies in order for the manager to achieve it. Critics of the MBO approach note that it focuses on ends versus means, and in the pursuit of achieving their goals, managers may overlook practical and ethical problems they create along the way (Barsky, 2007). For example, the manager focused on reducing readmission rates by 25% may directly or indirectly encourage billing staff to enter different codes for a returning patient so that it looks like the patient is being admitted for observation rather than for the same health problem the hospital originally treated, in order to avoid having the patient count as a readmission (Feng, Wright, & Mor, 2012).

How Individual Goals Work

According to Locke and Latham (2002), there are four ways in which employee performance can be enhanced through goal setting:

1. Goals focus attention toward relevant activities and away from goal-irrelevant activities.
2. Goals help energize employees, encouraging greater effort.
3. Goals affect persistence, and harder goals promote more time and intensity into the tasks required to achieve the goal.
4. Goals work indirectly by stimulating cognitive and motivational elaboration; in other words, goals encourage people to think beyond the task at hand and use their experience and problem-solving skills.

For example, if the manager of a hospital emergency department is given the goal of reducing average wait time in the emergency room (ER) by 30 minutes, the manager could use a variety of tools and strategies to accomplish the goal. Ideas could include improving patient flow, developing a more effective system of triage so that less-urgent cases are handled outside the ER, allowing more flexible provider scheduling, and reducing inpatient admission bottlenecks that keep patients stuck in the ER, among others. Senior management could have chosen to create separate goals for each of the above items—for instance, the manager could have been given the goal to "improve patient flow through the ER"; however, the higher-level goal of reducing the average wait time allows the manager more flexibility in solving an organizational problem that will serve the hospital's strategic objectives. In addition, the increased empowerment and flexibility that accompany appropriately set goals have been shown to have a positive motivational impact on employees, assuming sufficient resources are provided to accomplish the goal (Locke, 1991).

Clearly, in healthcare organizations, tasks become more and more complex each day, requiring employees to use their existing knowledge and new learning to devise appropriate problem solving methods. The ER scenario outlined above provides a good illustration of this complexity—in order to solve any of the specific problems that can cause long waits in the ER, issues outside the ER must be taken into consideration. For example, a bottleneck in inpatient admissions to medical-surgical beds occurs outside the scope of authority of the ER director, but it often causes backups in the ER, and thereby increases wait times.

Importantly, goals that are not easy to accomplish tend to motivate higher performance, up to a limit (Locke & Latham, 1990). The difficulty of the task is attenuated when employees are given specific goals instead of being instructed to simply do their best, and the presence of goals significantly improves the probability of success for difficult tasks. At some point though, the task can become too difficult for the employee to perform with his or her skill set, and the effect of goal setting diminishes. However, if employees succeed in achieving increasingly difficult goals, they can improve productivity and efficiency, accomplishing successive tasks at progressively higher levels. Locke and Latham (2002, p. 714) term this the *high-performance cycle*, setting the stage for leaders to establish a system of individual goals as an organizational management strategy. In many firms, leaders have used this phenomenon to set stretch goals that appear to be nearly impossible to reach, yet if people can reach them, they and the organization both benefit. Then, in theory, the organization can grow both quantitatively and qualitatively, getting better at meeting increasingly challenging goals, and thus becoming more successful than its competitors or peers.

Not all management researchers agree that goal setting should occupy such an important place in organizational management. Individual goals sometimes conflict with the goals of the work group or unit in which employees function, and sometimes with the goals of the company overall. Recent studies have suggested that the effects of individual goals are highly complex, especially in situations where employees work in groups or teams. Although individual goals encourage superior performance by employees working alone on specific tasks, such goals may prove counterproductive in work-group settings, and the presence of individual goals can actually lower performance when people work in groups on interdependent tasks. Employees who work in interdependent teams and are given individual goals tend to be more competitive and less cooperative, resulting in lower group performance (Mitchell & Silver, 1990). Furthermore, Zhang and Chiu (2012) found that selfish pursuit of individual goals reduced employees' commitment to their group, which poses a threat to the group's effectiveness. However, they also found that if individual and group goals are shared, employees become committed to both sets of goals.

The latter set of findings suggests that the dynamics of individual goal setting are complicated, and managing them effectively can be quite difficult. Ordonez, Schweitzer, Galinsky, and Bazerman (2009) warn against the overuse of goal setting as a management tool, noting that people often become too focused on goals that are designed to accomplish short-term wins, and that individual goals often produce undesired side effects in the same way that prescription drugs do. For example, goals that are too challenging can induce excessive risk taking, a problem that has created a number of disasters in business, including the collapse of Enron and the 2008 meltdown of the financial services industry related to the subprime mortgage market. In addition, a focus on individual goals can promote unethical behavior on the part of employees, especially when incentives are present. Sometimes the unethical behavior involves small but unmistakable cheating, such as moving sales orders from one quarter to another; at other times employees have engaged in serious instances of misrepresentation, misreporting, or deception (Jensen, 2003). Some healthcare organizations have attracted scrutiny from regulators who allege that they established goals for their physicians to admit certain numbers of patients into the hospital, raising ethical questions about the dilemma brought about by this practice. In some cases, physicians said that administrators praised doctors who met or exceeded their goals and exhorted better performance from (or even threatened) those who did not. This is an ethical issue that has received significant media attention, and several cases remain pending (Creswell & Abelson, 2012).

Individual goals can also produce perverse incentives, a phenomenon that occurs often in health care. The fee-for-service reimbursement system has been blamed for overuse of the healthcare system, excesses in billing for certain profitable services, and questionable referral practices (Goozner, 2012). Because healthcare providers are paid for every service they deliver to patients, a financial incentive exists to do more than perhaps is necessary. Doctors control all diagnosis and treatment decisions, and the medical profession takes seriously its responsibility to provide appropriate care to patients. Nonphysicians may not question the clinical decisions that doctors make. However, critics note that the financial pressures in the healthcare industry are filtering down to the bedside, especially as the industry continues to consolidate and more physicians are now employed by large hospital health systems. Fewer and fewer physicians work in independent practices, and large health systems have acquired many physician practice groups in order to vertically integrate their services.

Team considerations have become increasingly important in healthcare organizations, as patient care has become more interdependent, requiring careful coordination and better communication throughout a healthcare system that has traditionally operated in an individualistic fashion. This can be problematic for a management team that relies extensively on using goals to motivate people, because a focus on individual goals tends to promote competition over cooperation, and workers focus on their own roles rather than helping coworkers (Mitchell & Silver, 1990). Teamwork and cooperation are becoming critical to the success of contemporary healthcare organizations, as the industry's leaders have recognized that lapses in quality are often attributable to poorly functioning systems rather than poor performance by individuals (Institute of Medicine, 2000).

As Gawande (2011) has observed, the practice of medicine as well as the delivery of health care is rapidly transitioning from a culture of the cowboy (a single doctor relying on his or her own knowledge, skill, experience, and wits) to that of a pit crew (a carefully coordinated team of individuals who work expertly at their own task but remain focused on the team's goal). Inevitably, healthcare delivery must evolve toward the model of teamwork, coordination, and cooperation.

Cowboys and Pit Crews

In May 2011, Dr. Atul Gawande delivered the commencement address to the graduates of his alma mater, Harvard Medical School. He titled his talk "Cowboys and Pit Crews" to illustrate the ways in which the practice of medicine has changed and how doctors will need to adapt.

Gawande (2011) noted that until fairly recently, little was known about the causes or treatment of diseases, forcing doctors to rely on their training and personal experience to diagnose medical problems and prescribe remedies. He observed that this tended to produce a self-reliant "cowboy" culture among physicians, who worked alone and figured out the solution to problems on the fly. They had little use for the nurses, technicians, and administrators working alongside them, other than as assistants to carry out their orders. The unquestioned expertise of physicians gave them power, prestige, and authority.

However, with the scientific advances in medicine that have allowed us to understand the etiology of disease and how to treat it, this self-reliant culture has come under greater scrutiny. Rather than depending on personal experience and intuition, physicians rely on test results, clinical trials, and results from comparative effectiveness studies, as evidence-based medicine has begun to overtake the intuitive judgment of the individual physician. This has had profound effects on the ways in which medical care is delivered, many more professionals are now involved in the care of individual patients. In addition to nurses, other healthcare professionals and support personnel provide a wide variety of clinical services including imaging, lab work, nutrition counseling, and others, and good patient care now includes post-discharge planning, to ensure that patients remain healthy after leaving the hospital.

Thus, physicians find themselves working in highly interdependent group settings, more akin to a race car driver working with a pit crew. Everyone on a race car team shares the same goal, with members of the pit crew playing crucial roles in a highly coordinated effort in which each individual's contribution is essential to success. Gawande points out that physicians must adopt a new attitude, one in which they work as a member of the team, cooperating with a variety of coworkers, coordinating and communicating effectively to accomplish the team goal.

It means moving from cowboy to pit crew.

This discussion should not be interpreted as an indictment against individual goals in healthcare management, but rather a caution about using them appropriately. As Locke and Latham (2002) have shown, individual goals have great power to motivate employees (and leaders) to behave in ways that enhance performance, productivity, and effectiveness. However, that power can also work in ways unintended by the leaders who establish them, and the organization can suffer negative consequences. Thus, it is important that goals be properly managed to serve the purposes of the team, unit, and institution as a whole.

Organizational Goals

Organizations exist for a reason, and that reason is usually articulated in some statement of mission. What does the organization seek to accomplish?

A senior executive of a large diversified company once described his company's mission statement as the "circle outside which we shall not step." As such, a mission statement is a scope-limiting tool: it defines the area in which the organization will operate, and where it will not. Note that the circle can be as large or as small as the firm wants it to be; in fact, it must be large enough to allow room for growth and yet small enough to define a meaningful role for itself in the market, serving to establish an identity that both customers and employees can understand and relate to.

As Drucker (1974, p. 61) observed, "Only a clear definition of the mission and purpose of the organization makes possible clear and realistic business objectives." However, mission statements that are too vague or overly broad can set the stage for goals that may or may not make sense. For example, a children's hospital posted the following mission statement on its website: *Our mission is to eradicate pediatric illness.*

Although this statement draws a very large circle in which the hospital can operate, it does limit the scope to a segment of the population, namely children. However, the statement affords the hospital a great many strategic options. For instance, the hospital's leaders could invest in basic research to lead the effort to reduce children's suffering from a variety of afflictions that cause them and their families so much pain. They could decide to create an institute dedicated to researching the effectiveness of medical and surgical treatment of a particular disease category, such as pediatric cardiology. They could focus on health effectiveness and excellence in clinical treatment of children, becoming known as a hospital with superior outcomes in an area like neonatology. So while certainly laudable, this statement is so broad that just about any strategy can be considered valid in support of the mission, and although the mission statement is specific to children, it is unrealistic to think it can ever be accomplished. Thus, while it serves an aspirational purpose, it does not allow the hospital to focus on any particular set of goals, so it does not provide a strategic direction for the organization other than defining its patient population.

Management theorists distinguish between two kinds of organizational goals: official goals and operative goals (Daft, 2009). Official goals include not only the directional goals that are articulated in the mission and vision statements, but also ancillary goals that promise some benefits for the organization's constituency. For example, the mission of the children's hospital cited previously is to "eradicate pediatric illness." But in its annual report and community service plan, the hospital might also promise a commitment to being "a workplace that respects the dignity of each and every individual employee." Neither goal is specific. Official goals describe the general intent of the organization, and they tend to be more aspirational in nature, but usually there is no mention of how to get there.

Operative goals are the specific goals that the organization needs to accomplish in order to achieve its mission. They pertain to the actions that the organization will undertake, and leaders pay attention to their formulation and implementation when they relate to the core official goals of the organization, which involve financial and market metrics to which boards and managers pay close attention. For example, boards and senior management pay enormous attention to measures like market share in profitable service lines, inpatient census, average length of stay, cash flow, revenue cycle, operating margin, debt coverage ratios, and other metrics. Operative goals related to these metrics are established, and management is held accountable for reaching them. However, the official goals that promise benefits but are more peripheral to the organization seldom have corresponding operative goals, and accountability is not closely managed. A health system's official goals may mention respect for employees, environmental friendliness and stewardship, patient-first service, or community well-being, yet related operative goals are not usually considered or mentioned in the system's strategic and operational plans.

A Framework for Organizational Goals

The previous discussion illustrates the challenges of setting and managing goals that are highly interdependent across individuals and organizations. Intended or not, one goal and its associated strategies will affect other goals of the organization and its people; thus, goals must be carefully managed. A well-organized system of goals and strategies can operate effectively if they are coordinated and continually assessed.

The organization's mission serves as the directional goal, from which other goals are derived. Alternatively, the various goals that an organization tries to achieve are means to accomplish the ends described by the mission (Belasen, 2000). This fact helps shape the framework for strategic planning, which occurs at many levels of healthcare organizations and must adapt to constantly and rapidly changing environments, yet retain a mission that essentially remains fixed for a longer period of time. Swayne, Duncan, and Ginter (2006) depict this as a hierarchical framework of strategic planning in which healthcare institutions use lower-order strategies to accomplish the higher-order goals in a means-ends chain of actions designed to achieve the mission. Each level has a different focus, yet all relate to one another because they help execute the overall directional strategy of the healthcare organization.

Good strategy links the organization's mission to action, but good strategy also links actions to important organizational goals. For example, a community hospital may acquire a medical practice in its primary service area, and doing so would help the hospital achieve its mission of serving the population of the community. But strategically, acquiring the practice expands the scope of the hospital, extending its resources to achieve vertical integration, and enabling the hospital to provide coordinated care to its patients. However, the move also accomplishes the competitive goal of enhancing its market share by virtually assuring that a very high proportion of inpatient admissions (and revenue from ancillary services like labs, imaging, medications, etc.) will originate from this medical group. Thus, the hospital captures more of the market's healthcare business in two ways: (1) by providing primary care through a medical practice (upstream), and (2) by obtaining a higher proportion of the specialty referrals and inpatient admissions (downstream).

This framework helps leaders understand the relationships between decisions made throughout the strategic planning process: because every level of decision making is connected to both downstream and upstream strategies, the implications of strategies must be considered throughout the organization. Master leaders recognize this fact, and thus they include multiple levels of the organization in strategic planning. Of course, this requires much more investment in the planning process than that which many healthcare leadership teams are accustomed. Instead of simply providing analysis of the internal and external environment, planning teams and line managers must be fully involved in the strategic planning process, so that higher-level strategies can be articulated with a clear view of how they will be executed, in view of the impact they will have downstream.

Organizational goals come with many of the same risks as individual goals, and they need to be managed with the same care and caution (Ordonez et al., 2009). Just as managers sometimes set goals for individuals that can be counterproductive for the work team or company, organizations can set goals that benefit certain units or senior managers, while inadvertently undermining the strategic goals of the company as a whole. Organizations and their leaders are prone to focusing on short-term objectives at the expense of long-term goals, often leading to a myopic perspective and inferior performance over the long run. Many publicly traded firms have famously diverted their attention from R&D, innovation, and investment in their employees in order to meet quarterly earnings expectations, on which the leaders' bonus payments are based. In addition, organizations often focus on goals that are quantitative and measureable, while overlooking their overall purpose. For example, by focusing on compliance with specific quantitative metrics for quality (Centers for Medicare and Medicaid Services, 2014), a healthcare system may become distracted from working on the more important overall goal of delivering high-quality care and service to patients. Because hospitals have to meet certain benchmarks in order to qualify for full Medicare reimbursement under the CMS value-based purchasing (VBP) program, it is natural for their leaders to closely manage their organizations to meet those criteria (Rau, 2012).

Setting Organizational Goals Based on Strategic Position

In practice, organizational goals are frequently set by managers who create coalitions of noncompeting groups from among other units. Then, they engage in a process of negotiation among the different organizational unit leaders to establish the strategic direction of the organization. In this kind of planning process, those units with greater power will have more control over the direction of the company, which may or may not result in goals that operate in the best interests of the organization as a whole. Oftentimes, this happens when the CEO decides to build the strategic direction of the firm on the plans of individual operating units, letting unit management to decide the direction by consensus.

Rumelt (2011) points out the difficulty with this approach, namely that the goals of a firms' operating units may not coincide—and they sometimes conflict with one another. In this case, the leader needs to choose which direction to pursue, and failure to make this choice can result in disaster. He cites the famous example of Digital Equipment Corporation (DEC), whose CEO asked the unit heads of three operating divisions to come to consensus on which of their technologies the company should invest its future in. Though all three were in the computer technology space, they were very different businesses, and pursuing one meant selling off or discontinuing the other two. The unit heads could not come to consensus, so they created an almost meaningless goal statement: "DEC is committed to providing high-quality products and services and being a leader in data processing" (Rumelt, 2011, p. 7). This indecision cost DEC dearly, and they watched as competitors raced ahead with focused strategies that capitalized on technological advances in computing. Digital Equipment Corporation no longer exists.

It is critical for the master leader to establish the direction, but it is just as important to make sure that the direction relies on facts, evidence, and a true reading of the market and environment. It cannot be done in a vacuum, but as Rumelt's DEC example illustrates, the responsibility cannot be abdicated. From the perspective of the CVF in **Figure 7.1**, the vision-setter role must be played with extraordinary skill.

The Healthcare Organization's Position in the Marketplace

No two organizations are exactly alike, and each faces a different situation, both internally and externally. Not every healthcare organization has a dominant market share, nor do all institutions face a fragmented, competitive market. A thorough analysis of the market position is required to understand the kinds of goals that need to be accomplished.

Consider the following scenarios:

- ▶ **Scenario A.** A hospital health system is located in a rural area, 50 miles from a medium-sized metropolitan area of 2 million people. Within its service area, it has a large market share, but low population density. The population is not growing, and the average age is increasing. While the town is in the media market of the metro area and people see ads for hospitals there, the area is less attractive to outside competitors.
- ▶ **Scenario B.** A hospital health system is located in the middle of a major metropolitan area of 6 million people. Many competitors surround it, so it operates in a highly fragmented and competitive market, has a low market share, and has high population density. The population is highly diverse, the market is growing, and so are the healthcare needs of the area.

Figure 7.1 Leadership Roles (Top Managers)

Modified from: Hart, S. L., & Quinn R. E. (1993). Roles executives play: CEOs, behavioral complexity, and firm performance. *Human Relations, 46*(1993): 543–574.

Clearly, these two organizations face dramatically different situations, much of which their executives do not control. Neither health system can influence the number of people who choose to live in its service area, nor can they affect the age or demographic diversity of their population. They cannot dictate the general economic conditions of their market, which affect population migration (people move out when jobs are scarce, and they move in when the local economy is growing), their payer mix (stronger economic conditions mean higher employment, translating to larger numbers of insured patients), and community health (areas with higher unemployment rates usually see different health problems than regions with full employment). They also cannot control the population density of their services areas—one is rural and one is urban; by nature, the denser the population in a region, the more intense the competition for services will be. So, while they may have similar missions, these strategic goals of these two health systems must differ from one another to reflect the reality of the market situation each faces.

In Scenario A, the health system has the opportunity to become the dominant healthcare provider for the service area, so its goals may include expanding its scope of operations, vertically integrating to provide all the healthcare services needed by the people who live there. Thus, its executives may choose to acquire the region's primary care and specialty medical practices, as well as ancillary services that support the system. Downstream goals will be required to integrate these services into a coherent and effective system, and strategies must be carefully worked out to accomplish this goal, down to the unit level. The health system in Scenario B faces an entirely different set of challenges. Because of the size and nature of its market, it could decide to *narrow* its scope of operations to achieve competitive advantage, as it may see opportunities to establish leadership within a niche. For example, based on its own strengths and the capabilities of its competitors, the health system's leaders could choose to develop specialty service lines such as orthopedics or women's health, allocating resources to build these areas and differentiate them from the competition. Again, downstream goals and strategies would be built around the goal of defining the health system as a leader within a particular niche. These goals would include, for instance, building referral relationships and networks so that primary care providers and specialists would think of this health system's services first, and regard them as the best. It would not be necessary to acquire primary care practices to ensure this referral flow, because in a densely populated metropolitan area, there would be too many of them and the health system's focal service lines would represent a small proportion of referrals from a primary care practice. Note that such a strategy would not work for the system in Scenario A because its market is too small to support a niche strategy. By pursuing a goal to narrow its scope and focus, the health system in Scenario B has the opportunity build scale by capitalizing on its core competency.

Managing Long-Range Strategic Planning

Both example scenarios described previously require a great deal of thinking and planning by the boards of directors and executives who lead those systems. The planning effort relies on data and information about the external market and internal capabilities, but perhaps more importantly, it relies on the insights that the leaders can derive from their careful and thoughtful study of the business.

In practice, both boards and executives tend to focus on growth goals for their institutions, a trend that has contributed to a boom in constructing new facilities, adding clinical capabilities, purchasing new equipment, and acquiring other institutions. The competitive environment in which healthcare organizations operate has necessitated that executives attend to building market share of profitable service lines, which means acquiring the right kinds of medical practices, recruiting specialists, and providing first-rate facilities and equipment. Critics point out that hospital boards value growth goals over patient-oriented goals by rewarding executives with bonuses that are linked primarily to increases in volume and profits, and consequently they pay far less attention to quality of care, operational effectiveness, and patient well-being (Hancock, 2013).

As indicated in Figure 7.1, master leaders engage in both the vision-setter and the analyzer roles, so both the long-range strategic planning and the quality-safety needs of the healthcare organization can be met. However, in most healthcare organizations the growth goals overpower the operational goals at the senior management level, and at the operating unit level the needs of the moment tend to be especially demanding and draw much of the organization's brainpower, energy, and resources to operational necessities. At the same time, the environment is changing in ways that create uncertainty and unpredictability.

These problems have been recognized by Kaplan and Norton (1996), management theorists who proposed a *balanced scorecard* approach to strategic planning, in which the needs of multiple constituencies are measured when formulating plans and setting goals. They suggested a system of four fundamental perspectives to account for the different needs of the organization and its outside constituencies, with specific metrics or measurements that apply to each. These perspectives are the learning and growth perspective, the business process perspective, the customer perspective, and the financial perspective.

The *learning and growth perspective* focuses on employee training, organizational culture, and improvement through learning. Importantly, this perspective is designed to apply to the organization as a whole, not just individual personnel, so that organizations can improve their chances of success by learning from their experience, data, customers, and employees. Clearly, this requires an organizational culture that encourages communication, transparency, and information sharing from top to bottom. In many healthcare organizations, the traditional way of operating in silos has inhibited the system-wide ability to learn from experience, including mistakes (Tucker & Edmondson, 2003). As health care has become increasingly information-intense, this aspect of the balanced scorecard will take on greater importance.

The *business process perspective* involves assessment of the operational effectiveness of the organization, including the extent to which the needs of patients are being met. Healthcare executives have been forced to pay attention to these processes, because reimbursement is being linked to quality metrics by CMS under the VBP program. Notably, employers and private insurers are following CMS's lead by using quality data to move from paying providers for hitting general performance goals to paying for improved health outcomes for their employees and members.

The *customer perspective* recognizes the importance of a customer-centric approach as well as customer satisfaction. Again, CMS has taken the lead by requiring all acute care institutions that receive Medicare funding to participate in the Hospital Consumer Assessment of Healthcare Providers and Systems (HCAHPS) program, and publishing the results on a quarterly basis. Hospital leaders have begun to pay close attention to their HCAHPS scores, and have begun serious efforts to improve the patient experience. CMS has introduced a similar tool that measures patient experience and satisfaction with providers who practice in group medical practices (CG-CAHPS), but participation is not mandatory and few medical practices use it. Nonetheless, the customer perspective idea goes beyond participation in a survey program to receive reimbursement: Kaplan and Norton (1996) suggest that these measures serve as leading indicators, and if patients are not satisfied, they will eventually find other providers. In addition, by making public the scores of all hospitals, patients will be able to choose the provider that has the best track record based on experiences of other patients, and poor performers will be penalized by the marketplace.

The *financial perspective* involves timely and accurate financial metrics used to evaluate the performance of management. In Kaplan and Norton's formulation, this perspective is designed to represent the needs of a firm's shareholders. In health care, where many institutions are nonprofit hospitals, shareholders' interests are represented by boards of directors, who have fiduciary responsibility. So it is not surprising that boards focus heavily on financial metrics when they work with management. However, when boards focus almost exclusively on financials, it leads to an unbalanced situation with regard to other perspectives.

The balanced scorecard approach supports the CVF to help evaluate the performance of leaders, and if boards closely examine all perspectives from these two frameworks, they can guide senior leadership very productively.

Operating Unit Goals

Healthcare organizations face growing pressure to improve quality and lower costs. This is not a new trend. From the inception of managed care in the 1970s (Ellwood et al., 1971) to the quality metrics and measures of today, healthcare organizations have been pushed to study the effectiveness of what they do, as judged by the outcomes they produce relative to the costs they incur.

Like companies in most industries, healthcare organizations formulate goals for operating units on an annual basis. These goals are usually negotiated by the managers of the operating units and the financial management of the corporation, and in health care they usually include patient volume, cost, quality, referrals, and efficiency (White & Griffith, 2010). The annual planning process is used to generate these goals, after a review of the prior year's performance, historical trends, market data, and executives' judgment (Cote & Tucker, 2001). Thus, the goals of individual units are grounded in data rather than wishful thinking.

The analyses of prior performance and market data are critically important for goals at all levels of the organization because they can prevent the organization from establishing unrealistic goals and thus overshooting market potential. For example, if a hospital wishes to increase its inpatient census by 10%, it must look at its environment and assess market conditions to determine whether this goal is achievable; if the hospital is located in a small city whose population growth has stagnated and there are no population centers nearby, the idea that its census can grow by 10% is questionable. However, if the small city in which the hospital is located sits next to an expanding metropolitan area whose population is moving out from a central city into the surrounding region, a growth goal of 10% could be reasonable, perhaps even conservative. Importantly, data-based goals help prevent senior management from imposing unrealistic goals onto operating units, a phenomenon that emanates from leaders' sometimes overly optimistic confidence in their own and their organizations' capabilities (Montgomery, 2012).

Operating unit goals play an important role in the management of healthcare organizations. They provide a target for unit managers to reach, and a benchmark against which they will be judged by management. In a well-managed organization, such a process sets the stage for developing better processes, where unit managers can identify opportunities to improve the organization's competitive position in the market, enhance quality and efficiency, and control costs (White & Griffith, 2010). Because they are primarily financial, these unit goals roll up into the overall budget for the organization, linking to the strategic plan and mission. Throughout the year, unit managers, their supervisors, and financial managers can monitor the units' performance against the budget, taking action when necessary.

Note that setting yearly operating goals is never easy, as there are many constituencies to satisfy. The board and senior management want to see financial growth and profitability; patients demand first-rate care and service; employees want good pay, benefits, and working conditions; and the society at large needs greater cost efficiency along with better quality outcomes. All of these demands must get translated to goals that unit managers will be accountable for. Consequently, negotiations over the correct goals for an individual operating unit must be led with skill, balancing the concerns of the relevant parties.

Formulating and negotiating operational goals calls for master leaders to attend to the lower half of the CVF presented in Figure 7.1. Just as it is essential that the operational goals be realistic and based on market data, once they are established and agreed upon, it is essential for the healthcare organization to reach them. Everyone counts on the unit managers to hit their financial targets, as they fund the efficient operation of the organization and allow for long-range strategies to take root. When the organization fails to meet budget, the consequences are far-reaching: a crisis occurs, which distracts and consumes leaders at all levels of the organization.

For example, Denver Health, a municipal hospital that serves as the safety-net hospital for Denver, Colorado, had operating income of $5.5 million on patient revenue of $744 million in 2012, and in 2011, it posted net income of $18.3 million. The hospital projected $4.7 million in operating income in its 2013 budget. However, an unexpected increase in the number of uninsured and indigent patients, along with lower reimbursement from Medicare and Medicaid for observation, put the hospital in the red by over $2 million. While the Affordable Care Act (ACA) will alleviate some of these problems by bringing more uninsured patients into the Medicaid system, thus paying the hospital for the previously uncompensated treatment it has delivered, it is unclear whether the payments it receives from Medicaid will be sufficient to cover the costs of caring for the newly insured patients (Pear, 2014). For example, leaders of Denver Health set out to reduce costs by $10 million in 2013 through spending cuts, including staffing and operations (Booth, 2013).

This scenario plays out in many healthcare organizations across the United States, as leaders must put aside long-range strategic goals to focus on the crisis at hand. The healthcare environment is dynamic and highly unpredictable, so crises occur frequently, and leaders must step up to the challenges they pose. In some cases, crises can bring together diverse and opposite individuals as the effective leader rallies the troops to overcome the problem at hand. This process can actually energize the organization, if the leaders bring an array of others into the problem-solving process and people feel secure about their futures in the organization. However, if operating goals are not achieved year after year, the organization is forced into operating in a crisis mode on a continual basis, and the energy dissipates, people become dispirited, poor results become the norm, and the organization will likely fail. The leader's inability to move beyond this mode is a very serious problem.

Project-Based Goals

In many organizations, strategic plans are realized through projects that are completed by individuals working in teams, usually outside their formal day-to-day assignments. A *project* is a one time or infrequently occurring operation with a unique goal, a limited lifespan, and limited resources. *Project management* generally describes the activity of planning, organizing, and controlling resources to achieve specific goals. There are basic components of project management, including statements of work, project selection, team building, communication, budgeting, resource scheduling, metrics, and closure. On a practical level, goals are essential for project management undertaken by business units or work groups because milestones need to be reached both successively and simultaneously in order for the project to move forward, so the steps in the process serve as intermediate goals for the project team to reach on the way to the final goal, completion of the project (Gido & Clements, 2010).

It is important to note that the temporary nature of projects contrasts with business as usual or the regular daily operations of the business or unit. The latter are repetitive and permanent activities that the business needs to produce in order to satisfy its customers, and these can usually be scaled up or down, as the firm requires. The management of discrete projects differs from the management of ongoing operations, though the same individuals often assume roles in both, switching roles between their day-to-day responsibilities and the requirements of the special project. This is a frequent occurrence in healthcare organizations, in which the skills of clinicians and administrators are needed for patient care during regular business hours, but they must also focus on how to build new facilities, services, or equipment. As many executives have learned, project management teams must include those who will be responsible for managing and using the end product of the project.

Goals established as part of a project plan are often inserted into Gantt charts, which depict the project's plan and progress on a timeline that extends through project completion and review stages (Wilson, 2003). Checkpoints are built into the chart to make sure the project remains on schedule, and when each stage is reached, a goal is accomplished. If the goal is not going to be reached by the date on the project schedule, the plan must shift to accommodate the delay, and the end date for project completion may need to be altered. Many tasks within a project are interdependent and must be accomplished sequentially (that is, one task must be completed before another can begin). The greater the interdependence of the project's intermediate goals, the greater the pressure to complete them on time.

While first applied to construction and civil engineering projects, the practice of using Gantt charts in health care has been applied to quality improvement projects, assessments of surgical procedures, infection control, patient flow, and a great many other needs. Once the project is completed and the project goal is achieved, the organization benefits only if the results are rolled out into the organization and implemented across a larger scale.

Goals and the Competing Values Framework

Hart and Quinn (1993) developed a model of four archetypal leadership roles that correspond with four domains of managerial action, and we apply this model to healthcare organizations to illustrate the complexity of superior leadership performance. These roles (and domains) are depicted in the inner circle of Figure 7.1: taskmaster (performance), vision-setter (direction), analyzer (conformance), and motivator (inspiration). As vision-setters, master leaders in health care must clarify the strategic vision for their organizations, while simultaneously serving as the motivator, inspiring managers and employees to see themselves within that vision. However, master leaders must also recognize the interdependent nature of goals and strategies, so that the vision can be realized.

While this underscores the importance of the vision-setter and motivator roles (which overlap the transformational roles), the leader must also perform analyzer and taskmaster roles in order for the system of goals to be effective. As Hart and Quinn (1993) discovered, superior firm performance is achieved by organizations when their executives play *all four* roles in a coordinated fashion. Master leaders succeed by focusing on broad visions for the future (directional goals) while also analyzing and evaluating how the organization will achieve them. They also pay attention to relational issues while simultaneously addressing tasks and action plans. When managers overemphasize one set of values (or play certain roles extensively without considering the other roles) the organization may become dysfunctional. We often see this occurring among leaders—inside and outside of health care—who focus almost exclusively on broad vision and directional goals, leaving the hard work of implementation to others within the organization (Rumelt, 2011). We also see it when leaders become too focused on the day-to-day routine of operations, and they fail to discern external events that will bring rapid and significant changes to the environment in which they operate. Such a single-minded pursuit of one set of goals without paying needed attention to the other values or roles creates conditions of suboptimization (Quinn, 1988).

The process of goal setting requires leaders to be keenly aware of the various roles outlined in Figure 7.1. When setting organizational goals, leaders must ensure that they are consistent with market data and the competitive environment, and that they can be achieved by operating units that are provided with the correct resources. When setting individual goals, leaders need to be mindful of the potential unintended consequences that result from poorly formulated goals, where individual managers or employees focus on accomplishing their goal without regard to their team or organization. And when setting project goals, leaders must make sure that intraproject deadlines can be met, so that interdependent tasks can be accomplished along the way to project completion. The CVF proves to be a useful tool for leaders to assure that goals are appropriate at all levels of the organization.

Conclusion

Goals have proven to be very useful management tools, both for managing performance of employees and operating units, and for guiding the strategic and operational plans of organizations.

Three types of goals are commonly used in contemporary healthcare organizations: individual goals, organizational goals, and project goals. Individual goals have a strong motivating effect because they allow people to focus on a specific target, and they have been shown to promote increased effort, creativity, and task accomplishment. At the same time, there is a significant downside to individual goals, namely their specificity: people focus so much attention on the goal that they may ignore the needs of their work team, fellow employees, or the organization at large. Thus, leaders must use great care in formulating and assigning individual goals, so that an employee's successfully achieving them will support the team's and organization's goals as well.

Organizational goals apply to the enterprise as a whole, and they are often set by boards of directors and top management. These goals directly relate to the organizational mission, which defines its scope. A strategic framework illustrates the varying levels of relationships between goals, and strategies serve the means used to accomplish the goals an organization sets for itself. Operating unit goals are required to deliver specific results, usually by meeting financial targets that are negotiated and agreed upon annually by unit managers and the financial leadership. The goals must be realistic—based on market data and analysis of the competitive environment in which the healthcare organization operates.

Project goals relate to short-term, one-time projects initiated to support the strategic plan. Though there is an end-goal of completing the project, intermediate goals are used to map the steps and complete the project, and they are often interdependent and successive. Goals related to projects are distinct from the regular goals of operating units that must be achieved in day-to-day operations.

Finally, the ubiquitous nature and frequent use of goals by healthcare organizations means that leaders must consider the multidimensional nature of goal setting and motivation. The version of the CVF we present in Figure 7.1 illustrates how leaders can balance the various roles as they manage the goal setting process, using the vision-setter role to establish broad organizational goals, while using the taskmaster role to make sure project goals are appropriate and timely. Leaders must play the analyzer role to ensure that the goals reflect market reality through data, and they rely on the motivator role when they establish individual goals for managers and employees.

Review Questions

1. What is management by objectives?
2. Briefly summarize the difference between individual goals and organizational goals, and discuss the purpose of each.
3. What are the advantages of setting individual goals for employees? What are some disadvantages to this approach?
4. How do individual goals work to enhance employees' performance? Do you think that individual goals work differently in health care than they do in other industries?
5. What is the balanced scorecard? How is the balanced scorecard different from traditional organizational goals that companies have historically used to measure their performance?
6. Give an example of a project goal for a hospital that is expanding its emergency department.
7. Some chief executives believe that their main responsibility is to outline a broad vision and directional goals, leaving it to others in the organization to figure out how to get there because those people are "close to the action." What do you think? What are some advantages and disadvantages of this management style?

References

Barsky, A. (2007). Understanding the ethical cost of organizational goal-setting: A review and theory development. *Journal of Business Ethics, 81*(1), 63–81.

Belasen, A. T. (2000). *Leading the learning organization: Communication and competencies for managing change.* Albany, NY: SUNY Press.

Booth, M. (2013, June 24). Denver Health sinks into red again, cites cases others avoid. *The Denver Post*. Retrieved from http://www.denverpost.com/ci_23524476 /denver-health-sinks-into-red-again-cites-cases

Centers for Medicare and Medicaid Services. (2014). *Quality measures*. Retrieved from http://www.cms.gov/Medicare/Quality-Initiatives-Patient-Assessment-Instruments /HomeHealthQualityInits/HHQIQualityMeasures.html

Cote, M. J., & Tucker, S. L. (2001). Four methodologies to improve healthcare demand forecasting. *Healthcare Financial Management, 55*(5), 54–58.

Creswell, J., & Abelson, R. (2012, November 30). A hospital war reflects a bind for doctors in the U.S. *New York Times*. Retrieved from http://www.nytimes.com/2012 /12/01/business/a-hospital-war-reflects-a-tightening-bind-for-doctors-nationwide .html?pagewanted=all

Daft, R. L. (2009). *Organization theory and design* (10th ed.). Independence, KY: Cengage.

Drucker, P. F. (1974). *Management: Task, responsibilities and practices*. New York, NY: Harper & Row.

Ellwood, P. M., Anderson, N. N., Billings, J. E., Carlson, R. J., Hoagberg, E. J., & McClure, M. (1971). Health maintenance strategy. *Medical Care, 9*(3), 291–298.

Feng, Z., Wright, B., & Mor, V. (2012). Sharp rise in Medicare enrollees being held in hospitals for observation raises concerns about causes and consequences. *Health Affairs, 31*(6), 1251–1259.

Gawande, A. (2011, May 26). Cowboys and pit crews. *The New Yorker*. Retrieved from http:// www.newyorker.com/news/news-desk/cowboys-and-pit-crews

Gido, H., & Clements, J. P. (2010). *Successful project management with Microsoft® Project 2010* (5th ed.). Independence, KY: Cengage.

Goozner, M. (2012, August 17). Incentives spike fee-for-service health costs. *The Fiscal Times*. Retrieved from http://www.thefiscaltimes.com/Articles/2012/08/17 /Incentives-Spike-Fee-for-Service-Health-Costs

Hancock, J. (2013, June 16). Hospital CEO bonuses reward volume and growth. *Kaiser Health News*. Retrieved from http://www.kaiserhealthnews.org/stories/2013/june/06 /hospital-ceo-compensation-mainbar.aspx

Hart, S. L., & Quinn R. E. (1993). Roles executives play: CEOs, behavioral complexity, and firm performance. *Human Relations, 46*(5), 543–574.

Institute of Medicine. (2000). *To err is human*. Washington, DC: National Academy Press.

Jensen, M. C. (2003). Paying people to lie: The truth about the budgeting process. *European Financial Management, 9*(3), 379–406.

Kaplan, R. S., & Norton, D. P. (1996). Using the balanced scorecard as a strategic management system. *Harvard Business Review, 74*(1), 75–85.

Latham, G. P., & Budworth, M. H. (2006). The study of work motivation in the 20th century. In L. L. Koppes (Ed.), *Historical Perspectives in Industrial and Organizational Psychology* (pp. 353–382). Mahwah, NJ: Lawrence Erlbaum Associates.

Locke, E. A. (1991). Goal theory vs. control theory: Contrasting approaches to understanding work motivation. *Motivation and Emotion, 15*(1), 9–28.

Locke, E. A., & Latham, G. P. (1990). *A theory of goal setting and task performance*. Englewood Cliffs, NJ: Prentice-Hall.

Locke, E. A., & Latham, G. P. (2002). Building a practically useful theory of goal setting and task motivation. *American Psychologist, 57*(9), 705–717.

Mitchell, T. R., & Silver, W. S. (1990). Individual and group goals when workers are interdependent: Effects on task strategies and performance. *Journal of Applied Psychology, 75*(2), 185–193.

Montgomery, C. A. (2012, July). How strategists lead. *McKinsey Quarterly.* Retrieved from http://www.mckinsey.com/insights/strategy/how_strategists_lead

Ordonez, L. D., Schweitzer, M. E., Galinsky, A. D., & Bazerman, M. H. (2009). *Goals gone wild: The systematic side effects of over-prescribing goal setting.* Working Paper 09-083, Harvard Business School, Retrieved from http://www.hbs.edu/faculty /Publication%20Files/09-083.pdf

Pear, R. (2014, September 24). Affordable Care Act reduces costs for hospitals, report says. *New York Times.*

Quinn, R. E. (1988). *Beyond rational management: Mastering the paradoxes and competing demands of high performance.* San Francisco, CA: Jossey-Bass.

Rau. J. (2012, December 20). Medicare discloses hospitals' bonuses, penalties based on quality. *Kaiser Health News.* Retrieved from http://www.kaiserhealthnews.org /stories/2012/december/21/medicare-hospitals-value-based-purchasing.aspx

Rumelt, R. (2011, June). The perils of bad strategy. *McKinsey Quarterly.* Retrieved from http://www.mckinsey.com/insights/strategy/the_perils_of_bad_strategy

Shalley, C. E. (1995). Effects of coaction, expected evaluation, and goal setting on creativity and productivity. *Academy of Management Journal, 38*(2), 483–501.

Swayne, L. E., Duncan, W. J., & Ginter, P. M. (2006). *Strategic management of healthcare organizations* (5th ed.). Malden, MA: Blackwell.

Tucker, A., & Edmondson, A. C. (2003). Why hospitals don't learn from failures: Organizational and psychological dynamics that inhibit system change. *California Management Review, 45*(2), 55–71.

White, K. R., & Griffith, J. R. (2010). *The well-managed healthcare organization* (7th ed.). Chicago, IL: Health Administration Press.

Wilson, J. M. (2003). Gantt charts: A centenary appreciation. *European Journal of Operational Research, 149*(2), 430–437.

Zhang, Y., & Chiu, C. (2012). Goal commitment and alignment of personal goals predict group identification only when the goals are shared. *Group Processes and Intergroup Relations, 15*(3), 425–437.

PART D ▶

Community and Credibility

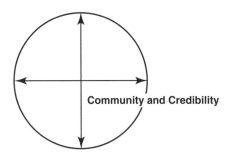

Community and Credibility

The lower right quadrant of the competing values framework (CVF) focuses on the relationships between an organization and internal and external stakeholders. The master leader is a skilled facilitator who is able to keep the organization actively and progressively focused on satisfying consumer needs while developing strategies and coordinating efforts with other organizations to ensure comprehensiveness of attention to those needs. Leaders proficient in this quadrant will demonstrate critical skills for engineering partnerships with community resources in order to promote a growing capacity for achieving high levels of patient satisfaction and improved clinical outcomes.

It may seem obvious that leaders in health care have always had to exercise mindfulness with respect to satisfying consumers and building relationships with other providers to advance the organization's capabilities to achieve care delivery goals. Historically, however, the preponderance of organizational attention was on internal tasks and processes. In the past several years, incentive structures have been reorienting: systems of rewards and penalties require organizations to ensure that consumers' impressions of care and service are favorable and that they participate in community-oriented networks to promote consumer access and strengthen continua of care practices.

Master leaders recognize that strategies for enhancing their organizations in this domain must be carefully balanced with the need to maintain operations and integrity of organizational identity. Failure to do so—by moving too aggressively or too swiftly or without a workable strategy—can result in a loss of credibility or put a strain on the organization. For example, promises to move patients through an emergency room visit within a particular timeframe, while noble in intent, can fall short if the organization lacks the operational capacity to deliver. Similarly, rapid integration into a healthcare system without effectively considering all the critical human resource issues can result in identity confusion and diminishment of employee and consumer loyalty. Conversely, moving too slowly in the development and implementation of patient satisfaction and system integration initiatives can render a healthcare organization's future bleak.

Hence, the chapters in Part D, Chapter 8, Chapter 9, and Chapter 10, focus on the need for today's healthcare leaders to evaluate and institute strategies for achieving a coordinated response to a community's healthcare needs and for building and sustaining a patient-centered culture.

CHAPTER 8 ▶

Healthcare Delivery:
A Community-Based Perspective

LEARNING OBJECTIVES

Students will be able to:

- Explain the evolution of the modern healthcare system and the historical context for a community-based perspective
- Define *community* as a multidimensional concept and discuss its application to the delivery of healthcare services
- Identify current economic trends and clinical and technological advances that are stimulating community-based approaches to healthcare
- Explain the components and essential conditions for a community-based approach to healthcare delivery; identify how healthcare alliances are distinct from consolidations, which occur through mergers and acquisitions
- Identify the characteristics of a healthcare alliance as well as the risks and limitations associated with such an approach
- Describe the role of leadership in promoting effective community orientations in healthcare systems

A Hospital Closes Its Doors

In April 2010 the board of St. Vincent Catholic Medical Centers voted to shut down its main facility, St. Vincent's Hospital–Manhattan, which served a large community in Greenwich Village. The 400-bed hospital had run up a prohibitive debt. The governor of New York, David Paterson, pumped $6 million of state funds into the hospital to help it meet its payroll and other financial obligations, but after an exhaustive search for a partner did not produce a positive result, the board concluded it had no choice but to cease operations. St. Vincent's had been in existence for over 150 years, and during that time the neighborhood underwent multiple transformations, serving almost every conceivable cultural and socioeconomic group. And it earned a place in history: throughout the years, St. Vincent's provided care to people who suffered during noteworthy crises, including "the cholera epidemic of 1849, the sinking of the Titanic in 1912, the 9/11 attack...the Hudson River landing of US Airways Flight 1549" (Otterman, 2010). The poet Edna St. Vincent Millay was named to honor the hospital for saving her uncle's life (Poemhunter, n.d.). Given its place in history, the board's decision would have been unthinkable until recently.

The plan was for most of St. Vincent's services to phase out relatively soon after the decision to shut down. But many in the community experienced significant unease about the closing of key medical services. After all, the area of Manhattan served by St. Vincent's was densely populated. Residents of the community would have to make alternative arrangements for their healthcare needs. Thus, the closing of St. Vincent's created a good deal of apprehension, and many who had a stake in the matter—including physicians, community residents, politicians, and neighboring hospitals—anticipated that a gap in care could be devastating. This feeling was exacerbated by the fact that there were few other comprehensive medical centers that had trauma and neurosurgery services in the lower part of Manhattan. Dr. Charles Carpati, chief of the ICU and hospital executive committee member, observed: "Once we go, this part of town will be isolated and dependent on traffic to gain these services in emergencies. Even in common emergency diseases such as heart attack and stroke, time is of the essence" (Hartocollis, 2010). Moreover, what would be the fate of the approximately 60,000 patients who went to St. Vincent's Hospital each year for emergency care? How would other area hospitals manage the influx of some of those patients? Thus, not only would the immediate community be affected, but so would neighboring communities.

But a look at how the healthcare needs of the community were met during the years following the closing of the hospital suggests that the void may have been largely filled. And more importantly, the way in which it was filled may portend how healthcare delivery systems may look in the coming years, particularly in urban centers. The solution did not lie in a big hospital replacing the big hospital that shut its doors. Rather, a mix of providers came together in a manner reminiscent of links in a chain—in a continuum of care. For example, the number of walk-in clinics increased, expanding the primary care base in the community. With easier access to care than a hospital-based setting, a potential spike in wellness and health-related programs could be feasible. Some pharmacies introduced or expanded their traditionally low level of health services. For example, their service base had generally been limited to taking blood pressure and giving flu shots. Now some provide a broadened range of basic primary care services, including diagnosis and treatment for bacterial infections and minor respiratory ailments.

Emergency care capacity was bolstered at neighboring hospitals, including Beth Israel Medical Center, a member of Continuum Health Partners, and the North Shore–Long Island Jewish Health System. According to Gibbons (2012), "Beth Israel had already doubled the size of its emergency room after the closing of Cabrini Medical Center in 2008, so it was well prepared for the St. Vincent's surge; other local hospitals also expanded and adapted to pick up the slack." Moreover, these hospitals sought partnerships with clinics and other primary care providers in an effort to gain a share of the market that was now up for grabs. In so doing, they added to the network of linkages in a system which made it more convenient for patients to seek different levels of care and move more seamlessly from one level of care at one venue to another level of care at another.

While the closing of St. Vincent's was viewed by some stakeholders as devastating when it occurred, the gap it created provided an opportunity to experiment; as Hartocollis (2012) suggests, it "turned Lower Manhattan into a laboratory for healthcare reform." Moreover, observes Hartocollis, "The new clinics and the maneuvering by large chains are anticipating an expansion of the number of people with insurance and changes in the way that health care is delivered and paid for." In the end, the loss of a big hospital paved the way for new thinking about the best way to deliver healthcare services to a community.

Introduction

What was it that occurred since April 2010 that may have significantly influenced attitudes and beliefs about the effectiveness of healthcare delivery in a densely populated area following the closing of the area's premier, not to mention largest, medical facility? Again, Hartocollis's (2012) account suggests that the affected section of Manhattan became a "laboratory for healthcare reform."

As we will explore in this chapter, the transformation of health delivery in that area of New York City may portend something of a broader metamorphosis in health care. The traditional and, indeed, prevailing way of conceiving of healthcare institutions is that they are independent entities—structures that begin and end at their lobbies and back doors, respectively. The boundaries of healthcare institutions are their perimeter walls. And while no provider has ever existed in a vacuum, all providers have had relatively fixed institutional parameters. This has been the case since the very late 1800s, when the hospital began to replace the home as the venue of choice for those suffering from serious illness or with a need for surgery. Hospitals are fixed buildings. As patients, we collect together within them when the need for a medical care arises.

The experience of St. Vincent's, and particularly the events that have occurred since it closed, are instructive in a most powerful way. Undoubtedly, hospitals will continue to exist and no one is suggesting they will disappear. But we may be on the threshold of a paradigm shift in which the healthcare system begins to reorient itself in a way that moves services closer to the patient, where access is more immediate and nearer to where patients live—more interwoven into our communities. We are witnessing providers linking together, broadening their collective scope and reach, and assuming a more widespread and integrated presence in the communities they serve. When this occurs, patient movement throughout the system becomes more fluid, and transitions from and to more acute settings are feasible. This chapter identifies the various collaborative arrangements healthcare organizations are undertaking, the reasons for doing so, and the leadership challenges associated with such endeavors.

A Community Perspective

Three conditions must be met in order for a community model to achieve a high level of effectiveness. First, the range of services and number of venues must be sufficiently broad in order to accommodate a considerable array of healthcare needs. Second, entry points into the system must be located close to or be easily accessed by the patient. Third, coordination and management of patient throughput must be such that transitions throughout the system feel seamless.

In this regard, the notion of community may have two points of reference. It may, at once, refer to the healthcare system, that is, the caregiving community, and it may simultaneously refer to the public it serves. A definition that encompasses both perspectives is, ultimately, the most serviceable; when a provider system and the consumer public it serves are genuinely integrated, there would exist a continuous exchange of communication such that the needs of the latter are always in the process of being better understood and more capably addressed by the former. The more accommodating approach to the definition allows for the inclusion of a broad range of stakeholders, including but not limited to practitioners and provider organizations, patients and their families, community residents, suppliers, employers, the workforce, government agencies, third-party payers, and a full range of social service and support agencies. The notion of a community suggests that members may belong to multiple stakeholder groups, even simultaneously; for example, practitioners and agency employees may also be patients.

Therefore, the purpose of this chapter is to identify a community perspective for health care, provide examples of how a community orientation is taking root, and define the role of leadership in a community-oriented healthcare system as follows:

> *A community healthcare orientation is defined as the continuous striving to make readily available, and facilitate access to, a comprehensive range of healthcare services through the formation of continua of care networks—or alliances—of providers that are integrated into the neighborhoods in which patients live and work.*

A community healthcare orientation is not new. Rather, it is part of a long-established trend and represents a next logical phase in the evolution of our healthcare system, albeit one that may be taking shape on a relatively accelerated basis. Ironically, the shift may represent more of a return to how things looked just as the 19th century gave way to the 20th. As the title of a popular film suggests, the trend may be akin to "Back to the Future." A look back will provide some context on where we may be heading and why, and shed light on why the disaster that was predicted with the closing of St. Vincent's did not occur.

An Historical Perspective

During the approximately 100-year period that began in the late 1800s, say around 1875, a massive number of hospital buildings were constructed. In this era, Americans developed the increasingly unshakable expectation that in order to get medical care they must to go to a place where it could be provided. Prior to that period, up until the very late 1800s, hospitals were generally places to be avoided. Hospitals emerged largely as extensions of charitable organizations, which went a step further than providing shelter for the indigent and homeless by also offering some healthcare-related services. While accurate statistics were not recorded, it is estimated that there were a few hundred hospitals in operation in the mid-1880s. Those who could afford to remain in their homes to receive medical attention did so. After all, hospital environments could not provide or ensure effective disease and infection management, and the probability of getting sick was as great as having illness managed successfully. Separating the very sick from the rest of the population evolved from a medieval mindset in which such segregation—even quarantine—was necessary to protect society. Consider for example, the "colonies" that were established centuries ago to house those suffering from leprosy. More recently, dangerous and contagious diseases such as tuberculosis, smallpox, and polio persisted well into the 20th century. Specialty clinics were built to house, treat, and comfort patients suffering from these serious illnesses, and comprehensive efforts were undertaken to study the nature of those diseases and to try to contain or eradicate them.

Thus, the early years of the 20th century were characterized by considerable apprehension about the prospect of receiving care in a hospital. People went there to die. However something was astir in the world of surgery; as newer technologies and modes of practice were coming to fruition for surgeries, it was becoming increasingly difficult for surgeons to perform their work outside of the controlled setting of a hospital. For example, anesthesia had become more reliable and effective, the practice of antisepsis was beginning to be employed on a widespread basis, and x-ray technology was being developed. So in a relatively brief period culminating in the early years of the 20th century, a movement toward hospitalization was well underway, stimulated by improvements in surgical care and the realization that improved outcomes are more possible if procedures were conducted in hospital settings.

As surgeons began to use hospitals more regularly, they began to develop standards of care. In 1918, the American College of Surgeons initiated a program of hospital inspections intended to ensure that hospitals were properly equipped to support surgical procedures and instill confidence in patients that the hospital was competent. An additional benefit of performing work in a hospital was that pathologists could more readily evaluate disease by performing autopsies and studying tissue, thereby advancing the capabilities of healthcare professionals to respond more skillfully to illness and disease. In order for this to occur, hospitals had to move quickly to ensure that the environments in which surgeons and physicians practiced were effectively resourced and could support their efforts. Therefore, administrators, too, began to collaborate as a means of strengthening their professionalism and upgrading their field, and an organization formed for such purposes in 1899, which later became the American Hospital Association (AHA).

Economics, politics, technological modernization, and sociological shifts came together during the first half of the 20th century in a manner that fueled the trend of hospital growth. By the mid-1920s, it was estimated that the United States had 4,300 hospitals. A downturn in growth took place during the period of the Great Depression, but the tide began to slowly turn in an upward direction in the latter part of the 1930s. World War II marked an important turning point with respect to the expansion of hospitals. For one thing, because employers were not permitted to raise wages during this period, they ushered in an era of employer-based healthcare insurance as a means of luring employees. Such employer coverage grew rapidly, providing millions of citizens with insurance for the first time. In addition, the proliferation of suburbs, resulting from the post-war period of prosperity and the large-scale acquisition of automobiles, required the construction of many new hospitals throughout broad swaths of the country.

Much of the construction of hospitals was made possible by the Hill-Burton Act, a federal law passed in 1946, which provided federal matching funds to support building of hospitals. The availability of such funds, coupled with the healthcare needs of burgeoning communities in the country, meant that hospitals of many types could come into existence, including hospitals that were erected and managed by municipalities, religious groups and charitable organizations, private for-profit enterprises, and those managed on a not-for-profit basis. The ability to produce penicillin on a large-scale basis was perfected during the 1940s. Hospitals could then go further in preventing the spread of infection, adding yet another layer of reassurance to patients. By 1960, there were almost 5,800 hospitals in the United States.

As the 1960s unfolded, Medicare and Medicaid were implemented. These programs, serving the healthcare needs of the elderly and the poor respectively, significantly expanded the pool of Americans who could seek health care without having to worry about paying for it. The availability of such programs was bound to increase longevity, meaning that future generations of Americans would live longer and, thus, increase the subscribership of these programs. In addition,

Medicare and Medicaid guaranteed that hospitals would receive payment for treating elderly and indigent patients, which not only relieved them of having to write off charges for their services, but also ensured a predictable future cash flow. This permitted hospitals to use future cash flow to secure bank loans and bond financing, and many hospitals accessed new capital to expand their facilities and services. A hospital building boom resulted (Sultz & Young, 2014).

By the time we reached the last quarter of the 20th century, the very concept of hospitals had been reengineered from the thinking that had prevailed 75 years earlier. By the second half of the 20th century, hospitals had become ubiquitous, had replaced the home as the desired place to be treated for medical care, had emerged as a relatively infection-controlled environment, and were available for use by large segments of the population who were not required to self-pay for the majority of care they received. It is little wonder that healthcare costs rose at what seem like astronomical rates in the past 50 years, from approximately $10 billion in 1960 to over $2.5 trillion today (**Figure 8.1**).

The growth of hospitals began to slow about 10 years following the passage of Medicare and Medicaid. Expansion cannot occur ceaselessly, and in this case a series of phenomena converged to halt the tide of growth and, to some extent,

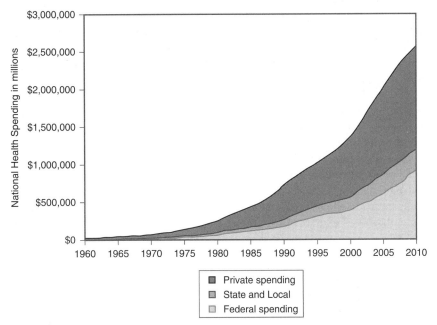

Figure 8.1 U.S. Spending on Health Care, 1960–2010

U.S. National Health Spending. (2012). *U.S. national health expenditures*. Retrieved from http://sambaker.com/econ/classes/nhe10/

even reverse it. Advances in arthroscopy and endoscopy and other clinical developments meant that a number of procedures that had required hospitalization could now be performed in outpatient facilities. Economic pressures spurred the development of managed care, which sought to limit hospitalizations to those truly necessary. Prospective payment programs, led by the implementation of Medicare's Diagnostic Related Group program in 1983, began to replace the fee-for-service model that had prevailed for decades. Hospitals responded by joining forces to consolidate and achieve economies of scale, seeking efficiencies, and devoting more time and attention to quality improvements. As a result, the massive expansion of hospitals and hospital beds that occurred throughout the majority of the 20th century began to reverse. As shown in **Table 8.1**, the number of hospitals has declined by 19% in the period of 1975–2009 and the number of hospital beds was reduced by an astonishing 35.6%.

And yet, during the same period of time that beds and hospitals were decommissioned, changes were occurring in the population that might have otherwise required the system to *add* beds. First, the population grew by a sizable one hundred million citizens (**Figure 8.2**).

Second, and perhaps even more important with respect to health needs, the population aged significantly. From 1980 to 2011, the percentage of people aged 65 and above grew by almost 15% (**Figure 8.3**). Given the greater propensity for illness and disease among the elderly—according to the Agency for Healthcare Research and Quality, those over 65 years old consume over one-third of the nation's healthcare resources (Stanton, 2006)—the need for acute care environments could have conceivably manifested in a need to increase the number of beds in hospitals, all other things being equal.

Yet, all other things were not equal. The emergence and compounding impact of seven trends created conditions under which hospital and bed downsizing made sense and, correspondingly, are now paving the way for a more pronounced community-oriented approach in the provision and delivery of healthcare services. These trends include (1) the development of electronic medical records, (2) a shift to outpatient venues for an increasing range of healthcare needs and increasingly important role of primary care, (3) cost containment pressures, (4) the increasing emphasis on evidence-based outcomes, (5) the continuing growth of mergers and system formation in health care, (6) the institutionalization of Accountable Care Organizations (ACOs), and (7) a growing recognition that patient proximity to healthcare resources is meaningfully related to effective consumption. Each trend is briefly discussed.

Trends Influencing the Development of a Community Orientation

Medical records. Electronic medical records (EMR) may be described as "computerized medical information systems that collect, store and display patient information" (Boonstra & Broekhuis, 2010). The movement to an EMR system is

Table 8.1 Centers for Disease Control and Prevention Data

Type of Ownership and Size of Hospital	1975	1980	1990	1995	2000	2008	2009
Hospitals				Number			
All hospitals	7156	6965	6649	6291	5810	5815	5795
Federal	382	359	337	299	245	213	211
Nonfederal[1]	6774	6606	6312	5992	5565	5602	5584
Community[2]	5875	5830	5384	5194	4915	5010	5008
Nonprofit	3339	3322	3191	3092	3003	2923	2918
For profit	775	730	749	752	749	982	998
State/local government	1761	1778	1444	1350	1163	1105	1092
6–24 beds	299	259	226	278	288	389	402
25–49 beds	1155	1029	935	922	910	1151	1164
50–99 beds	1481	1462	1263	1139	1055	995	991
100–199 beds	1363	1370	1306	1324	1236	1070	1063
200–299 beds	678	715	739	718	656	596	582
300–399 beds	378	412	408	354	341	355	348
400–499 beds	230	266	222	195	182	184	192
500 beds or more	291	317	285	264	247	270	266

(continues)

Table 8.1 Centers for Disease Control and Prevention Data (continued)

Type of Ownership and Size of Hospital	1975	1980	1990	1995	2000	2008	2009
Beds				**Number**			
All hospitals	1,465,828	1,364,516	1,213,327	1,080,601	983,628	951,045	944,277
Federal	131,946	117,328	98,255	77,079	53,067	45,992	44,772
Nonfederal[1]	1,333,882	1,247,188	1,115,072	1,003,522	930,561	905,053	899,505
Community[2]	941,844	988,387	927,360	872,736	823,560	808,069	805,593
Nonprofit	658,195	692,459	656,755	609,729	582,988	556,651	556,406
For profit	73,495	87,033	101,377	105,737	109,883	120,887	122,071
State/local government	210,154	208,895	169,228	157,270	130,689	130,531	127,116
6–24 beds	5615	4932	4427	5085	5156	6726	6894
25–49 beds	41,783	37,478	35,420	34,352	33,333	37,142	37,338
50–99 beds	106,776	105,278	90,394	82,024	75,865	71,477	71,012
100–199 beds	192,438	192,892	183,867	187,381	175,778	153,488	152,655
200–299 beds	164,405	172,390	179,670	175,240	159,807	144,895	141,920
300–399 beds	127,728	139,434	138,938	121,136	117,220	122,363	120,201
400–499 beds	101,278	117,724	98,833	86,459	80,763	80,815	84,783
500 beds or more	201,821	218,259	195,811	181,059	175,638	191,163	190,790

Occupancy rate[3]	Percent						
All hospitals	76.7	77.7	69.5	65.7	66.1	68.2	67.8
Federal	80.7	80.1	72.9	72.6	68.2	67.9	69.1
Nonfederal[1]	76.3	77.4	69.2	65.1	65.9	68.2	67.8
Community[2]	75.0	75.6	66.8	62.8	63.9	66.4	65.5
Nonprofit	77.5	78.2	69.3	64.5	65.5	68.4	67.4
For profit	65.9	65.2	52.8	51.8	55.9	57.8	57.7
State/local government	70.4	71.1	65.3	63.7	63.2	66.1	65.0
6–24 beds	48.0	46.8	32.3	36.9	31.7	33.8	33.6
25–49 beds	56.7	52.8	41.3	42.6	41.3	46.7	46.0
50–99 beds	64.7	64.2	53.8	54.1	54.8	56.6	55.9
100–199 beds	71.2	71.4	61.5	58.8	60.0	61.9	61.3
200–299 beds	77.1	77.4	67.1	63.1	65.0	66.4	65.5
300–399 beds	79.7	79.7	70.0	64.8	65.7	69.4	67.9
400–499 beds	81.1	81.2	73.5	68.1	69.1	74.2	70.1
500 beds or more	80.9	82.1	77.3	71.4	72.2	74.9	74.0

[1]The category of nonfederal hospitals comprises psychiatric hospitals, tuberculosis and other respiratory diseases hospitals, and long-term and short-term general and other special hospitals.

[2]Community hospitals are nonfederal short-term general and special hospitals whose facilities and services are available to the public.

[3]Estimated percentage of staffed beds that are occupied. Occupancy rate is calculated as the average daily census (from the American Hospital Association) divided by the number of hospital beds.

Reprinted from: Centers for Disease Control and Prevention, NCHS, Table 116: Hospitals, beds, and occupancy rates, by type of ownership and size of hospital: United States, selected years 1975–2009. Retrieved from http://www.cdc.gov/nchs/data/hus/2011/116.pdf

[Data are based on reporting by a census of hospitals.]

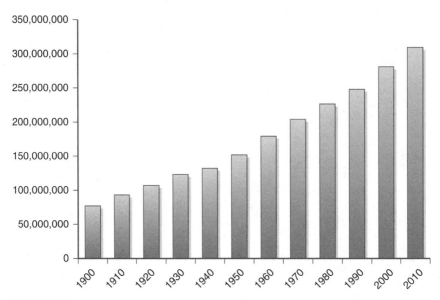

Figure 8.2 United States Population, 1900–2010

Courtesy of: Progressives for Immigration Reform. *Environmental impact statement (EIS) on United States immigration policy.* Retrieved from http://www.immigrationeis.org /eis-documents/us-demographic-history

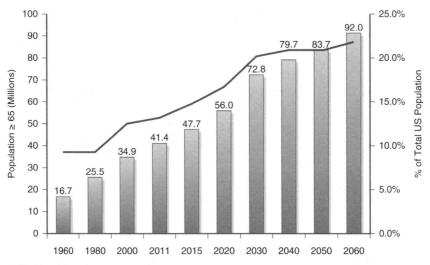

Figure 8.3 US Population 65 Years and Older

Courtesy of US Census Bureau.

underway; and notwithstanding resistance and fits and starts, the implementation of a broad, national (and, conceivably, eventually universal) implementation in which information about patients will be routinely amassed, managed, and exchanged in an electronic manner is inevitable.

According to the US Department of Health and Human Services (HHS) Office of the National Coordinator for Health Information Technology, EMR must satisfy two conditions essential for coordination and effective use of data related to patients' health. HHS employs the concept of *interoperability* as the basis of their contention. Borrowing the definition of interoperability from McGlynn et al. (2003), Rosenbaum (2010) observes that interoperability is generally accepted to mean the ability of two or more systems or components to exchange information and use the information that has been exchanged. That means that there are two steps to interoperability: (1) the ability to exchange information, and (2) the ability to use the information that has been exchanged. The Department of Health and Human Services (HHS) recognizes that the actual exchange of health information needs to be both interoperable and electronic across a myriad of information systems for us to realize a patient-centered, value-driven healthcare system (U.S. Department of Health and Human Services, 2013).

It is only when both conditions are satisfied that transitions from one part of a system to another will easily be accomplished and meaningful for all parties— for example, practitioners, healthcare managers, third-party payers, suppliers of medical equipment and pharmaceutical products, and, of course, patients.

Shift to outpatient venues and continued growth of primary care. The trend away from inpatient toward outpatient care has been well underway for at least three decades. VMG Health (2010) reports that outpatient procedures accounted for approximately 15% of surgical cases in 1980, 50% 1990, 60% in 2000, and 65% in 2008. This trend is expected to continue.

Advances in minimally invasive procedures such as arthroscopy, improvements in home care management, and progress with respect to anesthesia administration have all contributed to the trend. Furthermore, trends in reimbursement have also fueled this growth, as payers have encouraged providers to use outpatient procedures by refusing to pay for inpatient hospitalization for procedures that can be performed on an outpatient basis. While the change is more pronounced in some states than others (**Figure 8.4**), it is noteworthy that all regions of the country have experienced this development.

Primary care has also grown in importance. According to the American Academy of Family Physicians (n.d.), "primary care is provided by physicians specifically trained for and skilled in comprehensive first contact and continuing care for persons with any undiagnosed sign, symptom, or health concern (the "undifferentiated" patient), not limited by problem origin (biological, behavioral, or social), organ system, or diagnosis."

Thus, primary care—with its emphasis on health management, disease prevention, and initial treatment of a vast array of acute medical problems—is at

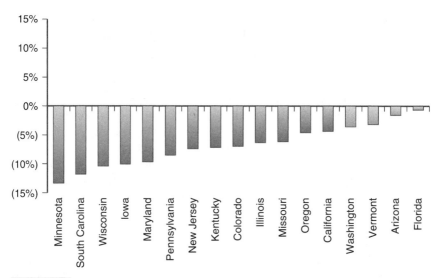

Figure 8.4 2006–2011 Change in Inpatient Use Rates per 1000

Grube, M.E., Kaufman, K., York, R. Decline in utilization rates signals a change in the inpatient business model. Retrieved from http://healthaffairs.org/blog/2013/03/08/decline-in-utilization-rates-signals-a-change-in-the-inpatient-business-model/. Kaufman Hall Point of View, © Kaufman, Hall & Associates, Inc., April 2013. Used with permission.

the front line of the health service system and functions as the gateway into the system. As the range of health needs that can be addressed in primary care and outpatient settings continues to increase, communication between generalists and specialists, including between primary care practitioners and surgeons, will continue to become more routine and essential. Coupled with the fluidity of information exchange achievable through EMR, opportunities for advanced levels of collaboration in terms of the overall management of patients' health are more prevalent. The community of caregivers is aided by proximity and mechanisms of communication. As such, the community can function more like a cohesive group—that is, more like a community—than a disparate set of practitioners.

Cost containment. Trends over the past few years have suggested that health-care spending has slowed (**Table 8.2**). Cuckler et al. (2013) posit that annual spending growth has been in the range of 4.0% in the period from 2009 to 2011 and can be expected to grow at an annual rate of 5.8% in the 10-year period concluding in 2022. The recent growth levels have been far more consistent with general economic growth than in previous years, as indicated by the considerably higher levels of spending from 2000 to 2008.

Many healthcare economists suggest that Americans are not likely to experience a highly inflationary period for some time to come because the forces

Table 8.2 US Healthcare Expenditures Annual Percentage Increase, 2000–2011

Year	Percentage Increase from Previous Year
2000	7.1
2001	8.4
2002	9.7
2003	8.4
2004	7.1
2005	6.8
2006	6.5
2007	6.2
2008	4.7
2009	3.9
2010	3.9
2011	3.9

Data from: Centers for Medicare and Medicaid Services. (2013). *National health expenditures*. Retrieved from http://www.cms.gov/Research-Statistics-Data-and-Systems /Statistics-Trends-and-Reports/NationalHealthExpendData/Downloads/tables.pdf

keeping costs down are likely to remain in effect. For example, according to Grube, Kaufman, and York (2013),

> federal and state fiscal challenges, and the growing proportion of US gross domestic product consumed by health care, ensure that the downward pressure on use rates is here to stay. Factors lowering utilization will be cumulative and interdependent. In addition to macroeconomic forces, drivers bending the utilization/cost curve include:
>
> 1. changes in medical practice that focus on coordinated, collaborative care across the continuum;
> 2. increased use of standardized care approaches to reduce care variation;
> 3. care process redesign to reduce every bit of unnecessary work in all care settings;
> 4. optimized service distribution to ensure the right care at the right site; and
> 5. financial incentives of new value-based payment models that reward elimination of waste and redirection of patients to lower-cost settings.

It is noteworthy that each of the forces identified by Grube et al. (2013) requires some measure of collaboration among providers. Plainly stated, achieving efficiency in care delivery—and the cost benefits associated with such efficiency—cannot occur without a team approach. Each element in the delivery system or delivery chain is dependent on the work conducted by those that precede and follow it. Accordingly, lack of collaboration in which the components of a health delivery system can maintain a high level of interdependence, cost containment goals cannot be achieved.

Evidence-based outcomes. Taking an evidence-based approach to decision making relative to conducting diagnoses and developing treatment plans is not new. In a landmark article in 1996, Sackett, Rosenberg, Gray, Haynes, and Richardson indicate that "the practice of evidence-based medicine means integrating individual clinical expertise with the best available external clinical evidence from systematic research" (p. 71). This can constitute quite a challenge as clinicians and researchers often occupy different provinces of the healthcare world, and integrating their activity involves building bridges that are not easy to sustain. But those bridges possess enormous value for the future of medicine and the health of patients. Sackett et al. emphasize the value of assessing a patient's clinical status relative to bodies of data and research: "External clinical evidence both invalidates previously accepted diagnostic tests and treatments and replaces them with new ones that are more powerful, more accurate, more efficacious, and safer" (p. 72). In this context, evidence-based practices have been based on published research, including laboratory studies as well as controlled clinical trials, which physicians have been encouraged to use for making decisions about appropriate treatment of their patients. However, as noted, a gap exists between research and practice: even the best research that demonstrates statistically significant positive impacts of a therapeutic intervention applies almost exclusively to a population, not necessarily to every individual patient. For example, a well-designed clinical trial could demonstrate that a new drug benefits 45% of the patients who received it, significantly more than the control group; but 55% of patients received no benefit. Individual physicians can take these findings into account, but they must still rely on their intuition and judgment to treat individual patients. However, evidence-based medicine is rapidly moving beyond the application of laboratory and clinical research studies. Today, the concept and practice of evidence-based approaches to healthcare management are broadening, in part because of the increasing emphasis on quality and reliability and because of the advanced capabilities for incorporating data into medical decision making. Frankovich, Longhurst, and Sutherland (2011) describe the application of EMR to evidence-based initiatives: "Real-time availability of data to guide decision-making has already transformed other industries, and the growing prevalence of EMRs along with the development of sophisticated tools for real-time analysis of deidentified data sets will…advance the use of this data driven approach to healthcare delivery" (p. 1758).

As the clinical database expands, and to the extent that relevant data may be easily and readily accessed, clinical decisions can be made that take into account the experiences reported by colleagues. Each medical intervention holds the potential to contribute meaningful information about the health status of a given patient. Each constitutes a link in the chain of information. To the extent that links are missing, the practitioner will be required to engage in some guesswork with respect to the diagnosis and treatment plan. This is not to suggest that medical practitioners have not brought a sound knowledge base, good judgment, and a strong skill set to the clinical context. Rather, the focus on and movement toward an evidence-based system will mean that the practitioner will have an extensive history of that patient and a readily accessible repository of diagnostic and treatment protocols that yield best practice approaches. The benefits to the patient are immeasurable.

But of equal importance is the organization of *epidemiological mapping,* a phrase we employ to characterize the robustly developing database regarding illness, disease, and injury management (Lawson, 2006). Such a database, whether servicing the immediate objective of supporting decision making relative to a particular patient, or the longer-range objective of contributing information to a clinical database, is dependent on active involvement of all practitioners. It will be as good as the commitment of the community to not only use it but to add to it. Best practice models will emerge to the extent that sufficient information is exchanged.

In the long run, such an evidence-based system will enable consumers to judge the value and quality of practitioners. Such scorecards will become increasingly easy to obtain and interpret. But the very fact that practitioners will be required to contribute will bind them in ways that are new and that fortify the notion of interdependence.

System formation. The coalescing of healthcare organizations into systems has been occurring without substantial interruption for the past couple of decades (Galloro, 2011). As shown in **Figure 8.5**, in the period from 1998 to 2010, 2177 hospitals were involved in some sort of merger.

Many in the healthcare community anticipate that the pace will accelerate. According to Creswell and Abelson (2013), "the consolidations are being driven by a confluence of powerful forces, not least of which is President Obama's signature healthcare law, the Affordable Care Act. That law, many experts say, is transforming the economics of health care and pushing a growing number of hospitals into the arms of suitors." Citing Booz and Company, Creswell and Abelson suggest that up to 1000 mergers could occur in the 5-year period ending in 2018. The prolonged period of mergers, beginning in the 1980s as a response to the implications of the increasing ubiquity of managed care, including the need to achieve economies of scale and the security of a competitive advantage, has forced hospitals to function as members of systems.

Some systems have functioned as relatively loose confederations of independent hospitals or vertically integrated structures comprising multiple organizations that complement rather than duplicate service offerings. Other systems have gone further in formalizing by instituting policies and standards that all system members are required to follow. Nevertheless, hospitals throughout the

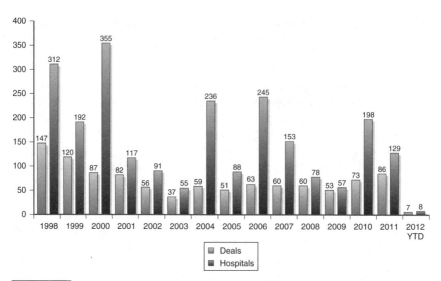

Figure 8.5 Hospital Mergers and Acquisitions, 1998–2011

Reproduced from: Burns, J. (2012 April). Reform forces health insurers to reinvent themselves.
Managed Care. Retrieved from http://www.managedcaremag.com/archives/1204/1204
.healthplan2020.html

country have had to adjust, in some fashion, to functioning on an interconnected
basis. Where much integration has occurred, sharing of staff, joint purchasing,
admitting privileges, the movement toward programmatic complementarity, and
cooperative strategies to achieve system-wide market share goals have all been
undertaken. Even in systems characterized by less assimilation, organizational
entities are typically bound to support corporate goals; adopt a system-wide
identity and, perhaps, brand; and abide by corporate-wide budget, financial,
and capital improvement guidelines as well as corporate policies and programs
related to risk management, quality improvement, and human resources.

Therefore, at this point in time, a great many hospitals have already experienced the phenomenon of managing, albeit to varied extents, in the context
of a system (Kaufman, 2011). They bend to the larger system while gaining the
benefit of being part of the whole. Leaders capable of steering their organizations
in such contexts will have an advantage (Eisenberg, Belasen, & Huppertz, 2013).
But more particularly, the experience of functioning as part of a larger system
has undoubtedly positioned providers to more capably embrace the community
model that will demand a more concerted effort to assimilate and integrate—to
engage one another on a more collaborative basis. The community model will be
effective to the degree that work processes, data sharing, and patient movement
through all sectors of the system occur effectively and efficiently.

Accountable care organizations. The concept of the accountable care organization (ACO) precedes the Affordable Care Act (ACA). In one of the more respected accounts, Fisher, Staiger, Bynum, and Gottlieb (2006) describe the phenomenon as a coordinated effort by hospitals and physicians to provide care. The ACA extends and formalizes the concept through the development of criteria related to leadership, monetary incentives for achieving quality and efficiency goals, and the number of patients served by the ACO (American Hospital Association Committee on Research, 2010). Miller (2009) observed that it is essential that healthcare providers form binding relationships in order to achieve a range of critical healthcare goals: "These include improved prevention and early diagnosis, reductions in unnecessary testing and referrals, reductions in preventable emergency room visits and hospitalizations, reductions in infections and adverse events in hospitals, reductions in preventable readmissions, and use of lower-cost treatments, settings, and providers" (p. 5).

By bringing together healthcare resources and by establishing models of coordination among them, ACOs seek to reduce or eliminate barriers to care from a given population. Financial incentives are organized around volume, efficiency, and quality criteria, requiring the ACO to provide attention to and demonstrate effectiveness in the areas of access, throughput, outcomes, and expense. Accordingly, it is only in the context of collaboration that the goals of ACOs may be achieved.

Experimentation regarding the model's effectiveness will continue, and ACOs are not risk-free entities. For example, an oversized ACO holds the potential to provide the ACO with excessive influence over pricing; an undersized ACO could fail to achieve goals of volume and access. Getting it right will demand trial and error, considerable monitoring of ACO experience, and extensive reporting of successes and failures. As the body of data expand, so too will best practice approaches to ACO formation, maintenance, and goals achievement. Nevertheless, ACOs represent another factor in encouraging coordination, collaboration, and resource pooling.

Neighborhood presence. Writing in *The New Yorker*, Gawande (2011) begins an account of the neighborhood model of health care this way:

> If Camden, New Jersey, becomes the first American community to lower its medical costs, it will have a murder to thank. At nine-fifty on a February night in 2001, a twenty-two-year-old black man was shot while driving his Ford Taurus station wagon through a neighborhood on the edge of the Rutgers University campus. The victim lay motionless in the street beside the open door on the driver's side, as if the car had ejected him. A neighborhood couple, a physical therapist and a volunteer firefighter, approached to see if they could help, but police waved them back.
>
> "He's not going to make it," an officer reportedly told the physical therapist. "He's pretty much dead." She called a physician, Jeffrey Brenner, who lived a few doors up the street, and he ran to the scene with a stethoscope and a pocket ventilation mask. After some discussion, the police let him enter the crime scene and attend to the victim. Witnesses told the local newspaper that he was the first person to lay hands on the man.

"He was slightly overweight, turned on his side," Brenner recalls. There was glass everywhere. Although the victim had been shot several times and many minutes had passed, his body felt warm. Brenner checked his neck for a carotid pulse. The man was alive. Brenner began the chest compressions and rescue breathing that should have been started long before. But the young man, who turned out to be a Rutgers student, died soon afterward.

Brenner was intrigued and, presumably disturbed, by the relatively passive role the healthcare system plays. It waits for health problems to occur and is then called into action to respond. Brenner was determined to institute a more proactive approach:

Besides looking at assault patterns, he began studying patterns in the way patients flowed into and out of Camden's hospitals. "I'd just sit there and play with the data for hours," he says, and the more he played the more he found. For instance, he ran the data on the locations where ambulances picked up patients with fall injuries, and discovered that a single building in central Camden sent more people to the hospital with serious falls—fifty-seven elderly in two years—than any other in the city, resulting in almost three million dollars in healthcare bills. "It was just this amazing window into the healthcare delivery system," he says.

So he took what he learned from police reform and tried a Compstat approach to the city's healthcare performance—a Healthstat, so to speak. He made block-by-block maps of the city, color-coded by the hospital costs of its residents, and looked for the hot spots. The two most expensive city blocks were in north Camden, one that had a large nursing home called Abigail House and one that had a low-income housing tower called Northgate II. He found that between January of 2002 and June of 2008 some nine hundred people in the two buildings accounted for more than four thousand hospital visits and about two hundred million dollars in healthcare bills. One patient had three hundred and twenty-four admissions in five years. The most expensive patient cost insurers $3.5 million.

Brenner wasn't all that interested in costs; he was more interested in helping people who received bad health care. But in his experience the people with the highest medical costs—the people cycling in and out of the hospital—were usually the people receiving the worst care. "Emergency-room visits and hospital admissions should be considered failures of the healthcare system until proven otherwise," he told me—failures of prevention and of timely, effective care.

Reproduced from Gawande, A. (2011). The hot spotters. *The New Yorker*, January 24.

The neighborhood model Brenner sought to implement included three important elements. One involved locating services more closely to residents and making them more accessible. The greater the number and the more formidable the barriers between the patient and the provider, the less likely patients will be to use them. This is especially true for those who lack the resources to overcome those barriers, whether it is distance to the provider, the financial wherewithal to pay for healthcare services, an ability to recognize health issues as well as an understanding of how to go about addressing them, and some familiarity with the healthcare system that would enable the person to seek the appropriate provider or resource. These patients will be more likely to wait until the health problem intensifies before engaging the system.

The second element involves the practitioner initiating contact with the patient, including visiting patients in their communities, their homes, and their workplaces, where and whenever possible. Again, this reverses the passive role ordinarily assigned to healthcare system practitioners—rather than waiting for the patient to initiate contact, that responsibility shifts to the provider. The nearer the provider can get to the environment of the patient, the more data can be collected about lifestyle choice and environmental impact on health—for example, dietary habits, stressors, sleeping patterns, work and leisure pursuits, and interactions with family members.

Third, the practitioner can record observations and interventions and input these into the epidemiological repository, thereby building a database about patterns of health and the manner by which community residents attend to them. However no single practitioner can do this in a vacuum, even someone with the perseverance and determination of Dr. Brenner. The more individualized attention a patient receives, the less time that practitioner has to attend to other patients. A community model will be effective to the extent there is a distribution of roles and responsibilities, and that complementarity—the coming together of services that provide different levels or types of care—constitutes the organizing principle of that allocation.

A Community-Based Model: The Emergence of the Alliance

The closer the healthcare system can locate itself to the consumer, the greater the opportunity to perform a broad range of healthcare activities and achieve a set of critical health-related objectives, including the following examples:

- ▶ Monitor health status
- ▶ Provide wellness, health maintenance, and a broad array of primary care services
- ▶ Assess the effectiveness of health services and medical interventions, thereby adhering to principles of continuous quality improvement
- ▶ Foster patient engagement of the system at earlier disease and illness stages
- ▶ Provide important information to practitioners about each patient to support diagnostic and clinical decision making
- ▶ Strengthen our understanding of patterns of illness and disease and the factors that contribute positively or adversely to health (Minkler & Wallerstein, 2010)
- ▶ Contribute to the development of an evidence-based approaches, and forecast long-term health needs of patients

Observing the benefits of a community-based model employed in under-served regions around the world, Paul Farmer, a medical anthropologist and physician noted, "The quality of care that we can deliver with this system that goes from community to clinic to hospital, when necessary, can provide better rates of retention, better outcomes than any other model in the world" (Chu, 2012).

While the term *merger* relates to the formal organizational process of achieving a common or unified management structure and governance, the term *alliance* may more properly characterize the relationships among those healthcare organizations that serve a particular community. Any healthcare organization may belong to multiple alliances. The nature of the formal relationships among the alliances may vary, that is, they may or may not have common management elements or structures. Nevertheless, alliances borne of a common commitment to a community model will have certain features:

- ▶ **The community as organizing principle.** The term *community* may be defined in multiple ways. The most typical is the definition associated with geographical boundaries and secondarily by demographic, socioeconomic, and sociocultural characteristics. For example, an alliance may serve those qualifying for Medicaid in a particular municipality. The definition of the community and its healthcare needs provide the basis for the establishment of the alliance.

- ▶ **Continuum of care/service complementarity.** All alliances must have a primary care presence as well as an acute care capability. The more links in between, generally speaking, the better; for example, orthopedic, pediatric, maternity, geriatric, and ambulatory care all add to the comprehensiveness of the alliance's services. There should be a sufficiency of access points into the system that match the care needs of the consumers. As noted in the CHP model referenced earlier (Hartocollis, 2012), teaming with pharmacies might even take hold, given their neighborhood presence and the one-stop shopping capability for health and pharmaceutical products. Nevertheless, the critical point is that the alliance will provide healthcare services that cut across a continuum of care; therefore, alliances will tend to be vertical (different, but complementary, services) as opposed to exclusively horizontal (offering the same services).

- ▶ **Employer involvement.** Situating services in or near the workplace, for example, in concert with an employee health service (if available), provides exceptional opportunities to evaluate health risks, advise employers on how to manage them, facilitate corporate wellness and accident and illness prevention goals, and establish common objectives for health insurance programs.

- ▶ **Stakeholder participation.** The more the full range of stakeholders—providers, consumers, and those who support their efforts, including local government, medical suppliers, third-party payers, employers, pharmacies, laboratories—contribute to the development of the alliance's goals, the more effective the alliance will be in carrying out its mission.

▶ **Quality initiatives.** The U.S. healthcare system is placing continued emphasis on quality and on determining whether quality has been achieved through evidence-based measures. Alliances are encouraged to pool their expertise to evaluate how each component of the alliance contributes to quality goals and abides by the notion that striving for improvements in quality is never ending.

▶ **Information management tools.** Alliances will have systems for sharing data that are easily linked and that facilitate effective and immediate information exchanges. The databases serve multiple purposes, but three in particular are essential. First, the system must achieve the full range of EMR goals. Second, databases in which aggregate and longitudinal information are assembled must allow for assessments of the clinical effectiveness of the alliance and facilitate the development of epidemiological mapping. Third, the system must allow for the reporting of its work to the full variety of stakeholders as well as to relevant government agencies, accreditation bodies, and the public.

▶ **Communication effectiveness.** The flow of information across the alliance must be managed with great care. Building and promoting an "alliance perspective," that is, the understanding on the part of all staff of the vital nature of the alliance in serving the community's health needs, is essential. Roles and responsibilities of employees across the alliance must be defined in such a manner that all understand and actively support the purpose of the alliance and act in accord with its principles and mandate.

An excellent example of these kinds of alliances is the "Health Home," a program initiated by the Centers for Medicare and Medicaid Services (Centers for Medicare and Medicaid Services, 2013a) that encourages states to bring together providers and community supports for Medicaid patients with chronic conditions. As Dr. Brenner discovered in Camden, these patients account for a large proportion of the community's medical expenses, mostly because of failures to manage their health conditions. The Health Home, a program each state tailors to its own Medicaid population, offers a team approach to not only the healthcare needs of Medicaid patients, but also to the social and economic conditions that prevent them from managing their health.

Population Health

An important concept related to the community health model is "population health," which generally refers to understanding the epidemiology of a particular population and aligning the community's healthcare resources to not only treat illnesses and heal injuries, but also to keep the population healthy (Kindig

& Stoddart, 2003). Although many public health officials and practitioners have discussed the importance of population health, the healthcare profession has lacked a consistent definition and different players interpret the concept in different ways. From a public health perspective, the providers, payers, and stakeholders should take responsibility for the health of the entire community, as defined by geographic boundaries (Hacker & Walker, 2013). In this view, everyone in a community plays a part in the health of all, and healthcare professionals should cooperate to ensure the health of the people residing in their service area. On the other hand, many payers and providers interpret the population health construct more narrowly. Payers—commercial health plans, managed care organizations, self-insured companies, and so on—define the population as their enrolled members or covered lives. Providers—hospitals, multispecialty medical groups, primary care practices, and so forth—define the population as *their* patient population, namely the patients enrolled in their network.

This understanding of the concept has gained momentum as providers are accepting responsibility for a broader spectrum of care for their patients through patient-centered medical homes (PCMH) and ACOs. Under these models, providers take on additional risk, agreeing to be held responsible for making sure that patients remain healthy after being treated and managing their chronic conditions. In return, they receive additional payments, bonuses for reaching agreed-upon targets, and shared savings from avoided costs of ER visits and hospitalizations. In order to accomplish these goals, they must do more than simply treat the conditions of patients who present at their doors. Because so many health problems result from social and economic conditions, these providers must collaborate with a variety of community agencies and other healthcare organizations to accomplish the goal of keeping their populations healthy.

Regardless of the definition, managing population health requires a new mode of leadership and a new way of thinking about the problem of providing health care to the community. The traditional boundaries that separate healthcare organizations from those that provide social services have begun to blur, just as the integration of providers has necessitated new ways of working that require greater collaboration and communication across the spectrum.

Leadership: The Key to a Community Model

Quite naturally, organizations develop their own cultures and tend to focus on their own agendas. Getting organizations to mesh around a broader system-wide goal is among the more challenging tasks of an organization's leadership. This may be particularly difficult for healthcare organizations given the history of a silo culture, which can be traced back, in part, to the highly specialized nature of the various professions that make up the base of the system. Nevertheless, as discussed throughout this text, industry trends along with environmental forces are coming together in such a way as to make it practically impossible to avoid collaboration. The community health model represents a next stage of this movement as we move into a more intensive phase of need for integration. It will require leaders who can steer their organizations through the parochial inclination to focus so much attention on their own organizations that the network of collaborators cannot achieve its potential. The skills associated with the master leader, as presented throughout this text, are essential for leaders who plan to organize and participate in alliances to serve the good of the community.

Finding ways to achieve balance between the need to manage internal processes and a burgeoning need to engage partners to most effectively deliver care to the community is quickly emerging as the mandate for leaders in health care. The competing values framework (Belasen, 2008) is instructive on this matter. Leadership, which cannot both negotiate with prospective partners to identify opportunities for alignment and advance stakeholder interests, will face potentially serious challenges as the healthcare system continues to evolve. The skills associated with alliance formation and participation are distinct from those that may serve the operational necessities of the organization. As shown in **Figure 8.6**, an integrated approach to leadership requires a skill profile in which the various and even conflicting roles are brought into a state of equilibrium.

It is important to emphasize that master leaders will be characterized by the capability to develop and constructively contribute to alliances. At the same time, those leaders must guard against the risks associated with alliances. There are at least three. First, as alliances come into existence and expand, the possibility exists

Figure 8.6 Alliance Leadership: An Integrated Approach

that they will crowd out providers that are outside the alliance or make it challenging for other providers to enter the area served by the alliance. In the event competition is diminished, pricing may increase beyond what is reasonable and achieving high levels of quality could be challenging to sustain. Despite the ACA's incentives to join forces and collaborate, the Federal Trade Commission remains on guard against pricing increases resulting from less competition among healthcare entities (Kendall, 2012). It will have its work cut out for it. As reported by Drum (2013) in reference to the supersizing of hospitals and healthcare systems, "'the rhetoric is all about efficiency,' said Karen Ignagni, the chief executive of America's Health Insurance Plans, a trade group that represents insurers. 'The reality is all about higher prices.'"

Second, the smaller organizations in the alliance may see their autonomy compromised in the event that control over the direction of the alliance becomes too centralized. For example, an outpatient clinic with an emphasis on orthopedic care may become pressured to focus more on primary care in the event the largest organizational entity in the alliance deems it to be in best interests of the alliance.

Third, the needs of communities change; alliances that lack the nimbleness or agility to respond to changing needs and environmental conditions may discover their services to be out of alignment with the community's healthcare requirements.

Case Study: A Midwest City Undergoes Change

A moderate-sized city in the Midwest had 14 acute care hospitals, a few hundred group practices, 122 rehabilitation facilities, dozens of pharmacies with basic capability to measure vitals like blood pressure, and, like so many cities around the country, a dwindling population of solo medical practices. The acute care hospitals were organized into three systems: one was comprised of five hospitals, a second had three (one of which was a trauma center), and the third had six (though this system had the fewest number of registered beds).

Patient mix patterns had begun to shift, in large part because of two trends. The first involved the influx of large numbers of younger professionals who were attracted to career opportunities as a result of the city's effort to lure high technology businesses. For several years, the city had worked extensively with local universities, the chamber of commerce, financial institutions, state officials, and local businesses to create an environment in which high technology development could flourish. The second trend involved the accelerated growth of the elderly population. Unlike other cities around the country, particularly those in colder climates, a significant percentage of people over

65 years old – and especially those over 75 – remained in the city. The comfortable climate and longstanding family ties made the need to relocate less desirable for city residents as they considered options following retirement. Thus, the city had a robust compilation of assisted living and nursing home facilities. Over an eight year period, the growth of the 25-35 and 65-85 age groups increasingly dwarfed the 35-45 age group. As a result of these changing demographic patterns, the health needs of the city's residents changed. Most notably, the need for acute care beds declined, the need for employee health increased, and the rehabilitation service composite began to place more emphasis on sports medicine, pain management, and geriatric care; similarly, intensive care and palliative care programs were on the rise.

The model of delivering healthcare in this city had to change. But how significantly? How rapidly? How could change be accomplished? How incremental or fundamental should it be? Who would lead the change? Who would be involved? And, quite critically, how could providers work more collaboratively to satisfy emerging health needs and remain viable.

All three hospital systems had a very powerful investment in understanding and adapting to what the future would bring. So did every other provider in the city. The hospital systems' leaders met several times and agreed on the need to study short-term and long-term demographic patterns and the healthcare needs associated with these population changes. They arranged to hire a consulting firm specializing in demographic change and population health. While they concurred about the need for good data, they also understood that their systems were not equally well-positioned to adapt to the changes in care delivery that might be required. But first things first – study the problem!

While the consultants were doing their work, each system independently organized a preliminary list of strategic issues which would need to be carefully evaluated as their understanding of the city's health needs became clearer. The strategic issues included:

▶ Given the importance of promoting continuity of care and partnerships with employers, how can the system more effectively engage employers with health wellness, maintenance, and risk management programs?

▶ What health delivery and health service goals overlap with providers of non-acute services? Most particularly, what health service needs will be desired by and essential for younger professionals and their families? How can this stakeholder group be afforded easy access to basic primary care services? What portals or gateways into the system will be most convenient and most attractive, and will provide easy transition to a hospital system in the event tertiary care becomes necessary? What non-acute providers should be consulted with now? Why?

▶ One of the hospital systems has a religious tradition. How might this influence an interest in building common ground among the systems in the event some sharing of services or service distribution becomes desirable or necessary? What other traditions, values, and historical imperatives of the various hospitals constitute challenges for alliance building among the systems?

▶ What will the stakeholder profile and composite look like in three years? Five years? Ten? Fifteen? What characteristics and services of an alliance will be essential to effectively serve the needs of these stakeholder groups? Where do the needs of stakeholders come together? Where do they diverge? How will these commonalities and differences change in five year increments?

▶ How can geriatric services occupy a more prominent place in the collection of care giving activities? What financing mechanisms are available for service growth in this area, especially in the context of anticipated Medicare limitations? Where is the overlap among services for younger professionals and older residents? Are there provider skill sets common to both? If so, what are they, and how can they be leveraged?

▶ What strategies can be employed to facilitate consumer engagement of the alliance? How do different consumer groups and subgroups respond to different approaches to encourage engagement? More broadly, what are the goals of engagement with each group and subgroup?

▶ Reimbursement could pose a thorny problem given the growth of the older population and the stable (if not shrinking) middle age segment of the population? As older people consume more and more healthcare dollars, how can the younger population continue to subsidize their healthcare services without promoting generational animosity?

▶ How can the systems and alliances build political support?

▶ The formation of alliances will have public reporting responsibilities. How can the components of an alliance work toward defining common ground even their goals may be somewhat disparate? How can the larger components of the system or alliance support the development of data base utilization among smaller components?

▶ To what extent can healthcare programs across systems and alliances achieve more significant levels of integration?

▶ What standards of quality will be employed as alliances form on horizontal bases?

▶ Components of the healthcare systems and anticipated alliance differ across a wide band of human resources and administrative activity. For example, in eight of the 14 hospitals, more than 50% of the work force is unionized, and there is no union representation in three of the hospitals. Nine hospitals have three 12-hour shifts for nurses and other clinical professionals; three do not. Vacation day allotments vary among the hospitals. Management structures vary. Purchasing consortia are different? And on and on. What are the implications for increased integration?

Case Study Review Questions

1. How would you define the community or communities you serve? What are the physical parameters and population characteristics of the community? What are their principal healthcare needs? How are these needs changing?
2. What providers serve your community's needs? Which providers offer services that are complementary? How will working in concert allow community residents to access healthcare services more readily and effectively?
3. What barriers could interfere with the formation of an alliance in your community (for example, incompatible systems of information management; different reimbursement opportunities and financial management objectives; competing priorities; different organizational cultures)? How might they be overcome?
4. What are the long-term care objectives that could be more fully served by collaborative efforts of providers?
5. From a strategic perspective, what options for alliance management are available? Which option would best serve the interests of your organization?
6. What skills do you possess that would enable you to participate effectively in a healthcare alliance? What skills would you like to develop to strengthen your ability to participate effectively?

Conclusion

The future of healthcare—if we view it as moving steadily toward a period when it works comprehensively to care for people both proactively as well as responsively—demands that providers work in concert with one another. We may be hard pressed to address the health problems that emanate from disparity of care in our healthcare delivery system unless we find ways to pool resources and move them right into the neighborhoods where people live and work. Although it may be both morally and practically advantageous to begin with underserved communities, the principle of community-based health care applies to all. It is as close as we can get to the concept of health care without walls. As the term implies, *walls* may function as barriers. Taking them down is tantamount to enabling patients to easily enter and engage the healthcare system. That is the goal of the community-based approach to health care. Master leaders will, over time, increasingly devote their energies and attention to such collaborative models.

Review Questions

1. Why is a community-based model considered a next logical step in the evolution of the healthcare system in the United States?
2. Why is it important to understand that a community health model is a multidimensional concept? What are the dimensions and how do they relate to one another?
3. What economic, clinical, and technological trends are coming together to create a climate conducive to community-health models?
4. What is the role of a healthcare alliance and how does an alliance model differ from the more traditional corporate consolidation model? What are the benefits and limitations of the alliance model?
5. What challenges will healthcare leaders confront as they consider having their organizations participate in an integrated community health model?
6. What skills will master leaders need to transition their organizations into a community-based health alliance successfully?

References

American Academy of Family Physicians. (n.d.). *Primary Care*. Retrieved from http://www .aafp.org/about/policies/all/primary-care.html

American Hospital Association Committee on Research. (2010). *AHA research synthesis report: Accountable care organization*. Chicago, IL: American Hospital Association. Retrieved from http://www.aha.org/research/cor/content/ACO-Synthesis-Report.pdf

Belasen, A. T. (2008). *The theory and practice of corporate communication: A competing values perspective*. Thousand Oaks, CA: Sage.

Boonstra, A., & Broekhuis, M. (2010). *BMC Health Services Research: Barriers to the acceptance of electronic medical records by physicians: From systematic review to taxonomy and interventions* [Full text]. (n.d.). Retrieved from http://www.biomedcentral .com/1472-6963/10/231

Burns, J. (2012, April). Reform forces health insurers to reinvent themselves. *Managed Care*. Retrieved from http://www.managedcaremag.com/archives/1204/1204 .healthplan2020.html

Centers for Disease Control and Prevention. (2011). *Table 116: Hospitals, beds, and occupancy rates, by type of ownership and size of hospital: United States, selected years 1975–2009*. Retrieved from http://www.cdc.gov/nchs/data/hus/2011/116.pdf

Centers for Medicare and Medicaid Services. (2013a). *Health Home Information Resource Center, Medicaid.gov*. Retrieved from http://www.medicaid.gov/State-Resource -Center/Medicaid-State-Technical-Assistance/Health-Homes-Technical-Assistance /Health-Home-Information-Resource-Center.html

Centers for Medicare and Medicaid Services. (2013b). *National health expenditures*. Retrieved from http://www.cms.gov/Research-Statistics-Data-and-Systems/Statistics-Trends -and-Reports/NationalHealthExpendData/Downloads/tables.pdf

Chu, L. (2012, October 23). *Global health pioneer Paul Farmer touts community-based health care model to combat infectious diseases*. Retrieved from http://www.ucsf .edu/news/2012/10/12984/global-health-pioneer-paul-farmer-touts-community -based-health-care-model-combat

Creswell, J., & Abelson, R. (2013, August 13). New laws and rising costs create a surge of supersizing hospitals. *The New York Times*, B1.

Cuckler, G., Sisko, A., Keehan, S., Smith, S., Madison, A., Poisal, J., ... Stone, D. (2013). National health expenditure projections, 2012–22: Slow growth until coverage expands and economy improves. *Health Affairs, 32*(1), 1820–1831.

Drum, K. (2013, August 12). Quote of the day: "The reality is all about high prices." *Mother Jones*. Retrieved from http://www.motherjones.com/kevin-drum/2013/08 /quote-day-hospital-mergers-price

Eisenberg, B., Belasen, A., & Huppertz, J. (2013) *The "ambidextrous leader": An integrated model of healthcare management for the future*. Association of University Programs in Health Administration Annual Meeting. Monterey, CA, June 20–23, 2013.

Fisher, E. S., Staiger, D. O., Bynum, J., & Gottlieb, D. J. (2006). Creating accountable care organizations: The extended hospital medical staff. *Health Affairs, 26*(1), 44–57.

Frankovich, J., Longhurst, C., & Sutherland, S. (2011). Evidence-based medicine in the EMR era. *New England Journal of Medicine, 365*(19), 1758–1759.

Galloro, V. (2011). Picking up speed: Health reform among the drivers cited for recent mergers and acquisitions. *Modern Healthcare, 41*(3), 22–26.

Gawande, A. (2011, January 24). The hot spotters. *The New Yorker*. Retrieved from http:// www.newyorker.com/magazine/2011/01/24/the-hot-spotters

Gibbons, D. (2012, June 28). Urgent care centers fill in some of the gap for former St. Vincent's patients. *NYPress*. Retrieved from http://nypress.com /urgent-care-centers-fill-in-some-of-the-gap-for-former-st-vincents-patients/

Grube, M., Kaufman, K., & York, R. (2013, March 8). Decline in utilization rates signals a change in the inpatient business model [Web log]. Retrieved from http://healthaffairs.org/blog/2013/03/08/decline-in-utilization-rates-signals-a-change -in-the-inpatient-business-model/

Hacker, K., & Walker, D. K. (2013). Achieving population health in accountable care organizations. *American Journal of Public Health, 103*(7), 1163–1167.

Hartocollis, A. (2010, April 8). Nearby hospitals to fill gap when St. Vincent's closes. *The New York Times*, A29.

Hartocollis, A. (2012, October 10). New style of care emerges to fill hospital's void. *The New York Times*, A1.

Kaufman, N. (2011). Changing economics in an era of healthcare reform. *Journal of Healthcare Management, 56*(1), 9–13.

Kendall, B. (2012, March 18). Regulators seek to cool hospital-deal fever. *Wall Street Journal*. Retrieved from http://online.wsj.com/news/articles/SB10001424052702303863404 57728607183774083

Kindig, D., & Stoddart, G. (2003). What is population health? *American Journal of Public Health, 93*(3), 380–383.

Lawson, A. (2006). *Statistical methods in spatial epidemiology*. San Francisco, CA: John Wiley & Sons.

Lund, C. (2013, July 11). *United States facing major shortage of geriatricians* [Web log]. Retrieved from http://www.elderbranch.com/blog/shortage-of-geriatricians/

McGlynn, E. A., Asch, S. M., Adams, J., Keesey, J., Hicks, J., DeCristofaro, A., & Kerr, E. A. (2003). The quality of health care delivered to adults in the United States. *New England Journal of Medicine, 348*(26), 2635–2645. doi:10.1056/NEJMsa022615

Miller, H. D. (2009) How to create accountable care organizations. *Center for Healthcare Quality and Payment Reform.* Retrieved from http://www.chqpr.org/downloads /HowtoCreateAccountableCareOrganizations.pdf

Minkler, M., & Wallerstein, N. (Eds.). (2010). *Community-based participatory research for health: From process to outcomes.* San Francisco, CA: John Wiley & Sons.

Otterman, S. (2010, April 6). St. Vincent's votes to shut hospital in Manhattan. *The New York Times*, A23.

Poemhunter. (n.d.). The biography of Edna St. Vincent Millay. Retrieved from http://www .poemhunter.com/edna-st-vincent-millay/biography/

Progressives for Immigration Reform. (n.d.). *Environmental impact statement (EIS) on United States Immigration policy.* Retrieved from http://www.immigrationeis.org /eis-documents/us-demographic-history

Rosenbaum, R. (2010). Data governance and stewardship: Designing data stewardship entities and advancing data access. *Health Services Research, 45*(5 Part 2), 1442–1455.

Sackett, D. L., Rosenberg, W. M. C., Gray, J. A. M., Haynes, R. B., & Richardson, W. S. (1996). Evidence based medicine: What it is and what it isn't: It's about integrating individual clinical expertise and the best external evidence. *British Medical Journal, 312*, 71–72.

Stanton, M. W. (2006). "Healthcare 411." *The high concentration of U.S. health care expenditures.* n.p., n.d. [Web]. 19 Dec. 2013. Retrieved from http://www.ahrq.gov /research/findings/factsheets/costs/expriach/index.html

Sultz, H. A., & Young, K. M. (2014). *Health care USA: Understanding its organization and delivery* (8th ed.). Burlington, MA: Jones & Bartlett Learning.

U.S. Department of Health and Human Services. (2013, August 7) *Principles and strategy for accelerating health information exchange (HIE).* Retrieved from http://www.healthit .gov/sites/default/files/acceleratinghieprinciples_strategy.pdf

U.S. National Health Spending. (2012). *U.S. national health expenditures.* Retrieved from http://sambaker.com/econ/classes/nhe10/

VMG Health. (2010). *Intellimarker: Ambulatory surgical centers financial and operational benchmarking study.* Retrieved from http://www.vmghealth.com/Downloads /VMG_Intellimarker10.pdf

CHAPTER 9 ▶

Patient Satisfaction and Quality Care: The Role of Leadership Communication

A Lesson on Patient Satisfaction Learned the Hard Way

Community General Hospital (CGH) was experiencing a problem: declining scores on key measures of patient satisfaction. The hospital was particularly concerned because it instituted a comprehensive quality improvement program that focused on service just three years earlier. The program was based on an extensive analysis that included gathering input from a variety of key sources—patients, their families, staff, and physicians. Based on their analysis, CGH determined that two areas would be addressed. One involved a concerted effort to schedule tests, procedures, and services on a more coordinated basis. The other involved providing communication training to all staff; key topics included empathy, managing stressful interactions, overcoming cultural differences, and delivering bad news.

For about two years, data from patient surveys showed steady improvement. Then, beginning about eight months ago, the overall patient satisfaction level began to slip. What's more, the decline cut across practically all areas of the hospital—quality of care, concern for the patient, food, timeliness of response, friendliness of staff.

CGH examined several hospital functions in which previously high scores were now showing signs of a downturn. The food had not changed, delivery times were the same, the appearance of the food and characteristics such as temperature had not changed at all. Most interestingly, a review of other functions in which measures of satisfaction showed a loss of favorability by patients revealed actual improvements; for example, response time to call bells had decreased and complaints to patient representatives had diminished in frequency.

Hospital management was puzzled. They reviewed every change that had been made since the satisfaction scores began to slide. Only one significant change was implemented, and this occurred about a year earlier. In an effort to elevate the quality of the patient's experience, CGH promised that the discharge time would be before noon—before lunch. It was common, therefore, for the family member or friend who would take the patient home to arrive in the morning.

As it happens, this promise of a noon deadline for discharge was difficult, if not outright impossible, to guarantee. The lack of complete control over the unfolding of events in a clinical environment was simply too much. Approximately one-third of all discharges occurred after 12:00 noon, and about 25% of those occurred after 1:30 p.m. It was common for those patients to be sitting in their rooms, all dressed and ready to leave, getting hungry and impatient—not to mention the aggravation experienced by the person who came to provide the transportation home. Staff were also affected. In their haste to meet the discharge deadline, staff often communicated discharge instructions quickly, displayed stress, and failed to provide patients with adequate time to ask questions.

Within a couple of days of discharge, the patient received a survey asking for their impressions of care and services.

The CGH management team scrutinized the data carefully, and they discovered a fascinating trend. Patients who scored the discharge experience as low tended to downgrade the hospital in other areas. Somehow, the impression of the final event—the discharge—colored their impressions of the entire hospital experience. It is quite possible that all else with the hospitalization went well, yet it seemed that many patients who had a negative experience with the discharge were not able to isolate other elements of their experience when completing the satisfaction survey.

The early discharge guarantee was intended to further promote the hospital's commitment to service. Instead, it backfired by creating an expectation the hospital was unable to satisfy. CGH learned three valuable lessons. First, the management of consumer expectations is an enormously powerful factor in determining the degree to which consumers will be satisfied. Second, an organization must be operationally prepared to deliver on its promises; a lack of alignment between goals, commitments, staff capabilities, and work processes is a recipe for failure. Third, a consumer's negative experience with one part of the organization can influence, often significantly, their impressions of other parts of the organization even when experiences with those other parts might have otherwise been positive.

Introduction

Considerable advancement has been made by healthcare organizations in recent decades to monitor, measure, and strengthen patient satisfaction. However, particular trends, and most especially their cumulative effect, hold significant potential to disrupt such progress. These trends include the growing shortage of primary care physicians, shrinking percentage of solo practices, aging population, increasing percentage of international medical graduates (IMGs), expanding reliance on technology, and growing emphasis on outcomes measures. As the role of the healthcare leader continues to broaden to accommodate shifting policy, economic, technological, clinical, and demographic conditions, research indicates that healthcare leaders must also be mindful of the importance of sound interpersonal and communication practices that affect patient satisfaction. An evaluation of these trends and factors, as well as strategies for overcoming obstacles to patient satisfaction, is presented in this chapter. Suggestions for the enhancement and application of monitoring systems, incentives, communication practices, and training programs are also provided.

Patient Satisfaction: A Complex Undertaking

Where does patient satisfaction fit into the matrix of priorities for medical practitioners? The question may evoke some confusion because the answer seems so obvious. The majority of us would undoubtedly agree that patient satisfaction should reside in the top tier of priorities for practitioners. Simply put, it is not likely to be viewed as controversial that patients occupy a special category of consumer and deserve conduct from providers that produces satisfaction. It may even be argued that attention to patient satisfaction is a moral imperative. The American Medical Association (AMA) affirmed this notion in its code of ethics by declaring that "the patient has the right to courtesy, respect, dignity, responsiveness, and timely attention to his or her needs" (American Medical Association [AMA], 2001). While the AMA is a relatively modern organization, the obligations of providers to their patients have been the subject of deliberation for centuries. Whether the call is to "do no harm," as mandated by the Hippocratic Oath ("Greek Medicine," 2012), or to take a more active curative or healing approach to managing the welfare of patients, the obligations of providers to ensure patient satisfaction are grounded in the realm of moral commitments (Buckingham, 1978; Clements, 1992; Moskop, Marco, Larkin, Geiderman, & Derse, 2005; Pellegrino, 1993; Sohl & Bassford, 1986; Tung & Organ, 2000).

But there are surrogate outcomes to ensuring patient satisfaction as well. Consider just a few phenomena that trend favorably with patient satisfaction as supported by research: compliance with medical directives increases (Brown, Stewart, & Ryan, 2003; Jha, Orav, Zheng, & Epstein, 2008), predisposition to ask follow-up questions of a provider strengthens (Brown et al., 2003), the inclination to initiate litigation against a provider decreases (DuPre, 2010), and 30-day readmission rates decline (Boulding, Glickman, Manary, Schulman, & Staelin, 2011; Press Ganey, 2012). More and more, research is validating a seemingly obvious proposition: evidence is showing that patient satisfaction is significantly related to quality of care (Manary, Boulding, Staelin, & Glickman, 2013).

The notion of what constitutes satisfaction has been the subject of considerable discussion over the past 20 years. According to Press Ganey, the largest firm that conducts surveys of healthcare organizations, patient impressions of care, service, and the environment are critical indicators of overall patient satisfaction (Press Ganey, 2013). Consistent with the literature on corporate communication and organizational effectiveness (Belasen, 2008), it is not uncommon for patients to rate the effectiveness of their medical care based on their estimations of how caring, sensitive, empathic, and communicatively adept their practitioners are. In a fashion, the interpersonal experiences with providers serves a gatekeeping role with respect to patients' perceptions of their medical care, and in so doing shape and influence their beliefs about how well the medical treatment or procedure went.

The quality of practitioner communication also influences the degree to which patients actively participate in the care-receiving experience and abide by medical directives. Consider the example of patient compliance regarding medications. The estimated annual cost of hospital admissions for patients who do not take their medications as prescribed is $8.5 billion ("Just What the Doctor Ordered," n.d.). According to the Center for Health Transformation (2010), approximately 125,000 people with treatable ailments die annually because of a failure to take prescribed medications properly or because they fail to take them at all. The reasons for such ill-advised or faulty decision making are often complicated, and include such causes as a willful disregard of physician instructions (for example, because of an inability to afford the medications). However, Torrey (2011) reports that miscommunication is a central factor—patients may not understand the prescription protocols or the consequences of failure to abide by them. For example, what is meant by the common directive *take as needed*? Does this term mean take when pain occurs? When pain is anticipated? How much pain should be felt to justify the medication? What is the risk of taking too much when the dosing instruction is open-ended? What is the risk of taking too little? Is there a point at which the medication should no longer be consumed? Patients who have favorable feelings about the provider are more likely to ask questions and to seek clarification, thus affirming the positive relationship between communication effectiveness and quality of care. DuPre (2010) describes the concept of *collaborative communication* in which caregivers seek to empower patients by removing barriers to status distinctions; when accomplished, patients participate more fully and actively in the exchange and depart with an enhanced understanding of, motivation for, and ability to carry out care management requirements.

Many Initiatives Are Underway

In recognition of the relationship between good communication, patient satisfaction, and quality of care, the healthcare industry has undertaken far-reaching programs to strengthen the measurement of patient satisfaction and to provide healthcare practitioners with the skills essential for promoting improved relationships with patients. Consider just a few:

- ▶ Over 65% of medical schools now have some form of communication training in their curricula (Kalet et al., 2004).
- ▶ The Accreditation Council for Graduate Medical Education, which sanctions post-medical training programs in the United States, has broadened its competency criteria to include "professionalism," "teamwork," and "communication" (Partners Healthcare, n.d.).
- ▶ Today, almost 60 US medical schools provide an MBA option to medical students in order to develop their management skills, including their aptitude for empathy, team-building, and relationship management (Association of MD MBA Programs, n.d.).
- ▶ Hospital tracking of patient satisfaction has become widespread; in fact, Press Ganey alone consults with and/or measures patient satisfaction in over 50% of hospitals in the United States (Press Ganey, 2013).
- ▶ Third-party payers employ communication effectiveness in their criteria for judging a practitioner's performance and for issuing or withholding incentives (Adamy, 2012).

Thus, the industry has been building toward a wide-ranging approach of addressing patient satisfaction by instituting educational programs on communication and related human relations skills, obtaining ever more feed-back from patients about impressions of their healthcare experiences, rewarding practitioners who produce higher levels of patient satisfaction, and penalizing those who do not.

Yet, despite the inroads made toward improving the communication climate between practitioners and patients, and despite all the efforts to establish patient satisfaction as a vital goal of the caregiving process, particular trends are emerging that add considerable challenge to the achievement of this goal. Accordingly, a more vigorous approach to ensuring patient satisfaction than has occurred is warranted.

The purpose of this chapter is threefold: (1) to identify trends that could impede progress toward patient satisfaction, (2) to suggest means for overcoming institutional and interpersonal barriers to achieving better outcomes, and (3) to examine the roles and responsibilities of healthcare leaders in sustaining their organizations' ability to achieve patient satisfaction objectives.

Emerging Risks to Achieving Patient Satisfaction

The image of the family doctor arriving at the family's home to tend to a sick child has become part of the annals of folklore, a charming scene that may well have been filled with horses and buggies from a period that preceded an era of mass communication. Much emphasis back then was on "TLC"—tender loving care—and the centerpiece of the relationship between physician and patient was trust. In the period around World War II, a transformation began to take shape. As mobility and economic opportunity expanded, an increasing emphasis on technology and clinical development began to replace TLC as principal focal points of the healthcare experience. A good doctor began to be defined more by reputation for clinical prowess than by proclivity for inculcating trust and exercising empathy (Schiavo, 2007). Not that the latter became unimportant; rather, their importance had become dwarfed by the emerging prominence of other—scientific, medical—factors. Metaphors for identifying the assets of a physician began to shift from interpersonal strengths to clinical expertise. The very term *clinical* may evoke connotations of sterility and dispassion, rendering TLC to a more quaint position in the realm of what we regard as important in a physician. Bedside manner was relegated to a "nice extra," and not a necessity of health care.

As researchers continue to examine the connections between the quality of the social experience and quality of care, the healthcare industry has instituted efforts to focus providers' attention on the importance of achieving high levels of patient satisfaction. Individual providers and hospital leaders who ignore the responsibility to furnish patients with a constructive and meaningful interpersonal experience are likely to fall behind in meeting their objectives (Bensing, 1991;

Bensing, Kerssens, & Vanderpasch, 1995; Roter & Hall, 1993; Street & Millay, 2001). It is not surprising, therefore, that the manner by which communication is practiced in healthcare contexts is being elevated to priority status. Healthcare leaders need to be aware of possible systemic barriers to effective communication and develop means to overcome them. These obstacles include the following:

- ▶ Shortage of primary care physicians
- ▶ Shrinking number of solo practices
- ▶ Aging population
- ▶ Increasing percentage of International Medical Graduates
- ▶ Increasing reliance on technology
- ▶ Greater emphasis on outcomes measures

Moreover, it is the cumulative impact of these factors that intensifies the potential for undercutting the gains made by the industry to promote increased satisfaction among consumers. A brief examination of each factor follows.

Shortages of Physicians

Primary care physicians have been routinely described as the backbone of the US healthcare system—the group at the frontlines of health care, and those stationed at the forefront of the system. In this regard, primary care physicians play a most vital role in the healthcare system of the United States. In particular, two roles of the primary care physician may be highlighted. First, the primary care physician is generally the point of contact for patients entering the healthcare system. According to the American Academy of Family Physicians (AAFP), a primary care physician is "specifically trained for and skilled in comprehensive first contact." Second, by virtue of the primary care physician's responsibility for initial contact, he or she is well-positioned to manage a majority of health issues, including prevention and wellness, as well as attending to the tremendous array of healthcare needs that might be considered routine. Again, according to the AAFP, the primary care physician provides "continuing care for persons with any undiagnosed sign, symptom, or health concern (the 'undifferentiated' patient) not limited by problem origin (biological, behavioral, or social), organ system, or diagnosis" (American Academy of Family Physicians, n.d.). In this capacity, the primary care physician holds the relatively distinct responsibility for navigating the patient through the healthcare system and coordinating the care provided by specialists—at least in theory. Under the fee-for-service reimbursement system, primary care providers may receive little or no compensation for their navigation and care coordination activities, and because their reimbursement rates are significantly lower those of specialists, they must quickly refer patients for specialty care and move on to the next patient. In order to break even, primary care physicians can spend only a few minutes with each patient, seeing many patients every day, with little time to build a relationship or even answer detailed questions.

Furthermore, the United States is confronting what is considered a critical, potentially long-term shortage of primary care physicians. Petterson et al. (2012) estimate that over the coming decade, an additional 52,000 primary care physicians will be necessary to keep pace with population growth, the aging population, and the need to accommodate the citizens who will become eligible for healthcare coverage as a result of the Affordable Care Act. But the incentive to pursue a specialty area, such as cardiology, orthopedics, oncology, or radiology, is powerful; whereas the approximate compensation level for primary care physicians such as internists or family practitioners is $170,000, the earning potential of specialists is significantly greater (Medscape, 2012).

If the ratio of primary care physicians to patients declines, a number of problematic consequences can occur. For example, wait times for appointments may lengthen, examinations may be less comprehensive, support personnel may be required to assume increasing levels of responsibility for obtaining patient information and conducting medical exams, the physician's ability to negotiate on behalf of the patient with other entities in the healthcare system could suffer, and the responsibility for providing primary care may increasingly shift to specialists like cardiologists or pulmonologists. Each of these occurrences carries possible costs in terms of both quality of care and patient satisfaction. As wait times for appointments lengthen, the potential for illness intensification correspondingly increases. Similarly, less time with the physician may mean the curtailment of opportunities for patients to ask questions or for a thorough examination to occur. Less time spent with the physician could also interfere with the development of trust toward the physician. The patient may be constrained from enlisting sufficient support from the physician for follow up tests or appointments with specialists or with the management of relationships or problems with third-party payers. Finally, as a result of their training, and by virtue of how their practices are oriented, some specialists may prove unable to execute a full range of primary care functions. Their practices may be more capable of doing tests and procedures specific to their specialty, and patients may be directed to other venues for routine tests and procedures that could otherwise be performed in an internal medicine or family practice facility.

Fewer Solo Practices

In 1970, approximately 60% of male physicians were self-employed, and many of them worked in solo practices. Today, the percentage of self-employed male physicians is about 30%. The percentage of female physicians who are self-employed declined from approximately 30% in 1970 to 20% in 2007 (**Figure 9.1**). The AMA estimated that in 2012, only 18.2% of physicians worked in solo practices (Kane & Emmons, 2012).

As **Figure 9.2** shows, the fastest growing medical groups are those with three or more physicians, and increasing numbers of doctors are becoming employees of hospitals, academic medical centers, and other kinds of providers.

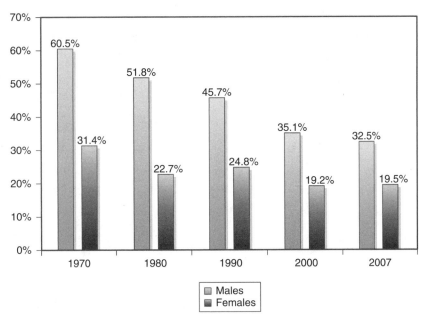

Figure 9.1 Physician Self-Employment, 1970–2007

Data from: American Community Survey. (2012). U.S. Census. Retrieved from http://factfinder2 .census.gov/faces/nav/jsf/pages/searchresults.xhtml?refresh=t.; U.S. Census of Population. (2010). Retrieved from http://www.census.gov/2010census/

In light of the economics of health care, these trends are far from surprising. Financial considerations have rendered solo practices relatively impractical (Goldin & Katz, 2011). The operating costs of multispecialty medical practices have increased dramatically in the past decade, putting a squeeze on doctors in independent practices. Multispecialty practices that are not owned by hospitals or health systems saw operating costs increase by 52.6% from 2001 to 2010 (Elliott, 2011). By comparison, the consumer price index (CPI), a common measure of inflation, increased by 23%, but even more importantly, Medicare and Medicaid reimbursements to doctors did not keep up with inflation throughout the decade, and Medicare payments to physicians have been cut by CMS using a formula known as the Medicare sustainable growth rate (Centers for Medicare and Medicaid Services, 2013). Under this formula, Medicare first cut payments to physicians for professional services by 4.8% in 2002, and was scheduled to further decrease payments by 21.3% in 2010 and 24.4% in 2014 (Fiegl, 2013). However, vigorous lobbying by the AMA and by individual physicians has forestalled these cuts through acts of Congress, preventing CMS from implementing them.

Physicians in multispecialty practices have responded to the market changes by reducing their operating expenses in recent years. In a recent study, the

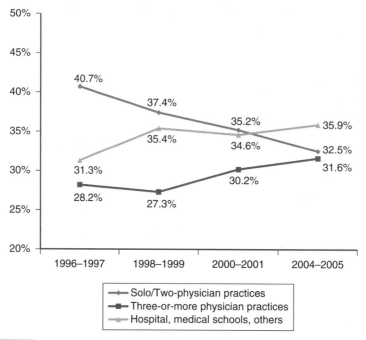

Figure 9.2 Percentage of Physicians by Type of Practice

Data from: Liebhaber, A., & Grossman, J. M. (2007, August). Physicians moving to mid-sized, single-specialty practices. Center for Studying Health System Change. Tracking Report No. 18. Retrieved from http://www.hschange.com/CONTENT/941/?topic=topic22%20-%20ib1

Medical Group Management Association reported that the operating costs of these practices declined by over 2%, as physicians and practice managers cut expenses by negotiating prices with vendors, deferring purchases of equipment and furniture, and closely managing staffing costs (Elliott, 2011). Nonetheless, relentless financial pressure on physician practices will continue to force many out of independent practice and into health systems, fueling the trend toward hospital-owned medical practices.

In addition to the challenges created by the gap between expenses and revenue, it is not unusual for medical school graduates to enter the profession with debt that takes on prohibitive dimensions (according to the Association of American Medical Colleges [2013], average debt is approximately $170,000), making clearer the choice between joining an established practice, with its guaranteed salary, and the unpredictable future of, not to mention considerable investment requirements for, a solo practice.

Practices with multiple physicians offer benefits not as readily available to solo practitioners. The collective nature of the practice members' expertise contributes to a more informed and expansive knowledge base; moreover, physicians have opportunities to validate diagnostic and treatment decisions. A broader range of services, including preventive and wellness care, may be offered. Generally, there is an increased capacity for capital investment, translating into a more robust technological environment in which a wider array of tests and treatments can be offered. Information systems are more readily afforded, acquired, installed, operated, and maintained. While the accelerated shift to multispecialty groups has occurred during only the most recent 10-year period, there are already some indications that particular clinical outcomes are better for patients treated in multiphysician practices than those treated in solo-physician practices (Meyer, 2012; Pham, Schrag, & Hargraves, 2005). And, of course, there is the benefit of providing call coverage, producing a greater likelihood that a patient will have a physician available on a more regular and reliable basis, and allowing physicians to experience greater peace of mind when planning vacations or needing to take time off for personal reasons.

Yet it is important to acknowledge the other side of the coin. Curoe, Kralewski, and Kaissi (2003) examined cultural distinctions between multiphysician and small medical practices. Their findings suggest that "the most pronounced cultural differences were found to be between single and multispecialty group practices. Multispecialty groups have cultures that are less collegial (sense of belonging), have less organizational identity, are less cohesive, and have less organizational trust. Their cultures are also less oriented toward quality of care. It seems that the addition of specialties greatly changes the practice culture and that those changes diminish physicians' orientation toward their colleagues and the practice as a 'group practice'" (p. 396). There is also evidence that charity care disparities exist between solo practitioners and members of group practices. Cunningham and May (2006) report that approximately 70% of physicians who own their practices or are part of a two-person practice provide charity care, while about 50% of those employed in larger practices do so. Finally, physicians in a solo practice possess greater capability for establishing more exclusive relationships with patients. Such exclusivity is believed to contribute to the formation and maintenance of trust, a phenomenon noted by Elliott (2009).

Aging Population

The fastest growing segment of the population comprises people aged 65 and over. Projections indicate that this group will double in size, from approximately 35 million in 2000 to over 70 million by 2030 (**Figure 9.3**), and increase from 12% of the population to 20% during that same period (**Figure 9.4**). The healthcare needs of older people are considerable compared with those of younger people. The majority of healthcare needs generally occur in the latter stages of life; approximately 30% of Medicare disbursements for care are spent in the final year of a patient's life (Riley & Lubitz, 2010).

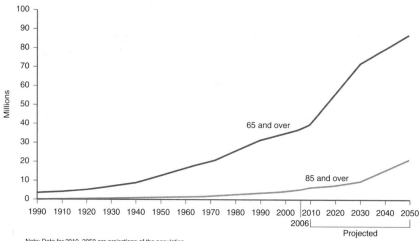

Number of people age 65 and over, by age group, selected years 1900–2006 and projected 2010–2050

Note: Data for 2010–2050 are projections of the population.
Reference population: These data refer to the resident population.
Source: U.S. Census Bureau, Decennial Census, Population Estimates and Projections.

Figure 9.3 Aging Population Trend

Reproduced from: Federal Interagency Forum on Aging-Related Statistics. (n.d.). Older Americans 2008: Key indicators of well-being. Retrieved from http://www.agingstats.gov/Main_Site/Data/2008_Documents/Population.aspx

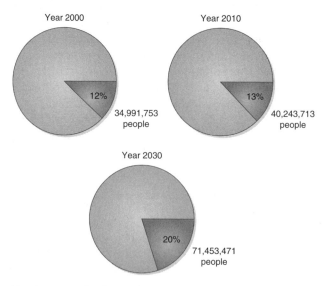

Note: Percentage of total population.

Figure 9.4 Percentage of Population over 65 Years Old

Data from the CDC U.S. Census Bureau, Population Division, Interim State Population Projections, 2005.

The complications of and challenges to communication between practitioners and older patients are significant. As cognitive, retention, and motor skills decline, so too does the capacity to abide by medical directives. Also, ailments may take longer to treat and they may produce a more debilitating range of side effects than would occur with younger people. Additionally, they could contribute to mental fatigue and deterioration, or fuel anxiety or depression. Further, it is not uncommon for caretakers, whether family members, friends, or trusted others, to serve as communication intermediaries between practitioner and patient. While this often helps, an untrained caretaker may misunderstand a medical directive or fail to carry out a healthcare plan as intended.

Managing the healthcare needs of an aging population represents one of the great tests of the country's healthcare system. It is all the more challenging because of the other trends identified in this chapter. The diminishing presence of primary care physicians coupled with (as discussed next) the increased percentage of IMGs and the expanding dependence on technology, intensify the communication problems particular to an aging population.

International Medical Graduates

IMGs have made critical contributions to the healthcare system in the United States. Indeed, during the past 70 years, the United States has welcomed IMGs from over 125 countries (AMA, 2010). It is safe to say that without IMGs, the United States would suffer a far more dangerous shortage of physicians than it presently faces, and it is likely that the greatest impact would be among vulnerable or underserved populations. The largest increase in the number of IMGs has occurred in internal medicine. In 1980, 13.4% of internal medicine physicians were graduates of foreign medical programs; by 2007, the percentage had swelled to 24.2%. (American Medical Association, 2010). As such, the most significant growth has occurred in areas of medical specialty that experience the greatest number of visits.

Examining the physician–patient encounter as an interpersonal context, Street (2003) argues that ethnicity influences the encounter in three ways. First, there may be differences in language or dialect that may manifest most vividly with respect to metaphors, idioms, and culture-specific uses of certain terms. Second, certain styles of communication are preferred over others as we move from one culture to the next. For example, Street references studies that suggest that individuals from western cultures—that is, those with more individualistic-oriented cultures—may be more prone to be expressive and assertive in their communication whereas those from more collectivist cultures may exhibit greater communicative restraint and more deference. Third, people from different cultures have different ways of explaining their health or may point to different factors that they believe may account for their health issues. Each level contains the potential to prevent the communication experience from flowing in a meaningful and productive manner. The accuracy of information transmission could be less than optimal, and all of the attending benefits of a constructive communication exchange could be compromised.

Other studies suggest there are acculturation challenges associated with the transition to practice in the United States (Maudsley, 2008; McMahon, 2004). For example, residency programs are periods of intense adjustment, and many fail to devote sufficient time and attention to support IMGs as they seek to learn ways of managing communication and cultural differences not only with patients, but with coworkers as well (Gozu, Kern, & Wright, 2009). Accordingly, IMGs may enter their profession in the United States at some disadvantage with respect to building communication bridges with a range of stakeholders. It is not uncommon for IMGs to pass through residency programs with few, if any, formal opportunities to learn how the health philosophies of their native countries may differ from those of the United States and how those differences may be overcome (Kales et al., 2006; Kramer, 2005; Searight & Gafford, 2006). The wider the cultural gap between provider and patient, the more challenging and potentially restrained the communication. As noted by Eisenberg (1997), given the relatively paternalistic presence of the physician, the patient may be reluctant to exercise the wherewithal necessary to establish a meaningful and productive communication exchange. Thus, any predisposition the patient may have to ask questions, seek clarification, or participate as a full-fledged participant in the communication experience may be compromised.

Increasing Reliance on Technology

Technology is ubiquitous in health care, its presence in every facet of the caregiving environment growing by the day. Inpatient and outpatient settings have become centers of technology, for example, making possible the retrieval of clinical information, including CT, MRI, and X-ray images, instantaneous from virtually anywhere in the facility (Ofri, 2011). Robots have entered the healthcare domain, performing a broadening range of functions from surgery to medication dispensing (Flowers, 2014) as well as to infection control, housekeeping, and disinfection (Laher, 2014). The expanding capabilities of video technology in operating suites have created opportunities to observe and display nearly every innermost facet of the body, sharpening the pinpoint accuracy of diagnosis and surgical correction, and minimizing the degree of surgical invasiveness; operating rooms today have the appearance of a state-of-the-art video game (Bloom, 2014). Not long ago, the patient registration process was time consuming and involved reams of paper assembled and clipped into a weighty chart; today, registration can occur quite literally in the blink of an eye through the use of biometric cameras (Laher, 2014). Breakthrough technologies involving sensors implanted in pills that, once ingested, allow for vital signs to be measured and transmitted to doctors; increasingly, the patient can be monitored and evaluated on a remote basis (Baulkman, 2014). Medical Records rooms, once repositories of endless compilations of medical files and microfiche films, have been transformed into sophisticated information centers, with rapidly increasingly capabilities for electronic transmission of data.

Health care has become so powerfully linked to and dependent on technology that every phase—diagnosis to treatment to post-treatment care, as well as all information management processes—are conducted, executed, captured, transmitted, or stored by some piece of equipment. Indeed, telemedicine—the process of communicating across distances for health-related purposes—is one of the more rapidly employed approaches for diagnosing illness, responding to health questions, and even receiving medical treatment (DuPre, 2010). Advances in technology have strengthened both the reach and quality of providing health care. And, technology is not only at the disposal of the provider. Technology has also made it possible for consumers to enter the healthcare context more informed and, therefore, more capable of communicating as a partner in the healthcare discussion.

Yet, because technology constitutes a mediating element in the provider—patient relationship, it can have a distancing effect on the parties. As Ofri (2011) observed: "But the presence of computers in the exam room has had another consequence. Both physically and psychologically it has placed a wedge in the doctor-patient relationship." Geist-Martin, Horsley, and Farrell (2003) report that while technological developments have immense capabilities for improving patient care, they could also interfere with the formation and maintenance of effective relationships between providers and patients. Surely, more frequent and timelier exchanges are made possible by the use of communication technologies. But opportunities for in-person contact as well as time spent in person could diminish. The full array of nonverbal signals that could indicate a lack of understanding will not be evident to the provider.

In a study that examined how the presence and use of technology influenced perceptions of empathy, Fonville, Choe, Oldham, and Kientz (2010) found that physician-interviewees felt that effectiveness of gathering information from patients was contingent on how well they understood and related to patients personally. But their results also acknowledge the complex nature of the phenomenon; for example, practitioners can reduce the adverse effects of a strong technological presence through a variety of interactional and environmental design strategies. Where and how equipment is placed, whether opportunities for direct interpersonal contact are available, how much information the patient is provided about the use of technology, and a host of other factors all influence the extent to which technology will be an ally or adversary in the quality of relationship building between physician and patient.

The steady march of technological advance is inevitable. Our understanding of how that occurs, and whether it complements or obstructs social, emotional, cognitive, and motivational aspects of the care-receiving experience, will benefit from considerable research in this era of profound technological progress.

Outcomes Measures

In the past, the focus of quality with respect to a medical procedure was on how faithfully the procedure adhered to established guidelines; quality assurance was a function of whether the conduct of the providers was appropriate and in concert with protocol and whether there was anything about the patient's condition immediately following the procedure that deviated significantly from what was expected. More recently, increasing emphasis has been placed on the quality of the outcome of the medical treatment or intervention. This focus is reflected in the evolving nature of measures employed by The Joint Commission (formerly the Joint Commission on Accreditation of Healthcare Organizations [JCAHO]) that link organizational accountability to evidence of quality outcomes (The Joint Commission, n.d.).

According to Manser and Walters (2001, p. 33), "The practice of evidence-based medicine involves the critical application of current best evidence to the care of individual patients. This process requires clinicians to be able to efficiently locate, critically appraise, and appropriately apply the best available evidence to particular clinical scenarios." It is generally agreed that evidence-based practice (EBP) or evidence-based medicine (EBM) may be traced back to 1992, when technological advances and best practice impetuses coincided in such a manner as to place greater emphasis on measuring outcomes as opposed to confining quality measures to the correctness and error-free nature of medical procedures (Hjorland, 2011). EBM is a data-driven, empirical process through which evidence is accumulated in order to assess the precise nature of the patient's condition following care, and it is being executed on an increasingly longitudinal basis. Moreover, there is a growing movement to make outcomes data publicly available.

The irony of EBM is that it could trigger something of a return to the period of the 1950s and 1960s with respect to a shift away from TLC to a focus more oriented to data and clinical acumen. After all, outcomes data serve to add objectivity to the measure of quality of care. If such a perception took hold, then the presence of "evidence" could obviate or, at the very least, lessen the tendency for patients to make judgments about the quality of medical care based on the quality of the interpersonal experience. Differences of opinion about the effectiveness of a practitioner may be resolved by a more "fact" based approach to determinations. The selection of healthcare provider could be driven more by impartial measures than bedside manner. With respect to one's health, this development has some very clear benefits. However, might the tendency for providers to let down their empathic guard occur? Might interpersonal complacency heighten?

In all likelihood, people will be disinclined to take a completely detached and unemotional approach to the selection of provider. An overriding tendency or desire to invest trust in the whole person, not just the clinician, will likely prevail, just as it does with each technological encroachment on the domain of human relations. Accordingly, it will be important to remain vigilant to the possibility for EBM to interfere with patient satisfaction goals that are dependent on the social dimensions of relationships with practitioners.

Implications for Leadership

The trends that could impair progress to patient satisfaction cut across a full range of healthcare system sectors, from entry points for providers (medical schools) to training and preparation phases (internships, residencies) to caregiving venues (medical practices, clinics, hospitals). Insufficient attention to patient satisfaction issues anywhere in the system creates a greater burden for the other parts of the system. For example, medical students who complete their programs without an opportunity to learn and practice how communication skills are essential to mitigating the effects of trends noted above will add to the challenge of the medical practices and hospitals they join. International Medical Graduates who complete residencies armed with sophisticated clinical skills, but ill-prepared to overcome cultural barriers with patients, will not be able to help their patients as fully as possible. Medical practices that employ several physicians may offer a strong clinical environment, but without implementing systems that encourage patients to feel welcome and at home, the social experience and clinical experience may feel out of sync for them. Similarly, hospitals that do not focus on ways to overcome the obstacles to patient satisfaction that could emerge from the trends discussed previously risk less-than-optimal patient perceptions of care and medical outcomes. Hospitalized patients who fail to ask questions or seek clarification may return to their physicians' offices to ask these questions later in the caregiving process than when such questions should have been asked. It is no wonder, then, that needless readmissions occur on a frequent and costly basis. In fact, $17.5 billion is spent annually on readmissions not considered medically necessary, and Shrake (2012) identifies patient satisfaction as one of the key factors that contribute to the phenomenon.

Those who lead healthcare organizations have the responsibility for designing, implementing, and overseeing systems, functions, processes, and activities that contribute favorably to patient satisfaction. Few would argue that responsibility for patient satisfaction is incumbent upon all people who commit to a profession in health care. But the leader—and this need not be confined to a particular job—sets the tone, establishes patient satisfaction objectives, monitors the extent to which those objectives are achieved, remains vigilant of environmental factors that influence patient satisfaction, and understands the vital role of communication in the sphere of human relations as well as the link between communication and the outcomes of care giving.

And yet, the role of the leader in health care has had a traditional focus elsewhere. Belasen and Eisenberg (2012) observe: "Prior to the 1990s, we may view the execution of leadership in health care as occurring largely within transactional parameters. Establishing systems of governance, ensuring compliance in a rule-laden industry, and building hierarchical organizational structures to achieve clarity of role and function—these were the hallmarks of leadership for much of the period from the 1960s through the 1990s." Eisenberg (1997) indicates that customer service, generically speaking, was prevented from penetrating this sphere of priorities largely because of four barriers with extensive traditions in health care: hospitals are highly governed by regulations, they possess a traditional resistance to entrepreneurship, they breed a culture of paternalism, and the medical model serves as a pretext for interactions between healthcare workers and consumers. While considerable advances have been made in the realm of patient satisfaction, these cultural elements have retained a vibrant presence in healthcare environments (Wright, Sparks, & O'Hair, 2008).

The need to generate high levels of satisfaction is intensifying and so are the barriers. It will be difficult for healthcare leaders to succeed without strengthening their acumen and aptitude for containing the impact of those obstructions. According to Belasen and Eisenberg (2012), the CVF provides a model for understanding the relationship between roles and tasks that have occupied the traditional leadership focus in health care and those that must receive more complete attention in environments increasingly sensitive to and influenced by consumer satisfaction. The CVF demonstrates that tensions may arise as a result of paradoxes that occur inevitably in organizational systems (**Figure 9.5**).

Eisenberg (1997) identified a basis for such tensions among leadership roles in healthcare environments:

> But beyond the psychological and medical model phenomena that can detract from customer service is the fact that healthcare work involves so technical an orientation. Health careers involve training in which the preponderance of focus is on scientific and technical skill acquisition. Customer service and patient relations receive disproportionately smaller levels of training, if at all. What's more, expectations form early that success in health care is more closely associated with technical performance than effective communication skills. For example, prospective trainees prepare for admission to health career programs by demonstrating proficiency in the fields of science and math. (pp. 23–24)

Historically, then, it is not surprising that the culture of healthcare organizations would focus on the mechanics of tasks, procedures, rules, and work processes. In the past 20 years or so, a broadening of healthcare leadership roles has occurred. Most particularly, this has involved the management of relationships between and among healthcare organizations because it has become practically impossible for such organizations to remain disconnected from partners of all sorts. Mergers and acquisitions, along with the formations of systems with vertical and horizontal relationships, have occurred at a dizzying pace (Galloro, 2011).

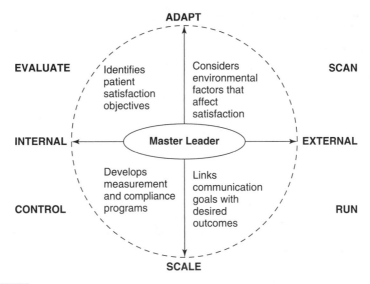

Figure 9.5 Ensuring Patient Satisfaction: The Master Leader

Belasen, A. T., and Eisenberg, B. (2012). The leadership challenge: Becoming master leaders in healthcare organizations. Academy of Management Annual Meeting, Boston, MA, August 3–7.

Competition has fueled the drive to secure relations with consumers as well as with practitioners. Much of this activity has generated role development of managers as brokers and as innovators.

Today, the trends of increasing dependence on technology, the expanding of medical practices, a growing percentage of IMGs, a shortage of primary care physicians, and the aging of the population point toward the need for a stronger set of human relations skills. In much the same way as the need to pursue organizational partnerships spurred the enhancement of brokering skills, the necessity to counter forces that can mar progress on patient satisfaction is generating a need to bolster social and communication skills.

The CVF highlights the complexity of the relationships among roles and the challenges associated with expanding roles. The traditional culture of healthcare organizations, especially hospitals, is hierarchical and control oriented. Channels of authority have been relatively clear and compliance requirements arguably more numerous and stringent than in many other industries (Belasen & Eisenberg, 2012). Therefore, empowering consumers by inviting them into the communication exchange as full partners may have a contrary sensibility in such an environment. There is much about the healthcare context that reinforces status distinctions between providers and recipients of service. Differences in their levels of education, dress, and language, along with the health vulnerability of the recipient (and other factors) can boost the patient's predisposition to acquiesce (Hall, Roter & Katz, 1988). Add to that the trends discussed in this chapter—the aging of the patient population, increasing cultural differences between practitioners and patients, the seemingly unending encroachment of technology, and a more depersonalized practice environment—and the challenge becomes that much greater.

We posit that there are at least four undertakings fundamental to leadership in health care for achieving high levels of patient satisfaction. They are briefly summarized below. However, each merits considerable development, and we encourage the healthcare community to study and evaluate how these can be most advantageously pursued.

- ▶ Reframe trends as opportunities rather than barriers.
- ▶ Institute or strengthen communication training at all levels.
- ▶ Construct or fortify incentives for achieving patient satisfaction objectives.
- ▶ Strengthen systems of monitoring patient satisfaction.

It is important to consider the interrelationships of these endeavors. A holistic approach—that is, one in which all undertakings are pursued and seen as complementary—provides some assurance that particular parts of the system will not have to compensate for the failings of others. As displayed in **Figure 9.6**, the organizing principle for a comprehensive approach is patient satisfaction. Mobilizing the energy, focus, skills, and knowledge to shift to a consumer-satisfaction perspective is rapidly emerging as a both a significant need and significant challenge.

We contend that healthcare leadership dedication, which begins with a vision and commitment to patient satisfaction, would benefit by evaluating how the following have pertinence to their organizations and how these endeavors would enable them to contribute to advancing the mission of patient satisfaction in the healthcare industry: reframing, communication training, reinforcement systems, and monitoring satisfaction. Each is discussed in the following sections.

Reframing

Any of the trends discussed in this chapter may function as a barrier to or an asset in achieving high levels of patient satisfaction. If ignored, in all likelihood they will function as obstacles. Yet leaders can help their organizations consider ways of adapting to and leveraging the inevitable. For example, Doyle et al. (2012) and Fonville et al. (2010) demonstrate that computers in the exam room can have a beneficial presence if—the key here is *if*—they are positioned properly in the setting and the physician makes a special effort to demonstrate how they can be helpful to the patient. Similarly, a large medical practice can counterbalance patients' feeling of being overwhelmed in an imposing environment by undertaking steps to promote a sense of familiarity and comfort.

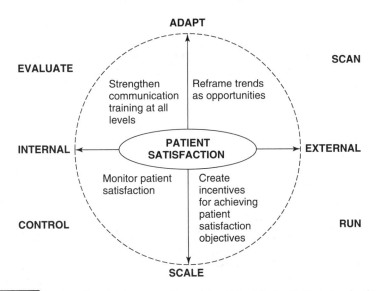

Figure 9.6 Patient Satisfaction as an Organizing Principle for Holistic Leadership

Belasen, A. T., & and Eisenberg, B. (2012). The leadership challenge: Becoming master leaders in healthcare organizations. Academy of Management Annual Meeting, Boston, MA, August 3–7.

"There is the potential for the patient experience to really suffer," said David Howes, MD, who once owned a small medical practice but is now president and CEO of Martin's Point Health Care in Portland, Maine. To prevent this, his 60-physician group has taken steps to ensure the practice is governed by doctors and works to maintain the autonomy of practices that join. "We are responsible for making wise decisions for our patients, and . . . patients feel that they have consistency in their patient-physician relationships." (Elliott, 2009)

This is accomplished through a variety of strategies, including patient orientation to the practice, maintenance of autonomy by the various practices that comprise larger multispecialty groups, and attention to environmental detail that allows for a large space to have a comfortable and manageable ambience.

Each barrier to patient satisfaction may be viewed as a stimulus for the organization to search for ways to move closer to, rather than detract from, patient satisfaction goals. In this respect, the trend is welcomed, not avoided or feared. For example, the fact that the population is aging could encourage a healthcare organization to examine how social needs and cognitive capabilities manifest in an older person. This could, in turn, help practices evaluate their ranges of services for such a population and potentially augment its service offerings (e.g., nutrition counseling). Not only is a patient need served, but an additional program could have a marketing benefit for the practice. Ultimately, while the idea for improvement can emerge from anywhere in an organization, it will fall to the leader to guide the organization from viewing a trend as a barrier to embracing it as an opportunity. It is not enough to figure out how to cope with a problem—especially when a problem bears the stamp of inevitability—the leader should inspire the organization to see it as a stimulus for positive change.

Communication Training

A critical factor in the effectiveness of healthcare delivery is the communication relationship between the patient and the healthcare provider. By focusing on the patient's specific issues and concerns and by giving and receiving reinforcing feedback, a trusting relationship between physicians and patients can be developed. Studies have shown that positive experience breeds higher commitment to quality care and better compliance, patient follow-ups, and overall increase in patient satisfaction (Bensing, 1991; Bensing et al., 1995; Roter & Hall, 1993; Street & Millay, 2001; Verlinde, De Laender, De Maesschalck, Deveugele, & Willems, 2012). Moreover, and as discussed throughout the chapter, optimizing physician–patient communication can lead to better patient health and outcomes (Cheraghi-Sohi et al., 2006; Duberstein, Meldrum, Fiscella, Shields, & Epstein, 2007; Jensen, King, Guntzviller, & Davis, 2010).

Yet while communication training for health professionals is expanding, teaching methods are often inconsistent, communication topics are squeezed into curricula frequently packed with a focus on technical skills, and learning activities take place outside the clinical setting. Moreover, such training may be targeted to different groups of healthcare personnel in different ways. Moving the training closer to the clinical setting, when feasible, offers advantages in that the application of training is more immediate. In so doing, trainees have opportunities to practice the newly acquired skills and can be coached on mid-course corrections. It also creates opportunities for different groups of professionals to participate in the learning environment together, thereby chipping away at the silo culture that has dominated healthcare environments.

A hospital system in New Jersey, committed to strengthening the communication practices of residents, implemented an on-site training program focused on upgrading residents' capabilities across various elements of communication behavior, including, for example, presenting information in a "user-friendly" manner and with sensitivity towards patients' aptitude for comprehension (Eisenberg and Rosenthal, 2013). Such curricular focus is essential, particularly since residents can be easily challenged by the complex responsibilities of administering care while serving in the new role of primary medical caregiver; the elimination of extensive and continuous supervision, which generally occurs at this stage in a physician's career, can prove daunting, potentially derailing a caregiver's intent to communicate clearly and emphatically. Moreover, the complications associated with working in a culturally diverse environment add to the demanding nature of the residents' interpersonal responsibilities. Training that occurs in the clinical setting can often take into account those contextual features which hold the potential for interfering with effective communication.

Of course, residents are not the only members of the care-giving team. Other clinicians, including nurses and physicians on the medical staff, were included in the training and were asked to support it in other ways, for example, by providing input into the curriculum. Not only was their expertise leveraged, but their involvement elevated the perceived credibility of the program. Ultimately, as discussed below, such support is essential in promoting the importance of the training program, establishing it as an institutional imperative, and securing the commitment of the participants to devote the time and energy necessary for achieving positive behavioral change.

Shifting to a culture that places a premium on sound communication practice in healthcare environments will always be difficult given its relatively unique mandate to serve people in need. For example, one resident in the NJ hospital system reported unease in working with elderly patients. He felt uncomfortable being "directive" with those whose life experience was so much greater. Discussions with the program facilitators revealed that his discomfort manifested in an aloof demeanor, exactly the opposite of what he intended to convey. Therefore, follow-up training focused on behaviors related to tone of voice, how and where he physically situated himself relative to the patient, eye contact, and what cues to look for in the patient's behavior to assess his or her understanding.

Other studies reported a positive relationship between a patient's social class and physician's level of responsiveness (Hall et al., 1988) as well as patient's communication style and ability to express opinions and ask questions (Street, 1991). A powerful sense of partnership is maintained when knowledge of a patient's background and concerns is combined with sensitivity and interaction skills (McKinstry, 2000). Physicians should pay close attention to personal attitudes, possible biases, and stereotyping and their effects on interpersonal communication and the patient's perceptions of fairness and equity. Likewise, affective communication and nonverbal communication such as posture, gesture, and facial expression influence patient perceptions of how well they are treated (Street & Buller, 1988). Physicians should encourage openness, invite questions, and actively listen to patients (Beach, Roter, Wang, Duggan, & Cooper, 2006; Piette, Bibbins-Domingo, & Schillinger, 2006; Simpson et al., 1991). By using an interactive communication style and developing a broader perspective, which includes the sociopsychological and physical needs of patients, physicians stimulate consultative decision-making processes, promote patient centeredness, and ultimately increase patient satisfaction (Mead, Bower, & Hann, 2002; Street, 2001).

This transformation to such a patient-centered perspective and a collaborative communication experience is not easy to accomplish. Because there is much to overcome in order to reduce the impact of the status-differentiating reinforcements when practitioners and patients get together, a concerted effort on the part of the providers is essential. As noted, while progress has been made, significant segments of the healthcare industry do not provide adequate training to practitioners. For example, most residencies do not have communication training activities; as noted, this could be especially problematic with respect to IMGs. Educational activities that focus on a broad spectrum of verbal and nonverbal strategies for managing cultural differences, increasing empathy, building trust, and encouraging the patient to ask questions should be instituted. Proven pedagogical strategies, including those in which facilitated simulation activities are employed (Eisenberg, Rosenthal, & White, 2009), are critical to the success of the training.

Rarely do continuing education requirements focus on social, communication, and environmental management skills. That means that established physicians may lack opportunities for such training, unless it is self-initiated or mandated by a third-party payer. Accordingly, such physicians may be unaware of the trends that interfere with patient satisfaction and with strategies for overcoming obstacles introduced by the trends. Research findings indicate that physicians overestimate their communication skills (Ha, Anat, & Longnecker, 2010), rendering it unlikely that self-initiated training will be pursued.

Most healthcare environments are replete with caregiving and ancillary professionals who must coordinate their activities effectively in order to deliver service that is efficient, friendly, and inviting for consumer participation. Therefore, communication skills training that focuses on team building and teamwork—for both practice-based and hospital-based staff—would not only facilitate operational effectiveness, but would sensitize participants to consider the perspective of others, an empathic orientation that would have transfer applicability to patients.

Reinforcement Systems

It will be challenging for the healthcare leader to mobilize his or her organization to be fully committed and able to consistently achieve high levels of satisfaction if systems are not in place to support this goal. That points to the importance of ensuring that all members of the caregiving organization understand the importance of providing patient satisfaction and are able to exercise the skills necessary to achieve it. Anything shy of a comprehensive approach to ensuring that policies and systems reflect the importance of patient satisfaction will produce gaps through which patient satisfaction can seep away. Plucking out one element of the system for fine-tuning may produce some beneficial change, but it may be short-lived. For example, providing communication training to some front line staff can be helpful in sensitizing them to the needs of people who enter the facility. However, consider how much more effective such training would be if the following elements were included as part of a comprehensive effort to strengthen communication conduct: performance standards and performance evaluation systems included criteria related to good customer relations; selection, recruitment, and interviewing practices reflected a commitment to hiring people with strong interpersonal and communication skills; supervisors were selected, in part, because of their aptitude to serve as role models with respect to communication effectiveness; orientation, in-service, and other training activities placed an emphasis on service; and managers at all levels discussed customer service at meetings and provided continuous feedback about the institution's progress relative to achieving patient satisfaction goals. All of these reinforce and operationalize the message and value that the organization views customer service as a core element of its mission (Eisenberg, 1997).

Monitoring Satisfaction

Monitoring patients' evaluation of care and service in hospitals is virtually universal, and now through the government initiative, hospital consumer assessment of healthcare providers and systems (HCAHPS), hospitals must comply with a standardized approach to capturing data (Hospital Consumer Assessment of Healthcare Providers and Systems, 2013). Moreover, with the efforts to make comparative data accessible to the public, patients will have a more informed basis on which to judge which facility may best serve their needs. Fewer requirements for such data gathering exist for medical practices or other venues, such as walk-in clinics, where health care is provided.

While the HCAHPS survey presents a standard set of questions to samples of patients who have been discharged after an inpatient stay, these data do not always present the complete picture of the patient's experience. Huppertz and Smith (2014) found that 20% of patients who completed HCAHPS surveys also wrote comments about the hospitals and their experiences—even though no space for comments is provided on the standard survey form. These comments amplified and in many cases went beyond the numerical scores reported publicly, providing important additional information that hospitals and consumers would find useful. Anecdotal comments and informal feedback by patients should not be overlooked.

At least three areas for improvement are offered. First, we encourage medical practices to strengthen patient feedback practices. Given the more intimate and ongoing associations that patients have with medical practices as opposed to hospitals, controlling for respondent biases will be problematic. Feedback systems will need to be carefully designed to ensure they can produce valid and meaningful data. Outsourcing the system and establishing controls for securing respondent anonymity are likely to constitute important conditions for the system's viability.

Second, feedback systems for all healthcare organizations should have longitudinal capability. The healthcare field is beginning to examine outcomes data on a long-term basis. For example, a patient may leave a hospital following a properly executed procedure. Assessments of care and service immediately postdischarge may show favorable results, but what about the long term? How is the patient faring 6 months following the procedure? One year following the procedure? Was there anything about the hospitalization that promoted changes in the patient's attitude and behavior that contributed favorably to a long-term health benefit? Was there anything that contributed unfavorably? Did the hospital enlist the right collection of follow-up practitioners, including those who could provide counsel on lifestyle education? Was the transition to follow-up care, including the acquisition of medically necessary resources, handled seamlessly or was the patient required to explain, clarify, or negotiate his or her aftercare needs with home medical supply companies, specialists for follow-up care, or home health agencies? Evidence suggests enormous opportunities for improvement exist with respect to this function (Kripalani, Jackson, Schnipper, & Coleman, 2007). Monitoring patient satisfaction on a longitudinal basis will not only enable healthcare organizations to learn where they are strong and where they need to improve, but will also enable the research community to examine the role of satisfaction in relation to outcomes on a long-term basis.

Third, healthcare leaders must ensure that satisfaction is fundamental to organizational policy making and strategic planning, and does not reside exclusively at the level of middle management. Many hospitals have made tremendous inroads in establishing patient satisfaction as a core element of their quality management programs. At the same time, hospitals are contending with an assortment of problems that could hinder operational effectiveness— most notably, shortages of key clinical personnel (particularly nurses) and shifts in levels and sources of reimbursement—such that patient satisfaction issues may be interpreted as yet another management problem needing to be addressed. When this occurs, it is not uncommon for quick fixes to be implemented at the unit or department level, with middle managers of the respective functions having the principal responsibility for coordinating efforts to produce constructive change. Certainly this is important, but it may not produce the organization-wide level of benefit that occurs when patient satisfaction resides in the domain of executive leadership.

Longest, Jr. & Darr (2008) employ the Japanese concept of *hoshin* to describe a strategic approach to quality and its relationship to satisfaction, which they describe as "customer oriented, externally focused, and seeks to achieve breakthroughs in performance, quality, and competitive position. It is a way of linking quality planning . . . to the overall strategic planning process" and "has six attributes: a focus for the organization . . . a commitment to customers . . . deployment of the organization's focus so that employees understand their specific contributions to it; collective wisdom to develop the plan through top-down bottom-up communication process; tools and techniques that make . . . the planning process and the plan helpful, clear; and ongoing evaluation of progress to facilitate learning and continuous improvement" (p. 341).

In this way, quality is elevated from a responsibility exclusive to middle management to a fundamental dimension of executive leadership, linking accountability lines with organizational outcomes (Belasen & Frank, 2010). Thus, it is fully integrated into the long-term planning and strategic direction of the organization. In light of the traditional top-down, paternalistic emphasis of healthcare organizations, the transformation to planning that is driven as much by consumers and through bottom-up channels, constitutes a challenge. But, environmental changes and the trends related to patient satisfaction demand that such a transformation occur.

Conclusion

In her blog, Doctor and Patient, at the *The New York Times*, Pauline Chen (2010), a New York City physician, observes that the increasingly technological nature of the patient care environment will require physicians to exercise more interpersonal skill such as listening and demonstrating empathy. If not, Chen cautions, "the risk remains that the presence of these physical—and technological—barriers will further eclipse some of the most effective ways in which doctors can alleviate the suffering of their patients."

There has always been tension between the need to treat the ailment and the need to manage the broader relationship with the person who has the ailment. It is not easy, and never has been, to find ways of bridging this gap. Strong forces enter the fray and create something of a mutually exclusive relationship between them. The current chapter highlights but a few of those forces. It may be that this is how it will always be, for it is relatively clear that this is the way it has always been. We put sick people in settings away from their most comfortable environs for the sake of helping them or preventing the spread of their illness. Centuries ago, the very sick were set aside—quarantined—from the rest of society. Today, the very notion of going to a hospital means that a person will be in surroundings that could be confusing, scary, uncomfortable—where they forfeit an ability to easily circumnavigate and exercise control.

The dilemma is not whether we should invent a new form of healthcare delivery. Rather, it is to ensure that we understand the importance of managing the relationship with the whole person while addressing the specific medical needs of that individual. Things have always gotten in the way of effectively attending to both sides of that equation. However, the moral imperative of caregiving instructs us to find ways to nullify, or at least contain, systemic and cultural barriers that can disrupt efforts to achieve high levels of patient satisfaction. It is the responsibility of healthcare master leaders (Belasen & Eisenberg, 2012) to create the tone and pave the way to ensure this occurs. They must inspire those they lead to understand why patient satisfaction is so important, not only because human beings deserve to be treated with kindness, compassion, and helpfulness, but because such treatment allows for relationship development that is more fully associated with positive medical outcomes. Master leaders must also employ pragmatism as they lay the foundation for the development of systems, processes, and practices targeted to achieving patient satisfaction goals.

There is an additional responsibility for the healthcare community, and that is to contribute to our understanding of how medical care can be augmented by the use of certain communication and relationship management skills. The precise nature of this relationship is not especially clear. Part of the problem is the relatively rapid change in some of the factors that influence patient satisfaction. For example, technological development is occurring so swiftly that it constrains our efforts to conduct studies and report results fast enough to be meaningful. As one case in point, the relatively recent widespread deployment of tablet computers allows physicians to have more mobility than can be provided by a personal computer or even a laptop (Mace, 2013). This technology allows physicians to enter data without having to reposition themselves at a desk outside the personal space of the examination. The technology is small and can be brought directly into the intimate sphere in which the exam occurs. As such, this technology may be helping practitioners reclaim some of the beneficial interpersonal territory the previous generation of information management technology took away.

Another area for study involves the longer-term impact of relationship development on medical outcomes. The healthcare field is making a more concerted effort to gather evidence about outcomes well after the time of treatment or procedure. This could occur 3 months, 6 months, 1 year, or more following the medical intervention. We do not have a database from which judgments can be made about the influence of the social experience on patients' attitudes and conduct that could materially affect outcomes on a long-term basis. Helping to shape a patient's predisposition to exercise proper care following a hospital experience may affect the medical outcome following even a significant passage of time. This is an area that merits further research.

Finally, we anticipate that research on the role of the master leader in health care will continue to be studied with vigor. As has been claimed elsewhere (Belasen & Eisenberg, 2012), the world of health care is changing in ways that will render the traditional knowledge and skill orientations of leaders inadequate in the coming years. But, as leaders contend with weighty issues of reimbursement, market development, and partnerships with other healthcare organizations, they must remain mindful that the bulk of healthcare delivery occurs in the interpersonal realm. We encourage the study of how healthcare leaders can integrate this notion into all phases of planning as they seek to strengthen their organizations' ability to thrive in an ever-changing environment.

Case Study: The Tip of the Iceberg

A hospital executive approaches you because she believes your management background lends itself to a problem her organization is facing. A group of five patients from one patient care unit made an appointment to see her about the poor interpersonal manner of one of nurses on the unit. This nurse was described by patients as brusque and insensitive. The executive asked for some examples. One patient said his wife was asked to leave at the end of visiting hours in a rude manner. Another patient said she is always nervous around this nurse because the nurse "yells at her for everything." Another patient said the nurse "never explains anything, like when I have to go for a test—it's just 'quick, get out of bed and into the wheelchair or you'll be late for your test.'"

This nurse has worked for the hospital for almost 8 years, and has had a generally good reputation. You begin to have doubts that the problem is confined to this one nurse's interpersonal manner, and ask for some background. The executive confesses that the hospital census has declined in the past few years from an average of 91% to 72%. Staff retention has slipped as well.

You ask if patient satisfaction is measured. The executive indicates it is and, further, every complaint is followed up with a letter. You ask what might be accounting for the census decline and staff turnover. The executive indicates that no real change has taken place other than the hospital's merger into a healthcare system that includes seven hospitals and four long-term care facilities. The merger, she claims, went smoothly. The executive is not certain why employees are leaving in greater numbers recently. You ask about the census at the neighboring hospitals. The executive indicates that despite some overall reduction they have remained more stable during this period.

You question the executive about what patients appreciated about the hospital prior to the decline in patient volumes. The executive reports that people in the community were "comfortable" in the hospital, they felt like it was an important part of the community, and they felt that when they spoke to a member of the staff they were speaking to a neighbor. The hospital is not a trauma center and does not do open-heart surgery. People elected to seek care at the hospital because it was friendly and comfortable.

You convince the executive that the problem might be more complex and involve important communication variables. The executive asks you to develop a plan. There are some things you might be able to do right away, others that require study. The executive asks you to develop a plan that encompasses communication strategies across a range of critical issues: relations with the public, employee relations, patient satisfaction, relations across departments, and other organizational issues that you believe may have relevance to the hospital's viability.

Case Study Review Questions

1. What information beyond that which is provided is essential for you to develop an approach to address the situation at this hospital?
2. What action, if any, would you recommend be taken to address the behavior of the nurse in question?
3. What underlying factors may account for anxiety in the work environment that manifests in unacceptable conduct on the part of some employees?
4. What immediate and long-term steps should be undertaken to restore the reputation of the hospital? To help the hospital achieve higher levels of quality care? To evaluate the census decline and determine how it may be reversed?
5. How might this situation lend itself to a continuous quality improvement effort? What measures and benchmarks may be employed to assess improvement?

Enrichment Exercise

Develop a communication training program based on principles in this chapter that take into account internal and external stakeholders.

- ▶ What would the design of the program look like?
- ▶ To whom should it be targeted and why?
- ▶ How should it be implemented?
- ▶ What resistance might you expect, and from whom?
- ▶ What strategies would you employ to ensure senior level support? Middle management support? Staff support? Support from external stakeholders?
- ▶ What mechanisms should be instituted to reinforce the skills employees acquire in the training?

Review Questions

1. Identify and provide examples of critical indicators of overall patient satisfaction.
2. What are the significant barriers to communication effectiveness in the healthcare field?
3. What steps has the healthcare industry undertaken to strengthen patient satisfaction? How will these help improve patient satisfaction?
4. What are some ways the healthcare industry has undertaken to improve the measurement of patient satisfaction?
5. What accounts for a shortage of primary care physicians? What are the consequences if the shortage continues?
6. How do cultural differences influence the physician–patient encounter? What can be done to neutralize the "barriers"?
7. How is the increasing reliance on technology affecting health care and patient satisfaction?
8. Why is a comprehensive organizational approach to communication training necessary to produce sustained results?
9. What are some ways patient satisfaction and evaluation of care are monitored?

References

Adamy, J. (2012, 14 October). U.S. ties hospital payments to making patients happy. *The Wall Street Journal*. Retrieved from http://online.wsj.com/news/articles/SB100008 7239639044389030457801026415607313 2

American Academy of Family Physicians. (n.d.). *Primary care*. Retrieved from http://www .aafp.org/about/policies/all/primary-care.html

American Medical Association. (2001). *Principles of medical ethics.* Retrieved from http://www.ama-assn.org//ama/pub/physician-resources/medical-ethics/code-medical-ethics/principles-medical-ethics.page?

American Medical Association. (2010). *International medical graduates in American medicine: Contemporary challenges and opportunities.* Retrieved from http://www.ama-assn.org/resources/doc/img/img-workforce-paper.pdf

Association of American Medical Colleges. (2013). *Medical student education: Debt, costs, and loan repayment fact card.* Retrieved from https://www.aamc.org/download/152968/data

Association of MD MBA Programs. (n.d.). Retrieved from http://mdmbaprograms.com/5.html

Baulkman, J. (2013, Nov. 2). High-tech medical advances could revolutionize healthcare. *University Herald.* Retrieved from http://www.universityherald.com/articles/5332/20131102/high-tech-medical-advances-could-revolutionize-health-care.htm

Beach, M. C., Roter, D. L., Wang, N. Y., Duggan, P. S., & Cooper, L. A. (2006). Are physicians' attitudes of respect accurately perceived by patients and associated with more positive communication behaviors? *Patient Education Counseling, 62*(3), 347–354.

Belasen, A. T. (2008). *The theory and practice of corporate communication: A competing values perspective.* Thousand Oaks, CA: Sage.

Belasen, A. T., & and Eisenberg, B. (2012). *The leadership challenge: Becoming master leaders in healthcare organizations.* Academy of Management Annual Meeting, Boston, MA, August 3–7.

Belasen, A. T., & Frank, N. M. (2010). A peek through the lens of the competing values framework: What managers communicate and how. *The Atlantic Journal of Communication, 18,* 280–296.

Bensing, J. (1991). Doctor-patient communication and the quality of care. *Social Science and Medicine, 32*(11), 1301–1310.

Bensing, J. M., Kerssens, J. J., & Vanderpasch, M. (1995). Patient-directed gaze as a tool for discovering and handling psychological problems in general practice. *Journal of Nonverbal Behavior, 19*(4), 223–242.

Bloom, J. (2014, May 28). First look at Kaiser's new high-tech East Bay Hospital. *ABC7 News.* Retrieved from http://abc7news.com/health/first-look-at-kaisers-new-high-tech-east-bay-hospital/82869/

Boulding, W., Glickman, S. W., Manary, M. P., Schulman, K. A., & Staelin, R. (2011). Relationship between patient satisfaction with inpatient care and hospital readmission within 30 days. *The American Journal of Managed Care, 17*(1), 41–48.

Brown, J. B., Stewart, M., & Ryan, B. L. (2003). Outcomes of patient-provider interaction. In T. Thompson, A. Dorsey, K. Miller, & R. Parrott (Eds.), *Handbook of health communication* (pp. 141–161). Mahwah, NJ: Lawrence Earlbaum.

Buckingham, W. B. (1978). Retrospectoscope: Ethical concerns and quality assurance—an historical overview. *Quality Review Bulletin, 4*(5), 21–23.

Center for Elders and the Courts. (2013). *Demographics of the aging population.* Retrieved from http://www.eldersandcourts.org/Aging/Introduction.aspx

Center for Health Transformation. (2010). *Saving lives and saving money by improving medication adherence through a coordinated approach to integrated healthcare.* The 21st Century Intelligent Pharmacy Project: The Importance of Medication Adherence. Retrieved from http://www.healthtransformation.net

Centers for Medicare and Medicaid Services. (2013). *Estimated sustainable growth rate and conversion factor, for Medicare payments to physicians in 2013.* Retrieved from https://www.cms.gov/Medicare/Medicare-Fee-for-Service-Payment/SustainableGRatesConFact/Downloads/sgr2013p.pdf

Chen, P. (2010, October 21). Losing touch with the patient, in *Doctor and Patient* [Web log]. *The New York Times.* Retrieved from: http://www.nytimes.com/2010/10/21/health/views/21chen.html?_r=0

Cheraghi-Sohi, S., Bower, P., Mead, N., McDonald, R., Whalley, D., & Roland, M. (2006). What are the key attributes of primary care for patients? Building a conceptual 'map' of patient preferences. *Health Expect, 9*(3), 275–284.

Clements, C. D. (1992). Systems ethics and the history of medical ethics. *Psychiatric Quarterly, 63*(4), 367–390.

Cunningham, P. J, & May, J. H. (2006, March). *A growing hole in the safety net: Physician charity declines again.* Tracking Report No. 13. Washington, DC: Center for Studying Health System Change.

Curoe, A., Kralewski, J., & Kaissi, A. (2003). Assessing the cultures of medical group practices. *The Journal of the American Board of Family Medicine, 16*(5), 394–398.

Doyle, R. J., Wang, N., Anthony, D., Borkan, J., Shield, R. R., & Goldman, R. E. (2012). Computers in the examination room and the electronic health record: Physicians' perceived impact on clinical encounters before and after full installation and implementation. *Family Practice, 29*(5), 601–608.

Duberstein, P., Meldrum, S., Fiscella, K., Shields, G., & Epstein, R. M. (2007). Influences on patients' ratings of physicians: Physicians demographics and personality. *Patient Education Counseling, 65*(2), 270–274.

DuPre, A. (2010). *Communicating about health: Current issues and perspectives* (3rd ed.). New York, NY: Oxford University Press.

Eisenberg, A., & Rosenthal, S. (2013, March 2). *Using specially trained actors in facilitated simulation experience (FSE) to achieve milestones.* 2013 Accreditation Council for Graduate Medical Education Annual Educational Conference, Orlando, Florida.

Eisenberg, A., Rosenthal, S., & White, T. (2009). Using drama to teach interpersonal and communication skills to residents and medical students. *Academic Physician & Scientist*, November/December, 7–9.

Eisenberg, B. (1997). Customer service in healthcare: A new era. *Hospital & Health Services Administration, 42*(1), 17–31.

Elliott, V. S. (2009, October 19). Ownership loses its luster: Physicians less likely to go solo. *American Medical News.* Retrieved from http://www.amednews.com/article/20091019/business/310199973/4/

Elliott, V. S. (2011, October 3). After years of big increases, practice costs drop 2.2%. *American Medical News.* Retrieved from http://www.amednews.com/article/20111003/business/310039961/6/

Federal Interagency Forum on Aging Related Statistics. (n.d.). Older Americans 2008: Key indicators of well-being. Retrieved from http://www.agingstats.gov/Main_Site/Data/2008_Documents/Population.aspx

Fiegl, C. (2013, July 22). Medicare proposes doctor pay for complex chronic care management. *American Medical News.* Retrieved from http://www.amednews.com/article/20130722/government/130729959/1/

Flowers, L. (2014, January 4). Hospital pharmacy relies on ADS pharmacy robot: Highly personalized care meets highly efficient technology. *Rx Medic.* Retrieved from http://www.rxmedic.com/blog/101-hospital-pharmacy-relies-on-ads-pharmacy-robot-highly-personalized-care-meets-highly-efficient-technology.html

Fonville, A., Choe, E. K., Oldham, S., & Kientz, J. A. (2010). *Exploring the use of technology in healthcare spaces and its impact on empathic communication.* Proceedings of the 1st ACM International Health Informatics Symposium (pp. 497–501), New York, NY.

Galloro, V. (2011). Picking up speed: Health reform among the drivers cited for recent mergers and acquisitions. *Modern Healthcare, 41*(3), 22–26.

Geist-Martin, P., Horsley, K., & Farrell, A. (2003). Working well: Communicating individual and collective wellness initiatives. In T. Thompson, A. Dorsey, K. Miller, & R. Parrott (Eds.), *Handbook of health communication* (pp. 423–443). Mahwah, NJ: Lawrence Earlbaum.

Goldin, C., & Katz, L. F. (2011). The cost of workplace flexibility for high-powered professionals. *The Annals of the American Academy of Political and Social Science, 638*(1), 45–67.

Gozu, A., Kern, D. E., & Wright, S. (2009). Similarities and differences between international medical graduates and U.S. medical graduates at six Maryland community-based internal medicine residency training programs. *Academic Medicine, 84*(3), 385–390.

Greek medicine: The Hippocratic oath (2012, July 2). U.S National Library of Medicine. Retrieved from http://www.nlm.nih.gov/hmd/greek/greek

Ha, J. F., Anat, D. S., & Longnecker, N. (2010). Doctor-patient communication: A review. *The Ochsner Journal, 10*(1), 38–43.

Hall, J. A., Roter, D. L., & Katz, N. R. (1988). Meta-analysis of correlates of provider behavior in medical encounters. *Medical Care, 26*(7), 657–675.

Hjorland, B. (2011). Evidence-based practice: An analysis based on the philosophy of science. *Journal of the American Society for Information Science & Technology, 62*(7), 1301–1310.

Hospital Consumer Assessment of Healthcare Providers and Systems (2013). *CAHPS Hospital Survey.* Retrieved from http://hcahpsonline.org/home.aspx

Huppertz, J. W., & Smith, R. (2014). The value of patients' handwritten comments on HCAHPS surveys. *Journal of Healthcare Management, 59*(1), 31–47.

Jensen, J. D., King, A. J., Guntzviller, L. M., & Davis, L. A. (2010). Patient-provider communication and low-income adults: Age, race, literacy, and optimism predict communication satisfaction. *Patient Education Counseling, 79*(1), 30–35.

Jha, A. K., Orav, E. J., Zheng, J., & Epstein, A. M. (2008). Patients' perception of hospital care in the United States. *New England Journal of Medicine, 359*(18), 1921–1931.

The Joint Commission. (n.d.). *Specifications manual.* Retrieved from http://www.jointcommission.org/specifications_manual_joint_commission_national_quality_core_measures.aspx

Just what the doctor ordered. (n.d.). EditorsWeb.org. Retrieved from http://www.editorsweb.org/wellness/doctor-ordered.htm

Kales, H. C., DiNardo, A. R., Blow, F. C., McCarthy, J. F., Ignacio, R. V., & Riba, M. B. (2006). International medical graduates and the diagnosis and treatment of late-life depression. *Academic Medicine, 81*(2), 171–175.

Kalet, A., Pugnaire, M. P., Cole-Kelly, K., Janicik, R., Ferrara, E., Schwartz, M.D., … Lazare, A. (2004) Teaching communication in clinical clerkships: Models from the Macy initiative in health communications. *Academic Medicine: Journal of the Association of American Medical Colleges, 79*(6), 511–520.

Kane, C. K., & Emmons, D. W. (2012). *New data on physician practice arrangements: Private practice remains strong despite shifts toward hospital employment.* American Medical Association. Retrieved from https://download.ama-assn.org/resources/doc/health-policy/prp-physician-practice-arrangements.pdf

Kramer, M. N. (2005). The educational needs of international medical graduates in psychiatric residencies. *Academic Psychiatry, 29*(3), 322–324.

Kripalani, S., Jackson, A., Schnipper, J., & Coleman, E. (2007). Promoting effective transitions of care at hospital discharge: A review of key issues for hospitalists. *Journal of Hospital Medicine, 2*(5), 314–323.

Laher, Y. (2014, March 24). *30 most technologically advanced hospitals in the world.* Top Master's in Healthcare Administration. Retrieved from http://www.topmastersinhealthcare.com/30-most-technologically-advanced-hospitals-in-the-world/

Liebhaber, A., & Grossman, J. M. (2007, August). *Physicians moving to mid-sized, single-specialty practices.* Center for Studying Health System Change. Tracking Report No. 18. Retrieved from http://www.hschange.com/CONTENT/941/?topic=topic22%20-%20ib1

Longest, B. B., Jr., & Darr, K. (2008). *Managing health services organizations and systems* (5th ed.). Baltimore, MD: Health Professions Press.

Mace, S. (2013, September 3). Say so long to PCs in hospitals. *Health Leaders Media,* Retrieved from http://www.healthleadersmedia.com/page-1/TEC-295905/Say-So-Long-to-PCs-in-Hospitals

Manary, M. P., Boulding, W., Staelin, R., & Glickman, S. W. (2013). The patient experience and health outcomes. *New England Journal of Medicine, 368*(3), 201–203.

Manser, R., & Walters, H. C. (2001). What is evidence-based medicine and the role of the systematic review: The revolution coming your way. *Monaldi Archives for Chest Disease, 56*(1), 33–38.

Maudsley, R. F. (2008). Assessment of international medical graduates and their integration into family practice: The clinician assessment for practice program. *Academic Medicine, 83*(3), 309–315.

McKinstry, B. (2000). Do patients wish to be involved in decision making in the consultation? A cross sectional survey with video vignettes. *British Medical Journal, 321,* 867–871.

McMahon, G. T. (2004). Coming to America—International medical graduates in the United States. *New England Journal of Medicine, 350*(24), 2435–2437.

Mead, N., Bower, P., & Hann, M. (2002). The impact of general practitioners' patient centeredness on patients' post-consultation satisfaction and enablement. *Social Science Medicine, 55*(2), 283–299.

Medscape (2012). *Medscape physician compensation report: 2012 results.* Retrieved from http://www.medscape.com/features/slideshow/compensation/2012/public

Meyer, H. (2012). Taking aim at America's number one killer—one key heart disease risk factor at a time. *Health Affairs, 31*(5), 895–898.

Moskop, J. C., Marco, C. A., Larkin, G. L., Geiderman, J. M., & Derse, A. R. (2005). Hippocrates to HIPAA: Privacy and confidentiality in emergency medicine. Part I: conceptual, moral, and legal foundations. *Annals of Emergency Medicine, 45*(1), 53–59.

Ofri, D. (2011, September 8). When computers come between doctors and patients [Web log]. *The New York Times.* Retrieved from http://well.blogs.nytimes.com/2011/09/08/when-computers-come-between-doctors-and-patients/?ref=healthcarereform&_r=1

Partners Healthcare. Interpersonal and communication skills teaching materials. Retrieved from http://partners.org/Graduate-Medical-Education/Curricular-Materials-And-Educational-Resources/Interpersonal-and-Communication-Skills.aspx

Pellegrino, E. D. (1993). The metamorphosis of medical ethics: A 30-year retrospective. *Journal of the American Medical Association, 269*(9), 1158–1162.

Petterson, S. M., Liaw, W. R., Phillips, R. L., Jr., Rabin, D. L., Meyers, D. S., & Bazemore, A. W. (2012). Projecting US primary care physician workforce needs: 2010–2025. *Annals of Family Medicine, 10*(6), 503–509.

Pham, H., Schrag, D., & Hargraves, J. (2005). Delivery of preventive services to older adults by primary care physicians. *The Journal of the American Medical Association, 294*(4), 473–481.

Piette, J. D., Bibbins-Domingo, K., & Schillinger, D. (2006). Health care discrimination, processes of care, and diabetes patients' health status. *Patient Education and Counseling, 60*(1), 41–48.

Press Ganey. (2012). The relationship between HCAHPS performance and readmission penalties. *Performance Insights.* Retrieved from http://img.en25.com/Web/PressGaneyAssociatesInc/PerformanceInsights_Readmissions_7871.pdf

Press Ganey. (2013). *About us: Our history.* Retrieved from http://www.pressganey.com/aboutUs/ourHistory.aspx

Riley, G. F., & Lubitz, J. D. (2010). Long-term trends in Medicare payments in the last year of life. *Health Services Research, 45*(2), 565–576.

Roter, D. L., & Hall, J. A. (1993). *Doctors talking to patients/patients talking to doctors.* Westport, CT: Auburn.

Schiavo, R. (2007). *Health Communication: From Theory to Practice.* San Francisco, CA: Jossey-Bass.

Searight, H. R., & Gafford, J. (2006). Behavioral science education and the international medical graduate. *Academic Medicine, 81*(2), 164–170.

Shrake, K. (2012, October 24). Hospital readmission penalties: Seize the opportunity. *Hospital Impact.* Retrieved from http://hospitalimpact.org/index.php/2012/10/24/p4151

Simpson, M., Buckman, R., Stewart, M., Maguire, P., Lipkin, M., Novack, D., & Till, J. (1991). Doctor-patient communication: The Toronto consensus statement. *British Medical Journal, 303*, 1385–1387.

Sohl, P., & Bassford, H. A. (1986). Codes of medical ethics: Traditional foundations and contemporary practice. *Social Science and Medicine, 22*(11), 1175–1179.

Street, R. L. (1991). Information-giving in medical consultations: The influence of patients' communicative styles and personal characteristics. *Social Science Medicine, 32*(5), 541–548.

Street, R. L. (2001). Active patients as powerful communicators: The communicative foundation of participation in care. In W. P. Robinson & H. Giles (Eds.), *The new handbook of language and social psychology* (pp. 541–560). Chichester, England: Wiley.

Street, R. L. (2003). Communication in medical encounters: An ecological perspective. In T. Thompson, A. Dorsey, K. Miller, & R. Parrott (Eds.), *Handbook of health communication* (pp. 63–89). Mahwah, NJ: Lawrence Earlbaum.

Street, R. L., & Buller, D. B. (1988). Patient's characteristics affecting physician-patient nonverbal communication. *Human Communication Research, 15*(1), 60–90.

Street, R. L., & Millay, B. (2001). Analyzing patient participation in medical encounters. *Health Communication, 13*(1), 61–73.

Torrey, T. (2011, February). *Why don't patients comply with treatment recommendations?* About.com. Retrieved from http://patients.about.com/od/decisionmaking/a/noncompliance.htm

Tung, T., & Organ C. H., Jr. (2000). Ethics in surgery: Historical perspective. *Archives of Surgery, 135*(1), 10–13.

U.S. Census of Population. (2010). Retrieved from http://www.census.gov/2010census/

Verlinde, E., De Laender, N., De Maesschalck, S., Deveugele, M., & Willems, S. (2012). The social gradient in doctor-patient communication. *Equity Health Journal.* Retrieved from http://www.equityhealthj.com/content/11/1/12

Wright, K., Sparks, L., & O'Hair, D. (2008). *Health communication in the 21st century.* Malden, MA: Blackwell.

CHAPTER 10 ▶

Strategies for Maximizing Leadership Effectiveness in Healthcare Organizations

LEARNING OBJECTIVES

Students will be able to:

- Recognize that the complexity of health care requires higher levels of cognitive complexity
- Appreciate the need for behavioral flexibility to cope with change leadership
- Balance microscopic and telescopic views of leading and transitioning healthcare organizations
- Realize the importance of developing leadership capacity to help choose and support the right roles to deal with internal and external stakeholders
- Learn to use systems thinking and navigate around the competing values framework
- Develop new competencies, adopt mobile technologies
- Train in weak areas to improve engagement skills
- Develop self-improvement activities, become customer focused
- Understand personality traits; use honesty and transparency
- Learn to frame leadership position, use influence skills
- Get a 360° review to inform self-development plans

A Medical Facility Confronts Its Future

Mark Reynolds is the administrator of a large orthopedic practice in Philadelphia. The practice has 4 outpatient facilities, 3 rehabilitation centers, a surgi-center, 18 physicians, and 44 other clinical and administrative staff. Reynolds has been the administrator for 7 years. He began as the coordinator of one of the outpatient facilities and replaced the prior administrator who left to become director of admissions at a nearby hospital.

The board comprises five physicians along with Reynolds, the chief financial officer, a financial advisor, an attorney, a risk management consultant, and three members of the business community. One of the board members thought it important to organize an information session on the Affordable Care Act (ACA) and begin to evaluate whether and how it might affect the practice. Denise Edwards, a consultant who advises healthcare organizations on health policy and implications for the management of healthcare systems, was invited to provide a review of the ACA and to facilitate the discussion.

Edwards spent an hour providing an overview of the ACA. She then suggested that the group focus on 10 important issues that held the potential of being affected, perhaps quite significantly, not only by the ACA but by other industry trends:

- Influx of new patients into the practice
- Migration of patients to other practices
- Pressures for affiliation, practice acquisition, merger
- Payer mix changes, reimbursement challenges, and revenue volume and stream
- Service mix changes
- Ensuring high levels of patient satisfaction
- Long-term quality and evidence-based outcomes
- Information management systems and practices, including electronic medical records (EMR)
- Corporate and organizational structure
- Quality improvement program

Moreover, Edwards emphasized, the practice must be prepared to measure the effectiveness of everything the practice does, including, for example, efficiency of work processes, quality of clinical outcomes, and assessments of patient impressions of care and services. Edwards suggested that they embark on the development of a strategic plan. She acknowledged that the vast majority of healthcare organizations are in a similar state of not knowing precisely how the ACA will affect them. However, waiting too long to get answers and develop a plan could put them at a strategic disadvantage.

After offering her suggestion, Edwards turned to Reynolds and asked if the practice had ever developed a strategic plan. Reynolds shifted uneasily in his seat and nervously adjusted his tie. "Not really," he replied, "There really hasn't been much need. We have held pretty steady for the last several years. Not much change in our patient base, insurance programs, and overall practice."

Reynolds appreciated that he couldn't count on things staying the same. But he understood that the forthcoming period would involve a level of change he had not previously addressed, and the management requirements referenced by Edwards seemed to him to be outside his comfort zone. He thought about what he had accomplished in the past year. The parking lot in the largest facility had been repaved; a new billing system was finally implemented; a physician's assistant was hired and had been getting very positive feedback from both physicians and patients; the scheduling system was updated; a new MRI was installed in a diagnostic center; staffing remained generally stable; despite some initial glitches, the block time schedule he negotiated with the local hospital's operating room was working out well; and no major issues occurred with the insurance companies and other third-party payers—all in all, a pretty good year.

But, thought Reynolds, how do these accomplishments compare with the list of issues the practice will need to focus on moving forward? The thought was unsettling to him. At that very moment, he felt ill-equipped to study such matters, let alone lead the organization on them—affiliation possibilities, service changes, comprehensive EMR systems, negotiating with new payers, studies on patient throughput, long-term clinical outcomes—all measured and documented!

Edwards reiterated that what may have worked in the past may not work the same way in the future. Healthcare organizations of all types—whether hospitals, healthcare systems, clinics, or practices—will need to evaluate what they must do to establish and sustain a competitive place in their market. She offered some detail on the challenges by explaining that EMR linkups will require collaboration and relationship building on operational systems as never before; patients may have different coverage options that may alter their consumption of services; new patients may enter the system who, because of lack of previous coverage, may not have much experience engaging providers; community demographics may create some shifts in patient composition; hospitals may accelerate the purchase of practices to solidify their place in the market; and so on and so on. Organizations that spend too much time looking in at the practice rather than devoting a proper amount of attention to what is occurring around them may discover that such a focus imperils their viability. Further, Edwards stressed that everyone who works in the practice would not only have to be part of the discussion, but part of the solution. Everyone would have to feel invested in the strategic direction for it to be effective.

This future sounded daunting to Reynolds. Everyone who worked in the practice would look to him as the point person across this broad spectrum of challenges. He thought of himself as a good manager—but not necessarily as a leader. It seemed to him that up until now, the practice may not have needed one. After all, for the most part the practice ran just fine; change was manageable. Not anymore—starting today, a leader would be essential. He wondered if he would be up to the task.

Reynolds looked around the room. The expressions on the faces of the people around the table suggested they understood a new day was dawning. It occurred to Reynolds that everyone knew something big had to begin, though they were not sure what it was. He recognized that someone had to take responsibility for defining what it would mean for their organization.

The group thanked Edwards and she left. Everyone came into the meeting with some understanding that the ACA, along with clinical, technological, and regulatory trends, would cause some change. But listening to a full explanation—with all the pieces tied together—put it into a far broader and comprehensible perspective. Until now, they had a sense that the changes forecast for health care, though not trivial, were something for them to consider when they had time, but did not rise to the level of importance that could shake their world.

Reynolds suggested that they all take a week to digest and reflect on Edwards's presentation and then regroup to discuss it. They agreed. As they walked out of the room, Reynolds understood that one thing was crystal clear: his role would never be the same.

Introduction

There is, at the very least, a little bit of Mark Reynolds in all of us. The issue at hand is not whether Reynolds has done an admirable job. Nor, and most especially, is the problem that Reynolds is the wrong person to lead the organization in the future. Reynolds has done a good job because he did what was necessary in all the years he served as administrator. He devoted most of his energies to ensuring that, proverbially speaking, "the trains ran on time." In this respect, Reynolds responded to the set of conditions and challenges in a relatively appropriate and reasonable manner. Could one argue that he should have exercised more forethought and looked more systematically at the trends occurring in the industry, the economy, and the world around him? Maybe? Possibly? But the more critical question is whether Reynolds can adopt a perspective more suited to what the future holds.

Let's face it, the world around us keeps changing rapidly, and no industry or profession can escape change. As Jack Welch famously pointed out during one of his famous encounters with his executives, "Change before you have to!" Accordingly, the healthcare industry is by no means unique with respect to the status quo being challenged. We need only to look around to see how quickly change is occurring in many industries. For example, telecommunications is advancing at a rate that makes today's products obsolete tomorrow. And while the computer industry is heading for collapse due to lack of adaptation, the aerospace industry is relying on technology innovation and collaborative research and development (R&D) to sustain competitive advantage.

Massive shifts toward natural gas and alternative fuel sources, as well as the trend for the United States to become less dependent on other nations for oil, are creating enormous change for the energy industry. The world of finance has been rapidly globalizing, and new rules and new markets keep everyone in that industry on their toes. Manufacturing, for decades a source of woe because of its exodus from the United States, has been making something a comeback. Retail has been transitioning from a model in which transactions occur on the retailer's premises to where they can occur in the home or workplace through technological advances that would have seemed unimaginable just a few generations ago. Even the world of education, long viewed as relatively stable, is experiencing a transformation—advances in education delivery are enabling many more people to obtain a degree in higher education without having to leave their homes.

Consistent with *disruptive innovation theory*, which places a great emphasis on the power of organizational processes and enabling technology to deliver products and services at lower costs than incumbent firms, innovative firms transform their markets by pulling in new customers (Belasen & Rufer, 2013; Christensen & Raynor, 2003). Key organizational functions with important synergistic effects for successful innovation include marketing, R&D, and operations/production. However, it has long been recognized that without open communication and joint accountability, the tension among these functions that is often triggered by conflicting communications with external stakeholders might lead to lower levels of organizational performance (Belasen, 2008). Indeed, resources and capabilities that are not translated into well-synchronized activities, best practices, or business processes cannot have a positive impact on a firm's performance (Ray, Barney, & Muhanna, 2004). The healthcare industry is no different. Master leaders must focus on identifying characteristics of adaptive culture and innovation communication that contribute to effective interfunctional collaboration.

Health care is not alone. Leaders in each industry are well-served by examining the trends that affect their world and identifying the skills that will be essential not only today, but tomorrow as well. The future of health care is approaching with a heavy foot on the gas pedal, so tomorrow is arriving ahead of schedule. Accordingly, Mark Reynolds will not have much time.

As we have discussed, health care began to metamorphose significantly as the 19th century gave way to the 20th. It was then that health care made a fundamental transition from something of an art to a full-fledged science, and practitioners organized standards of conduct and formed professional associations (Jennings, Bailey, Bottrell, & Lynn, 2007). In the roughly 100 years since, the principal responsibility of the healthcare manager was to create an environment in which standards could be properly followed. Standards related to all aspects of the healthcare environment but, above all, they provided a clear framework as to how clinical activity should be conducted in the organization. As the management profession matured, standards would naturally extend to other aspects of the organization including, for example, financial performance, human resources performance, risk exposure, legal vulnerability, governance, and operational soundness. The job of the healthcare manager required nothing less than devoted attention to all the details of the work context. During those years, more and more of the payment for services was made by a third party to the transaction, freeing the manager somewhat to concentrate on procedures and details. Such attention is no less important today. No manager can afford to take his or her eye off the ball and permit any slippage of attention to operational processes, standards of performance, and tasks that allow patient care to be delivered in the most effective and efficient manner possible.

Just as the very beginning of the 20th century brought about fundamental change, so too has the 21st introduced change on a level no less profound. Now that we are several years into the new century, the forces underlying the need for change have crystallized, as have the leadership roles and responsibilities essential to respond to those forces. The demands of a century ago required an intense, microscopic focus inward; that is, they required a dedicated examination of the myriad of details that add up to the delivery of health care.

The demands today require a telescope aimed outward—an ability to analyze not only the landscape but what lies beyond it—and this all while the microscope is still holding steady on all activity going on inside. Zooming in and at the same time zooming out allows effective leaders to see the forest and also the trees, to concentrate on details while simultaneously seeing the big picture (Kanter, 2011). Adopting inside-out and outside-in perspectives is an important 180° skill that, when applied effectively, helps mitigate unwise decisions and avert failure.

It is not news to anyone that health care is undergoing rapid and widespread change. The key theme of this text revolves around the new responsibilities that leaders of healthcare organizations must embrace for their organizations to succeed. Today's demands are far more complex, because they pull us in directions that seem at odds with one another. The more we understand those tensions and the underlying reasons for their existence, the more prepared we will be to diversify our skills to meet the challenges that lie ahead. This understanding is the purpose of this chapter, to provide a blueprint for change. More specifically, this chapter is intended to demonstrate how an analytical framework such as the competing values framework (CVF) can serve as both (1) a vehicle for understanding how the challenges the healthcare industry faces translate into a need for a more extensive skill set, and (2) a practical development tool that identifies how our competencies can be broadened.

Looking to the Future

Some leadership texts imply that leaders come to their roles with certain characteristics that make them more or less successful in their organizations, given the needs and contexts of the moment. For example, a company in fiscal crisis may benefit more from a leader who can focus on financial and operational details, while an organization in a stable environment with strong community support and few competitors may benefit from a leader who can maintain and optimize operational effectiveness. Likewise, a firm whose workforce has become demoralized as a result of negative publicity may benefit from a leader who relates to the needs of frontline employees, someone who empathizes with their concerns and can rebuild their confidence. And an organization that faces daunting challenges from new competition, shifting markets, fiscal uncertainty, and uncertain growth prospects may benefit from a leader who can visualize future opportunities and chart a path toward grasping them. In business, companies have sometimes handled these different requirements by changing their leaders to meet the challenges they face at the moment—reasoning that a leader who can take charge in a time of crisis and stabilize the company may not be the same person who is best suited to running the operation day-to-day once the crisis has been resolved. We have even given a name to an individual hired to take charge for a given period of time who is charged with the responsibility to effect considerable change—the *turnaround specialist*.

In health care, however, the environment is evolving too rapidly to change leaders to suit every situation. Healthcare organizations must adapt to a rapidly changing environment and uncertain future, yet they must also maintain flawless day-to-day operations. These trends put pressure on leaders to accomplish many goals simultaneously, some of which appear to conflict with one another. For this reason, the skills and competencies associated with a master leader are crucial to the modern healthcare organization.

In this text, we have seen that master leaders can rise to these challenges by understanding the shifting roles they must play, and the CVF describes the underlying paradoxes. We have emphasized that historically, healthcare managers have attended predominantly to operational issues, a focus that has not gone away but has in fact intensified due to more regulations, increased scrutiny by accreditation agencies, financial pressures that demand high levels of efficiency, as well as the considerable moral obligation associated with the need for meticulousness when caring for people who are sick. However, today's healthcare leaders cannot look internally for all the answers, because pressures from outside the institution will necessitate greater attention to relationships with external stakeholders, and how this plays out will require vision beyond the facility. Healthcare reform has turned the practice of caring for the sick and injured into a community-wide initiative, and the extent to which a leader coordinates and manages the health of the population served by his or her organization will set the stage for success. Leaders who demonstrate that they can integrate innovation and operations are able to build organizations with a more prosperous and enduring presence in the industry.

As we have observed throughout this text, managing and leading can no longer be regarded as separate skill domains, but rather essential complements for success. We maintain that these roles are different yet compatible, and integrating them will emerge as the paramount challenge for healthcare organizations into the future. Because leadership and management function differently and are guided by different goals, it takes considerable fortitude to prevent organizations from succumbing to the natural tensions between the two. Yet never has it been more important for healthcare executives to accomplish both successfully. As illustrated by the experience of Mark Reynolds, the orthopedic practice administrator whose story began this chapter, life will never be the same.

Let us summarize a few of the trends that are driving the changes that prompt such an important need for convergence of management and leadership.

Internal and External Collaboration

In health care, we are fond of saying that departments and units within organizations operate in silos, and in Chapter 1 we discussed how personnel in various units barely communicate or interact with those outside their unit. But the silo analogy extends beyond the internal departments of hospitals and health systems. The healthcare system has been described as fragmented, with many actors working independently and focusing on their own specific issues, patients, and economic realities. The concept of collaboration has been slow to catch on.

Historically, hospitals have traditionally operated as "workshops" for physicians (Shi & Singh, 2012). Doctors have worked independently, responsible to their peers in their discipline rather than to the hospital administrators who manage the facility. This created a dual hierarchy of governance (Liebler & McConnell, 2011), as well as silos defined by departments of the hospital and medical specialties of the physicians. Thus, doctors have treated patients, while hospitals have provided facilities and staffing to support the physicians' work.

Primary care physicians (PCP) have traditionally performed initial screening and diagnoses for patients, referring them to specialists for tests and treatment and often transferring their care to the specialists. Then they move on to see the next patient. After their patients complete a course of treatment with the specialist to whom they were referred, the PCP may receive a letter detailing what was done, the instructions given to the patient, medications prescribed, and follow-up appointments with the specialist. This letter usually goes into the patient's file, but the PCP receives no compensation for the time required to read it, and with a busy office full of patients needing to be seen, the letter often sits unread until the patient's next visit to the PCP. Effectively, the PCP is out of loop after the referral has been made. Given this, the burden for managing that loop often falls to the patient, the one party in all of the transactions who holds the least training necessary to understand how the clinical pieces fit together. What are the consequences of the patient's failure to formulate the correct questions regarding follow-up care? To have the confidence to ask them? To understand the answers? To organize and carry out a course of action based on those answers? To follow up on the next steps?

Almost by definition, specialists operate in silos, functionally organized units with pooled or sequential interdependence that minimizes interaction. They know a great deal about particular organ systems or medical conditions, and professionally they are accountable to their peers in the specialty. If the patient presents with multiple conditions, the specialist treating the first set of health problems usually refers the patient to another specialist (or set of specialists) for the others. Each layer of specialists treats the individual problem he or she is qualified to treat, prescribing medications and recommending procedures. Genuine coordination of care, while unquestionably desirable, is typically elusive—after referring the patient for specialty care, the PCP is far removed from that person's care, and even if the patient requested his or her involvement, no additional payment would be provided to the PCP for doing so. As has been pointed out earlier, quality care requires the integration of diverse specialties into patient-centered apparatuses in which physicians achieve coordination through reciprocal forms of interdependence that promote interprofessional collaboration.

In the new era, these patterns will inevitably evolve into more collaborative and team-oriented systems of care. There is widespread agreement that primary care will play an integral part in this transition, with PCPs at the center of coordinating care across multiple settings and providers (Commins, 2013). Patient centered medical homes (PCMH) have emerged as the means for paying PCPs to perform the coordinating role beyond the patient's visit to their office, allowing them and members of their teams to follow patients through the process of treatment and healing. The PCMH has brought health plans closer to the management of care. However, the PCMH model is only the first step toward integration, because it involves essentially the primary care practice's network and patient panel.

Payers have also operated in silos. After traditional HMOs leveled off in size and influence in the early 2000s, health plans have focused more narrowly on aggregating commercial business from employers who provide healthcare coverage to their workers and negotiating with networks of providers to deliver care. With access to utilization data from multiple providers in their markets, they have been able to provide useful information about the health and wellness of their members to their customers, and they have developed programs and advertising campaigns to encourage healthier lifestyles among their insured populations. However, their influence has been limited primarily to their customers, and their attention has focused on marketing the products they develop to meet their clients' needs. Hospital health systems and providers have been adversaries in negotiations over rates and services (Melnick, Shen, & Wu, 2011), rather than partners in providing care to the community.

In the new era, payers have a more important stake in taking care of the population. Through the establishment of Accountable Care Organizations (ACOs), payers will play a large role in providing care to the patients of the future, and they will be more involved in managing the care of those they insure (DeGaspari, 2013). Because the new care models require significant investments in data, technology, and infrastructure, partnerships between payers and providers are essential for establishing successful ACOs. In addition, the ability to use the huge volume of data relative to the populations targeted by the ACO necessitates closer cooperation between payers and providers than ever before. Payers can no longer operate in silos, because the savings offered by ACOs depend on integrating care; thus both providers and insurers share responsibilities for the health of their population.

At the same time that payers are getting closer to providers through PCMH arrangements, ACOs, and other means of integration, providers will be moving closer to payers. This is partly attributable to new reimbursement models that pay providers for delivering care to a population instead of individual patients, and in some cases, they will work under a capitated reimbursement model. Under these payment models, providers must shoulder some risk because they have to estimate how many people in the population will require care of varying intensity. This is traditionally a job that payers have undertaken, known as underwriting risk, and it requires a great deal of patient data and a high level of analytical sophistication.[1]

Leaders will also have to promote collaboration within and outside of their organizations. Within healthcare organizations, the increasingly complex nature of medical treatment involves many more individuals than in the past, each of whom has responsibility for some portion of the patient's care. The work of these people must be coordinated and managed, which Gawande (2011) likens to a NASCAR pit crew, in contrast to the traditional view of the doctor acting as a lone cowboy. Between organizations, the financial incentives are designed to promote closer coordination, a condition emerging as increasingly imperative for success. If one organization performs its task exceedingly well while another fails to execute satisfactorily, the results will suffer. Under the new value-based purchasing models adopted by the Centers for Medicare and Medicaid Services (CMS) and soon to be followed by private insurance plans, reimbursement will decline if metrics are not followed and the outcomes are not delivered.

An Interpretation Through the Lens of the Competing Values Framework

As we have emphasized in this text, healthcare leaders of the future will have to balance many agendas, often with contradictory expectations, and this will pose significant challenges. We will briefly discuss these in the context of the CVF.

Primary care serves as an excellent example. As noted previously, the importance of primary care providers will grow to unprecedented levels, and organizations of all kinds (medical practices, hospitals, health plans, etc.) expect to build more capacity in this area. As discussed previously, the leader must adopt the skills in the upper right quadrant of the CVF—that is, in the area of environment navigation and strategic relationship formation—in order to effectively develop and maintain partnerships throughout the community. The system must work together using the leader's primary care network as a management and

Figure 10.1 Competing Values Framework for Healthcare Leaders

Modified from: Hart, S. L., & Quinn, R. E. (1993). Roles executives play: CEOs, behavioral complexity, and firm performance. *Human Relations, 46*(1993): 543–574.

coordinating tool, and the leader must deliver results in a highly reliable and cost-effective manner, using skills in the lower right quadrant of **Figure 10.1**. Managing the work processes outlined in that quadrant involve teams of individuals that are usually associated with operations internal to a medical practice—PCPs,[2] nurses, and office staff—but in the modern care coordination scenario, the team expands to include social workers and other nontraditional support staff such as outreach and care coordinators.

As primary care grows in importance, a shortage of primary care physicians looms ever closer, prompting great concern among healthcare managers and medical leaders. Based on population growth, aging, and insurance expansion through the ACA, it is estimated that the United States will need an additional 52,000 primary care physicians by 2025 (Petterson et al., 2012). There are not enough primary care doctors being trained, and although physician extenders (nurse practitioners and physician assistants) increasingly pick up more of the primary care load, the task of care coordination requires a high level of clinical and managerial skill. It is easy to see how teams working in community settings may become overwhelmed by the increased demand for services, and it will fall to the leader to delegate operational roles to middle managers, as discussed previously, to maintain high morale and motivation among the team members, as well as to recruit more practitioners into the organization. Thus, the human relations skills depicted in the motivator role in the upper left quadrant of Figure 10.1 are necessary to keep people engaged and inspired. Earlier, we covered strategies and practical suggestions for engaging and motivating healthcare employees and staff specialists. Furthermore, analysis and planning for such shortages will demand that the leader call upon his or her analyzer skills of the lower left quadrant to ensure that quality and safety are maintained.

Whereas the main task of PCPs of managing the health of the population, and especially that of patients with chronic conditions in community settings, involves the strategic skills of building partnerships with external organizations (top right quadrant of Figure 10.1), on the acute care side, a similar issue involves coordinating care after discharge. As noted by many experts, too many needless readmissions occur—that is, after being discharged, a patient returns to the hospital for reasons that should have been avoidable. As healthcare reform provisions take root and pressure to reduce healthcare spending has intensified, attention has been focused on this problem, which is quite costly. An estimated $26 billion per year is spent on readmissions of just Medicare patients (Robert Wood Johnson Foundation, 2013). This happens for a number of reasons, but readmissions often result from patients' not receiving adequate follow-up instructions upon discharge, lack of understanding the instructions, not taking their medications properly, or not receiving proper medical care after leaving the hospital. These items are represented throughout the CVF. In particular, making sure that patients receive the correct instructions on discharge exemplifies the quality/safety role in the lower left quadrant. Staff need the right frame of mind to empathize and take time with patients who may not understand instructions, the importance of which resides in the upper left quadrant: inspiration. Often, discharged patients do not take their medications or receive follow-up care because they lack the resources, transportation, or assistance to obtain these important services; changing this will require vision-setting skills and creative strategies represented in the upper right quadrant to build and manage relationships with a variety of outside agencies that can help these patients overcome such obstacles.

Putting the CVF to Work

As we have discussed throughout this text, leaders will need to engage all of these skills simultaneously. This may seem like a daunting challenge, but the CVF can simplify the task by breaking it down into the four main areas a leader must attend to. Master leaders continually monitor their progress in each of the four dimensions, making adjustments as appropriate.

In this final section, we will make suggestions for executives and aspiring leaders to use the CVF to manage their own careers by assessing their own biases and skill shortcomings that can distort or hamper their performance, based on personal preference as opposed to the needs of the situation. For instance, some managers thrive with operational matters where they can coordinate and monitor progress toward measurable goals, while others relish the experience of mentoring and building strong professional relationships with junior staff members. Each of these brings benefits to the organization, but as we pointed out earlier, objective assessment of a leader on the CVF dimensions can illuminate imbalances of which he or she may not be fully aware.

In the following section we depict some archetypal profiles of the CVF applied to individual managers' assessments. As you can see, each individual has leadership strengths and weaknesses, a pattern that occurs commonly. The profiles portrayed in the figures that follow are representative of many leaders who bring important strengths to their jobs, but are deficient in a particular area, which renders their leadership profile suboptimal to deal with diverse stakeholders and complex healthcare issues. Usually, the lack of balance or the "bias toward action" occurs in a single domain of operations where a leader is too focused, narrow, or exclusive in his or her perspectives. Belasen (2008) terms this *leadership by omission* because their span of attention does not encompass the full scope of the CVF domains, and it appears as a "dent" in the leader's CVF profile.

What can you do if you have such a dent in your profile? Here we outline some recommendations.

In **Figure 10.2**, the dent occurs in the operationally focused, task-master quadrant, indicating that the leader is removed from the day-to-day operations to the extent that a disconnect occurs between the organization's strategy and the frontline staff who carry it out. This often happens when senior management

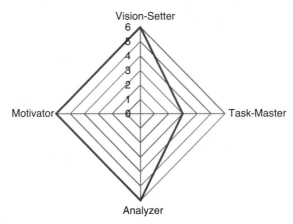

Figure 10.2 Task-Master Deficient

gets wrapped up in strategic planning processes, and they most frequently communicate with direct reports, board members, peers at other institutions and professional associations, consultants, and each other. Though they almost always rose through the ranks to reach their current positions, their attention is now focused elsewhere, and their former roles have changed so dramatically they would not recognize their former responsibilities (and sometimes even their former colleagues).

Leaders in this situation must reconnect. It will be awkward and hard to do at first, especially if people have not seen you in a while. They will wonder what went wrong to prompt such a visit, and they need reassurance that this will become a regular part of the routine—not every day, but done frequently enough for a deeper and more complete understanding of the issues and problems that take place. Some hospitals have begun to follow *management by walking around* (MBWA) practices (Belasen, 2000) requiring senior managers to engage in "executive rounding," where administrators visit units to learn about problems firsthand, enabling them to bring resources and solutions that improve quality and patient safety (Reinertsen & Johnson, 2010). In order for this to work, leaders must round frequently, and problems must be addressed quickly and effectively.

Another way in which executives' task-master quadrant can drop is when they pay too little attention to the work under their supervision. With the hectic pace in most healthcare organizations, it is easy to let some things slip, especially if they do not require immediate attention. For example, a service line manager recently complained that he had not received a performance review in over 2 years; the vice president (VP) to whom she reported said she was too busy, and no one held her accountable for missing the deadline to conduct the review.

Besides a need for accountability in the organization, this is an example of a lack of self-discipline on the part of the VP, who has let down the unit manager who reports to her. Recognizing her low level as a task-master, this VP should review all the basics of her job description, making sure that she and her direct reports have covered their responsibilities and that when stepping back and examining her performance, everyone would conclude that she runs a tight ship.

The next case, depicted in **Figure 10.3**, is exemplified by Mark Reynolds, the administrator of the orthopedic practice mentioned in the opening vignette. A highly competent operational manager who successfully manages a profitable business, Reynolds has been able to discern what the practice needed at any given time, as suggested by his high level of performance as an analyzer. He has experienced low turnover in great measure because of his skill as a motivator, and the practice's physicians respect him, the staff look up to him, and he takes pride in the fact that the office not only runs smoothly but also has a positive energy. But the consultant's report seemed to blindside him, leaving Reynolds to wonder what will be next.

A deficiency in the vision-setter role sometimes occurs when a leader is too inwardly focused—paying attention to operational and financial needs, as well

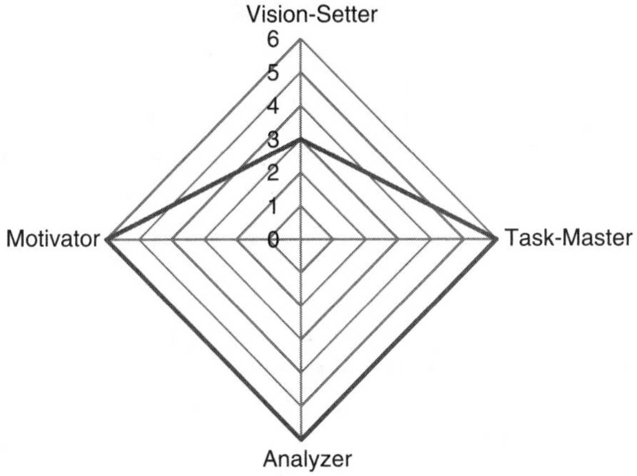

Figure 10.3 Vision-Setter Deficient

as managing the staff effectively. Again, these are important matters, and they cannot be ignored. However, the changes in healthcare press on everyone in the industry, and specialty medical practices face changing circumstances as much as hospitals, primary care practices, long-term care facilities, and community health services agencies do. The temptation among many leaders is to act with a sense of urgency rather than strategy. Also, historically, healthcare organizations lacked the marketing mind set essential to drive alignment between activity at the operational level and strategy at the senior level. Refocusing on mission and purpose and using that as the basis for strengthening consistency at the senior level and alignment between mission and organizational activity, as the text suggests throughout, is at the core of the master leader concept. As Montgomery (2012) points out, strategy links actions to the mission of the organization.

Executives like Mark Reynolds need to get more exposure to what goes on outside their own practice, hospital, or agency. Certainly, attending professional conferences helps—in fact, Reynolds had attended the Medical Group Management Association (MGMA) meetings every year, he served on the local MGMA chapter board, and he occasionally attended meetings of the Healthcare Financial Management Association's (HFMA) local chapter when the topic pertained to medical practice billing or claims denials. However, there is great benefit in going beyond one's own area of expertise and realm of responsibility. Certainly, attending meetings of organizations like the American College of Healthcare Executives (ACHE) would prove valuable. But in addition, other organizations with links to payers, employers, and providers outside the practice arena can provide useful insights that can help leaders think more broadly about the issues their organizations will face. For example, the Institute for Healthcare Improvement

(IHI) offers an array of programs and information related to patient safety and quality (www.ihi.org). Groups representing employers, like the National Business Group on Health (www.businessgrouphealth.org) can provide insight into the issues of concern among the people who pay the bills that providers generate. Examining larger-scale trends can help Reynolds and others develop a greater sense of vision beyond their own organizations, thus helping to guide them into an uncertain future.

Yet other leaders experience a deficiency in the analyzer quadrant, as depicted in **Figure 10.4**. This deficiency is usually marked by a tendency to shoot from the hip, and it results in making decisions without the benefit of all the available information. With the increasing amount of healthcare data among payers, providers, and information exchanges, pressure to use information for decision making will increase, especially because the promise of greater efficiency relies on better utilization of information. Just as physicians are being urged to base their judgments on evidence-based medicine, healthcare executives face pressure to engage in evidence-based management (Kovner, D'Aquila, & Fine, 2009).

Managers who demonstrate a deficiency in the analyzer quadrant sometimes deride reliance on information and data because they wish to avoid the pitfall of "paralysis by analysis." Clearly, some individuals are reluctant to make decisions, and so they put off the decision by asking for more data and more analysis. When requests for more information are used to avoid committing to a direction, the organization suffers and the manager comes across as a weak leader.

Executives who demonstrate a low analyzer level need to resist the temptation to make decisions quickly, even though the urgent pressures of the moment

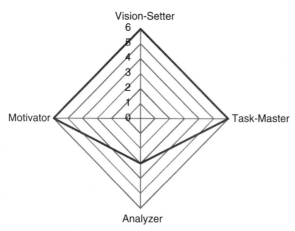

Figure 10.4 Analyzer Deficient

may push him or her into deciding something too quickly. Unless the matter is extremely urgent and a decision absolutely must be made on the spot, leaders should pause and ask a few questions: Is there information or data to support the decision? What do we know? What don't we know? How long do we have to decide this? How long will it take to get the data? Who has it? Who is working on it? What is the risk and cost of making the wrong decision? The industry's movement toward evidence-based decision making will render the executive unable or unwilling to ask these questions obsolete.

Another way for executives to improve their analyzer abilities is to bring others into the decision-making process. Asking for recommendations from people who are directly involved in the matter can not only help improve buy-in, but those on the front lines can often provide crucial understanding of the implications of the decision.

In **Figure 10.5** we illustrate the profile of a leader deficient in the motivator quadrant. This may prove to be the most difficult deficiency to remedy, because it relies on the individual's emotional intelligence and ability to empathize with others, especially employees.

Bosses have a tremendous impact on those who work in an organization. Recent surveys of employees have found extremely high levels of dissatisfaction with the workplace environment and more specifically managers they work for. A recent study by Gallup (2013) found that only 30% of employees are engaged and inspired at work. This study, which involved a survey of more than 150,000 full- and part-time workers during 2012, indicates that the vast majority, 70%, are not engaged with their employers, and productivity suffers as a result. Gallup suggests that while these workers are not necessarily hostile or disruptive, they

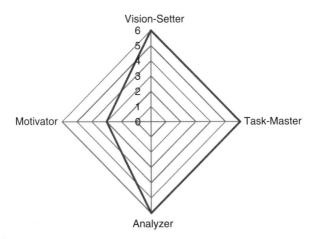

Figure 10.5 Motivator Deficient

are unproductive. Essentially, they have "checked out." Though the study did not identify workers in the healthcare industry, they were included in the survey, and this problem likely affects healthcare workplaces as well.

Executives and senior managers have an obligation to become, plainly stated, good leaders. Many common sense strategies exist for improving your effectiveness as a motivator—that is, specific actions leaders can take to improve their employees' effectiveness and their morale at the same time. In his book *Good Boss, Bad Boss*, Robert Sutton (2010) offers simple suggestions for becoming a better and more effective boss. Included in his suggestions are the following:

1. **Provide psychological security.** Create an atmosphere in which employees can feel safe to experiment with new ideas, try new things, and fail without threat of repercussions. (Note that this is extremely important in health care because people who are afraid of punishment for mistakes are less likely to report them, and this can cause enormous problems in healthcare organizations.)

2. **Shield people from problems and inefficiencies elsewhere in the organization.** Avoid, for example, bureaucratic or time-wasting meetings, problematic managers, disruptive physicians, or fellow employees who get out of line.

3. **Make small gestures of appreciation.** Thank people for their work and acknowledge the effort they contribute. This happens all too rarely; it is all too easy for a leader to forget, and it is all too easy to do.

At the same time, bosses need to ensure that human resources systems, policies, and programs are in place to support growth, development, productivity, and performance excellence. It is one thing for a leader to profess that effective communication with patients is essential (who wouldn't?), but if that same boss does not address staffing shortages or poor resources, the environment may evoke stress, which, in turn, manifests in less-than-effective communication practices. Similarly, if employment selection criteria, job descriptions, performance standards, and evaluations fail to specify how communication with patients is to occur, the employee may not appreciate the degree to which communication is a priority. Moreover, if employees do not receive relevant training or if patient feedback is not shared with employees, they may lack the skills or the motivation, respectively, to ensure that their communication practice is strong. In all, the leader must work to create an environment in which employees are motivated, but must also ensure that managers have the tools to define performance priorities and reward desired behavior.

Conclusion

Leaders are human beings and, like all of us, leaders have strengths, weaknesses, and many other skills that fall somewhere in between. Sometimes the mix of strengths and weaknesses may simply not be right for the task at hand. Not everyone is capable of growing in the areas most critical to the survival and success of an organization. But most are capable of growing far more than they might imagine. That is why we set out to write this text. More often than not, leaders have the capacity to make fundamental adjustments, to redirect and broaden their attention, to recognize that the world around their organizations is changing in ways that demand new approaches—all while keeping the basic work of the organization under control. Being a leader does not mean entering the fray fully equipped with an inflexible set of capabilities. Being a leader means adapting capabilities and adding new ones as the circumstances demand.

Leaders cannot expect their organizations to grow and develop if they themselves do not envision their own development as occurring on the same continuous basis expected for quality (that is why it is called *continuous* quality improvement). Leaders who do not adapt are prone to functioning in the hypereffective manner we discussed earlier; they revert to what they know, and fall prey to the confirmation paradox—seeking out information that confirms what they already know and doing more of the same. Developing a more comprehensive and effective skill profile requires an understanding of where strengths and weaknesses lie (through personal audits, comprehensive evaluations of their performance, self-reflection, and myriad other ways) and building development plans and strategies. In so doing, they become role models for their organization— their personal commitment demonstrates a willingness to grow and adapt—the same way that every healthcare organization must grow and adapt. Of course, this must be balanced against the need for resolve, the need to maintain a sense of direction, and the need to exercise decision-making that provides clarity and adherence to core institutional values.

So we return to a theme raised at the beginning of this text. Why the concept of *master leader*? Throughout this text we employ the term *gap* to refer to that space that exists between a particular ability and the desired and necessary skill. *Mastery* is the process of closing that gap and achieving a more well-rounded and balanced profile. Not every job requires this type of comprehensiveness. And, it can be argued, as we have in this text, that the conditions surrounding health care during many periods in the modern era have been such that leaders without such breadth could succeed.

However that is no longer the case. The industry has grown more complex— with new challenges for organizations to collaborate, prove their relevance, institute efficiencies, satisfy patients, embrace new technologies and clinical advancements, manage relationships with a shifting array of stakeholders, demonstrate that their efforts translate into improved health for the people they care for, and submit all their work to the universe of public scrutiny—and leaders must bring all challenges into alignment. A gap in a leader's ability can prove hazardous for the organization. The master leader has committed to mastering the broad range of complementary skills necessary for directing the organization through the web of challenges every healthcare organization faces today. The CVF provides a powerful and comprehensive tool for evaluating one's skill profile and for identifying where and how adjustments must be made.

Master leaders cannot shield themselves from feedback. Rather, they must seek it out. Growth cannot occur without knowing where one stands. Feedback is not only critical for the substantive information it provides, but on a meta level it forces engagement—closer ties—with employees, clinicians, consumers, and those who have a stake in the work of the organization. And this brings us to a key direction in health care—the need to work together. Whether occurring on the level of the patient care team or all the way to alliance and system formation, the master leader will, above all, create and leverage opportunities for collaboration. Reversing the long-standing characteristic of fragmentation and building a more systems approach to health care will undoubtedly occur. The health of our patients depends on it and the incentives are moving in place to encourage it. Master leaders will be on the forefront of this movement.

Becoming a master leader is tantamount to "actualizing" as a high performing manager. It is not easy, but few things in life worth achieving are. It takes hard work and an unwavering dedication to improve, but if we retain the conviction that by engaging in honest and effective assessment of our skills and the perseverance to maintain a continuous appreciation for the challenges confronting health care and the skill requirements to address them, each of us can move closer to becoming a master leader. As this occurs, above all else, we expect that those who will benefit the most will be those we serve—our patients. The transformation of health care and the emergence of master leaders will ensure that the integrity of the healthcare system and the profession of medicine will restore the trust and social contract between physicians and patients, with patients put above all interests and physicians performing collaboratively with high standards of excellence.

Review Questions

1. Develop an action plan for becoming a master leader. Discuss the challenges associated with your development plan.
2. What makes a master leader effective in leading healthcare organizations in environments of change? (Clue: Think about the types of roles that master leaders require to deal with change.)
3. Do you think that master leaders can emerge in all hierarchical levels?
4. Can you apply the concept of master leadership to organizations in different industries?

Notes

[1]The inability to accurately assess risk is one of the factors assumed to have damaged closed panel health maintenance organizations in the 1990s. With little actuarial expertise, many HMOs entered into capitation agreements that underestimated patient utilization, resulting in severe financial losses and bankruptcies.

[2]We include nurse practitioners and physician assistants in this definition of primary care providers.

References

Belasen, A. T. (2000). *Leading the learning organization: Communication and competencies for managing change*. Albany, NY: SUNY Press.

Belasen, A. T. (2008). *The theory and practice of corporate communication: A competing values perspective*. Thousand Oaks, CA: Sage.

Belasen, A. T., & Rufer, R. (2013). Innovation communication for effective inter-professional collaboration: A stakeholder perspective. In N. Pfeffermann, T. Minshall, & L. Mortara (Eds.), *Strategy and communication for innovation* (2nd ed., pp. 227–240). Germany: Springer.

Christensen, C. M., & Raynor, M. E. (2003). *The innovator's solution: Creating and sustaining successful growth*. Boston, MA: Harvard Business School Press.

Commins, J. (2013). Primacy of primary care. *Health Leaders*, October, 8–9. Retrieved from http://www.healthleadersmedia.com/page-4/MAG-297038/Primacy-of-Primary-Care

DeGaspari, J. (2013, June 11). Payer partnerships and population health. *Healthcare Informatics*. Retrieved from http://www.healthcare-informatics.com/article/payer-partnerships-and-population-health

Gallup. (2013). *State of the American workplace: Employee engagement insights for U.S. business leaders*. Princeton, NJ: Gallup.

Gawande, A. (2011, May 26). Cowboys and pit crews. *The New Yorker*. Retrieved from http://www.newyorker.com/news/news-desk/cowboys-and-pit-crews

Jennings, B., Bailey, M., Bottrell, M., & Lynn, J. (Eds.). (2007). *Health care quality improvement: Ethical and regulatory issues*. Garrison, NY: The Hastings Center.

Kanter, R. M. (2011). Zoom in, zoom out. *Harvard Business Review, 89*(3), 112–116.

Kovner, A. R., D'Aquila, R., & Fine, D. J. (2009). *Evidence-based management in healthcare*. Chicago, IL: Health Administration Press.

Liebler, J. G., & McConnell, C. R. (2011). *Management principles for health professionals*. Sudbury, MA: Jones and Bartlett.

Melnick, G. A., Shen, Y., & Wu, V. Y. (2011). The increased concentration of health plan markets can benefit consumers through lower prices. *Health Affairs, 30*(9), 1728–1733.

Montgomery, C. A. (2012). *The strategist: Be the leader your business needs*. New York, NY: Harper-Collins.

Petterson, S. M., Liaw, W. R., Phillips, R. L., Rabin, D. L., Meyers, D. S., & Bazemore, A. W. (2012). Projecting US primary care physician workforce needs: 2010–2025. *Annals of Family Medicine, 10*(6), 503–509.

Ray, G., Barney, J., & Muhanna, W. A. (2004). Capabilities, business processes, and competitive advantage: Choosing the dependent variable in empirical tests of the resource based view. *Strategic Management Journal, 25,* 23–37.

Reinertsen, J. L., & Johnson, K. M. (2010). Rounding to influence: Leadership method helps executives answer the "hows" in patient safety initiatives. *Healthcare Executive, 25*(5), 72–75.

Robert Wood Johnson Foundation. (2013, February). *The revolving door: A report on U.S. hospital readmissions.* Retrieved from http://www.rwjf.org/en/research-publications /find-rwjf-research/2013/02/the-revolving-door--a-report-on-u-s--hospital -readmissions.html

Shi, L., & Singh, D. A. (2012). *Essentials of the U.S. health care system* (3rd ed.). Burlington, MA: Jones & Bartlett.

Sutton, R. I. (2010). *Good boss, bad boss: How to be the best—and learn from the worst.* New York, NY: Business Plus.

INDEX

Note: Page numbers followed by *f* or *t* indicate material in figures or tables respectively.